Portugal

FODOR'S TRAVEL PUBLICATIONS

are compiled, researched, and edited by an international team of travel writers, field correspondents, and editors. The series, which now almost covers the globe, was founded by Eugene Fodor in 1936.

OFFICES
New York & London

Fodor's Portugal

Area Editor: Susan Lowndes
Contributors: Robert Brown, Mark Lewes, Elisabeth de Stroumillo
Drawings: Lorraine Calaora
Maps: Swanston Graphics
Cover Photograph: Owen Franken

Cover Design: Vignelli Associates

SPECIAL SALES

Fodor's Travel Publications are available at special discounts for bulk purchases (100 copies or more) for sales promotions or premiums. Special editions, including personalized covers, excerpts of existing guides, and corporate imprints, can be created in large quantities for special needs. For more information, write to Special Marketing, Fodor's Travel Publications, 201 East 50th Street, New York, NY 10022. Enquiries from the United Kingdom should be sent to Merchandise Division, Random House UK Ltd, 30–32 Bedford Square, London WC1B 3SG.

Fodor's 89

Portugal

FODOR'S TRAVEL PUBLICATIONS, INC.
New York & London

Copyright © 1988 by Fodor's Travel Publications, Inc.

Fodor's is a trademark of Fodor's Travel Publication, Inc.

All rights reserved under International and Pan-American Copyright Conventions. Published in the United States by Fodor's Travel Publications, Inc., a subsidiary of Random House, Inc., New York, and simultaneously in Canada by Random House of Canada Limited, Toronto. Distributed by Random House, Inc., New York.

No maps, illustrations, or other portions of this book may be reproduced in any form without written permission from the publisher.

ISBN 0–679–01687–2

MANUFACTURED IN THE UNITED STATES OF AMERICA
10 9 8 7 6 5 4 3 2 1

Contents

Facts at Your Fingertips

Exploring Portugal

vi CONTENTS

FOREWORD

Portugal is now very much on the tourist map again. The country has been through a series of social upheavals, but the commonsense and balance of the Portuguese people kept the ill effects of the disturbances down to a minimum where the visitor was concerned. Although prices are no longer as amazingly low as they were in the late 1970s, they are still very favorable in comparison with many other European countries. The Algarve rates have risen somewhat, but in most of Portugal you will find hotel and restaurant bargains that will add to the enjoyment of your visit.

For the many people who like the illusion of being transported into an utterly different setting, Portugal is still an enchanted world, where folkways and traditions have been lovingly preserved in all their sturdy authenticity. At every turn, there are reminders of the country's glorious past, side by side with the abundant signs of an awakening modernity. Portugal has always been the haven of genuine hospitality and heartfelt welcome. The innate courtesy and gentleness of the Portuguese people remain unchanged, even though their country has been swept by long-overdue reforms and their way of life struggles to move forward decades in a few short years.

*

We take this occasion to express our grateful acknowledgement to all those who have given so generously of their time and knowledge to help in the preparation of this volume. We particularly wish to thank the Director of the Casa de Portugal in London, and his staff, who were of great help to the editors.

In Portugal we were greatly assisted by Mr. Martiniano Laginha, Manager of the Tourist Information Department, to whom, and to whose staff we owe a debt of gratitude. As we do, also, to Mrs. Ronald Symington, Mrs. W. D. Thorburn, D. Inez Brattel Camilo dos Reis, D. Ana Marques Vicente, also to Mr. David Cranmer and Dr. Martim Cunha da Silveira, who put their unrivaled knowledge of the Azores at our disposal.

Finally we would like to thank Susan Lowndes, our Area Editor, for her patience and for putting her unparalleled understanding of—and deep affection for—Portugal at our service.

*

While every care has been taken to assure the accuracy of the information in this guide, the passage of time will always bring change, and consequently the publisher cannot accept responsibility for errors that may occur.

All prices and opening times quoted in this guide are based on information available to us at press time. Hours and admission fees may change, however, and the prudent traveler will avoid inconvenience by calling ahead.

Fodor's wants to hear about your travel experiences, both pleasant and unpleasant. When a hotel or restaurant fails to live up to its billing, let us know and we will investigate the complaint and revise our entries where the facts warrant it.

Send your letters to the editors of Fodor's Travel Publications, 201 East 50th Street, New York, NY 10022, or to Fodor's Travel Publications, 30–32 Bedford Square, London WC1B 3SG, England.

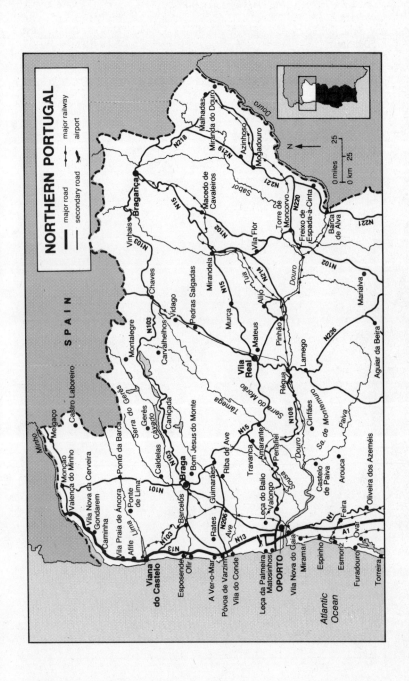

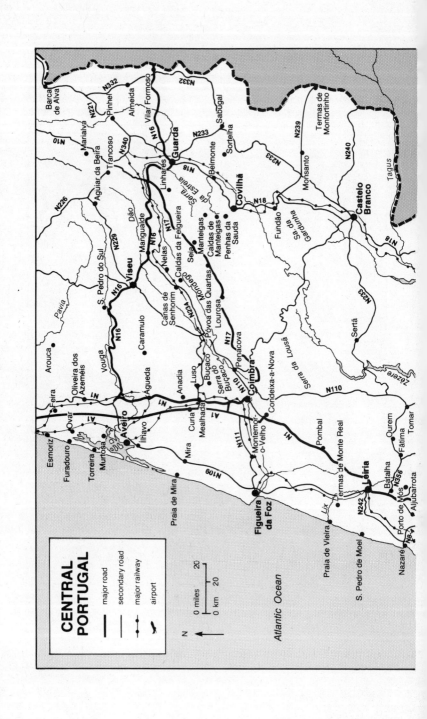

CENTRAL PORTUGAL

— major road
— secondary road
┼ major railway
✈ airport

N

0 miles   20
0 km   20

Atlantic Ocean

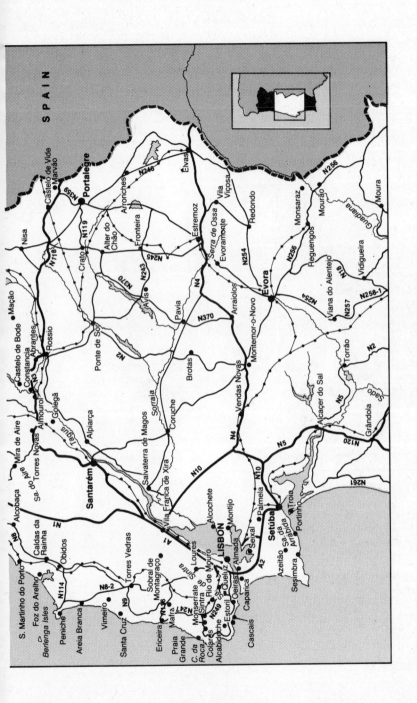

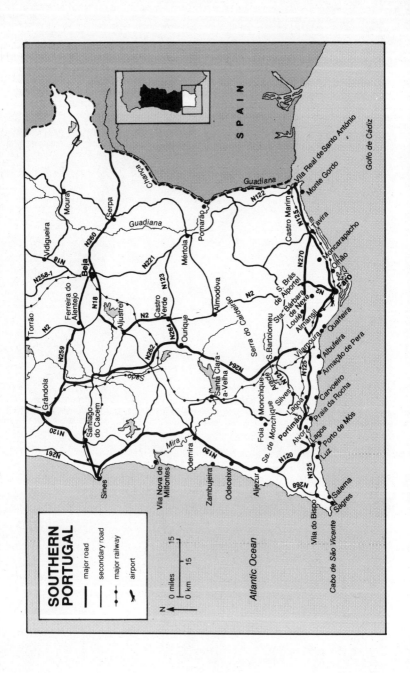

FACTS AT YOUR FINGERTIPS

FACTS AT YOUR FINGERTIPS

Planning Your Trip

WHEN TO GO. Portugal has a temperate climate, and the tourist season begins in spring and lasts through the autumn. It is never unbearably hot even in midsummer (except in parts of the Algarve and on the inland plains), and it is especially pleasant along the coast where a cool breeze springs up in the evening. Winter: mild except in the mountains. In the Algarve, springtime begins in February, and an Indian summer keeps its sunshine through November. The winter season in Madeira and the Azores has long been popular. Off-season travelers not only have the advantage of reduced hotel rates, but have a much better chance to see the Portuguese way of life than in the hustle of the full tourist season.

Average afternoon temperatures in Fahrenheit and Centigrade:

	Jan.	Feb.	Mar.	Apr.	May	June	July	Aug.	Sept.	Oct.	Nov.	Dec.
Lisbon												
F°	56	58	61	64	69	75	79	80	76	69	62	57
C°	13	14	16	18	21	24	26	27	24	21	17	14
Algarve												
F°	61	61	63	67	73	77	83	84	80	73	66	62
C°	16	16	17	19	23	25	28	29	27	23	19	17

NATIONAL TOURIST OFFICE. One of the very best sources of information, brochures and suggestions for helping you plan your trip in general, is the Portuguese National Tourist Office. Casa de Portugal information offices are located in—**New York:** 548 Fifth Avenue, New York, NY 10036 (tel. 212–354–4403). **Montreal:** 500 Sherbrooke O, Suite 930, Montreal, Quebec H3A 3C6 (tel. 514–843–4623). **London:** New Bond Street House, 1/5 New Bond St., London W1Y 0NP (tel. 493 3873).

TOURS AND TOUR OPERATORS. From the U.S. Tours of Portugal tend to be tours of Portugal and Spain; most include some time in the second with the first. *Maupintour,* for example, offers "Pousadas and Paradors," a 16-day tour of the Western Iberian peninsula, with stops in Lisbon, Buçaco, Vila Nova de Cerveira, Estremoz, and several other Portuguese cities, as well as Benavente, Segovia, Madrid, and Salamanca in Spain. Cost is $2,729–$2,798, but that doesn't include airfare.

"Unusual Spain and Portugal" is *Travcoa's* 18-day Iberian offering. The tour begins in Madrid and goes to Segovia, Toledo, Oviedo, León, Salamanca and several other Spanish cities before heading to Oporto, Buçaco,

Coimbra, Fátima, Nazaré, and Lisbon in Portugal. Travcoa's tours are small, usually 25 or less participants. The Spain/Portugal tour costs $3,495 per person, without airfare.

Hemphill Harris spends five days of its 22-day "Flamenco and Fado" tour in Portugal, stopping in Oporto, Coimbra, Lisbon, and Evora. The remaining days are spent in León, Segovia, Madrid, Toledo, Granada, Córdoba, and Seville, in Spain. Hemphill Harris offers a slightly higher level of luxury, and correspondingly higher prices: $5,860, without airfare.

For those who are determined to visit Portugal without setting foot on Spanish soil, *Abreu Tours* has several offerings, including "North of Portugal," which begins and ends in Lisbon and passes through Nazaré, Fátima, Coimbra, Sangalhos, Oporto, Viana do Castelo, Braga, Portalegre, Evora, and several other cities. Accommodations and most meals are included. Seven days cost $501; 11 days is $645.

If you'd prefer to try Portugal on your own, *Extra Value Travel* arranges Self-Drive Programs lasting a week or more that provide a rental car, unlimited mileage, accommodations, and a daily continental breakfast. The rest is up to you. Costs begin at $355 for a week.

Abreu Tours, 60 E. 42nd St., New York, NY 10165 (tel. 212–661–0555).

Cycle Portugal, Box 877, San Antonio, FL 34266 (tel. 800–282–8932). Accompanied bike tours staying in first class hotels in different parts of the country.

Extra Value Travel, 683 S. Collier Blvd., Marco Island, FL 33937 (tel. 800–255–2847).

Globus Gateway/Cosmos, 92–95 Queens Blvd., Rego Park, NY 11374 (tel. 718–268–1700).

Hemphill Harris Travel Corp., 16000 Ventura Blvd., Encino, CA 91436 (tel. 800–421–0454; in CA, 818–906–8086).

Maupintour, 1515 St. Andrews Dr., Lawrence, KS 66046 (tel. 800–255–6162).

Pinto Basto Tours, 1320 Hamilton St., Somerset, NJ 08873 (tel. 201–246–4947).

Portuguese Tours, 321 Rahway Ave., Elizabeth, NJ 07202 (tel. 201–352–6112).

Sun Pleasure Tours, 383 Rockdale Ave., New Bedford, MA 02740 (tel. 617–997–9361).

Travcoa, 4000 MacArthur Blvd., Suite 650E, Newport Beach, CA 92660 (tel. 800–992–2003).

From the U.K. For the special interest market, *Thomson Tours* have arranged a "Wine Routes of Portugal" tour which includes visits to Lisbon and Oporto, and excursion to the Sandeman port cellars, the Mateus estate, and the Dão wine cellars; it can be combined with 7 nights in Estoril. 7 nights £287–£317, 14 nights £412–£465.

Club Med have 40 acres of private parkland surrounding a hotel above a beach in the Algarve, at Balaia, Albufeira. All the usual Club Med facilities and attractions, with visits around the Algarve and to Lisbon, plus golf, which is an Algarve specialty sport. Prices for a week range from £419–£538, £575–£726 for two weeks, including flight from London.

And talking of golf, *the* firm for arranging golfing holidays to the Algarve is *Eurogolf,* who can customize your vacation on the greens with a wide range of prices and dates. Most of their programs come with Avis cars attached, so when the guy is putting his companion can explore. At the Penina Golf, Alvor, for example, 1 week would run from £539, 2 weeks from £899.

Hartland Holidays are one of the specialist firms dealing with holidays organized round pousadas. Their tours start from three major airports (Oporto, Lisbon, and Faro), and include a car rental. From Oporto (the most popular) there's a choice of 7 or 14 nights, with the cost ranging from £369–£428 for 7 nights, £669 for 14, depending on the time of year. Hartland has other offers which include Spain and its paradores as well as Portugal.

For those who really want to turn their vacations to advantage, *Roger Taylor Tennis Holidays* can provide excellent package deals—a week, including coaching, flights, villa accommodations (with maid service), car hire and insurance, from £350 per person, depending on the season, in the Algarve.

Club Méditerranée, 106–108 Brompton Rd., London SW3 1JJ (tel. 01–581 1161).

Eurogolf, 41 Watford Way, Hendon, London NW4 3JH (tel. 01–202 0191).

Hartland Holidays, Brunswick House, 91 Brunswick Cres., London N11 1EN (tel. 01–368 0343).

Roger Taylor Tennis Holidays, 85 High St., Wimbledon, London SW19 5EG (tel. 01–947 9727).

Thomas Cook Ltd., 100 Victoria St., London SW1E 5JR (tel. 01–828 0437).

Thomson Holidays, Greater London House, Hampstead Rd., London NW1 7SD (tel. 01–387 9321).

World Wine Tours, 4 Dorchester Rd., Drayton St. Leonard, Oxon. OX9 8BH (tel. 0865 891919).

WHAT IT WILL COST. The seemingly perpetual shaky state of Europe's finances, with consequent rising taxes and costs throughout and possible inflationary trends to come, make accurate budgeting long in advance an impossibility. Prices mentioned throughout this book are indicative only of costs at the time of going to press (mid-1988). Keep an eye open for fluctuations in exchange rates. At press time the exchange rate was about 136$50 escudos to one US dollar; 250$00 escudos to the pound sterling. (The dollar sign becomes an escudo sign in Portugal and stands between the escudo and the centavos—as 12$50.)

There is one simple answer to the uncertainties of advance budgeting for a trip—if you take a package tour, paid for before you leave, when the only extra expense is the amount of pocket money you allow yourself for drinks, gifts, postcards and postage, etc.

Whether on a prepackaged tour or traveling freelance, it is always more economical to divide your vacation between two centers rather than move around every two or three days. Staying for several days in one hotel means you can take advantage of pension or semi-pension terms.

According to your personal tastes, you can figure out from the approximate prices below just what you are likely to spend extra to your travel costs. You will probably travel on one of two levels in Portugal—deluxe or on what might be called the normal tourist level, which is somewhat above the usual local level. In Portugal, because of the definite difference in living standards, American, Canadian and British tourists generally do not tend to travel on the lower local level. Portugal still remains a far less expensive country to visit than France, Switzerland, Belgium or Scandinavia, for example.

For a breakdown of hotel costs, together with our grading system, see under *Staying in Portugal* later in this section.

Some Sample Costs. A cocktail costs about 500$00–600$00; a bottle of beer 150$00; a bottle of ordinary table wine (*vinho da casa*) 250$00, half bottle 150$00. Coffee after your meal is about 100$00 (also for expresso).

Local brands of cigarettes are about 140$00 for a pack of 20. Color film is 1,000$00. Man's haircut 500$00; for a woman, the cost of a shampoo and set starts around 750$00–1,000$00, a manicure 500$00; styling can cost 750$00. A shoeclean will cost 100$00.

A seat at the opera or theater costs about 1,500$00–2,000$00; at the movies 500$00, at a nightclub, allow for a minimum cover charge of 2,000$00–3,000$00.

TAKING MONEY ABROAD. Traveler's checks are still the standard and best way to safeguard your travel funds; and you still usually get a better exchange rate in Portugal for traveler's checks than for cash. In the U.S., many of the larger banks issue their own traveler's checks—just about as universally recognized as those of *American Express, Cook's* and *Barclay's*. In most instances there is a 1% charge for the checks, though some banks issue them free to regular customers. The best-known British checks are *Cook's* and those of *Barclay's, Lloyd's*, the *Midland Bank* and the *Nat West*, and of course *American Express*. It is also always a good idea to have some local currency upon arrival. Some banks will provide this service; alternately, contact *Deak International Ltd.*, 630 Fifth Ave., New York, NY 10011 (212–757–0100), call for additional branches.

Britons holding a *Eurocheque Card* and check book can cash checks for up to £100 a day at banks participating in the scheme and can write checks in hotels, restaurants and shops again for up to £100. Look for the distinctive blue and red symbol in the window. To obtain a card and check book, apply at your bank.

Credit Cards. The major credit cards—*American Express, Diner's Club, MasterCard* (incorporating *Access* and *EuroCard*) and *Visa*—are generally but by no means universally accepted in most larger hotels, restaurants and shops. We give details which of these cards is accepted by the hotels and restaurants we carry in our *Practical Information* listings. We have indicated them with the abbreviations AE, DC, MC, V. But always be sure to check before reserving your room or ordering a meal that your particular brand of plastic is accepted.

SPECIAL EVENTS. Religious festivals, pilgrimages and folklore events are typical of the Portuguese scene, as traditions run deep. We list here a selection of annual events throughout the country; for further details consult the *Practical Information* sections at the end of each chapter. *It is always advisable to check dates with Tourist Offices.*

January. National *golf championship* matches in Estoril, near Lisbon. In winter, and in spring, there is the *Gulbenkian Music Festival* in Lisbon, including ballet and recitals.

February–March. *Carnaval,* Monday and Tuesday before Ash Wednesday. Processions in many parts of the country.

Easter. *Holy Week* processions in Braga. The *Bullfighting season* opens on Easter Sunday. In Portugal the bulls are not killed and the highly trained horses go unscathed; bullfights take place usually on Sundays and Thursdays in addition to public holidays. The season continues through Oct. After Easter international *golf tournaments* are held at Penina, Alvor in the Algarve.

April. *April in Portugal,* with many different local folk celebrations and much pageantry; one day in April is specially set aside to honor visitors. Big *pilgrimage* at Loulé (Algarve), 2nd Sunday after Easter. One of the most interesting and unspoilt folk pilgrimages still held in Portugal is the *Romaria* or *Festival of Nossa Senhora do Almurtão,* four km. (two and a half miles) from Idanha-a-Nova (Beira Baixa), in mid-Apr.

May. 3, Barcelos (Minho), *Festival of the Holy Cross.* 4, Monsanto (Beira Beixa), historic procession of the *Marafonas.* 12–13, the largest *pilgrimage* of the year at Fátima. Mid-May in Coimbra, *Queima das Fitas,* ceremony at which university students burn their academic ribbon insignia, and dancing.

June. *Festival of São Gonçalo,* Amarante (near Oporto), 1st weekend; age-old fertility rites accompany this great folk pilgrimage. Festivals galore—*Whitsuntide, Corpus Christi, St. Anthony, St. Peter* and *St. Paul,* and particularly *St. John's Day* on June 23 are celebrated amid great festivities and an abundance of local color. In Lisbon, June 13, *St. Anthony's Day* processions and folk-dances, also many celebrations in city and suburbs till end of June. Whitsuntide, Sunday to Tuesday, *pilgrimage* at Matosinhos, near Oporto. *Romaria* at Penha Longa between Sintra and Estoril on Whit Monday. *King David's Procession* at Braga (Minho), 23–24. The biggest *fair* of the year at São Pedro de Sintra (near Lisbon) with local produce and handicrafts, 29.

July. Early July, *Festival of the Tabuleiros* in Tomar, biannually. Spectacular offertory procession. Vila Franca de Xira, *Festival of the Colete Encarnado,* "Red Vest," including cavalcade of the *campinos,* bullfights, bull-runs through the streets, folk dances, open-air feasting. Folklore Fair opens in Estoril, 1st week. *Festival of the Holy Queen* in Coimbra (Beira Litoral), 13–20. *Feira do Carmo,* Faro (Algarve), 3rd week, with procession on 16.

August. *Pilgrimage* at São Bento da Porta Aberta (Minho), 10–15. Music and Ballet Season at the Estoril Casino. 15, *Assumption Day,* is a national holiday, the main festivities occurring at Viana do Castelo. One entire week is devoted to the *Festival of Our Lady of Sorrows.* August 17, pet animals go on pilgrimage to Janas near Sintra. The 2-day colorful and noisy *Albufeira Festival* takes place around 27 and 28 (but check with the Tourist Office, as it is a movable feast).

September. 1st Sunday, *folk pilgrimage* to 17th-century chapel of Our Lady at Porto de Ave, Póvoa de Lanhoso (Minho). 6–8, *Pilgrimage to Our Lady of Nazo,* 11 km. (seven miles) from Miranda do Douro (Trás-os-Montes), with colorful Pauliteiros dances. At Lamego (Trás-os-Montes), *Romaria of Nossa Senhora dos Remedios,* early part of the month. Mid-month, great annual celebrations of *Our Lady of Nazaré* at Nazaré (Estremadura). 20–22, the *New Fair* (started in the 12th century) at Ponte de Lima (Minho), with produce, stock, farm implements. End Sept., *grape harvest and vintage festivals,* in the Douro Valley and all over the country. *Vindimas* or vintage at Palmela, with fireworks, etc.

October. 12–13, pilgrimage to Fátima. Third week, *Santa Iria's Fair:* country festival in the beautiful town of Tomar (Ribatejo). Monchique (Algarve), *Feira de Outubro,* end of month.

November. Annual *São Martinho horse fair* at Golegã (Ribatejo), 10–13.

December. 31, superb *fireworks display* at Funchal, capital of Madeira.

PILGRIMAGES. Probably the most famous pilgrimage center on the Iberian peninsula at present is the most recent—Fátima, in Portugal, whose fame dates only from 1917. From May till October inclusive, pilgrimages to Fátima occur on the 13th of each month, the dates of the apparitions of the Virgin to three shepherd children. The biggest celebration takes place on May 12–13. The second most important pilgrimage to Fátima is that of October 12–13.

Other pilgrimages are listed under *Special Events* and in the *Practical Information* sections of each chapter.

HIGHLIGHTS. Itinerary for History Mavens. From North to South—*Viana do Castelo,* stately manor houses, a King Manuel-inspired town square; *Guimaraes,* where Portugal was born; *Oporto,* capital of the North, center of history; *Leça do Balio,* scene of the tragic marriage that led to the fall of the First Dynasty; *Montemor-o-Velho,* Inês de Castro lived near here; *Buçaco,* Wellington's defeat of Napoleon's army; *Coimbra,* Independent Portugal's first capital, university founded in 1308; *Conimbriga,* early Lusitanian-Roman settlement; *Leiria,* King Dinis' favorite fortress home; *Batalha,* abbey commemorating Battle of Aljubarrota, tombs of the House of Aviz; *Aljubarrota,* Portugal's greatest victory over Spain, in 1385; *Alcobaça,* splendid 12th-century Cistercian monastery; *Tomar,* fief of the Order of Christ, which financed the Great Discoveries; *Obidos,* wedding gift to the queens of Portugal; *Mafra,* the Escorial of Portugal; *Sintra,* summer palace of Portugal's kings; *Queluz,* royal residence near Lisbon; *Silves,* where the Algarve was finally wrested from the Moors in 1189; *Sagres,* where Prince Henry the Navigator planned the voyages leading to the discovery of the sea route to the Indies by Vasco da Gama in 1498.

The Art Lover's Portugal. Five itineraries:—*Lisbon,* Jerónimos church and cloisters, Coach Museum at Belém, Museum of Ancient Art, Gulbenkian Museum, St. George's Castle, Pombaline Lisbon; *Mafra,* Machado de Castro's sculptures; *Queluz,* elegant 18th-century palace and grounds; *Sintra,* three castles.

2—*Lisbon–Obidos,* completely walled medieval town, Renaissance churches; *Alcobaça,* Cistercian monastery, tombs of Inês de Castro and King Pedro; *Batalha,* pantheon of the Royal House of Aviz; *Conimbriga,* Roman mosaics; *Coimbra,* university, Royal Library, ancient cathedral, best collection in the country of early polychrome statues in the Machado de Castro museum; *Caramulo,* museum; *Tomar,* ranks with Jerónimos and Batalha as one of the showplaces of Manueline, or the highly decorated Portuguese Gothic style.

3—*Lisbon–Alentejo–Setúbal,* Church of Jesus; *Evora,* museum town, the heart of the Alentejo, Roman temple of Diana; *Portale-gre–Elvas–Mertola,* mosque now a Christian church; *Vila Viçosa,* palace of the Dukes of Braganza; *Estremoz* and other picturesque, walled and castelated towns in the Alentejo.

4—Starting from Oporto: *Oporto,* churches, magnificent gold wood-work; *Viana do Castelo,* Renaissance town; *Braga,* churches, Baroque stairway of Bom Jesus; *Guimarães,* feudal castle, quaint streets, Iron Age Colossus of Pedralva in Martins Sarmento Museum; *Viseu,* Grão Vasco Museum, churches; *Aveiro,* tomb of the Infanta Santa Joanna; *Lamego,* another Baroque stairway to Nossa Senhora dos Remedios.

5—*Algarve: Faro,* cathedral, museums, Renaissance Arco da Vila; *Silves,* castle; *Milreu,* extensive Roman remains; *Lagos,* golden chapel of St. Anthony; *Vila Real de Santo António,* built in five months in 1774 by the Marquis of Pombal.

Portugal for Nature Lovers. Portugal is on the main route of migrat-ing **birds** so, particularly in the Algarve, there are a great many species to be seen. Dunlins, which breed in Iceland, fly south to the mudflats of the River Arade in Portimão; bee-eaters nest in Monchique; golden orioles and hoopoes are all over the country, as are flocks of white egrets following the plow. Azure-winged magpies, which can be seen only in Portugal and Spain, China and Japan, congregate in noisy flocks in wooded country, while storks nest in the eucalyptus trees and on the bell-towers of churches all over the Alentejo and the Algarve. Both great and little bustards are hard to find in the cornfields around Evora and Elvas in the Alentejo, and the flamingos which come to the upper reaches of the Tagus estuary are protected by its being a nature reserve. Golden eagles, Egyptian and black vultures, falcons and kestrels and other birds of prey hover over the wild country on the Spanish frontier. Warblers, terns, owls, tits and finches, as well as dozens of other species, can all be seen by keen ornithologists.

The **wild flowers** are equally diverse. March, April and May are the months in which to find several varieties of orchis, fritillaries, cistus, laven-der, tulips, gladioli, anemones, celandines, aquiligea, iris, asphodel and scillas, often at the sides of country roads. Arum lilies also grow wild in the many suitably damp situations.

Nature Reserves. The oldest nature reserve in the country is that of Peneda-Gerês in the extreme north. Wild boar, civet cats, wolves and a local breed of wild horse roam the huge mountainous area. There is anoth-er reserve at Montezinho, north of Braganza, where at the time of the full moon, small parties of three or four can go after wild boar in the early part of the night. Alvão is a lesser area near Vila Real, as is the Serra da Malcata on the Spanish frontier, east of the mountain range of the Serra da Estrela, all of which is a reserve.

Further south, the Serras de Aire and Candeeiros are preserved, as are the Serras da Sintra and Arrábida near Lisbon. Perhaps the most interest-ing is on the River Tagus above Alcochete where, as has been mentioned, the rare flamingos come and go. The estuary of the River Sado, south of Lisbon, is also a reserve, as is the coast of the Algarve from Faro to Vila Real de Santo António for the preservation of unnumbered waders and sea birds who make this coast a stop-over in their migration south.

WHAT TO TAKE. The first principle is to travel light, and fortunately for the present-day traveler this is really possible due to the manufacture of strong, light-weight luggage and drip-dry, crease-resistant fabrics for clothing. If you plan to fly, you have a real incentive forced on you by the restrictions on baggage size. Regulations concerning baggage on transatlantic flights vary slightly from airline to airline, so check with yours before you go. In general, however, these are the rules: passengers are allowed to check two pieces of luggage, and carry on one. Checked luggage is restricted by weight (the maximum is usually 32 kg., 70 lbs.) and by total dimensions (that is, the total of the piece's height, width, and depth) which should be no more than 1.57 meters (62 inches) for one piece and 1.47 meters (58 inches) for the second. Carry-on luggage must be small enough to fit under a seat, or in the compartment above the seats. These rules all apply to economy-class passengers; first-class travelers are often allowed a few extra inches' total dimension. If your bags are larger, heavier, or if you want to bring more than three pieces, you will have to pay an excess baggage charge, usually $66. Please note that these rules apply to transatlantic flights only. If, after breaking your journey, you fly on to the Continent or beyond, the rules may well be different. Again, check before you go.

Most bus lines as well as a few of the crack international trains place limits on the weight (usually 25 kg., 55 lbs.) or bulk of your luggage.

Even if you are traveling by ship, resist the temptation to take more than two suitcases per person in your party, or to select luggage larger than you can carry yourself. Porters are increasingly scarce these days and you will face delays every time you change trains, or hotels, go through customs, or otherwise try to move about with the freedom that today's travelers enjoy.

Motorists should limit luggage to what can be locked in the trunk or boot of the car when daytime stops are made. At night, everything should be removed to your hotel room.

Some Tips. If you want to save on baggage weight, then it means choosing carefully. Mix and match works well, and means that you can get extra mileage out of each item.

Choose well-broken-in shoes, walking around Portugal's cobbled streets and squares can be hell on the feet.

Take a sun or beach hat and the best shades you can find, as the sun in Portugal can be fierce.

Have a good shoulder bag to contain all your daytime needs— guidebooks, purse and so on. Get one with a strap that you can slip bandolier-fashion, to foil snatchers.

Men, remember that a battery razor, if you shave electrically, is always a good idea, the backwoods may not have outlets.

Tissue handkerchiefs, Kleenex and such, are very useful for all sorts of purposes undreamed of by the manufacturers. They can be pricey abroad!

A small flashlight comes in handy for peering into out of the way dark corners. And a pair of binoculars for high places—or a monocular is even better, less cumbersome.

If you need prescriptions for medicines, take a copy with you.

Remember a spare pair of spectacles.

Almost inevitably you will find yourself accumulating gifts, souvenirs, extra clothing, picture books, etc., on your travels. A good hold-all for these is a collapsible suitcase or a grip that can be packed in your ordinary luggage on the outward journey. Books can be posted back home, but don't leave this to hotel porters.

TRAVEL DOCUMENTS. Getting a passport should have priority in your plans. **U.S. residents** must apply in person and several months in advance of their expected departure date to the U.S. Passport Agency in Boston, Chicago, Honolulu, Los Angeles, Miami, New Orleans, New York, Philadelphia, San Francisco, Seattle, Stamford, Conn., Washington DC. Local county courthouses and some post offices are also equipped to handle passport applications. If you still have your latest previous passport issued within the past 12 years, you may use this to apply by mail. Otherwise, take with you your birth certificate or certified copy; 2 recent photographs 2″ square, on non-glossy paper, color or black and white; proof of identity that includes a photo and a signature, such as a driving license; and $35, plus a $7 processing fee (no processing fee when renewing your passport by mail). For those under 18 years old, passports cost $20, plus the $7 fee. Passports are valid for 10 years, 5 years for those under 18, and are nonrenewable. If you expect to travel widely you may ask for a 48- or 96-page passport instead of the usual 24-page one. There is no extra charge. Record your passport's number, date, and place of issue in a separate, secure place. The loss of a valid passport should be reported immediately to the local police and to the Passport Office, Dept. of State, 1425 K St., NW, Washington, DC 20524; if your passport is lost or stolen while abroad, report it immediately to the local authorities and apply for a replacement at the nearest U.S. Embassy or consular office.

If you are an alien (as opposed to a permanent resident) and are leaving from the U.S., you must have a Treasury Sailing Permit, Form 1040C or short Form 2063, certifying that all Federal taxes have been paid—apply to your District Director of Internal Revenue; you will also have to present a blue or green alien registration card, passport, travel tickets, most recently filed Form 1040, W2 forms for the last full year, current payroll stubs or letter—and maybe more, so check.

To return to the U.S., you need a re-entry permit if you intend to stay away longer than one year. Apply for it at least 6 weeks before departure in person at the nearest office of the Immigration and Naturalization Service, or by mail to the Immigration and Naturalization Service, Washington, DC.

Canadian citizens in Canada should apply in person to regional passport offices or write to Bureau of Passports, Complexe Guy Favreau, 200 Dorchester West, Montreal, PQ H2Z 1X4 (tel. 514–283–2152). A fee of $25, two photographs, a guarantor, and evidence of Canadian citizenship are required. Canadian citizens living in the U.S. need special forms available at their nearest Canadian Consulate.

British citizens: Apply through your travel agency. The application should be sent to the Passport Office for your area, as indicated on the guidance form, or taken personally to the nearest main post office. Apply at least 5 weeks before the passport is required. The regional Passport Offices are located in London, Liverpool, Peterborough, Glasgow, and Newport (Gwent). The application must be countersigned by your bank manager or by a solicitor, barrister, doctor, clergyman, or Justice of the Peace who knows you personally. You will need 2 full-face photos. The current fee is £15. Valid for 10 years. (Cost rise expected.)

British Visitor's Passport: This simplified form of passport has advantages for the once-in-a-while tourist to Portugal and most other European countries. Valid for 1 year and not renewable, it costs £7.50. Application must be made in person at a main post office; proof of identity and 2 passport photographs are required—no other formalities.

Incidentally, when you have your passport photos made, order about 6 extra prints. These come in handy for international driver's licenses and similar purposes that are difficult to foresee.

Visas. Neither American nor British citizens need a visa to visit mainland Portugal, Madeira or the Azores for stays up to 60 days. For longer stays, apply to the police for an extension, when the original 60 days is about to end.

Health Certificates. Not required for entry into Portugal. Neither the U.S. nor Canada requires a certificate of vaccination prior to re-entry. Because of frequent changes in law, we suggest you check up before you leave.

HEALTH AND INSURANCE. The first thing to do when considering your insurance needs for an upcoming trip is to look at the coverage you've already got. Most major insurers (*Blue Cross/Blue Shield, Metropolitan Life,* etc.) treat sickness, injury and death abroad no differently than they treat them at home. If, however, you find that your existing insurance comes up short in some significant way (most do not cover the costs of emergency evacuation, for example); or if you would like help finding medical aid abroad, as well as paying for it; or if you would like coverage against those most vexing travel bedevilments, baggage loss and cancellation of your trip, then you may want to consider buying travel insurance.

Your travel agent is a good source of information on travel insurance. She or he should have an idea of the insurance demands of different destinations; moreover, several of the traveler's insurance companies retail exclusively through travel agents. The *American Society of Travel Agents* endorses the *Travel Guard* plan, issued by *The Insurance Company of North America.* Travel Guard offers an insurance package that includes coverage for sickness, injury or death, lost baggage, and interruption or cancellation of your trip. Lost baggage coverage will also cover unauthorized use of your credit cards, while trip cancellation or interruption coverage will reimburse you for additional costs incurred due to a sudden halt (or failed start) to your trip. The Travel Guard Gold program has three plans: advance purchase, for trips up to 30 days ($19); super advance purchase, for trips up to 45 days ($9); and comprehensive, for trips up to 180 days (8% of the cost of travel). Optional features with the Travel Guard Gold program include cancellation and supplemental CDW (collision damage waiver) coverage. For more information, talk to your travel agent, or *Travel Guard,* 1100 Center Point Dr., Stevens Point, WI 54481 (tel. 800–826–1300).

The *Travelers Companies* has a *Travel Insurance Pak,* also sold through travel agents. It is broken down into three parts: Travel Accident Coverage (sickness, injury, or death), Baggage Loss, and Trip Cancellation. Any one of the three parts can be bought separately. Cost of the accident and baggage loss coverage depends on the amount of coverage desired and the length of your stay. Two weeks of accident coverage can cost approximately $20; baggage coverage for the same length of time costs $25. The cost of trip cancellation coverage depends on the cost of your travel; the rate is $5.50 per $100 of travel expenses. Again, your travel agent should have full details, or you can get in touch with the *Travelers Companies,* Ticket and Travel, One Tower Square, Hartford, CT 06183 (1–800–243–3174).

If an accident occurs, paying for medical care may be a less urgent problem than finding it. Several companies offer emergency medical assistance along with insurance. *Access America* offers travel insurance and the assistance of a 24-hour hotline in Washington, DC that can direct distressed travelers to a nearby source of aid. They maintain contact with a worldwide network of doctors, hospitals and pharmacies, offer medical evacuation services (a particular problem if you're hurt in an out-of-the-way spot), on-site cash provision services (if it's needed to pay for medical care), legal assistance, and help with lost documents and ticket replacement. Access America offers its services through travel agents and AAA. Cost ranges from $5–$10 per day. For more information, *Access America,* 600 Third Avenue, Box 807, New York, NY 10163 (tel. 1–800–851–2800).

Other organizations that offer similar assistance are:

Carefree Travel Insurance, c/o ARM Coverage, Inc., Box 310, 120 Mineola Blvd., Mineola, NY 11510, underwritten by the Hartford Accident and Indemnity Co., offers a comprehensive benefits package that includes trip cancellation and interruption, medical, and accidental death/dismemberment coverage, as well as medical, legal, and economic assistance. Trip cancellation and interruption insurance can be purchased separately. Call 800–654–2424 for additional information.

International SOS Assistance, Inc., Box 11568, Philadelphia, PA. 19116 (tel. 1–800–523–8930) charges from $15 a person for seven days to $195 for a year.

IAMAT (International Association for Medical Assistance to Travelers), 417 Center St., Lewiston, NY 14092 (tel. 716–754–4883); 188 Nicklin Rd., Guelph, Ontario N1H 7L5 (tel. 519–836–0102).

Travel Assistance International, the American arm of Europ Assistance, offers a comprehensive program offering immediate, on-the-spot medical, personal and financial help. Trip protection ranges from $35 for an individual for up to eight days to $220 for an entire family for a year. (These figures may be revised before 1989). For full details, contact your travel agent or insurance broker, or write Europ Assistance Worldwide Services Inc., 1333 F St., NW, Washington, D.C. 20004 (tel. 1–800–821–2828). In the U.K., contact *Europ Assistance Ltd.,* 252 High St., Croydon, Surrey (tel. 01–680 1234).

The Association of British Insurers, Aldermary House, 10–15 Queen St., London EC4 N1TT (tel. 01–248 4477), will give comprehensive advice on all aspects of vacation travel insurance from the U.K.

Medical Treatment. In Portugal, there is no free medical treatment for visitors unless their countries of origin have reciprocal health agreements, as with the U.K. there is Nationals and residents benefit according to their employment. There is a British Hospital at Rua Saraiva de Carvalho 49, Lisbon (tel. 602020 day; 603785 night), for both in- and outpatients, with English-speaking doctors and nurses. There are local hospitals with emergency services in all the larger towns.

HINTS FOR HANDICAPPED TRAVELERS. *Access to the World: A Travel Guide for the Handicapped,* by Louise Weiss, is an outstanding but somewhat dated book covering all aspects of travel for anyone with health or medical problems. It features extensive listings and suggestions on everything from availability of special diets to wheelchair accessibility. Order from *Facts On File,* 460 Park Ave. South, New York, NY 10016 ($14.95).

Tours specially designed for the handicapped generally parallel those of the non-handicapped traveler, but at a more leisurely pace. For a complete list of tour operators who arrange such travel send a SASE to the *Society for the Advancement of Travel for the Handicapped,* 26 Court St., Penthouse Suite, Brooklyn, NY 11242. The *Travel Information Service* at *Moss Rehabilitation Hospital,* 12th St. and Tabor Rd., Philadelphia, PA 19141, answers inquiries regarding specific cities and countries as well as providing toll-free telephone numbers for airlines with special lines for the hearing impaired and, again, listings of selected tour operators. The fee is $5 per destination. Allow one month for delivery.

The *International Air Transport Association* (IATA) publishes a free pamphlet, *Incapacitated Passengers' Air Travel Guide,* explaining the various arrangements to be made and how to make them. Write IATA, 2000 Peel St., Montreal, Quebec H3A 2R4.

In the U.K., contact *Mobility International,* 228 Borough High St., London SE1 1JX; the *Royal Society for Mentally Handicapped Children and Adults* (MENCAP), 117 Golden Lane, London EC1 0RT; the *Across Trust,* Crown House, Morden, Surrey (they have an amazing series of "Jumbulances," huge articulated ambulances, staffed by volunteer doctors and nurses, that can whisk even the most seriously handicapped across Europe in comfort and safety). But the main source in Britain for all advice on handicapped travel is the *Royal Association for Disability and Rehabilitation* (RADAR), 25 Mortimer St., London W1N 8AB.

CUSTOMS. If you propose to take on your holiday any *foreign-made* articles, such as cameras, binoculars, expensive time-pieces and the like, it is wise to put with your travel documents the receipts from the retailer or some other evidence that the item was bought in your home country. If you bought the article on a previous holiday abroad and have already paid duty on it, carry with you the receipt for this. Otherwise, on returning home, you may be charged duty (for British subjects, V.A.T. as well). One happy factor is that Portuguese Customs are almost non-existent for tourists.

Getting to Portugal

FROM NORTH AMERICA BY AIR. Two airlines fly from the U.S. to Portugal: *TAP Air Portugal* and *TWA.* TAP flies daily out of New York, and twice weekly out of Boston. TWA flies daily out of New York in the summer, less frequently other times of the year. From Canada, *Air Canada* will begin thrice weekly service from Toronto and Montreal to Lisbon in

October 1988; *TAP Air Portugal* has frequent services from both Montreal and Toronto.

In the past few years, airlines have beefed up security on international flights considerably. That translates into more time getting on and off a plane. Be sure to leave yourself plenty of time at the airport arriving and departing.

Air Canada, Place Air Canada, 500 Dorchester Blvd., Montreal, Quebec H2Z 1X5 (tel. 800–361–9620; in Montreal, 514–393–333).

TAP Air Portugal, 1140 Ave. of the Americas, New York, NY 10036 (tel. 800–221–7370).

TWA, 605 Third Ave., New York, NY 10158 (tel. 212–290–2141).

Fares. The ever-changing puzzle of international air fares is best put together with the help of a travel agent, who can unearth the newest bargain, and book your flight, at no charge to you. There are, however, one or two things you might know before setting out.

Fares generally come in four categories, which are, in descending order of expense, First Class, Business, Economy, and APEX. The first three are usually sold without restrictions; they can be bought, used, cancelled or changed at any time. They are distinguished from one another by where they seat you on the plane, and what sort of freebies are attached to your travel (e.g. champagne, etc.). They are also all quite expensive compared to the fourth, APEX.

APEX tickets are always round-trip, seat the passenger in the economy section, and are subject to several conditions. They must be bought well in advance of the flight (7–21 days); they limit the times and days one can fly, and they restrict the length of your travel; they usually require a minimum stay of seven days, and a maximum of three months. They are also quite inexpensive compared to the other tickets. In mid-1988, round-trip New York–Lisbon fares were: First Class, $3,726; Business Class (TAP calls it Navigator Class), $2,076; Economy, $1,362; APEX, from $492. Note that TAP Air Portugal does not offer First Class service.

For even greater savings, tickets on charter flights are sometimes available. Check with your travel agent. There are also a number of ticket brokers who sell seats on flights ordered by tour operators that are not quite completely booked. Note that these tickets are usually available only on very short notice. Among the brokers are: *Stand-Buys Ltd.,* 311 W. Superior, Ste 414, Chicago, IL 60610 (tel. 312–943–5737); *Moments Notice,* 40 E. 49th St., New York, NY 10017 (tel. 212–486–0503); *Discount Travel Int'l,* 114 Forest Ave., Suite 205, Narberth, PA 19072 (tel. 215–668–2182); and *Worldwide Discount Travel Club,* 1674 Meridian Ave., Miami Beach, FL 33139 (tel. 305–534–2082).

FROM NORTH AMERICA BY SEA. The chances of traveling by boat across the Atlantic reduce each year. Only Cunard's *Queen Elizabeth 2* makes trans-Atlantic crossings regularly between New York and Southampton, England and Cherbourg, France. The few cargo ships making the trip and accepting passengers are booked several years ahead. Even so, the persistent can be rewarded with passage on the rare freighter offering relatively comfortable one-class accommodations for a maximum of 12 people. For details, and to help you choose from the lines available, consult *Pearl's Freighter Tips,* Box 188, 16307 Depot Rd., Flushing, NY 11358, publisher of the *Trip Log Quick Reference Freighter Guide.* Or take the QE2 and make further land or sea arrangements from England or France. *Cunard,* 555 Fifth Avenue, New York, NY 10017.

FROM THE U.K. BY AIR. During the summer there are two flights daily from London Heathrow to Lisbon by *British Airways/TAP Air Portugal.* The flying time is two hours 35 minutes. There is also a flight every day (except Tuesday) from London Gatwick airport. Flying BA to Lisbon a roundtrip in Club Class costs around £396, £150–£207 for a Super-Pex return. Book and pay at any time before departure.

Oporto has a direct flight on Mondays, Wednesdays, and Fridays by British Airways from London Gatwick; and daily (though with varying departure times) by TAP from London Heathrow.

Faro is served by a British Airways scheduled flight on Tuesdays, Wednesdays, Thursdays, Saturdays, and Sundays from London Gatwick; and by TAP on three days (Thursday, Saturday and Sunday) from London Heathrow. However the fantastic boom in the popularity of the Algarve as a holiday destination has meant a large number of regular charter flights to Faro, and to a lesser extent Lisbon. This gives a wider choice, especially from regional airports in the U.K. For charter seats booked in advance expect to pay between £90 and £190, according to season. However, these seats are often sold off at a big discount at the last minute.

FROM THE U.K. BY TRAIN. Getting to Lisbon by rail takes two, or two and a half, days depending on which route you take. But it is much more comfortable than going by bus. First of all travel by day to Paris. The fastest connection is the *Hoverspeed City Link* rail–hovercraft–rail service from London Charing Cross. There are up to four departures daily to choose from. Alternatively take one of the through services using the conventional ferries via Dover–Calais, or Newhaven–Dieppe, with an increased journey time. But remember that in bad weather the Hoverspeed section's a non-starter.

From Paris the most comfortable connection is obtained by taking the luxurious overnight Paris–Madrid *TALGO.* This leaves the Gare d'Austerlitz at 8 P.M. and arrives at Madrid Chamartin station at 8.40 the following morning, in good time to transfer to Atocha station to catch the *Lisboa Express.* This leaves at 10.10 A.M., and reaches Lisbon just after seven in the evening. On the TALGO train there is no tiresome change at the frontier, and there is an excellent restaurant service. To guarantee a place book well in advance. Advance reservation is obligatory on both trains anyway.

Alternatively there is one train from Paris with through carriages to Lisbon and Oporto. But this really requires an overnight stop in Paris. The *Sud Express* leaves the Gare d'Austerlitz at 8.42 A.M., and has 2nd-class couchettes which run right through to Lisbon and Oporto (couchettes are carriages with seating compartments which convert at night to provide sleeping accommodations for 6 people). On these carriages the bogies are changed to the broad gauge at Hendaye on the Franco–Spanish border, so there is no need to change trains if you have booked in one of these. Otherwise there are 1st- and 2nd-class day carriages Paris–Irun, and first-class sleepers and day carriages Irun–Lisbon. But this means changing carriages at Hendaye. Lisbon is reached just after 9.30 in the morning.

Taking the fast Hoverspeed City Link service, the luxury Paris–Madrid TALGO, and the Lisboa Express the single fare London–Lisbon works out at around £200. This includes a sleeper berth overnight and breakfast on the TALGO, and all supplements. Using the ordinary ferries and the Sud Express with a second class couchette berth, budget around £125 single, £200 roundtrip.

FROM THE U.K. BY BUS. Portugal is poorly served by coach services from the U.K., and the situation's not likely to improve as the airways are deregulated. In the U.K. the coach companies who run scheduled international services have grouped together under the banner *National Express.* As part of National Express, *Eurolines* run three services to Portugal. From April through September there are two coaches a week to the capital Lisbon (Saturday and Tuesday); two to Faro and Lagos (Wednesday and Saturday) in the Algarve on the southern coast; and two to Coimbra (Saturday and Monday). The coaches leave London Victoria Coach Station in mid-evening, and the Channel crossing is made in the middle of the night. Paris is reached early the next morning and it is necessary to change coaches and coach stations on both the outward and return journeys (Porte de la Villettè to Porte Charenton and v.v.). The Paris–Portugal leg of the journey is operated by *SEAFEP Intercentro,* Coimbra is reached in the late morning on the third day after leaving London, Lisbon in the late afternoon, and Faro/Lagos in the early evening. No overnight stops are made en route so it's a pretty gruelling journey!

Fares are low compared with standard air fares, but high when compared with regular air charter prices, and extortionate when compared with last-minute air seat sales. An adult return to Lisbon works out at around £135, and to Faro at around £150. Barely any reductions are made for students. Please note that dated returns are not issued. Seats for the return journey must be reserved on arrival in Portugal with the local Eurolines/SEAFEP agent. Details from *National Express-Eurolines,* The Coach Travel Center, 13 Regent St., London SW1Y 4LR (tel. 01–730–0202); *Eurolines,* 52 Grosvenor Gardens, London, SW1W OAU (tel. 01–730–8235); or from any *National Express* appointed travel agent.

FROM THE U.K. BY SEA. There are no direct passenger services linking the U.K. with mainland Portugal but various cruise companies (*P&O* being the main one) call at Lisbon, as well as Madeira and the Azores.

Motorists can take advantage of the Santander ferry run by *Brittany Ferries* from Plymouth (see below). Santander, in Spain, is a long day's drive to the Portuguese border, but good if you want to start your vacation visiting the north of the country.

FROM THE U.K. BY CAR. From Calais to Lisbon is some 2,121 km. (1,318 miles) by main road through France and Spain. For a distance such as this, unless time is no option, it is best to consider going as far as possible by ferry, or using Motorail for part of the journey to reduce the tiring drive to a minimum.

Brittany Ferries currently operate a ferry service twice weekly throughout the year from Plymouth to Santander on the northern coast of Spain. The crossing takes 24 hours. For a car (up to 4.5 meters), driver and one passenger, with a comfortable two-berth cabin with shower/w.c., budget

FERRY CHART

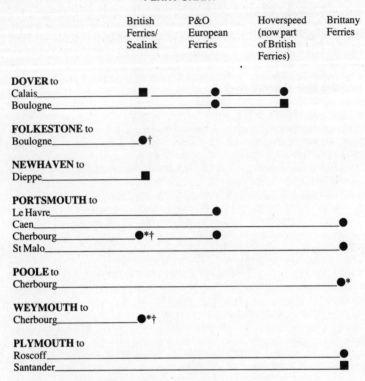

	British Ferries/ Sealink	P&O European Ferries	Hoverspeed (now part of British Ferries)	Brittany Ferries
DOVER to				
Calais	■	●	●	
Boulogne		●	■	
FOLKESTONE to				
Boulogne	●†			
NEWHAVEN to				
Dieppe	■			
PORTSMOUTH to				
Le Havre		●		
Caen				●
Cherbourg	●*†	●		
St Malo				●
POOLE to				
Cherbourg				●*
WEYMOUTH to				
Cherbourg	●*†			
PLYMOUTH to				
Roscoff				●
Santander				■

Key ● crossing only really suitable for motorists
     ■ crossing suitable for rail passengers as well—easy train/ship interchange
   * summer service
   † this service may have ceased to operate by 1989. Check for latest information with your travel agent.

for around £545 return excluding meals. However at press time (mid-1988) there was speculation that Brittany Ferries would either introduce a direct ferry service to Portugal, or increase the frequency of the Santander sailings for 1989. But their press spokesman was being very tight lipped! Going via Santander cuts the drive by half. Brittany Ferries offer a range of touring holidays for motorists to Spain and northern Portugal which are based on the famous paradores and pousadas, and are excellent value for money. Contact *Brittany Ferries,* Millbay Docks, Plymouth, PL1 3EW (tel. 0752 221321 for ferry reservations, 263388 for inclusive holidays).

There is a *Motorail* service from Paris (Gare Austerlitz) to Lisbon which runs daily throughout the summer. Passengers and their cars travel separately. Passengers are booked on to the Sud Express (see *By Train*) and arrive the next morning. However the cars are sent on a separate train from Paris Tolbiac, and arrive the day after. The cost for a car, driver and passenger, with couchette works out at around £275 single, £490 roundtrip. *French National Railroads,* Rockefeller Center, 610 Fifth Ave., New York, NY 10020, can provide schedules only; rate information and arrangements are handled in Europe. In the U.K., *French Railways,* 179 Piccadilly, London, W1V 9DB.

If going by road the choice is between using a daytime short crossing or a longer service. Taking one of the short cross-Channel services from Dover/Folkestone to Calais/Boulogne (or from Newhaven to Dieppe), it is best to go via Paris. Then take the toll Autoroute de L'Aquitaine from Paris via Orléans, to just beyond Bordeaux, crossing into Spain at Hendaye and then continuing via Burgos and Salamanca before entering Portugal. If you use one of the longer crossings from Portsmouth it is possible to drive south using the ordinary main roads via Rennes, Nantes, and La Rochelle before joining the Autoroute. From St. Malo to Lisbon it's around 1,765 km. (1,097 miles). For comfortable driving one should allow for at least two overnight stops en route in addition to a night on the ferry.

On a short Channel crossing, budget for £95 single for a car (up to 4.5 meters), driver, and a passenger in high season. From Portsmouth, budget for around £120 single including cabin. In addition, allow for autoroute tolls, overnight accommodation etc. en route.

Fly/Drive Holiday. This has proved one of the more popular touring holidays in Portugal, as it combines swiftness in getting to the country (in practice you can be driving along the roads of Portugal within three hours of leaving the U.K.) with total freedom of movement—plus the advantages of the "package" with none of its attendant restrictions. Prices are as a rule calculated per person, with two sharing both the car and the accommodation (if that is pre-booked), or if four go together, then the costs are lower. Fly/drive can start at all of Portugal's three mainland airports—Lisbon, Oporto and Faro, with Lisbon and Faro being the most popular. You can also arrange fly/drive in Madeira but in this case they are based on staying in one hotel and touring from there.

The prices include the flight, hire of the car on an unlimited-mileage basis with full insurance, often first and last nights' accommodation (or if required a fully-worked itinerary) and the necessary documentation. This, however, does not include accommodation other than the first and last nights. *British Airways* team up with *Avis* for this but there are a number of other car hiring companies in the market, prominent among them *Lane's Travel Service Ltd.,* of 251 Brompton Road, London SW3 2EY, who also operate in conjunction with Avis, and serve Funchal on Madeira, as well as the three principal mainland centers. In some cases (the Algarve in particular) a car is offered as part of the package deal when you rent a villa or apartment.

Full details from travel agents, car hiring companies and the airlines.

Arriving in Portugal

CUSTOMS. The principal Portugal/Spain frontier customs houses are located at Valença do Minho, coming from Vigo; Vilar Formoso, coming from Salamanca; Caia (Caya), coming from Merida-Badajoz; Rosal de la

Frontera, from Seville; and Vila Real de Santo António, from Seville-Huelva. Others are at São Gregório, Vila Verde da Raia, Quintanilha, Miranda do Douro, Segura, Galegos, São Leonardo, Portela do Homen, Vila Nova de Cerveira. Those at Valença do Minho in the north, and Vilar Formoso and Caia to the east, are open all the time. Opening times of the other frontier crossings vary: some open from 7 A.M.–9 P.M. in winter and 7 A.M.–midnight in summer (March 1 to October 31); others, such as Vila Real de Santo António from 8 A.M.–8 P.M. in winter, and 8 A.M.–11 P.M. in summer (May 1 to October 31).

You are allowed to bring into Portugal such personal possessions as typewriters, cameras, movie cameras, tape-recorders, portable radios, tents and camping equipment, sports equipment like fishing gear, hunting rifles with 50 cartridges, a kayak 5.5 meters (18 ft.) long (maximum), tennis racquets, etc. You are also entitled to bring in 200 cigarettes or ½ lb of tobacco, a bottle of wine, a quart of liquor, an ordinary amount of perfume. If you wish to bring in a dog, you must be able to produce a recent veterinary's certificate attesting that the animal has had anti-rabies and anti-distemper shots; this must be endorsed by a Portuguese consulate prior to departure. But dogs cannot return to Britain without 6 months in quarantine.

MONEY. As exchange rates are currently so volatile, we suggest you check on them while planning your trip, and keep a very close eye on what the escudo is up to while you are traveling. There are 100 centavos to an escudo.

Note: the symbol for the escudo is a $ sign, written between the escudo and the centavo units—thus 100$00.

The smallest unit is now 50 centavos. You must anticipate differences in buying and selling rates, and a percentage charge for conversion.

We would like to suggest that you take with you some small denomination Portuguese money to help with porters, taxis and such on arrival. It is not always possible, or convenient, to change travelers' checks immediately.

There are notes of 5,000, 1,000 and 100 escudos, and coins of 50, 25, 29, 10, 5, 2½ and 1 escudos and of 50 centavos.

Staying in Portugal

HOTELS. Hotels are graded into categories based on quality and prices: 5-star (deluxe), 4-, 3-, 2-, and 1-star. These roughly equate to our usual Fodor categories of Deluxe (L), Expensive (E), Moderate (M), and Inexpensive (I). Hotel prices are no longer state controlled.

Daily Bed and Breakfast Room Rates

Approximate High-Season Rates for Two in Escudos

Deluxe (L)	25,000–30,000
Expensive (E)	15,000–20,000
Moderate (M)	9,500–15,000
Inexpensive (I)	6,000–8,000

Service and tourist taxes are usually included.

Hotels in the (L), (E) and (M) price categories will have all rooms with bath, while those in the (I) category will have most rooms with bath.

If breakfast is not included in the hotel rate, this will cost from 300$00. Lunch or dinner at a good restaurant will run from around 5,000$00 each, depending on the wines chosen. Service and taxes are usually included in the bill but a 5% to 10% tip should be given. All restaurants have their price lists displayed outside. Only in 5-star and luxury restaurants can you book tables.

Note: These are the rates as we go to press in mid-1988. In the present financial situation they may well have risen by the beginning of 1989, so check in advance.

If you haven't reserved any hotel accommodation in advance, you can make enquiries as follows: in *Lisbon,* at the Information Service of the Direcção-Geral do Turismo, Palacio Foz, Praça dos Restauradores or Ave. António Augusto Aguiar 86; at *Portela airport,* the branch office of the above; in *Oporto,* at the Delegação do Direcção-Geral do Turismo, Praça D. João 1, 25; and in all the country towns.

In addition to conventional hotels—and apartment hotels in resorts—Portugal has a variety of establishments offering accommodation, ranging from simple pensions to luxurious *pousadas.*

Pensions. Pensions exist in most towns and only occasionally have restaurants, serving breakfast only. A room without bath is likely to cost from 3,000$00 to 4,000$00, and a room with bath, from 3,500$00 to 4,500$00. The Portuguese word is *pensão.*

Residências, some serving breakfast only, are now to be found in most towns, ranging in price from 2,500$00 a night without bath, to 4,500$00 with bath. Between November 1 and mid-March there is a 15% reduction. *Albergarias* are also pension-like establishments, generally in the Moderate price range.

Country Houses. A venture named *Turismo de Habitaçao,* or Country House Tourism, by which a few visitors are received in private houses, is now in operation. The majority are in the north and are often beautiful manor houses. Not all give dinner, but those that do will be included in the Hotel and Restaurant lists at the end of each chapter. A simple dinner costs around 1,500$00 and for several courses can go up to 3,000$00. Prices for a double room and breakfast are lowest in the north of the country, starting at around 7,000$00, and highest in Evora, in the Alentejo. Full particulars of all the country houses available for this unusual accommodation can be obtained from Ave. António Augusto de Aguiar 86–3, 1000 Lisbon (tel. 575493) or call Ponte de Lima, (tel. 058 942335), for houses in the Minho in the north of Portugal.

Pousadas. In and outside many towns, but usually easily accessible, are government-controlled *pousadas,* which are mostly in the Expensive price category and sometimes in the Deluxe, and also private *estalagems* (usually Moderate). These attractive tourist inns offer the motorist a chance to rest in typical Portuguese surroundings. Any traveler may stop for a meal and the food is generally excellent. Varying in architecture from historic through bucolic to modern, the standard of comfort and service in both types of establishment is likely to be excellent. In summer always book ahead, as accommodation is limited; to be sure, book ahead at any time.

In the following list of pousadas, organized by town, the name in italics after each entry is the title of the chapter in whose *Practical Information* section you will find the pousada listed.

Águeda. Pousada de Santo António. *The Three Beiras.*
Alijó. Pousada do Barão de Forrester. *Trás-os-Montes.*
Almeida. Pousada Senhora das Neves. *The Three Beiras.*
Amarante. Pousada de São Gonçalo. *Minho.*
Batalha. Pousada Mestre Afonso Domingues. *Estremadura.*
Bragança. Pousada de São Bartolomeu. *Trás-os-Montes.*
Caniçada. Pousada de São Bento. *Minho.*
Caramulo. Pousada de São Jerónimo. *The Three Beiras.*
Castelo de Bode. Pousada de São Pedro. *Ribatejo.*
Elvas. Pousada de Santa Luzia. *The Alentejo.*
Estremoz. Pousada da Rainha Santa Isabel. *The Alentejo.*
Evora. Pousada dos Loios. *The Alentejo.*
Guimarães. Pousada de Santa Maria da Oliviera. *Minho.*
Guimarães. Pousada de Santa Marinha da Costa. *Minho.*
Manteigas. Pousada de São Lourenço. *The Three Beiras.*
Marvão. Pousada de Santa Maria. *The Alentejo.*
Miranda do Douro. Pousada de Santa Caterina. *Trás-os-Montes.*
Murtosa. Pousada da Ria. *The Three Beiras.*
Obidos. Pousada do Castelo. *Estremadura.*
Palmela. Pousada de Palmela. *Environs of Lisbon.*
Póvoa das Quartas. Pousada da Santa Bárbara. *The Three Beiras.*
Sagres. Pousada do Infante. *The Algarve.*
Sao Brás de Alportel. Pousada de São Brás de Alportel. *The Algarve.*
Sao Tiago do Cacém. Pousada de São Tiago do Cacém. *The Alentejo.*
Serém. Pousada de São António. *The Three Beiras.*
Serpa. Pousada de São Gens. *The Alentejo.*
Setubal. Pousada de São Filipe. *Environs of Lisbon.*
Torrao. Pousada de Vale do Gaio. *The Alentejo.*
Valença do Minho. Pousada de São Teotónio. *Minho.*
Vila Nova de Cerveira. Pousada de Dom Diniz. *Minho.*

CAMPING. In Portugal, camping has been on the upswing over the past few years, and over 100 good camping sites are available all over the country. One of the largest is the *Monsanto Parque Florestal* site run by the Lisbon Municipality, not far from city center, along the Estoril autostrada, with tennis, swimming pool, bank, restaurant, cafés, chapel, library, game-room, mini-market, etc. For information, apply to the *Turismos* or *Federa-çao Portuguesa de Campismo,* Rua Voz do Operario, 1, 1100 Lisbon (tel. 862350).

Another very pleasant site is 5 minutes from Guincho beach, Cascais, operated by *ORBITUR,* Avenida Almirante Gago Coutinho 25, Lisbon, (tel. 892938), who also have several other well-equipped camps, some with 4-person chalets to rent.

Other good sites are at Caminha, Esmoriz, Espinho, Guarda, Viana do Castelo and Vila Real in the north; Castelo Branco, Coimbra, Evora,

Figueira da Foz, Nazaré, Tomar and Viseu in the central part of the country; Caparica, Ericeira, Oeiras, Palmela, Praia de Santa Cruz (Torres Vedras), Sesimbra and Setúbal near Lisbon; and Albufeira, Alvor, Armação de Pera, Faro, Ferrugado, Lagos, Monte Gordo, Praia da Luz, Quarteira and Vila Nova de Cacela in the Algarve.

The camping guidebook *Roteiro Campista* can be obtained from the Portuguese Travel Office in your home country. Campsites are graded by the Ministry of Tourism and are Inexpensive.

YOUTH HOSTELS. The *Pousadas de Juventude* hostels are open to young travelers of all nationalities who have valid membership cards bearing the current year's stamp of a Youth Hostel Association belonging to the International Federation of Youth Hostels. There are youth hostels in: Areia Branca (Lourinhã), Braga, Coimbra, Evora, Leiria, Lindoso (Gerêz), Lisbon (Rua Andrade Corvo 46, tel. 01 532696), Oeiras (Catalazete), Oporto, Penhas da Saude, Portalegre, Sagres, São Martinho, São Pedro de Moel and Vila Real de Santo António. The official limit is 3 consecutive days in any one hostel, but sojourns can be prolonged on a space-available basis. To join the International Federation of Youth Hostels, apply in the US to: *American Youth Hostels, Inc.,* P.O. Box 37613, Washington, DC 20013; in Canada to *Canadian Hostelling Association,* 333 River Rd., Tower A, Vanier City, Ottawa, Ontario, K1L 8H9; in Britain to *Youth Hostels Association,* 14 Southampton St., London WC2E 7HY.

RESTAURANTS. Although we grade our restaurant listings Expensive (E), Moderate (M), and Inexpensive (I), as usual, there are very few Expensive restaurants outside the major towns or main tourist areas. In comparison with the States or Britain, eating is very reasonable in Portugal, highly seasoned and hearty. Portions are generally large, except in really top-class places, and you'll find yourself having only one big meal a day without any problem at all.

Our grading is aligned to the following price ranges—(E) 7,500$00–10,000$00, (M) 4,000$00–6,000$00, (I) 1,500$00–3,000$00 per person, but these are very flexible as you travel around the country.

Unlike many European countries, Portugal doesn't have the practice of set menus. With prices so low, you hardly need them anyway. A few very up-market hotels will have a *table d'hôte,* such as the Seteais at Sintra, but it is fairly rare. The Seteais set menu has the extra luxury of several choices per course, and, at only 4,000$00 a head, it's a bargain.

The soup is always a good bet in Portugal, rich and filling. If you are eating in an (I) restaurant, you can easily share a fish dish and then a meat dish between two, and still come away feeling full. Beef and mutton are generally to be avoided—the pasture doesn't make for succulent meat— pork and chicken are usually good. Fish is excellent almost everywhere, but, times being what they are, and catches dropping all over the European seaboard, any fish dish will run expensive. *Tascas* make a good meal, and, when washed down with local wine, will help you to feel that you have really discovered Portugal.

Our *Portuguese Cuisine* chapter will tell you more about what to look for. But one last word of cheer—don't be afraid to eat in an out-of-the-way little eatery in a backwoods village. It may look rough and ready, but the food will almost certainly be excellent.

TIPPING. Hotel service charges cover everything. But give 100$00 per bag to whoever brings the luggage up. A nightclub waiter expects 10% in addition to the service charge. Station porters expect 100$00 per bag, hatcheck girls, theater ushers, the same; 50$00 escudos for bootblacks. Taxi drivers get 15 to 20%. Gas station attendants 10$00. In barbershops, men give 50$00 or 100$00, while in average beauty salons women tip 100$00, in more elaborate ones 200$00.

Although a service charge is usually included in the check at restaurants, cafés, etc., a small tip is always welcome (about 5% in a moderate restaurant). Especially wise if you intend to return.

SPAS. Especially in the north, many places have excellent thermal waters. In the smaller spas, hotels are rather simple. In the more famous stations, they are first class. Most of the spas are open only from May to October, a few from June.

Caldas da Rainha: near Lisbon, is known world-wide for its rheumatic treatment as well as for the legend that Queen Eleanor discovered the curative powers of these potent, smelly waters. Always open.

Caldas de Monchique: a few miles inland from the Algarve coast, for rheumatism, and respiratory ailments. Overlooks the Algarve plain.

Caldelas: in the Braga district, for gastric troubles. These waters are known to have the same mineral content as those of the famous Bad Kissingen in Bavaria.

Cucos: near Torres Vedras, the only natural mud baths in Portugal; excellent against rheumatic complaints.

Curia: between Coimbra and Aveiro, for circulatory troubles as well as for gout and rheumatism.

Entre-os-Rios: near Oporto, sulphur baths for asthma and bronchitis.

Gerêz: in the north, for diabetes, corpulence and metabolic complaints.

Luso: between Coimbra and Aveiro, is a well-known spa, for liver, digestive and respiratory ailments.

Monfortinho: near Castelo Branco, for liver, intestinal and kidney troubles.

Monte Real: near Leiria, for rheumatism, liver and digestive tract.

Pedras Salgadas: in the north, for liver and kidney complaints.

Vidago: in the north, for allergies, liver, digestive tract and kidneys.

Vimeiro: about 80 km. (50 miles) north of Lisbon, for kidneys and livers. Always open.

MUSEUMS. Both the Gulbenkian and the Coach Museums in Lisbon are justly world famous. The other Lisbon museums contain fine and unusual exhibits such as the 15th-century polyptych panels of St. Vincent by Nuno Gonçalves and the silver table service made for King John by the Germain brothers, in the Ancient Art Museum. It is a relief that no museum in Portugal is very large, so visitors do not easily become exhausted, as they do in the Louvre, Prado or Metropolitan.

Oporto has several delightful collections, as have all the major towns, and there is an unusually large number of small, personal collections all over the country. These are shown in the former owners' houses, some of which, like the Castro Guimarães in Cascais and the Casa dos Patudos at Alpiarça, are well worth seeing.

Museums usually open at 10, close for lunch and shut at 5; they are closed Mondays and holidays; palaces in Lisbon close on Tuesdays. Entrance fees vary wildly from 150$00 to 300$00. The major collections are listed in the *Practical Information* sections at the end of each chapter.

CHURCHES. The churches of Portugal are of course Roman Catholic; however, there are a few Anglican (Episcopalian) churches as well as some caring for English-speaking Roman Catholics. *Anglican:* St. George's, Lisbon; St. Paul's, Estoril; St. James's, Oporto; St. Vincent's, Algarve; English Church, Funchal, Madeira. *Roman Catholic:* Corpo Santo, Lisbon, run by Irish Dominicans; St. Mary's parish center, São Pedro do Estoril; St. Sebastian's Chapel, Cascais. For further details, see *Practical Information* sections at the end of each chapter.

SHOPPING. As an introduction to the varied handicrafts of Portugal and so to shopping for unusual things, a visit to the Museum of Folk Art at Belém (Lisbon) is recommended. In every province there are ethnographic museums with displays of the local Portuguese products, for example in Oporto, Ílhavo, Estremoz and Faro.

Air travelers who are careful of weight should look at the superbly made baskets on sale, not only in local markets, but also in both specialized and general shops. The beautifully hand-embroidered table linen does not weigh much, and there are also blouses and dresses in the finest lawn or organdy, a specialty of the women of Madeira, as are initialled and embroidered handkerchiefs. Each part of Portugal goes in for different patterns and colors for their hand-work. In the north, Viana do Castelo is noted for stylized hearts in red, blue or natural; Guimarães for floral motifs in white on natural or beige on white and blue or white in simple patterns come from the Azores. Traditional embroidered silk bedspreads are still made in Castelo Branco and real lace in Vila do Conde near Oporto. The variety is endless.

The country is famous for glazed tiles (*azulejos*) either in patterns or pictorial panels. Some of these are lovely and can be sent home by freight. Names and addresses of suppliers can be found in the Practical Information sections.

Smaller items of porcelain or pottery can be very attractive. *Vista Alegre* is the most famous and oldest porcelain factory, with works near Aveiro and shops in Lisbon, Oporto and Coimbra. Pottery differs widely from place to place. The brightly colored roosters are made in Barcelos, black pottery in Vila Real, polychrome in Aveiro, blue and white in Coimbra and Alcobaça. Caldas da Rainha is famous for green glazed plates and dishes made in the form of leaves, vegetables, fruit and animals. There are also more conventional pieces in a soft white. Mafra and Sobreiro near Lisbon specialize in vessels made with a gray pearl-like finish. But it is in the Alentejo, particularly in Estremoz, that you will find the early Etruscan and Roman shapes reproduced in unglazed red water pots and jars, while there is a big range of glazed cooking pots in all shapes and sizes, and colored figurines. Marinha Grande is the center for glass ware of every kind.

The Alentejo is also the home of natural cork; products such as the *tarros,* a kind of lidded bucket in which food can be kept hot or cold, are light to carry and make original and unusual ice containers. Lamb and goatskin slippers, carpets and jackets are also made in this province, as are wooden carved spoons and boxes.

Tin, brass, copper and other metals are turned into attractive lanterns, fire screens and door furniture in the Algarve and Trás-os-Montes. Primitive as well as sophisticated musical instruments are made in the Minho, Trás-os-Montes and the Beiras. Coimbra is famous for guitars, and clay whistles are made in Estremoz.

Fine leather shoes, handbags and belts can be bought all over the country, as can materials, mainly manufactured in and around Oporto and other textiles such as cotton and wool blankets in cheerfully colored stripes are to be found everywhere. Embroidered carpets and rugs are the specialty of Arraiolos in the Alentejo, and Portalegre has the finest tapestry workshops in Portugal.

Genuine antiques are getting harder to find, but perfect copies are made at the *Espirito Santo Foundation* in Lisbon and in Braga and Viseu in the north. Incidentally, the Portuguese are excellent at repair work and old jewelry, watches, silver and plate are superbly restored. Book-binding in fine leathers is another specialty.

LOCAL MARKET DAYS AND FESTIVALS. Market days are an attraction anywhere, and Portugal's no exception. They include the Thieves Market, Tuesday and Saturday behind the Church of São Vicente de Fora in *Lisbon*. Near *Lisbon:* every Wednesday and Saturday in *Cascais;* 2nd and 4th Sunday of the month in *São Pedro de Sintra;* every Thursday at *Malveira* near *Mafra;* and *Carcavelos* on the Cascais line; south of the river 1st Sunday at *Azeitão*. In the north: every Thursday at *Barcelos*. In the Algarve: 3rd Sunday at *Albufeira;* 1st Saturday at *Lagos;* 1st Monday at *Portimão;* 3rd Monday at *Silves;* 3rd Monday at *Tavira;* every Saturday at *Loulé* and in *São Braz de Alportel*.

Festivals called *romarias,* which are all religious in origin, are held all over the country. They are listed at the end of each chapter.

CLOSING TIMES. Banks are open 8:30–11:45 and 1–2:45 Mondays to Fridays. Shops usually open from 9 to 1 and 3 to 7 Mondays to Fridays, 9 to 1 Saturdays. There are now shopping centers and supermarkets in every big town, many of which are open till midnight and also on Sundays. Museums in Lisbon and most other places are closed Mondays and holidays, open 10–5 other days, including Sundays, but usually close for lunch. Palaces in Lisbon close on Tuesdays.

NATIONAL HOLIDAYS. January 1 (New Year's Day), February 7 (Carnival), March 24 (Good Friday), April 25 (Anniversary of Revolution), May 1 (Labor Day), May 25 (Corpus Christi), June 10 (National Day), August 15 (Assumption), October 5 (Republic Day), November 1 (All Saints Day), December 1 (Restoration of Independence), December 8 (Immaculate Conception), and Christmas Day.

MAIL. Postal rates, both domestic and foreign, increase from time to time, especially in the present uncertain economic climate. Sub-post offices open 9–12:30, 2:30–6 on weekdays. Main offices stay open at lunchtime; that in the Restauradores in Lisbon is open 24 hours.

Stamp collectors may find treasures, or simply enjoy a leisurely visit to the *Clube Filatélico de Portugal,* 70 Ave. Almirante Reis, 5th floor, or to *Numifilarte,* Calçada do Carmo 25, *Molder,* Rua 1 Dezembro 101, 3rd floor, *Eládio de Santos,* 27 Rua Bernardo Lima, all in Lisbon. Look under *Filatelia* in the Yellow Pages for further addresses.

ELECTRICITY. Voltage 220 AC. In a few remote areas, 110 volts.

DRINKING WATER. Water is usually safe to drink, but use one or other of the excellent mineral waters if you want to play safe. *Luso* is still (*sem gas*), *Agua de Castelo* fizzy (*com gas*). Pasteurized milk is available in most towns.

HINTS FOR BUSINESSPEOPLE. Normal office hours in Portugal are from 9 to 5 or 5:30 with a 2-hour break for lunch from 1 to 3, but don't expect to see the managing director before 10. Coffee is often offered to clients, but no one minds if it is refused. Smoking is declining, but again no one minds if you smoke.

Although the Portuguese are an easy-going race, they have very high standards of manners. Shake hands wherever you go, turn as you get out of sight to bow or wave to your host who will be standing at the door until you are out of his vision and do the same to him if he comes to your office or hotel.

Men should normally be addressed as Senhor Doutor if they are lawyers or medical men, as Senhor Engenheiro if they are engineers and Senhor Arquitécto if they are architects, women as Senhora Doutora, Senhora Engenheira or Senhora Arquitécta. Indeed, every university graduate is called Senhor Doutor or Senhora Doutora, so it does no harm and is flattering to do so if in doubt.

The *Hospedeiras de Portugal,* Rua Borges Carneiro 63–3D, Lisbon 1200, (tel. 01 604353), will provide interpreters, translators and secretarial assistance.

It is now considerably cheaper and more satisfactory to telephone abroad than to send cables. All good hotels have telexes.

FISHING. Portugal's almost 800 km. (500 miles) of coast, plus its rivers and streams, make it a fisherman's paradise, offering one of the greatest variety of catches. For sport fishermen, the season is April–November, with deep-sea fishing available all year. For about 3,500$00 per person for four hours, you can rent a professional fishing boat, complete with dinghy and action-seat, with bait and tackle included, at Peniche, Ericeira, Nazaré, Cascais (through *TIP Tours,* Avenida Costa Pinto 91A, tel. 2865150), Sesimbra and several places in the Algarve.

Off-shore there are swordfish, skate, ray, and the twice-yearly tunny runs to and from their spawning banks beyond Gibraltar are sensational. The Fishing Service for licenses is at Avenida João Crisostomo 9, 1000 Lisbon, but most sea fishing in Portugal is free for all.

The best fresh-water fishing is in the Minho and Lima rivers (lamprey, trout, salmon); in the Vouga river, and the Serra da Estrela lakes and streams (trout).

Off Madeira and the Azores, the Gulf Stream ensures some of the best deep-sea fishing in the world.

There is good *undersea fishing* all along the coast and the waters around the Berlenga Islands are notably good for gaffing the big ones. The many lagoons along the eastern part of the Algarve are exceptionally rewarding. Apply to the *Centro Português de Actividades Subaquáticas,* Rua do Alto do Duque 45, 1495 Lisbon (tel. 01 616961). This club organizes expeditions along the Algarve coast and out of Arrabida, Sesimbra, etc.; open to non-members.

Itinerary for Fishermen. *Lisbon–Cascais–Ericeira–Peniche* for bream, bass, mullet, swordfish; *Berlenga Islands,* 16 km. (10 miles) out from Peniche, as above, also conger, seasonal tunny; *Nazaré* for bream, mackerel, sole, silver eel; *Póvoa de Varzim,* best bass area; *Foz do Arelho,* bream, flounder; *Sesimbra,* a fisherman's paradise, big game, shore and seabed fishing, swordfish, tunny, conger, red mullet, sole etc.; *Sines,* for bass, bream, sole; *Sagres* for deepsea, shore rock fishing, gray mullet, bream, bass, etc.

Fishing grounds are excellent all along the Algarve coast: the Naval Clubs at Lagos in the Algarve, Espinho near Oporto, and Cascais gladly advise visitors.

GOLF. There are some excellent golf links all over the country, at Estoril (an 18- and 9-hole course), another very pretty 9-hole course near the Estoril-Sol Hotel at Linhó between Estoril and Sintra, at Cascais an 18-hole course at the Quinta da Marinha, designed by Robert Trent Jones, as was that at Troia near Setúbal, at Oporto, at the Lisbon Sports Club, Belas, and the famous International Championship Course at the Algarve Penina Golf Hotel between Portimão and Lagos, designed by Henry Cotton, three times British Open Champion. This is an 18- and 9-hole course, the scene of many International Tournaments, as are the other Algarve courses—Vilamoura, designed by Frank Pennick, as was the adjoining Dom Pedro (both near Albufeira), both are 18 holes, with fine views of the sea; Vale de Lobo near Faro, another Henry Cotton course, three distinct 9-hole courses which are said to be the most scenic in Portugal; Palmares, near Lagos, also by Frank Pennick, with five of its 18 holes sited on dunes as was the original golf course at St. Andrew's in Scotland; Quinta do Lago, near Almansil, American-designed course of 27 holes, permitting 18-hole play in three different combinations, with lakeside trees, and the latest at Parque da Floresta near Budens, by Pepé Gancedo. Vidago, Vimeiro, Miramar near Oporto, Santo da Serra in Madeira, Furnas in São Miguel in the Azores are all 9-hole courses. There is an 18-hole course on Terceira island also in the Azores.

Package Tours for Golfers. If you are a keen golfer you should investigate the program that *Eurogolf* have to offer. See the earlier *Tour Operators* section.

BULLFIGHTS. The Portuguese version of bullfighting is a combination of elegance, daring, and skill. The combat is waged between the bull and the *toureiro,* the latter on superbly trained horses. The bull is not killed. Season from Easter Sunday through October, on Sundays, sometimes also Thursdays.

Portugal boasts over 30 bullrings. The main one is Campo Pequeno in Lisbon. The biggest names in the bullfighting world usually appear at Santarém in June, in Vila Franca de Xira in July.

Traveling in Portugal

BY AIR. The internal services of Air Portugal are remarkably good considering that it is a comparatively small country. Lisbon is linked at least four times daily with Oporto and Faro, daily (more at peak periods) with Funchal (Madeira) and weekly with Porto Santo—the smaller of the two inhabited islands in the Madeira group—and several times a week to Terceira and São Miguel in the Azores. There are also small aircraft on "second level" internal flights to Viseu, Vila Real, and Bragança on the mainland, and several flights weekly between Oporto and Faro via Lisbon. Main services are all by jet, mostly 727s.

BY TRAIN. The Portuguese railway system is surprisingly extensive for a small country. However, the physical geography greatly hindered the development of north–south communications, and it must be said that there is room for modernization. Although trains are clean and leave on time, many of those away from the Lisbon–Oporto main line are slow, old-fashioned and infrequent. Diesel engines haul trains which are not yet electrified. Many of the branch lines serving the agrarian interior, especially in the north, are meter gauge.

Some expresses between Lisbon and Oporto run virtually non-stop and have either restaurant or buffet facilities. They are first class, require supplementary fares and reservations are obligatory. Other trains have an extra-fare saloon car attached. The fastest trains take under three hours for the 350 km. (215 miles).

Several of the Oporto–Lisbon trains take cars, as does one train a day between Lisbon, Castelo Branco, Regua and Guarda, as well as some of the Algarve trains, though the latter only in the summer. Prices are reasonable, but remember that cars must be at the station an hour beforehand, and tickets must be purchased then or in advance.

There is a secondary route between Lisbon and Oporto which goes via the coastal route through Figueira da Foz rejoining the main line at Pampilhosa. To the Algarve there is a daily so-called express between the Barreiro Station just across the Tagus (ferry links) from Lisbon, the "Sotavento," leaving just after lunch, with buffet car, taking four hours through beautiful country. A supplement is payable, and reservation is obligatory. In addition there are slower trains.

From the Cais do Sodre station in Lisbon there is an excellent service of electric trains along the north bank of the Tagus estuary to Estoril and Cascais, taking around half an hour for the entire 27 km. (17 mile) route. Services every 15 minutes, less frequent at off peak periods. From the city's Rossio Station there is also a good service to the lovely hill town of Sintra (30 km., 19 miles).

In the north there is a regular service (about a dozen trains daily) between Oporto and Braga, taking about an hour and a half for the 60 km. (37 miles). A fascinating scenic line goes from Oporto up the River Douro to Barca de Alva on the Spanish border.

Be sure to buy tickets at the station as there is a huge surcharge if bought on the train. Timetables are the same on Saturdays and Sundays as on weekdays, except on suburban trains. Passengers aged 65 and over get half-rate fares on production of Europrail cards, but only out of rush hours on the Cascais and Sintra lines.

The times of the main trains are contained in the *Thomas Cook European Timetable*. This can be obtained by mail in the U.S. from *Forsyth Travel Library,* Box 2975, 9154 W. 57th St., Shawnee Mission, KS 66201. In the U.K., over the counter from any branch of Thomas Cook, or by post from Thomas Cook Ltd., P.O. Box 36, Peterborough.

Portuguese Railways (C.P.) are covered by the Eurailpass. Details of the Eurailpass and up to date prices can be obtained in the U.S. from *French National Railroads,* Rockefeller Center, 610 Fifth Ave., New York, NY 10020. *Wasteels Expresso,* Ave. António Augusto de Aguiar 88, 1000 Lisbon (tel. 01 579180), is reliable for all local and international train tickets and reservations.

BY BUS. The nationalized bus company and tourist office called *Rodoviaria Nacional* has passenger terminals in Lisbon at Ave. Casal Ribeiro 18 (tel. 01 577715); and at Ave. Santos Dumont 57 (tel. 01 775245). The company runs regular services throughout Portugal. Other recommended companies are *Mundial Turismo,* Ave. António Augusto de Aguiar 90–A (tel. 01 553710); *Novo Mundo,* Rua Augusto Santos 9 (tel. 01 555959); *Sol Expresso,* Rua Entrecampos 1 (tel. 01 773748), for the Algarve and Alentejo. *Capristanos,* Ave. Duque de Loulé 47 (tel. 01 542973), and *Citirama,* Ave. Praia da Vitória 12 (tel. 01 575564), for well organized bus tours. All these are in Lisbon. Bookings can be made in hotels or travel agencies. Various inter-urban lines are served by private companies.

BY CAR. As is the case for most countries, the motorist bringing his car into Portugal should be in possession of an international driving license, car insurance (green card) and nationality plates. Spare parts for American and British cars are available.

The Portuguese automobile club is *Autómovel Clube de Portugal,* Rua Rosa Araujo 24, Lisbon (tel. 01 563931).

At the time of writing (mid-'88) fuel prices were approximately 115$00 per liter; super 119$00 per liter; oil 365$00 per liter. But these prices may well rise. A table of highway distances is given opposite.

Driving is on the right, and on the very few kilometers of motorway the country possesses, the speed limit is 120 kph (74 mph). On other open roads it is 90 kph (56 mph) and in built-up areas 50–60 kph (31–37 mph) according to traffic density. Main roads have priority, but do not rely on that. At the junction of two roads of equal size, traffic coming from the right has priority. The roads are good but narrow, with many curves and an incredible variety of surfaces; but traffic, except in a few cities, is light. You should however be prepared to encounter people walking on the road, often—if they are women—carrying loads on their heads. Seat belts are now obligatory. Horns must not be used in built-up areas. A red warning triangle must be carried. Portuguese drivers are notoriously rash.

Car hire. If you choose neither to bring your own car nor to buy a fly-package, cars may be rented on arrival, though it is cheaper, and bookings more certain, to pay for them from abroad. The following are some of the hire firms available—

Avis, Praça dos Restauradores 47, (tel. 01 361171); *Europcar,* Ave. Antonio Augusto de Aguiar 24, (tel. 01 524558); *Hertz,* Ave. 5 de Outubro

TABLE OF DISTANCES BY ROAD (IN KILOMETERS)

	Aveiro	Beja	Braga	Bragança	Castelo Branco	Coimbra	Évora	Faro	Guarda	Leiria	Lisbon	Oporto	Portalegre	Santarém	Setúbal	Valença do Minho	Viana do Castelo	Vila Real	Vila Real de S. António	Vilar Formoso
Beja	380																			
Braga	121	502																		
Bragança	343	589	230																	
Castelo Branco	217	281	329	308																
Coimbra	58	332	170	312	159															
Évora	302	78	424	511	203	254														
Faro	502	154	624	724	416	454	213													
Guarda	181	387	263	203	107	168	309	524												
Leiria	114	265	238	379	168	67	187	387	235											
Lisbon	244	192	366	508	258	196	150	298	364	129										
Oporto	67	449	53	254	276	117	371	571	219	184	313									
Portalegre	297	209	409	388	80	239	131	344	186	168	231	313								
Santarém	186	195	307	448	170	138	117	299	278	69	78	254	154							
Setúbal	294	141	416	558	265	246	103	249	371	179	50	363	193	121						
Valença do Minho	192	578	91	321	405	242	500	700	347	313	442	123	485	383	492					
Viana do Castelo	139	525	51	279	352	193	447	647	294	260	389	70	432	330	438	53				
Vila Real	184	544	107	139	263	202	466	660	157	273	402	115	343	343	452	198	155			
Vila Real de S. António	504	626	713	405	456	203	53	53	389	389	316	573	333	319	266	702	649	688		
Vilar Formoso	230	436	312	253	155	217	358	571	50	284	413	267	235	329	420	396	343	206	560	
Viseu	96	472	186	248	191	96	394	607	86	163	293	133	271	233	342	262	209	110	184	135

10, (tel. 01 579027); and *InterRent*, Ave. António Augusto de Aguiar
124–A (tel. 01 542133); all in Lisbon. In addition, these four have branches
at the airports and all over the country. Prices range from 4,500$00 to
10,000$00 a day, with unlimited mileage.

Exploring by Car

The most enjoyable way to see the country is by car. Secondary roads
are sometimes poor, but as most of the principal sights are located on main
roads, you rarely need to leave them. As has already been said, visitors
driving in Portugal should be particularly careful as the local driving is
of a low standard. Safety belts are obligatory.

A fairly low volume of traffic and easy city parking—except in Lisbon
and Oporto—make Portugal a very relaxed motoring country. But beware
the trunk road north from Aveiras de Cima where the motorway from
Lisbon ends. It is probably the only road in Portugal, apart from the Estrada Marginal between Lisbon and Cascais, that is overcrowded.

"Averaging out" is not really possible on journeys in Portugal. You
can't say that a journey of so many kilometers will take so long, at so many
kilometers an hour. The quality of the roads, the nature of the traffic—
anything from huge trucks to donkey-drawn loads—and the kind of driving you might encounter, make it necessary to allow the maximum possible time for any trip, especially around the north of the country.

Portugal is sufficiently individualistic that, looking at the tiled façades
and heavily decorated houses, you could never imagine yourself anywhere
else, and the *pousadas* have a characteristic elegance that sets them apart.
In the north, no inch of cultivatable ground is wasted, which means that
the roads are lined and sometimes arched with vines, or flowering shrubs
and trees.

The whole of Portugal can be explored from north to south entering
from Spain across the Minho and leaving through the Algarve across the
Guadiana again into Spain, or vice versa, with several alternative border
crossings in the west. But unless you arrive by car, you will probably start
from Lisbon.

Portugal obligingly divides itself naturally into four distinct geographical, and therefore cultural areas; and because it is small and with little
traffic it is possible to move selectively from one area to another.

The Algarve. Clearly, the best-known holiday area of Portugal is the
Algarve, which has in the last 20 or so years become the playground of
the British and Germans in particular. Sheltered in the north by a long
line of accommodating, not too high, mountains, its splendid beaches are
warm throughout the year. The old inland villages with distinctly Moorish
characteristics are less overwhelmed by hotels and leisure centers than the
seaside resorts, though the government's continuing efforts to control
building are often unsuccessful. If you want sun and sea as a short break
in a motoring tour, there is nowhere more pleasant to have it.

The Alentejo. Immediately north of those mountains that shield the
Algarve is the Alentejo, a mildly wooded, undulating, agricultural country
stretching as far up as Setúbal. The Rio Guadiana flows down in the east,
forming the frontier with Spain from below Badajoz to Monsaraz and then

again when the river reaches the Algarve. The stretch of the Guadiana which flows through the Alentejo is particularly beautiful, the country remote and the great river only disturbed by half-ruined water mills and a dam near Moura. There are but five bridges over it throughout the Portuguese part of its considerable length, so there are few towns or even villages. Wild flowers cover the land with great swathes of purple and white and yellow in the spring, and rare birds fly overhead.

Equally, there are very few roads down to the Atlantic on the west coast, which does have some beaches in the Algarve, but in the Alentejo—apart from the Praia de Melides, the Costa de São André, Almograve, Caxuleira, Zambujeira, Porto Covo and the lovely estuary of the River Mira at Vila Nova de Milfontes—there is almost inaccessible sand up to the Troia peninsula opposite Setúbal on the River Sado. A regular car-ferry service goes between Setúbal and Troia, but the queues for embarkation are apt to be long in the summer. A fast motorway with a modest toll leads from Setúbal to Lisbon across the Tagus bridge (toll over, free return). The bridge has opened up the northern part of the peninsula of Setúbal to commuters, but once off the main roads the country is still unspoilt. The Alentejo is the granary of Portugal and towns and villages are few. Evora, Estremoz, Elvas, Portalegre and Beja are all attractive and well worth visiting. The last named, the capital of the Southern Alentejo, has become very industrialized.

Estremadura and Ribatejo. These two provinces extend north and east of Lisbon, almost to the university city of Coimbra, and along the wide valley of the River Tagus. The country is highly populated and has some of the most famous monuments such as the great Abbeys of Alcobaça and Batalha, and the Templars' Castle of Tomar. The coast is studded with beaches and fishing towns including Nazaré and Peniche. Obidos is a perfect example of a walled town, and at Torres Vedras start the famous Lines constructed by the Duke of Wellington to defend Lisbon in the Peninsular War against Napoleon. Fátima, one of the main pilgrimage centers of Europe, is also in Estremadura, 130 km. (80 miles) north of Lisbon.

Ribatejo is the home of splendid horses and fighting bulls centered on Vila Franca de Xira. Santarém is one of the main agricultural cities and Abrantes, hanging over the river near the island castle of Almoural, is a good place from which to explore this part. The roads are good and a motorway (toll) goes up from Lisbon to Aveiras de Cima, not far from Santarém.

The North. Northwest of Lisbon is another seaside area. Inland, on the River Mondego is Coimbra, with its university founded in 1308, and north is Aveiro with its many canals. Northeast the mountains begin again, but present no difficulty to the driver. North again is the Rio Douro, up which is the Port-producing district. The neat vines on darkly rich earth in terraces falling down to the green river are extremely attractive, and Oporto, the strange mixture of ancient riverside slums and modern elegance, is at the mouth of the river.

All the far northern part which is loosely classified as the Minho is full of interest. Braga is the capital of Baroque architecture and Guimarães the cradle of the Portuguese nation as the first king, Afonso Henriques, was proclaimed there in 1139. The grapes for the lightly sparkling *vinho verde,* the green wine, come from vines trained up tree trunks and pergolas, thus ensuring that the grapes are green when pressed and not fully ripened from heat rising from the soil as in conventional vineyards. Up the Douro and the Minho there are wild mountains and great man-made lakes for generating electricity.

Trás-os-Montes in the northeast, with fine buildings, is still very remote, and little visited by travelers. The adventurous will find good pousadas, adequate hotels and lovely country in this sparsely populated area.

Conversion Chart. The simple chart below will serve as a quick and easy guide to converting miles into kilometers and *vice versa.* If you want to convert from miles (m) into kilometers (km), read from the center column to the right; if from kilometers into miles, from the center column to the left. Example—5 miles = 8 kilometers, 5 kilometers = 3.1 miles.

m		km	m		km
0.6	1	1.6	37.3	60	96.6
1.2	2	3.2	43.5	70	112.3
1.9	3	4.8	49.7	80	128.7
2.5	4	6.3	55.9	90	144.8
3.1	5	8.0	62.1	100	160.9
3.7	6	9.6	124.3	200	321.9
4.3	7	11.3	186.4	300	482.8
5.0	8	12.9	248.5	400	643.7
5.6	9	14.5	310.7	500	804.7
6.2	10	16.1	372.8	600	965.6
12.4	20	32.2	434.9	700	1,126.5
18.6	30	48.3	497.1	800	1,287.5
24.8	40	64.4	559.2	900	1,448.4
31.0	50	80.5	621.4	1,000	1,609.3

BY TAXI. All Portuguese taxis are uniformly black with green roofs—there's no mistaking them. They are fast and comfortable, their drivers are skillful. Taxi drivers not only know their way perfectly through the maze of Lisbon's and Oporto's twisting back streets, up and down steep inclines, but are usually courteous, accommodating, knowledgeable, and somehow always manage to understand exactly where you want to go. Best of all, fares are still reasonably cheap compared with other countries. Tip 10% to 15%.

BY BIKE. *Tip Tours,* Ave. Costa Pinto 91, Cascais (tel. 2865150) hire out bicycles.

Leaving Portugal

CUSTOMS. Americans who are out of the United States at least 48 hours and have claimed no exemption during the previous 30 days are entitled to bring in duty-free up to $400 worth of articles for bona fide gifts or for their own personal use. The next $1,400 worth of material will be assessed a flat 10% duty. After that, the rate varies, depending on the value of the merchandise. The value of each item is determined by the price actually paid (so save your receipts). Every member of a family is entitled to this same exemption, regardless of age, and the allowance can be pooled.

Not more than 100 cigars and 200 cigarettes may be imported duty-free per person, nor more than a quart of wine or liquor (none at all if your passport indicates you are from a "dry" state, or if you are under 21 years of age). Only one bottle of perfume that is trademarked in the United States may be brought in, plus a reasonable quantity of other brands.

Gifts which cost less than $50 may be mailed to friends or relatives at home, duty-free but not more than one per day (of receipt) to any one addressee. Mark the package "Unsolicited Gift/Value less than $50." These gifts must not include perfumes costing more than $5, tobacco or liquor. However, they do not count as part of your $400 exemption.

Do not bring home foreign meats, fruits, plants, soil, or other agricultural items when you return to the United States. To do so will delay you at the port of entry. It is illegal to bring in foreign agricultural items without permission, because they can spread destructive plant or animal pests and diseases. For more information, request the U.S. Customs brochures *Know Before You Go,* and *Travelers' Tips.*

Antiques are defined, for customs purposes, as articles 100 years old and over, and are admitted duty-free. If there's any question of age, you may be asked to supply proof.

If your purchases exceed your exemption, list the items that are subject to the highest rates of duty under your exemption and pay duty on the items with the lowest rates. Any articles you fail to declare cannot later be claimed under your exemption. To facilitate the actual customs examination it's convenient to pack all your purchases in one suitcase.

Purchases intended for your duty-free quota can no longer be sent home separately—they must accompany your personal baggage.

Canadian residents. In addition to personal effects, the following articles may be brought in duty-free: a maximum of 50 cigars, 200 cigarettes, 2 pounds of tobacco, and 40 ounces of liquor, provided these are declared in writing to customs on arrival and accompany the traveler in hand or checked-through baggage. These are included in the basic exemption of $300 a year. Personal gifts should be mailed as "Unsolicited Gift—Value Under $40."

British Citizens. There is now a two-tier allowance for duty-free goods brought into the U.K. due to Britain's Common Market membership. **Note:** The Customs and Excise Board warn that it is not advisable to mix the two allowances.

If you return from an E.E.C. country (Belgium, Denmark, France, W. Germany, Greece, Holland, Italy, Luxembourg, Ireland, Britain—and, since 1986, Portugal and Spain) and goods were bought in one of those countries, duty-free allowances are: 300 cigarettes (or 150 cigarillos, or 75 cigars, or 400g tobacco); 1.5 liters of alcoholic drinks over 22% vol. (38.8° proof) *or* 3 liters of alcoholic drinks not over 22% vol. *or* fortified *or* sparkling *or* still wine, plus 5 liters of still table wine; 75g perfume and .375 liter of toilet water; gifts to a value of £250.

If you return from a country outside the E.E.C. *or if the goods were bought in a duty-free shop on ship, plane or airport* the allowances are less: 200 cigarettes (or 100 cigarillos or 50 cigars or 250g tobacco); 1 liter of alcoholic drinks over 22% vol. (38.8° proof) *or* 2 liters of alcoholic drinks not over 22% vol. *or* fortified *or* sparkling *or* still wine, plus 2 liters of still table wine; 50g perfume and .25 liter of toilet water; gifts to a value of £32. Note that tobacco allowances are double if you live outside Europe.

INTRODUCING PORTUGAL

By
ELISABETH DE STROUMILLO

Elisabeth de Stroumillo has been Travel Correspondent of Britain's The
Daily Telegraph *for almost 20 years, but she has been traveling the world
for far longer than that—since her infancy, in fact. Her early childhood
was spent in India; her mid-teens, thanks to having an American mother,
in New York and Massachusetts, where she went to school. She still manages
to fit at least one U.S. trip a year into her busy travel schedule (which has
included over half a dozen visits to Portugal). She is married, with two
grownup daughters, and lives in London.*

Portugal is possibly the most under-rated country in Europe, far too frequently thought of merely as a long, thin buffer of land between Spain
and the Atlantic: a place from which the only escape was seaward. Given
this unenviable situation, no wonder her most glorious sons were explorers
or navigators—or so runs the usual train of thought.
　Like many another time-worn train of thought, this one peters out a
fair way short of the whole truth. Yes, Portugal has given birth to more
than her share of ocean-conquerors, starting with the half-English Prince
Henry the Navigator who in 1415, as a young man, took part in the conquest of Ceuta, in North Africa, and then retired to Sagres in southwestern
Portugal to found a school of navigation whose ultimate objective was to
work out a sea route from Europe to the Far East. And yes, it was thanks

to his work and inspiration that the 15th-century Portuguese mariners roamed so far and wide; Bartolomeu Diaz round The Cape of Good Hope; Cabral westward to Brazil; Vasco da Gama eastwards to India and Magellan, in his wake, penetrating as far as Indonesia. (Here he died, but one of his ships went on to become the first vessel to sail round the world).

All this is true enough, but it is very far from the whole truth. For a start, emphasizing this aspect of Portuguese history carries with it an underlying inference that Portugal was a country from which escape was the most desirable option—and it is this that has led to its being so seriously under-rated. In fact, its very length and narrowness make for the most extraordinary amount of variety: I would venture to say that, for its area, it has more geographical and climatic variations than any other country in Europe, and although there are no deep ethnic divisions among the Portuguese, the almost Celtic character of the northerners make them quite different from the southern people of the Algarve, who still retain more than a trace of their Moorish antecedents.

From the Atlantic to Spain

I have been visiting Portugal regularly for nearly 20 years, and I never fail to be astonished by the number of new facets it reveals each time, nor by the ease and speed with which you can move from one landscape into a totally different one. Just crossing the country (and a very short stretch of often choppy sea) from west to east—a distance of about 150 miles—affords a whole spectrum of contrasts that can, if you are energetic, be encompassed in a day.

First, take the little boat from Peniche, north of Lisbon, to the Berlenga Islands. Never heard of them? Nor have most people, who think only of Madeira and the Azores when they think of Portuguese islands. The Berlengas are no competition to them, being little more than rocky outcrops patched with grass and lashed by creamy-topped Atlantic rollers, but they have an oddly haunting beauty and they swarm with graceful sea-birds who will dive-bomb you for your lunchtime picnic and soar off again, screaming triumphantly. Just up the coast from Peniche is the fishing-village of Nazaré, its long beach crowded with fishing boats that are as artfully painted as chorus-girls' faces. The people of Nazaré have long been famous for their colorful local costumes: floppy stocking-hats and baggy checked pants for the men, full skirts and elaborately-tied kerchiefs for the women. Not so long ago, everyone wore these clothes as a matter of course; now you will only see them en masse on feast days. On ordinary days, I rather suspect that different groups of locals take it in turns to wear traditional dress and to walk among the boats and whitewashed streets, ready to pose for tourists' photographs (and to accept a little tip in return).

Head inland from Nazaré and you cross low, rolling hills and come down into the valley of the Tagus, full of market gardens and rice fields, stud farms and cattle ranches. Just a little further east, a quite different landscape unrolls: flat at first, where fields of grain stretch as far as the eye can see, punctuated by the sculptural shapes of cork-oaks, their trunks glowing orange in the afternoon sun, and by the softer, silver-gray outlines of millions of olive trees. This is the Alentejo, Portugal's granary, where large white farmhouses sun themselves on the summits of low hillocks, and where sheep and rangy black pigs forage, and it ends at the Spanish border in the shapely hills of the Serra de São Mamede.

Another cross-country journey yields another series of contrasts, this time starting from the wine-capital of Oporto or, more precisely, from the coast just west of it, where on sultry days the Atlantic fogs mass offshore looking as solid as a wall. There are long fine beaches to north and south, and some pretty resorts, but at the mouth of the River Douro Oporto has straggled downwards and outwards from its old steep-perched site to cover most of the surrounding hills as well. Oporto is full of stately buildings, many of them associated with the British and the port-wine trade, but the real center for the wineries themselves is across the river in Vila Nova de Gaia.

Make your way eastwards from either and you come first to the vineyards where the pale, faintly sparkling *vinho verde* wines are grown and then, by way of the villages of Resende and Barro, to the famous port-growing area of the Douro valley, where vineyards clothe the slopes like ruched velvet coverlets. Roads are narrow and winding (if you are there in the fall, when the grapes are being harvested, and get stuck behind a vehicle stacked high with them, you could get drunk on the aroma before you had a chance to overtake). Turn north through the little administrative town of Regua and there are more vineyards, this time the Mateus Rosé ones; pass through pleasant Vila Real and the countryside suddenly opens out again with gentle terraces of fig and almond trees.

In a little garden in the center of Murça stands a very ancient, impudent-looking, stone-carved boar and then, after Mirandela, cork-oaks and olive trees appear and the landscape widens out further still into hills that in spring are aflame with flowers. Beyond, almost on the Spanish border, Braganza lies among the Trás-os-Montes mountains, on the edge of a region deeply forested with chestnuts, interspersed by sharp bare fells and stretches of reddish earth; it boasts, among other things, two more carved stone boars, one of them dating back to the Iron Age and incongruously supporting a pillory.

From North to South

Traveling from north to south, scenes change just as rapidly and rewardingly. Up in the far north, wooden grain-stores are perched on stone mushroom-shaped props that deter marauding rats; cottage gardens and small fields display well cared-for rows of potatoes and the tall, thick-stalked local cabbages that together go to make the famous *caldo verde* soup; there are pinewoods and hills covered in heather and gorse, and huge hydrangea-hedges. So lush is this part of the country that the grass grows tall and thick along the roadsides and frugal farmers' wives lead their cows along the verges to graze, reluctant to waste a single blade, while the farmers scythe their fields and pile the hay into conical shapes around tall poles or tree trunks, creating what look like gigantic spindles sheathed in greeny-gold.

Southwards again, and there are fine towns with ornate churches like Braga and Guimarães, deliciously pretty Amarante and Viseu, whose cathedral square was so peaceful when I was last there that I could actually hear the pigeons coo as they fluttered from statue to statue on the building's west front. South of it is the cool Buçaco forest, laced with streams

and waterfalls, where in 1810 the Anglo-Portuguese army under Arthur
Wellesley (later Duke of Wellington) defeated Napoleon's forces under
the command of Masséna. Alongside the simple monastery where Wellington slept in a cork-lined cell is a fantastically-conceived former royal
hunting-lodge, now converted into an hotel.

Next points of interest are the ancient university town of Coimbra and
the great 15th-century monastery of Batalha, rising in a succession of
pinky-gold arches to a forest of pinnacles and dominating even the new
highway that sweeps past it. By then you are almost in Lisbon, that elegant, gentle and most manageable of European capitals, with its biscuity-
colored pantile roofs stacked up the hill around St George's castle to the
east of the harmonious, 18th-century Baixa, or lower town, and the lively
Bairro Alto quarter rising above it to the west.

The landscape between Lisbon and the Algarve in the extreme south,
a distance of some 320 km. (200 miles), is perhaps the only monotonous
one Portugal has to offer, but even here there are compensations. The
bridge across the Tagus and the broad motor-road beyond it sweep you
across the Arrábida peninsula almost before you realize it, and it is only
too easy to bypass Setúbal, judging it merely another industrial town from
the face it presents to the road. It isn't: the old core of the town is delightful, with pebble-mosaic alleyways and handsome buildings. Alcaçer do
Sal, beyond it, is a sleepy, whitewashed town bedecked in springtime with
myriads of untidy storks' nests; take a little time to sit on a bench and
watch the family squabbles as the young jostle each other crossly for space.

The new motorway, bypassing Grandola, will take you to Messines in
the Algarve in a couple of hours with good stopovers for lunch at Canal
Caveira. But if you are not in a hurry, go on the old road through Santiago
do Cacém, a pleasant town with an imposing castle. Off the road to seaward is Sines, birthplace of Vasco da Gama, and just south of it, another
castle dominates the seaside village of Vila Nova de Milfontes. In the early
19th century, when the English poet Southey visited it, it had been "half-
converted into a poor dwelling house"; some 150 years later, the elderly
and aristocratic owner had made it into a discreet and exclusive retreat
(hotel is not the right word for it) to which politicians and diplomats came
from Lisbon for a few days' relaxation. His widow carries on the tradition.

Past Odemira lie the shapely hills of the Serra de Monchique, which
cut the Algarve off from the rest of the country: there are lovely villages
up there, like Monchique itself, Silves, São Brás de Alportel, Almansil,
and Loulé, and some staggering views. Beneath the hills, and sheltered
by them from the north winds, the Algarve coast is reminiscent of the
Mediterranean: a string of resorts stretching away to the Spanish border.
In early spring, the country between and behind them is blanketed with
white almond-blossom; later the wattle hedges burst into bloom, and from
then on the coastal strip is ablaze with the colors of oleander, bougainvillea, hibiscus and scores of other flowers.

At the western extremity of this coast, which is in fact the westernmost
point in Europe, lies Cape St Vincent, its perpendicular cliffs rearing out
of the ocean in a flurry of spume. It is a tremendous sight, dramatic in
the extreme, and it is the spot on which to ponder the stories of all those
great Portuguese navigators, for just up the road is Sagres, not a particularly distinguished-looking town today, but secure in the annals of Portu-

guese history as the place where Prince Henry the Navigator founded his school.

Castles and Palaces

Castles in Spain are the traditional landmarks of travelers' fantasies, but Portugal has her fair share of castles too. There is a striking, half-ruined fortress-castle a little way from Cape St Vincent with a modest café-restaurant built into part of it, where you get superb views of the wave-lashed cape. I have already mentioned the castles of Santiago do Cacém and Milfontes and there is another fine castle just northwest of Evora at Montemor-o-Novo, while to the north of Lisbon the castle of Leiria, near Batalha, is perhaps the most dramatically-sited of them all.

Much further inland, near the Spanish border, there are—as you would expect—a whole string of castles that were originally built as defenses. Many of them have crumbled away or been used as quarries for building houses within their once-stout walls, but as many again are still formidable-looking: Beja, in the lower Alentejo, is a beauty with its fat square tower; so are Terena, Alandroal, Marvão and Castelo de Vide, further to the north; so too are Monsanto, Sabugal, Belmonte, Castelo Rodrigo and Almeida, farther north still, and Chaves with its fang-crenelated keep.

Some of these old border castles have, as they lost their strategic importance, been transformed over the centuries into fortified villages of striking picturesqueness. One such is hill-perched Monsaraz, its crenelated walls spiked with white turrets; you leave your car outside the imposing gateway and walk through an arch into the main street, cobbled and lined with whitewashed houses whose often elaborately-carved portals signify that they were originally designed for grander surroundings. All that remains of the castle proper, at the end of the street, is the keep, around whose base chickens scratch the dust; the views from the top are marvelous. There are more marvelous views from the top of the castle keep at Evora-monte, and the architecture of the keep itself is remarkable, for it consists of four fat stone towers encircled by two thick, dressed stone bands carved into knots on the four sides. The citizens of the village that has been made from the rest of the original castle are evidently proud of it: when I visited, a quartet of busy ladies, their broad-brimmed straw hats secured with kerchiefs, were assiduously hoeing the weeds from between the street-cobbles.

There are castles and palaces open to the public, preserved as museums, like Lisbon's 17th-century Azuara Palace, housing the Espirito Santo Foundation's fine decorative arts collection and Belém's splendid former royal palace of Ajuda. Oporto has its Palácio das Carrancas, now the Soares dos Reis Museum; Sintra its former royal residence, the National Palace, and also the extraordinarily flamboyant 19th-century Gothic Pena Palace; Queluz, nearer to Lisbon, rejoices in what is perhaps the prettiest palace of them all, while the nearby Fronteira Palace is renowned for its gardens.

The Bragança family, who ruled Portugal for over 300 years, are associated with two palaces apart from the one in Bragança itself: at Vila Viçosa, in the Alentejo, where the huge edifice and the monumental square in front of it, flanked by two mausoleum-churches, completely dwarf the unassuming town alongside; and at Guimarães in the north. Guimarães is one of the places where you can stay in a palace, for several of Portugal's state-owned *pousadas* (inns) are installed in historic buildings. One of the two at Guimarães occupies an 18th-century town palace of great elegance while the Estremoz pousada has been converted from the rugged castle that crowns the summit of the town, and from the bedroom windows you can look out upon swallows wheeling back and forth above the rooftops far below: a bird's-eye view of birds. Within an hour's drive south of Lisbon, on the Arrábida Peninsula, both Setúbal and Palmela have castle-pousadas, the latter incorporating some former monastic buildings; north of Lisbon, the charming white-walled town of Obidos also has a pousada in its castle.

Decoration Run Riot

The pousada of Evora, in the Alentejo, is not in a castle but a former convent (Portugal has far fewer redundant ecclesiastical buildings than castles). As you eat your dinner in the former cloister, now the dining room, you will notice delicately spiraled columns supporting horseshoe-arches: they are typical of the late Gothic architectural style that is unique to Portugal, the Manueline, named for the then-reigning King Manuel. This exuberant style flowered in the 16th century, when Portugal was reveling in the discoveries made by her great explorers, and many of its motifs have a nautical feel about them: the twisted columns suggest ropes, and there are embellishments based on knots, anchors, and even seaweed.

Portugal has far too many fine churches to mention here, let alone to visit even in the course of several trips, but the Manueline style is so unusual and fascinating that it is rewarding to follow up, and I cannot resist naming a few examples. One of the oldest is the Church of Jesus in Setúbal, where the ceiling is supported by barley-sugar columns and is ribbed with rope-like patterns. Others include the sacristy door at Alcobaça and the Royal Cloister at Batalha; the chancel of Guarda cathedral and the vaulted roof of Viseu's; Coimbra's University Chapel and Santa Cruz cloister, and the Jerónimos church at Belém. They do not all look the same—far from it. The Manueline style adapts itself good-humoredly to all sorts of artistic variations, and one of the most peculiar of these is the grotesque window that takes the place of a west door in the church of the Convent of Christ in the delightful town of Tomar. This is a riotous stone-carved composition of twisted ropes, seaweed, coral, and other patterns wreathing around representations of the monastic order's Cross and the royal coat of arms, and all supported by the grimacing figure of the Old Man of the Sea; it is a real treat.

Portugal's other unique art-form is *azulejo* work, made up of hand-painted and glazed ceramic tiles, originally always blue and white, though yellow and other colors gradually crept into the designs. You see glazed tile-work everywhere in Portugal, on house fronts, public fountains and park benches; in patios, halls, reception rooms and up stairways in all types of domestic buildings, but the best of the old ones are to be found in palaces, museums, and churches. Sometimes they depict religious scenes, sometimes they are purely decorative (the latter type look wonderful when they form a background to gray cloister arches), and again I cannot resist naming a few favorites. They include the Misericórdia church by Chaves castle and two churches in Barcelos, the pretty town where those attractive pottery cockerel-figures originated: Senhor da Cruz and the Terço; the Santa Maria church in Obidos and the castle chapel in Estremoz. These latter depict the story of the Miracle of the Roses when Queen Isabel, later Saint Elisabeth, was carrying gold in her apron to distribute to the poor. Her husband, the King (whose gold it presumably was), asked her what she was carrying—and when she opened her apron, the coins had turned into roses. Three more of my favorites are in the Algarve: the churches of São Franciso and São Pedro in Faro, and São Lourenço, near Almansil, but there are others to be seen almost everywhere.

Romans and Moors

Like most of the rest of Europe, Portugal has a long history going back to the Iron Age and earlier, and there are legacies of it the length and breadth of the country. Some of the finest ones were left by the Romans: the excavated ruins of the city of Conimbriga, south of Coimbra, with some fine mosaic floors; and of Medobriga, near the Spanish frontier, and Miróbriga in the lower Alentejo. One of the most imposing is the second-century Temple of Diana in Evora, which was adapted to all sorts of other purposes down the centuries, including that of a slaughter-house; as a result it stands proudly outside the pousada on a high platform, its pediment running round all but two of its granite columns. There are more modest traces of the Roman occupation to be noticed in many an odd spot, too, like the bridge with a milestone at its center in Chaves; and there are some that are all but disappeared, like those of Troia and Vilamoura, the former half submerged beneath the ocean, and the latter removed to make way for a marina.

The Moors occupied Portugal for some 500 years, too, and there are relics of their civilization to be seen here and there: they were responsible for the original building of many a castle that was later rebuilt and strengthened. If you look carefully about you as you wander the streets of provincial towns, you will see the occasional horseshoe-arched window that still retains its plasterwork tracery, or an oddly frivolous balcony or patio designed on Arabesque lines. Those famous Algarve chimney-pots, shaped and pierced with innumerable patterns, are also inspired by Moorish designs and you can see their forerunners in the wind-towers that still grace a few old mansions in Dubai and other parts of the Middle East.

An Old Alliance

Britons feel a particular affinity for Portuguese history, for they have played a part in it for so long—over 600 years. A band of English Crusaders, bound for the Holy Land in 1147, were persuaded to stop off and help drive the Moors out of Portugal instead. It was basically the same enemy they were fighting, but in a different place, and many of them went no further, thus beginning the trade links between the two countries. The first official treaty between them was signed in 1386, and has never been broken. (Its 600th anniversary was celebrated in 1986 with special ceremonies at Windsor Castle). The treaty was cemented by a royal marriage preceded by a series of circumstances that would make a fine basis for a musical comedy, when John of Gaunt, brother to the English king, decided to lay claim to the Spanish throne of Castile by virtue of his marriage to a Spanish infanta. He sailed off to Northern Spain with a great retinue, including

of course his wife and daughters, and on his arrival sent word that he
would welcome the assistance of his Portuguese ally, offering the king the
hand of one of his daughters in return. The Portuguese king chose the
eldest, Philippa, and among their children was Prince Henry the Navigator. John and Philippa were eventually buried at Batalha where their effi-
gies lie hand in hand; Henry and four of their other sons are also buried
there. There was another royal link between the two countries nearly 300
years later, when Catherine of Bragança married King Charles II of
England, bringing with her a rich dowry that included a large chunk of
India; sadly, she bore him no children, and returned to Portugal to end
her years in widowhood there.

A high-point of the Anglo-Portuguese alliance came in the early 19th
century when Napoleon occupied Portugal and the king was forced to escape to Brazil with an escort of British warships. The following year Sir
Arthur Wellesley, later Duke of Wellington, brought a British force to
Portugal and in 1808 started the long campaign that not only drove Napoleon's armies out of the country but inexorably forced them back across
the entire Iberian peninsula and over the Pyrenees into France. To wander
about Portugal with even the sketchiest knowledge of that campaign
brings many a scene more vividly to life. Vimeiro, nowadays a peaceful
little spa-cum-seaside resort, is hard by Wellington's Torres Vedras defense lines, built to protect Lisbon from the north; Buçaco was where Wellington, assisted for the first time by re-trained Portuguese troops, defeated
Masséna . . . and so on. I had a mildly embarrassing encounter at Buçaco
with a Frenchwoman who had left her guide-book in her car; waiting together for opening-time at the monastery in which Wellington spent the
night after the battle, she asked me to translate the plaque by the door.
It is beautifully florid: "The glorious general Arthur Wellesley, Viscount
Wellington, Baron Douro, and after Count of Vimeiro, Marquês of Torres
Vedras" (and a lot more titles besides) "spent the night following the victory of Buçaco over the invading army of Masséna, on the 27th September
1810, in this convent"—but it was hardly the sort of stuff to gladden the
ears of a Frenchwoman.

Before, after, and no doubt during this period, trade between Britain
and Portugal flourished, notably the port trade, but also many another,
and there are signs everywhere of the British connections: a red letter-box
in Elvas (and others elsewhere, no doubt); an English cemetery and
English-style buses in Lisbon; street and shop-names.

The Good-Humor Men

If there is one slight shadow across this picture (and there generally is),
it is the language problem. They say that the Devil must have invented
the Basque language; if so, then one of his apprentices was showing prom-
ise when he came up with Portuguese. Even if you speak one or more of
the Latin languages reasonably well, such as French or Spanish, and can
therefore manage to read and understand a bit of written Portuguese, the
pronunciation will defy you until you have put in long practice. What is
one to make of a tongue that renders a nice place like Setúbal as "Shtoo-
ble"?

Fortunately, there is an antidote when no one is about who understands
a word you are saying, or who can make him- or herself understood to

you: the extraordinarily patient good nature of the ordinary people. This has not consistently manifested itself throughout Portuguese history: they were stern and sometimes harsh colonists—and they reaped a bitter harvest when the African colonies were granted independence and thousands of refugees flooded back into the mother country in the 1970s. I remember landing at Lisbon airport during that period and at first being shocked to see between 60 and 100 people camping in a corner of the arrivals hall; then I noticed how tidily they had installed themselves, and how placidly the children were playing while their mothers did the ironing on makeshift beds, or sat sewing. Patient good humor had asserted itself in that situation and, now that the cruel aftermath of the 1974 revolution has become a thing of the past, patient good humor is once more the norm.

It was often manifest even during those difficult times. I visited the Alentejo in the late 1970s, when many of the big farms, or *quintas,* were still occupied by the workers, and on the advice of Susan Lowndes made a detour to try to see the Quinta dos Loios, just outside Arraiolos, whose church has fine azulejos that include one of the English king, Edward the Confessor. I arrived to find the church firmly locked up and two rustic ladies devouring a sandwich lunch on the porch. With toothy grins, they informed me that the church was shut "for ever," miming the action of someone putting the key into a pocket and departing—and then offered me a wedge of bread and cheese and a swig of their wine.

A language barrier is supposed to make real enjoyment of a country impossible, but thanks to the amiable disposition of the Portuguese, this simply does not apply there. My experience at Arraiolos is just one instance, and there have been dozens of others, when kindly policemen or local citizens have gone to endless trouble to help me. Sometimes the results have been little short of hilarious, as on one occasion in Tomar, where I was anxious to see the monks' dormitory-corridors in the Convent of Christ. They are in a part of that great complex not normally shown to visitors except by special permission, which I had not realized, and I could not manage to make the guardian on duty understand what it was that I wanted. Eventually he decided that it was lodgings I was after ("dormitorio," which I kept repeating, must mean "somewhere to sleep") and he triumphantly sent me back into town, accompanied by one of his friends. This started off a Pied-Piperish situation in which my retinue was gradually swollen by the addition of two students, one tobacconist (who spoke a little English but knew nothing of monastic dormitories), one parish priest and one cavalry officer, and which ended in a very jolly party indeed, in a local bar. I have never regretted not seeing the monks' dormitory; it cannot be half so much fun.

Fish Supreme

If the Portuguese language is hard to get the tongue around, Portuguese food is emphatically not. Fish is, of course, supreme, and one of the great Lisbon experiences is to visit the fish-market early in the morning, when dawn has hardly broken, and the shouts of the auctioneers and bidders seem to be emanating from a seething mass of shadowy phantoms. As the first light gets stronger, you can watch the fishwives washing off their purchases at incredible speed and arranging them in elaborate patterns in huge flat baskets, which they then balance on their heads and stride off to start their morning's work. What delicious fish it is, too, from the fat fresh sardines that are grilled along the Algarve quaysides and eaten straight off the fire, to the aromatic *caldeiradas,* or fish stews, that differ slightly from region to region, and the hundred-and-one very different dishes that are all based on cod in one form or another. The Portuguese also mix fish with meat with great success: try pork with oysters or mussels, flavored with Madeira wine—which, along with their mainland wines, they use lavishly in cooking. And, of course, try the wines by themselves: all of them.

THE PORTUGUESE EPIC

A mild, salubrious climate on the coast of a sea teeming with fish; great rivers, beautiful forests and deep, sheltered valleys; few carnivorous beasts or poisonous snakes—everything about Portugal favored a flourishing primitive existence whose only remaining traces are ancient idols, iron-age settlements, dolmens, and mounds of seashells along the shores. The dark-skinned, thick-set Iberians were the primary racial strain in a widely scattered population; later, as a result of foreign trade and invasions, their blood would mingle with that of the Celts, the Phoenicians, Jews and Moors, all of whom were easily absorbed as can be seen in the faces of the Portuguese men and women of today.

Until the middle of the 12th century A.D., the history of Portugal is one with the general history of the Iberian Peninsula. For the Ancients, Cape St. Vincent in the province of Algarve marked the end of the earth, for there they could see the sun swallowed up by the sea. Not far away, the commercially-minded Carthaginians and Greeks set up trading posts on Portugal's southern shore.

The Romans annexed the Iberian Peninsula, with its wealth of olive oil and wine, around 200 B.C. Whereas Gaul had been quickly conquered and Romanized, Lusitania mounted a stubborn resistance. A chieftain from the hills named Viriathus, the Hannibal of the Iberians as Lucilius said, held the Roman legions at bay for years; he embodied the ferocious attachment to the native soil and the blind, desperate heroism which have always been constant factors in the history of Portugal.

Rome's relationship with her far-off province was one of exploitation rather than development. She did, however, construct roads, bridges and

aqueducts, some of which still exist; she also founded cities, of which nothing remains today but their names. The beautiful Temple of Diana at
Evora and, above all, the ruins of Conimbriga, near Coimbra, which had
been buried for centuries, bear witness to an affluent and peaceful lifestyle.
Christianity easily took root in such soil. The bishopric of Braga was established as early as the third century.

The Invasions

Then came the Barbarians. At Conimbriga, a hastily built wall (you can
still see the broken statues and columns of porphyry used to fortify it)
failed to protect the city against the onslaught of the Suevi. The next invad-
ers, the Visigoths, imposed a warlike regime but, little by little, they were
won over by the pious and pastoral existence of the people they thought
they had conquered. By the sixth century, the Church had greatly increased its influence and chapels and monasteries sprang up on the banks
of the Douro and the Mondego rivers.

Wamba, the 30th king of the Visigoths who had reluctantly accepted
the crown in 672, demanded to be consecrated at Toledo. He repulsed an
invasion force of 260 ships which the Moors, Turks and Arabs, the new
masters of North Africa, launched against the peninsula. After Wamba's
death, quarrels among the barons and the criminal spite of Julian (who
had betrayed the invasion route to Tariq, the Emir of Africa) enabled the
Moors to defeat Rodrigo, last king of the Goths, at Guadalete in the year
711. Rodrigo took refuge in a hermitage on the Asturian coast, and the
Moorish tide rolled on as far north as Poitiers. Alone, a small band of
Christian noblemen under the leadership of Pelayo entrenched themselves
in the mountains of Asturias and began the arduous reconquest which was
to endure for centuries.

The Moorish domination of Portugal was fruitful: orchards sprang up
from irrigated land, indeed, their methods of irrigation are still being used
in Portugal today; white and fawn-colored cities came to life and pros-
pered. The tolerant Moors welcomed Jews and even protected the studious
meditations of Christian monks. A Moorish–Arabian culture spread outward from the cities of Coimbra and Kelb, now Silves in the Algarve. The
very name Algarve is a Moorish survival, it was originally al-Gharb.

First Dynasty: the House of Burgundy (the Founders)

Meanwhile, north of the River Douro, Christian counts and barons
from Galicia, León and Asturias kept watch and waited for an opportunity
to renew the offensive which had already enabled them to liberate Burgos,
Toledo and Santiago de Compostela. Portugal was about to be born as
a separate country at the height of the 12th century, amid the bellicose
and religious exaltation of the reconquest.

The younger sons of the great families left frequently to fight abroad.
The excitement of the Crusades drew many of them to the Holy Land;
however, some of them considered that it was more important to liberate
Europe and to hurl the Infidel back into the sea before setting out to rescue
the Holy Sepulcher. The Cid captured Valencia. Among his comrades-in-
arms was a Count of Burgundy who had received the hand in marriage
of one of the daughters of the King of León in Spain for services rendered.

Her dowry consisted of lands located between the Douro and the Minho rivers, at that time a country called Portucale. Their son, Afonso Henriques, seized the throne from his regent mother in 1128. He freed himself by pushing the Moors to the south.

With foolhardy courage, and seconded by knights cut from the same cloth as himself, Afonso captured seven Moorish strongholds—a feat he commemorated by incorporating them into the Portuguese coat-of-arms. You can see the ramparts of these fortresses today at Lisbon, Leiria, Santarém, Sintra, Palmela, Montemor and Evora.

Afonso's descendants brought order to their kingdom, defending and enlarging its frontiers. Dom Dinis, the poet-king, founded the University of Coimbra in 1308 and built the first Portuguese fleet. He had pine trees planted in the sandy soil between the sea and Leiria, dominated by his hill-top castle, in order to stabilize the land and conserve the crops. He married Isabella, the Infanta of Aragon, later known as St. Elizabeth of Portugal for her devotion and concern for the poor. Her piety is celebrated in many legends, mostly concerning the conversion of gold to roses and vice versa. Apart from the one we have already related in the Introduction, there was the occasion, upon completion of the Church of Santa Clara-a-Velha which she had ordered built in Coimbra, when she had nothing but a rose to offer the workmen as payment—which turned to gold in their hands.

The son of this Holy Queen was the stormy Prince Afonso, whose rebellion darkened the last years of his father's reign. After Afonso became king, he received the same kind of treatment at the hands of his own progeny. He gave his son Pedro in marriage to Constança, a princess of Navarre. Constança had a beautiful Galician friend and cousin named Inês de Castro as a lady-in-waiting. Inês and Prince Pedro soon became entwined in an ill-fated affair. Constança died alone and unloved in giving birth to a son, but Pedro cared only for the children presented him by Inês, whose brothers were adept in the art of courtly intrigue. Their ambitions frightened the old King Afonso, whose councillors pressed him to sacrifice Inês in the interests of the kingdom. He resigned himself to the bitter necessity of this course of action and had her murdered in the garden of the Quinta das Lágrimas in Coimbra. The stones in the spring by which she died show dusky red through the bright water to this day. After Inês's death, when Pedro became king, he wreaked a horrible vengeance upon her murderers, and crowned her corpse before having it transported to Alcobaça in a great funeral procession. She was laid to rest in a magnificent tomb which Pedro ordered to be placed opposite his own so that the first sight each should see on the Day of Resurrection would be the beloved face of the other. The last of the Burgundians died with no male heir, and the King of Castile marched on Lisbon with a powerful army to back up his claim to the throne.

Second Dynasty: the House of Aviz (the Explorers)

The threatened capital placed itself in the hands of João, one of Pedro's illegitimate sons, who was head of the military and religious Order of Aviz. He was named Defender of the Realm, and then elected king by popular acclaim. All Portugal united around him to preserve its independence. Lisbon suffered a cruel siege; but then, led by João I and his young captain

Nuno Álvares Pereira, the Portuguese army fought courageously in a clash
with the Castilian cavalry. The battle took place on August 14, 1385, on
the Plain of Aljubarrota, and 14,000 Portuguese infantry and crossbow-
men with 3,000 English archers and horsemen routed 30,000 Castilian soldiers and horsemen. This battle secured the independence of Portugal for
almost two centuries. The spoils of victory were immense. As an act of
gratitude for his victory, João erected the monastery of Nossa Senhora
da Vitória at Batalha, not far from the battlefield. He was later buried there
with his wife, Philippa of Lancaster, daughter of John of Gaunt; their marriage confirmed the Portuguese pact with England—the oldest continuing
alliance in Europe. This Treaty of Windsor, signed in 1386, was invoked
by Britain in World War II to obtain fueling facilities for ships and aircraft
in the Azores Archipelago, which were duly granted. The sixth centenary
of the treaty in 1986 was widely commemorated in both countries.

Philippa bore six children to João, one of whom, the Infanta Isabella,
married Philip of Burgundy, Grand Duke of the Occident. But the most
famous of this "noble generation" was Henry the Navigator. His wise and
learned face appears in the celebrated polyptych in the Lisbon Art Gallery
painted by Nuno Gonçalves, a disciple of Van Eyck.

After having played an important role in the conquest of Ceuta in 1415,
Henry retired to the arid promontory of Sagres, in Algarve, where he surrounded himself with seamen, map-makers and astronomers. Using their
vast experience and original calculations, these scholars at Sagres were the
first to establish the principles of navigation on the high seas. Here also
the caravelle was developed—the first sailing ship capable of being navi-
gated in a cross wind. None of these long-range expeditions would have
been possible without the painstaking and inspired research of Henry, the
"Prince of the Sea."

The Atlantic archipelagos (Madeira in 1420 and the Azores in 1431)
were the first discoveries of Henry's explorers; the latter were colonized
for a while by the Flemish, after Faial had been given to Isabella of Burgundy in 1466. These islands proved to be excellent stepping stones for
the exploration of the west coast of Africa. Henry, unlike Columbus, was
certain that a sea route to India could be found by circumnavigating this
still-unknown continent.

The caravans from the Orient, which carried the precious stones, spices,
silks and gold of which Europe had always been so fond, were becoming
exposed to ever-increasing dangers. Although their safe conduct had previously been assured by paying protection money to the Arabs of the Middle East and the pirates of the Mediterranean, the caravans now found
themselves subject to attacks by the Turks.

It was therefore of vital importance to the European economy to have
direct access to those countries that produced spices, silk and gold.

The Discoveries

Christopher Columbus, who had lived for over a year on the island of
Porto Santo off Madeira, and who had often sailed with Prince Henry's
captains, sought this mythical westward route to India (on the last and
most desolate of the islands of the Azores, a mysterious weathered stone
still points toward the setting sun). It was while seeking this route to India
that Columbus accidentally discovered America in 1492.

Bartolomeu Dias rounded the Cape of Storms at the southern tip of Africa in 1488, 28 years after the Navigator's death; it was immediately rechristened Cape of Good Hope, since this momentous event confirmed the certitude of Henry and his followers that here indeed lay the route to India and the Spice Islands. Finally, in 1498, Vasco da Gama reached Calcutta.

Portuguese explorations opened up a multitude of new worlds to the Old World. In 1500 Pedro Álvares Cabral discovered Brazil. The following year Corte-Réal landed at Greenland, while Cabrilo and João Martins explored the coasts of California and Alaska, respectively. The Portuguese were the first white men to reach the Moluccas, China, Japan and Ethiopia and, thanks to the voyage of Magellan in 1520, the first to circumnavigate the globe.

An immense Portuguese empire now spread over four continents. Missionaries like St. Francis Xavier and Father Manuel de Nobrega carried the word of Christ into the jungles and the deserts, to pagan tribes and to the ancient civilizations of Asia. Trading posts were established in Guinea, Malacca, Ceylon and Oceania; fortresses were built to protect them, and a Portuguese monopoly was maintained throughout the Indian Ocean—often at a bloody price.

Nevertheless, the great Afonso of Albuquerque was not as proud of having conquered Ormuz and Malacca as he was of having founded at Malabar a new race of Christians—the Luso-Hindus of Goa. In the Congo, 12 Christian churches graced the city of San Salvador, capital of the black King Afonso (godson and ally of the King of Portugal). Everywhere—from Madeira to Macau, where Portugal had established the first European settlement in China in 1557, from Cape Verde to Mozambique—Portuguese was spoken by a mixture of races, making it the universal language of the time. Hundreds of Portuguese words are still found today in many of the dialects of Africa and Asia.

The Lisbon of Manuel the Fortunate

Lisbon had gotten the better of its major commercial rivals: first Bruges, then Venice. It was the richest city of Europe. Using revenues from the lucrative tax on pepper, King Manuel (called "the Fortunate Monarch") built the church and monastery of the Jeronimites at Belém on the same shore from which Vasco da Gama had set sail. Manuel chose the armillary sphere as his emblem, to indicate that his realm extended around the world—or at least a good half-way around the world, since a treaty signed at Tordesillas with Spain (and confirmed by the Pope) had divided the new world between them: the two spheres of influence were defined by a line passing 370 leagues to the west of Cape Verde.

Intoxicated with the riches of this universal empire, Portugal decorated buildings and public monuments with emblems of its conquests on the high seas and in the jungles of the tropics: representations of anchors, seaweed and rigging mingled with exotic animals and strange symbols. Belém, Batalha, Tomar—all bear witness, sculptured in stone, to the fact that the Portuguese of the 16th century envisioned their empire as a grand fusion of diverse races and civilizations, with Christianity and the Portuguese language as their common bond.

This sudden prosperity of Portugal was, like its new-found power, more apparent than real. Their senses reeling with the spirit of adventure, the Portuguese lost sight of the more solid virtues of their race: endurance, sobriety and tolerance. They wasted their wealth in idle luxury, cultivating a false pride fraught with danger for the future.

King Sebastian, the frail and unstable end-product of a once great but now worn-out bloodline (he was the grandson of the flamboyant Manuel and the all-powerful Charles V of Spain), hurled himself into an absurd and fatal crusade in Morocco (1578). During the massacre of Al-Kebir, the king perished along with the flower of the country's youth. This event left Portugal ruined and drained of its last drop of royal blood—an easy prey for its powerful neighbor, Spain.

Camões, the great Portuguese poet who had sung of the era of discovery in his *Lusiads,* died the same year that Portugal fell into the hands of Philip II of Spain; his last words are said to have been, "I am dying at the same time as my country."

Third Dynasty: the House of Bragança (the Restoration)

The Spanish domination lasted for 60 years. The three Philips who wore this double crown cared little about the interests of Portugal, who lost many of her overseas possessions and was dragged into all of Spain's quarrels—with France, with Holland, and even with England, Portugal's traditional ally.

In 1640, with the overwhelming support of popular opinion and the approval of the various enemies of Madrid, a group of Portuguese patriots expelled the Spanish. They installed on the throne the most powerful nobleman in Portugal, the Duke of Bragança—descended from the old royal family through his grandmother—who took the title of João IV. During his entire reign he had to contend with the armed intervention of Spain. Six years after his death in 1656, his widow confirmed Portugal's alliance with England by giving their daughter, Catherine, in marriage to Charles II.

These constant wars ruined the country, but the unswerving loyalty of the Brazilian colony retained for Portugal a source of gold, diamonds and precious wood. João V helped himself to this wealth with both hands: he launched dazzling projects, such as the Aqueduct of the Free Waters in Lisbon; heedless of cost, he erected buildings on an irrationally grand scale, the monastery at Mafra and the University Library at Coimbra among them. The Chapel of St. John the Baptist in Lisbon's Church of St. Roque, constructed mainly of lapis lazuli, is another example of the appetite for magnificence of the Maecenas-like king. He was infatuated with foreign styles: his architects were Italian or German, while his furniture and tableware came from France. Grotesque though his extravagance was, this prodigal king added many churches and Baroque palaces to the architectural wealth of Portugal.

The Earthquake

João V had been dead for five years when, on November 1, 1755, a terrible earthquake shook the entire country and destroyed a large part of Lisbon. In the cruel years that followed, Pombal, a great statesman and powerful minister of King José I, succeeded in raising Portugal from its ruins. A cruel and unrelenting but enlightened despot, Pombal held the nobility in check, limited the power of the church (expelling the Jesuits), and breathed new life into commerce and industry. He rebuilt Lisbon in the beautiful, austere architecture clearly derived from the Queen Anne style in London, where Pombal had served as Portuguese Minister, but here lightened by the local temperament. The streets between the Rossio and the great colonnaded riverside square, the Praça do Comércio, or Terreiro do Paço are an early example of town planning and show one facet of Pombal's many-sided genius. After the death of José I, Pombal fell into disgrace; his religious changes were overturned by the new, pious queen, and he died in the town which bears his name.

In the years covering the turn of the century, the Peninsular War (1808–14) proved crucial to Napoleon's fortunes. In order to deprive England of her overseas naval bases, he invaded Portugal on three separate occasions. Under the generalship of Sir Arthur Wellesley, later the Duke of Wellington, Britain carried the war into Portugal itself, and, after a series of hard-fought campaigns from 1808–11, the French were finally forced to retire, as much by starvation as by the force of arms. The war shifted over into Spain, and Portuguese troops fought side by side with the British until Napoleon was at last defeated.

After the Peninsular War, Napoleon left the country devastated and vulnerable to the destructive influences of internal strife. João VI was in Brazil for most of his reign, during which his younger son Miguel plotted against his elder brother Pedro, and started a civil war. But on the accession of the young Maria II in 1826, Miguel was made regent; he then usurped the throne, causing further strife until he was expelled from the country in 1834. The monarchy had by now become unpopular; it was blamed for all the ills of a country which had been abandoned to political intrigue.

While Portugal was thus wasting away, the other European powers were actively seeking new outlets for their commerce—especially in Africa. England decided to unite Africa from the Cape to Cairo. At the Congress of Berlin, France, Prussia and Italy divided among themselves a continent in which Leopold of Belgium had taken the lion's share. In order to pacify the Bantu tribesmen, who had risen, being cleverly manipulated and armed by outside interests, troops were sent from Portugal to reinforce the local garrisons in Angola and Mozambique.

In Lisbon, popular agitation reached fever pitch. On February 1, 1908, King Carlos and Crown Prince Luis were assassinated by anarchists on the Terreiro do Paço. Two years later the monarchy, in the person of Manuel II, was overturned, the Bragança family was banished, and a republic proclaimed. Manuel withdrew to England where he lived in retirement until his death in 1932, leaving all his properties in Portugal back to the State. These properties, notably the palace and chase at Vila Viçosa are managed by an independent body, the Casa de Bragança.

However, simply becoming a republic did not restore peace and prosperity. A costly and confused participation in World War I (in Africa and northern France) at the request of the Allies, further aggravated Portugal's social and economic problems.

The Modern State

Between 1911 and 1926, 44 governments attempted to raise the country from the morass into which it had sunk. A *coup d'état* in 1926 brought General Gomes da Costa to power as President, followed by General Carmona—the latter retained the nation's confidence until his death in 1951. He appealed to António de Oliveira Salazar, professor of political economy in the Law Faculty at the University of Coimbra, to rebuild the national economy and take Portugal's destiny in hand. From 1928, first as Minister of Finance, then as Prime Minister, Salazar was in effective charge of the country, maintaining a parallel dictatorship to Franco's in next door Spain. After having maintained, in the face of many pitfalls and calculated risks, an active neutrality during World War II, Portugal made considerable economic progress, but at the expense of any social modernization.

After suffering a severe stroke in 1968, Dr. Salazar was succeeded, after a constructive dictatorship of almost 40 years, by Dr. Marcello Caetano, a Professor of Law at Lisbon University. Caetano was respected and might have been able to bring his country into a more democratic way of life had he had the courage to replace the then President, Admiral Americo Tomas, by a man more aware of the problems caused by the 13 years of colonial war, waged to retain control of Portugal's great African empire of Angola and Mozambique. Although fatal casualties were remarkably few, many members of the armed forces were injured by landmines and boobytraps, which did not improve morale and both the privates and officers were very badly paid.

So it was not surprising that a military uprising took place in the mother country, led by 64-year-old General António de Spinola in April 1974. This Carnation Revolution—so called because the soldiers put red carnations in the barrels of their rifles—was a bloodless one, fewer than 20 people being killed, and those almost by accident, in the few disturbances which ensued. Spinola was appointed President of a predominantly Left-wing government, but he was shortly replaced and banished to Brazil where Marcello Caetano and Admiral Américo Tomás had been allowed to go directly after the coup. Both former Presidents were allowed back into Portugal, where Admiral Américo Tomás died. Marcello Caetano returned to academic life in a Brazilian university and died in 1980.

Free elections have since shown that the great majority of the Portuguese people want to build a new nation in peace and on foundations of commonsense. The massive aid and loans from the United States and other nations have largely revived the economy, and the election of a Social Democratic government by a large majority in 1987 augurs well for a better future.

Some 700,000 refugees, a large proportion of them black (which is a tribute to Portuguese rule overseas), poured into the country in 1975 from the African possessions which had been granted independence, and from Timor in the Far East, annexed by Indonesia. This is almost a tenth of the total population of the country. The government rapidly formed a special department to succor these unfortunate "returned ones" as they were called. At first those who had no relatives in Portugal were lodged free in hotels and boarding houses, but eventually those who had not found jobs and accommodation were moved to army barracks and unused buildings, so that tourism could get under way again, which it has done in a big way. Many of the refugees have started their own businesses and they are all becoming fully integrated.

Joining the European Common Market in 1986 would, it was believed, bring industry up to date and above all improve the very backward state of agriculture, which should be able to produce enough to feed the whole country. The condition of the people has greatly improved since the revolution in spite of unemployment. Wages have increased, inflation, which rocketed for some years, is slowing down, and the social services are improving, with health care operating all over the country and pensions for the disabled and elderly.

The really amazing thing is that a country so strictly controlled for over 40 years should burst into the light of free speech and free association with so little actual violence and bloodshed. It speaks well for the inherent qualities of the Portuguese people that, in spite of pressures from outside and hysteria from within, they are building themselves a place in the Europe of Today.

CREATIVE PORTUGAL

The Portuguese language, which is spoken today by over 100 million people in various parts of the world, never fails to astonish anyone who is hearing it for the first time. When the Romans conquered Lusitania some two centuries before the Christian era, they acquired the embryo of a nation; the desperate resistance of the soldiers of Viriathus, Chief of the Lusitanians, who had a fierce desire for independence, demonstrated a moral unit, a kind of ethnical solidarity. That solidarity grew during the fight against the Moors and brought about such a strong national consciousness that Portugal emerged from among the rival kingdoms fighting the Moors as a nation having exactly the same frontiers in 1139 as today.

Despite its Slavic-sounding inflections and nasal intonations, so elusive to the unpracticed ear, Portuguese is essentially a Romance language. The unity of the Portuguese language dates back to the 12th century. Henry of Burgundy—the father of Afonso Henriques, Portugal's first ruler—had brought with him to the peninsula a considerable retinue of French noblemen and scholars. No wonder that early Portuguese literature is like a renewal of Provençal poetry. At that time, the use of prose was restricted to the chronicling of historically significant events.

Sancho I, the son of Afonso Henriques, was a poet and, some 100 years later, Dom Dinis was also composing his love poetry and songs of friendship. Both of them had been taught by French troubadours. Duarte I, whose courtiers—including the ladies—were learned scholars, proficient in both Greek and Latin, developed a stricter literary form, the essay. Subsequently, there were the chronicles of Fernão Lopes, the historian of Portugal's tragic Middle Ages, and those of Azurara, who accompanied the explorers of Sagres in their wanderings.

54

Portuguese literature, as a diversion of princes, ran the risk of remaining too restrained and too affected, since the period demanded preoccupation with form. However, the 15th century brought to it what had been lacking—virility, strength, the discovery of new horizons, a taste for observation, and inspired exaltation. When Pedro Vaz da Caminha described the arrival of Pedro Alvares Cabral's ships in Brazil, he was merely reporting, but when, a half century later, Camões sang of the arrival of Vasco da Gama's fleet in India, he did so in an epic poem. The primary reason for the change is that during those 50 years Portugal had written one of the most extraordinary, romantic, and heroic chapters of history. Oceans were conquered, islands and lands discovered, and continents outlined.

Literature was inspired by the history with which everyone was surrounded. Great men of letters, such as Pedro Nunes, essayist and mathematician, André de Resende, humanist, Damião de Gois, historian, Sá de Miranda, poet, Bernardino Ribeiro, a poet who wrote a novel, António Ferreira, also a poet, and Fernão Mendes Pinto, adventurer, lived during this half-century and made it illustrious.

But not until Gil Vicente's time do we find a typically Portuguese lyric inspiration. His *autos,* or "mysteries," skillfully express many different kinds of themes, including the serious, the truculent, the heroic, and occasionally the prophetic. There are excellent translations available of his works. However, the outstanding representative of Portuguese literature is Luiz de Camões, a not unworthy contemporary of Cervantès and Shakespeare. The *Lusiads* sing of the people whose glory and wretchedness he shared: allegory and myth mingle with the prodigious epic of the Discoveries, blending facts, heroes, and legends into the masterpiece of a genius. However, many readers prefer—instead of the bright fanfare of the famous *Ten Songs*—the pure, artfully contrived harmonies of the *Sonnets,* tinged with melancholy, that sing so sweetly of love.

The Spanish domination between 1580 and 1640 naturally led to a decrease in Portuguese writing, though the Jesuit António de Vieira, who went to Brazil, wrote fascinating letters from that immense and then largely unexplored country. His work is now becoming a popular source of study among academics.

The *Love Letters from a Portuguese Nun* are imbued with love and sadness: they were supposedly written by Mariana Alcoforado, a nun at the Beja convent of Conceição, now a museum, to a dashing French officer. First published in France in 1669 and since translated into many languages, these letters remain a fascinating literary mystery. The Portuguese originals have never been found and little is known of either the writer or of the Chevalier de Chamilly, who is believed to have received these moving epistles.

Bocage, who died in 1805, was the leading satirical and lyric poet of the 18th century. He left some admirable sonnets conveying exquisite bitterness and despair. In the same century Francisco Manoel do Nascimento was an early opponent of rhyme in poetry.

The Romantic Movement came late to Portugal, only around 1825. The most brilliant of the writers of that time was Almeida Garrett, who died in 1854. He was not only a novelist and dramatist, but also a poet who influenced a whole generation in a century prolific in remarkable writers whose works are little known outside their own country. These include Camilo Castelo Branco and Julio Dinis, both novelists, the historians Alexandre Herculano and Oliveira Martins and the poets Antero de Quental and António de Castilho.

The latter half of the last century almost exactly covered the life of the greatest Portuguese novelist, Eça de Queiroz. He was an early realist and his books, all translated into English, are well worth reading for their brilliance and vivid writing.

Fernando Pessoa, who died in 1935, was a prolific poet, the author of diversified works distinguished by their classic form and by surrealistic flashes in their synthetic expression and imagery. His reputation is becoming established, and deservedly so, in many countries. His followers in the "modern movement" include José Regio, Almada Negreiros, Miguel Torga and Natalia Correia.

Mention must also be made of other writers who rank among the Portuguese classics, including Trindade Coelho, Ana de Castro Osório (Portugal's first woman novelist), Ferreira de Castro, Fernando Namora and Aquilino Ribeiro. Among contemporary writers are José Gomes Ferreira, Sofia de Melo Breyner, José Cardoso Pires, Joaquim Paço d'Arcos and Luis Sttau Monteiro. Although novelists have not yet found inspiration in the revolution of 1974, a great number of political studies have been published and several books of memoirs and autobiographies.

Architecture

The relics of the Roman occupation of Portugal are many though few have been excavated: splendid bridges (Chaves and Ponte de Lima), the old roadbeds, several thermal springs and, notably, the Evora temple (second-century), with its marble-topped granite colonnade. And at Conimbriga you will find intact the highly picturesque remains of a Lusitanian settlement looking much as it did before the barbarian hordes overran it. Prehistoric *citanias* or hill cities can still be seen in the north. The most fully excavated is that of Briteiros near Guimarães.

Many Visigothic vestiges remain: pilasters, columns, etc., in the museums. Although considerably damaged and inexpertly restored, St. Frutuoso, near Braga (seventh-century), stands out as the purest example of Byzantine art in the peninsula (it is laid out like a Greek cross). The Templars' Shrine at Tomar (12th-century) derives its octagonal shape from the temple of Jerusalem.

Portugal's churches mark the various stages in the process of reconquest during which the Christians gradually pushed the Moors southwards. Numerous Romanesque chapels, utterly touching in their humbleness, sturdy as the faith that inspired them, artlessly adorned with simply carved capitals and portals, cover the landscape between Minho and Douro, all the way to the Mondego. Those at Rates, Fonte Arcada and Bravães merit special consideration. The early bishops, who were often French, built cathedrals on the model of Cluny (notably at Braga, Oporto, Lamego, and Coimbra). Some of these edifices have preserved their fortress-like appearance (at Lisbon and Guarda).

The Gothic Style

South of the Mondego, art forms evolved towards the Gothic, but the sobriety and vigor of the Romanesque style so accurately suited the prevailing Portuguese temperament that Alcobaça, despite its ogival arches, is a witness to a certain characteristic restraint.

At the end of the 13th century, King Dinis, a prodigious builder, began replacing the transitional Gothic with a more typically Portuguese style, as evidenced in churches (Santa Clara-a-Velha, in Coimbra, Leça do Balio and the monastery at Odivelas), fortresses, and castles (Leiria, Estremoz, Beja). Handsome cloisters have survived from this period, at Guimarães, Coimbra, Lisbon, and Evora.

The Portuguese ogival style found its highest development at Batalha, which was influenced by English perpendicular Gothic and had grafted on to it that most original and expressive of styles, the Manueline.

The latter seems to have sprung forth spontaneously, as a kind of exaltation of the extraordinary epic of the Portuguese Discoveries. The magnificence of the Manueline style was made possible by the gold and spices that poured into the country. Exotic new worlds, either just discovered or integrated into the Christian universe, gave it its exuberant and occasionally pagan shapes. The stone, for all its rigidity, throbs with an inner dynamism, a hidden pulse, that makes the very columns contort and writhe in the Church of Jesus at Setúbal; the cables twist themselves into knots in the roof at Viseu; and the lace foams and froths in Batalha's Unfinished Chapels. Unlike the sprawling Spanish *plateresque,* Manueline art gathers itself up into medallions set against the stark simplicity of bare expanses. In the ultimate analysis, the window of Tomar's Chapter House of the Order of Christ is but a single outsized votive offering.

Art—from Renaissance to Modern

The Manueline style failed to survive beyond the lifetime of the man responsible for giving it both its name and its impetus. Almost as a reaction, João III introduced a classicism that found its expression in the Tomar cloisters. An Italian architect, Felipe Terzi, was entrusted by Philip II of Spain with all the royal projects: the coastal fortifications, the aqueduct at Vila do Conde, and the churches of São Vicente de Fora and São Roque in Lisbon (end of the 16th century).

In the early 18th century, a German, Frederic Ludwig, won the favor of King João V, the "magnificent king." Ludwig's feeling for spaciousness and generous proportions manifested itself in Mafra (1730). His Portuguese disciples had a greater sense of gracefulness. The earthquake in 1755 razed the center of Lisbon to the ground. For the rebuilding of the city, an elegant but restrained style known as "Pombaline" was introduced: the masterpiece of this period is Lisbon's Praça do Comércio (formerly the Terreiro do Paço).

The richest expression of church decoration is in the Rococo retables made of polychrome and gilded carved wood. Angels, birds, branches, shells, trophies, and pinnacles embellish the altars of churches rebuilt in the late 17th and 18th centuries, finding their way even into Romanesque and Gothic sanctuaries. The most extraordinary example of this strange and lovely art is to be found in the church of São Francisco in Oporto, where a late Gothic church has been entirely covered—pillars, arches, groined ceiling—in a plethora of superb carved and golden wood. It is fortunate that these 17th- and 18th-century additions were not removed when a passion for restoring churches and other buildings to their original state struck Portugal in the first half of this century. The great golden interior of Alcobaça was only removed around 1910, leaving that fine structure evocative but bare. However, there is still splendid Baroque and Rococo work in churches all over the country, many of which will be mentioned in their respective chapters. This golden fantasy is often allied to bright blue and white tiled panels of scriptural subjects, and strangely enough the two fantasies complement each other.

Apart from ecclesiastical art, this style did produce charming private residences (*solares, palacetes,* and *quintas*), frequently tinted in delicate shades—pinks, grays, and whites—and accented, in the Minho, with granite festoons and tiles of many hues. Landscaped gardens complete with fountains, pools, and statuary provide a setting for, or a prolongation of, these exquisite houses that can be seen both in Lisbon and in some out-of-the-way villages. The most interesting examples are found in the north, at Viana do Castelo, Vila Real, and Braga.

Until the end of the last century, Portuguese artisans and working masons built beautifully proportioned houses and little cottages by some strange inner instinct. Then, after a brief flirtation with art nouveau after World War I, examples of which can be seen all over Lisbon, the modern love of concrete took over. Even so, the acres of apartment houses outside Lisbon and other large towns are often painted in bright colors, the balconies alive with climbing geraniums, and natural stone is used for window and door frames which gives a certain dignity to the most uninspired buildings.

Sculpture and Painting

A number of Iron Age sculptures have been found in the north of the country in the course of the last hundred years. The best collection is in the Martins Sarmento Museum in Guimarães, of which the outstanding exhibit is the Colossus of Pedralva. This huge seated figure in granite with its powerful face and limbs, is one of the most remarkable prehistoric statues in Europe, yet seems to be almost unknown, even in Portugal.

Although in the pre-Romanesque portals and capitals Portuguese sculpture remained somewhat awkward and barbaric, it found its first ideal outlet in funerary monuments. The visitor to Coimbra is struck by the mannered realism in the recumbent figures of the kings and bishops on the tombs in Santa Cruz, and the original Gothic tomb of St. Isabel of Portugal in the choir of Santa Clara-a-Nova as well as the tombs in the cathedrals of Lisbon, Guarda, and Braga. These sculptures are a foretaste of the masterpiece of their kind, the tombs of Pedro and Inês at Alcobaça (circa 1367). The rich sarcophagus embellishments give full rein to the Portuguese feeling for expressive form, much more so than do the carved portals and altarpieces. The attitudes of the reclining figures—many of them are portrait-like—are stirringly eloquent: the perfect union of João I and Philippa, symbolizing also the English alliance, expresses itself in the two figures clasping each other by the hand as they lie under the high ceiling of the Founder's Chapel in Batalha.

The finest retables are the work of the French sculptors Nicholas Chantarene, Jean de Rouen, and Houdart. Their masterpieces may be seen in Coimbra, Evora, and Guarda.

An 18th-century Portuguese sculptor named Machado de Castro produced the greatest equestrian statue of his time: that of King José I, on Lisbon's Praça do Comércio. Responsible also for the impressive figures at Mafra, Machado de Castro was equally successful with miniatures: in his Nativity groups, the innumerable tiny clay figures reveal details that provide invaluable insight into the everyday life of the time (costumes, tools, utensils, accessories). His crowning achievement in this branch of art, the world's largest and finest Nativity scene, is in the Estrela Basilica in Lisbon.

In modern Portuguese sculpture, as exemplified by such craftsmen as Canto da Maia and Barata Feio, the outstanding feature is restraint, the attitude of a figure sufficing to delineate the personality of the subject—see the work of Francisco Franco (statues of Queen Leonor at Caldas da Rainha and of King Duarte at Viseu) and of Alvaro de Brée (statue of João III at Coimbra University). The work of Artur Rosa, João Cutileiro and Fernando Conduto is also of interest.

Portuguese painting came into being in the 15th century with Nuno Gonçalves. In his polyptych of São Vicente now in Lisbon's Museum of Ancient Art, this artist, obviously under Flemish influences, outshines his teachers by his use of composition, the deep brilliance of his coloring, and the amazing accuracy of his portraiture. This picture is a masterpiece that immortalizes on its panels the princes and knights, the monks and fishermen, the great names and the anonymous people of Portugal at the time of the Discoveries. *Ecce Homo,* noted for its filmed eyes, dates from the same period. Camões sang of this time, Nuno Gonçalves painted those who lived it. This was also the period of Frei Carlos of Evora, Gregorio Lopes, and Cristovão de Figueiredo.

The paintings by the Manueline artists also testify to the glory of their epoch. Caravelles sail up the Rhine on the panels of Santa Auta, and one of the Three Wise Men in the Adoration scene at Viseu is a Tupi Indian. The great Vasco (Vasco Fernandes) is harsher and more earthy. His style is distinguished by the vigor of its compositions, its expressive naturalism, plus a certain awkwardness.

The 18th century was one of decorative art: artists painted ceilings *à la* Quillard, frescos *à la* Pillement; they painted carriages, and family portraits. Living his formative years in the war-torn time of the Napoleonic invasions, Domingos Sequeira developed certain distinguishing traits of style set off by a Goyaesque bitterness.

The Victorian age saw a flowering of landscape painting, a branch of art which previous Portuguese painters had ignored. The work of José Malhoa, Miguel Angelo Lupi, who painted in the pre-Raphaelite manner, Silva Porto, Columbano, Luciano Freire and João Reis is a revelation. Their work is best seen in the José Malhoa Museum at Caldas da Rainha.

Contemporary Portuguese painting, which ranks among its pioneers such artists as Amadeu de Sousa Cardoso, who was a friend of Braque and Modigliani, and Almada Negreiros, has achieved world fame with Vieira da Silva. Other well-known painters are Noronha da Costa, Bartolomeu dos Santos, Lourdes Castro, Mário Eloy, Júlio Pomar, Paula Rego, Eduardo Nery, Francisco Smith and Menez.

Decorative Arts

Throughout the centuries, the ceramic tiles of Arabic origin known as azulejos have continued to develop. Early examples of this art have designs in relief, often geometrical motifs, as shown at Bacalhoa or in the old *Paço* in Sintra. By the 17th century the relief patterns had disappeared and been replaced by whole panels of smooth, glazed tiles with religious or secular motifs which decorated churches, palaces and private houses. In some places patterned tiles were joined together so as to look like Persian carpets. (The most beautiful tiles are in the Fronteira Palace and gardens at São Domingos de Benfica on the outskirts of Lisbon.)

The 18th century was characterized by landscapes, allegories, Biblical scenes, hunting excursions, pleasure parties (see the rare collection at the old University in Evora). In rebuilding Lisbon, polychrome tiles were used for the decoration of standard constructions and to conceal unsightly restorations. They are to be seen even covering the whole façade of a house. Emerging from the mass production of the last century, the azulejo, under the fresh impetus of such talented ceramists as Cargaleiro, Jorge Barradas, Maria Keil, Júlio Pomar, Carlos Botelho, Sá Nogueira and Querubim Lapa, has been restored to its proper place in decoration and architecture.

Wrought Gold and Tapestries

Portuguese wrought gold is outstanding in religious and other forms. The treasures in cathedrals (Evora, Viseu) and museums (Lisbon, Oporto, Coimbra) trace the development of this art from the early Romanesque crosses and chalices through to the Germanic-type vessels, including the era of Manueline splendor. The 16th-century monstrance in the Museu Nacional de Arte Antiga (Ancient Art Museum) in Lisbon, made with the first gold to reach Portugal from the Orient, is a superb example.

The Arraiolos carpets were originally wool embroideries based on Oriental rug designs, subsequently developing their own distinctive themes and colorings. They are now being produced from original designs or patterned after early models. You will see strikingly beautiful examples in all the museums.

The Portalegre tapestry studios are flourishing, and are using designs by both Portuguese (Lapa, Camarinha, Tavares) and foreign artists (Lurçat). Tapestries are used in the decoration of many public buildings and luxury hotels.

Porcelain, Pottery and Glass

The Vista Alegre porcelain works near Ílhavo were founded in 1824 by José Ferreira Pinto Basto and are still owned by the same family, many of the highly skilled craftsmen being descendants of the original workers. The porcelain is the same kind of hard type as that produced by the Berlin factory and the works still makes lovely things—not only table services but vases and ornaments in both traditional and modern styles. There are other porcelain factories in the country, but none of them approach Vista Alegre in quality.

Pottery, as has been indicated, is made all over the country and differs widely in design and color according to the clay from which it is fashioned.

Near Lisbon at Sobreiro between Mafra and Ericeira, José Franco makes original pottery pieces, as well as beautiful, simple pearl-gray plates and jugs for which the district has long been noted. Potters in the Alentejo specialize in red earthenware vessels, still modeled on traditional Roman forms, though those from Nisa are decorated with small pebbles. At Barcelos in the north they use a black clay as well as making the gaily-colored roosters for which the town is famous. Caldas da Rainha is noted for vivid green leaf plates and dishes, and these are also made in off-white. Perhaps the best known to visitors is the Olaria Pottery in the Algarve, three km. (two miles) west of Porches on the main road from Faro to Lagoa and Portimão. The Pottery was started by an Englishman, the late Patrick Swift, and specializes in high-quality hand-painted ceramics in a wide variety of both modern and traditional designs.

The Marinha Grande Glass Factory was also started by an Englishman, John Beare, in 1748, but was enlarged and developed in 1769 by William Stephens, who with his brother John left the business to the Portuguese state. The factory still produces fine table glass and decorative pieces.

PORTUGUESE CUISINE

The Western world has adopted many boringly standardized attitudes to life—jeans, jazz and junk food among them. Everywhere on the continent of Europe the hamburger reigns supreme, with Coke and, for the delectation of the British, fish and chips close behind. This omnipresence of dull, safe food has forced the adventurous traveler to acknowledge what was once one of the less vital facts of touring—that local produce, cooked according to centuries-old recipes, can provide a fascinating and real contact with the essential character of a nation. This is especially true of Portugal, where a varied and idiosyncratic cuisine reflects the nation's rich past. Meats and fish are usually marinated with wine, olive oil, garlic or herbs before being cooked, which adds much to the flavor.

The northern dietary tradition rests on butter and fats, but Portugal belongs to the civilization of oil *(azeite)*. Olive oil, naturally, but it is stronger and less refined than most varieties used in Spain. It may happen that olive oil does not really agree with you, and in that case, local dishes cooked in butter or corn oil *(oleo)* will always be found available.

It is readily conceded that, speaking generally, the quality of meat is indifferent but that game is excellent, and that fish, and all that the sea has to offer in the way of seafood, is superb. Vegetables are cropped early in the season, fruit is abundant, and desserts are a revelation. Fruit and vegetables are not usually imported, so one eats what is in season and freshly gathered. These considerations are intended for the fainthearted, the hesitant, and mothers of traveling families. Having said this, let us review in detail some local specialties fully deserving of the gourmet's attention.

Soups and Entrées

The mainstay of all festivities and formal occasions is soup, made of vegetables in season, boiled together and sieved with a spoonful of olive oil added at the end, or it may be *canja.* This consists of the liquid in which a chicken and the chopped liver and gizzard have been boiled. When the chicken is removed a handful of rice is thrown in. The broth of the Portuguese boiled dinner, *cozido,* in which meat, poultry, fat bacon, smoked sausage, rice and chick peas are simmered together, is a delicious and very sustaining soup. It is more a main dish than a soup, as is *açorda,* from the Alentejo, which can be likened to a kind of porridge but is based on wheat bread oiled and garlicked and offering the following alternatives: white fish (such as cod) with boiled eggs (which must be soft), and flavored with herbs such as coriander. The *açorda* is a complete repast in itself; fragrant, filling without being in the least heavy (babies—even delicate ones—are brought up on it). In Evora, you should try those offered at the *Pousada dos Loios,* which are delicious.

Very different is the true Alentejo soup, where chopped-up fat bacon is melted with a little smoked ham in a pan with two or three sliced onions; water is then added and salt and pepper to season. When the water boils, eggs are then broken in; when these are poached, a piece of bread is placed in each soup plate and the liquid poured onto it with an egg in each plate. For another Alentejo soup which requires no cooking, a good deal of garlic and fresh coriander leaves are chopped with olive oil into the bottom of a soup tureen—boiling water is then added and a few pieces of bread, and eaten at once.

The *caldo verde* from the Minho in the north is served in a bowl. Basically it consists of green cabbage shredded thinly into a clear potato broth and with slices of smoked, peppery sausages. Wholesome chunks of corn bread are eaten with it. Fish soups are also good, made by adding a little rice, onions, tomatoes, potatoes and a tablespoon of olive oil to the stock in which fish has been boiled.

The hot entrées are fine indeed: meat or fish croquettes, rissoles of seafood, stuffed pancakes or fritters. Rice *(arroz)* is equally delicious: garnished with mussels, shell fish, tunny, chicken, rabbit or simply onions, tomatoes, pimentoes or turnip tops.

Seafood

There was a time in Portugal when crayfish was served with every meal. Highly valued, it is now exported and has become scarce. Specialists in eating places still offer it today but at prices that not everyone is prepared to pay. Portuguese crayfish are so fleshy that they can be enjoyed just boiled, although some prefer them grilled or steamed *(lagosta suada),* and served with hot sauce such as will be offered on the beaches at Guincho or Peniche. Specialist restaurants display windows of seashells arranged in intriguing mosaics in Lisbon (around the Rossio) and on the far bank of the Tagus, at Cacilhas. Crabs *(santolas),* which are consumed stuffed, crayfish, prawns and shrimps *(camarões)* all entice the gourmet. Shellfish abound along the coastal regions at all times. Bringing to your lips the very taste of the waves are the astonishing *percebes,* but only of course when they are in season.

There are, however, hardly any oysters at all, and in the past they were eaten cooked. The celebrated "Portuguese" oysters, with which the oyster-beds of the Vendée were seeded, are now beginning to be offered in their natural state. Somehow neither the conveyance of these delicacies, nor their preservation in their own water has really been achieved successfully, and care should be taken to check their freshness before eating them. Oysters from the Tagus or the Sado are flat and insipid. Far more tasty are mussels *(mexilhões)* and the tiny shellfish known as *ameijoas.*

When in Algarve, you should try a *cataplana:* cockles served with chicken or sausages and bacon, bringing to the table the scented fragrance of the herbs with which they are sprinkled, and cooked in an intriguing circular tin or copper utensil with a close-fitting lid, brilliant like a miniature radiant sun or moon.

Fish is available everywhere in almost confusing abundance. If you are a lover of the outdoors, you will relish grilling your own catch of mackerel in their blue spotted jackets, gray mullet or sea bream, on those little earthenware fire-pots in which charcoal is kept aglow with a small fan woven in straw. In their humble ways, sea fishermen also have kept their own special recipes such as *caldeiradas,* a type of stew that demands an abundance of onions, fresh tomatoes, as many fish as are available, potatoes, oil and a sweetish paprika named *colorão.*

Among the many tasty fish available are sole *(linguado),* bass *(robalo),* brill *(cherne),* merou *(garoupa)* and hake *(pescada).* It is best to eat them grilled or *meuniére.* At Setúbal you should ask for red mullet *(salmonetes).* The nacrous flesh of the swordfish *(peixe espado* or *espadarte),* smelt *(carapau),* tunny steaks *(atum)* and the sea or conger eel *(safio)* are well worth going a long way to find. As for the sardine *(sardinha),* long ago it brought Portugal fame on the tables of the world. When they are fresh, try them grilled over charcoal, accompanied by a salad of tomatoes and green peppers. Another way of cooking them when they are fresh is to fillet them, roll them in oatmeal, and then fry them—it takes away some of the richness.

Do not allow the thought of cuttlefish *(chocos)* and squid *(lulas)* to intimidate you, but eat them cooked in butter with lemon, stuffed or stewed. The octopus *(polvo)* is even more impressive, and if tender, in pilaw or with tomatoes, it will confirm the general opinion that it is far superior to the best tinned crayfish. Smoked swordfish *(espadarte)* can well support comparison with smoked salmon.

High in the fish league is dried cod *(bacalhau).* The Portuguese simply love this strange dried salt fish which has to be soaked in water overnight before it is possible to cook it. It has now become expensive so few can afford to eat it often, though it is usually to be found on the menus of both simple and grand restaurants.

Every true Portuguese relishes a dish of boiled dried cod with cabbage, turnips, large onions, potatoes and a hard-boiled egg, covered in olive oil with crushed garlic and olives. But, perhaps fortunately, there are 364 other ways of dealing with this fish, some of which may be noted. First in rissoles *(pasteis de bacalhau):* when offered in taverns and snack-bars they are usually cold, and therefore less tasty than when served hot from the frying pan when they are deliciously light and melting.

Bacalhau Gomes da Sá is made by flaking the boiled fish and melting it in a deep pan with olive oil, sliced boiled potatoes, sliced onions and stoned black olives. When everything is tender the dish is served with sliced hard-boiled eggs and chopped parsley on top. It is also excellent with boiled chick peas used instead of potatoes. A lighter way of preparing this bacalhau is to add a small amount of shredded boiled cod to a couple of chopped onions melted in butter with half a dozen beaten eggs. This delicious variant of scrambled eggs should not be over-cooked.

A wealth of fresh-water fish inhabit the rivers of Portugal: lampreys *(lampreias)* and salmon *(salmao)* in the Minho, eels *(eiroz* or *anguias)* from the marshlands, the incomparable trout *(trutas)* of the Serra da Estrela or from the torrents of Madeira but now only too often from trout farms, and shad *(savel)* from the Tagus and the Douro. In the spring, in Oporto they smoke shad *(savel fumado),* using for the process venerable oak wine barrels still gorged with the memory of brandies of long ago. It is delicious, as is the smoked eel.

One last word concerns wines: sardines and dried salt cod are consumed with red wine, contrary to all other fish dishes.

Meat, Poultry and Game

Portugal is not favored as regards grazing land, which explains the scarcity of red meat. Beef, which responds to the uncompromising name of *carne de vaca,* is seldom tender enough for the ordinary grill except in the Ribatejo, in the Azores, or understandably, in the grill rooms of the leading restaurants. Nevertheless, you will find in taverns some juicy *bifes à portugesa* with a sweet paprika and red wine sauce, served sizzling hot in an earthenware dish, and perhaps topped with a fried egg. In Madeira you may try an interesting recipe for *espetadas,* consisting of a kind of kebab of beef marinated in oil, wine and garlic, then skewered on to branches of the bay tree. This is set to roast in the fragrance of wood fires and eaten in the open. If in a hurry, you will enjoy a *prego,* a sandwich of hot beefsteak, sometimes associated with smoked ham.

The *cozido* is a boiled dish, interesting because of all that goes into it: meat, poultry, fat bacon, a diversity of sausages, rice and chick-peas. The liquid makes the soup referred to above. Veal *(vitela)* can be disappointing.

Here and there in the countryside one sees sheep *(carneiro)* eating meagerly off arid and bitter pastures. The poor fellow remains thin, with too little meat and scarcely any fat. In the country regions both sheep and goat are made to serve some purpose in the kitchen. In Beira they stew the meat at great length in a wine sauce. This is the *chanfana* of Buçaco. More tender and therefore preferable, is the kid *(cabrito)* and lamb *(borrego),* either cooked together in a sort of spring stew such as *ensopado* or *sarapatel,* or soaked in herb juices and skewered as they eat it in Ribatejo.

But if all this talk of skinny sheep and stringy beef bodes ill for the carnivorous reader, do not despair yet, for in complete contrast, pork *(carne de porco)* is excellent and abundant. Both in the cork-oak forests of Alentejo and the rocky heaths of the north are healthy breeds of pigs. In the Alentejo they find that succulent diet of acorns and white truffles which they relish, and the aromatic shrubs of the heathlands make the meat sweetscented and firm. The cooked meats for instance are quite special. Quite apart from the more esoteric fancies such as sugared black pudding, you must try the dried ham *(presuntos),* smoked loin of pork rolled into a tight bolster *(paios* and *salpicoes),* and the lean or fat meat, which form the basis of some of the best typical dishes.

In the popular taverns of Lisbon one may be served panfuls of liver with onions *(iscas).* In Alentejo, they roast lean pork fillets with cockles over charcoal, or embers of the cork-oak. Shellfish, tasting of the sea, go admirably with the fragrant juices of the pork. Around Coimbra you must taste suckling-pig, sizzling and straight from the oven. Deliciously browned and crackling, generous helpings of pepper relieve the insipidity of the tender meat. This is a further pretext for indulging in the sparkling local wine *(Bairrada).* In Madeira pork is occasionally perfumed with cinnamon.

The sausages differ slightly in every part of the country, but they are almost always smoked and should be eaten in stews, as a relish with rice or spaghetti, in an omelette, or sliced in a sandwich. Generally speaking, the smoked varieties are better not eaten neat as they are very rich, though delicious flambéed in brandy.

One specialty to note is smoked pigs' tongues, which are unknown outside Portugal. These should be soaked all night and then slowly boiled till tender, when they make an unusual dish that can be eaten either hot or cold. Other pig products are trotters stewed with dried beans, and liver or kidneys.

Barbecues *(churrascos),* particularly chicken barbecues, are the "in" thing. African pepper, known as *piripiri,* can be used excessively on such occasions—perhaps because it stimulates the thirst and helps to get the party going with an alcoholic swing. You will be better off when the chicken has been cooked without the gunpowder. The *dobrada à moda do Porto* consisted originally of tripe and beans; it dates back to the days when the Infante Dom Henrique, preparing his father's expedition against Ceuta, slaughtered and salted all available cattle in the area, and left the unfortunate inhabitants only the offal and tripe. Today, the recipe is infinitely more sophisticated, and includes chicken, sausages, carrots, and tomatoes; it is very tasty indeed. You should keep an eye open for turkey *(peru).* In Portugal the bird is fed with bread soaked in brandy before it is killed, which not only makes the bird dizzy but is supposed to improve the flavor and make it tender. When the bird is ready for cooking, it is rubbed with coarse salt and lemon and stuffed with a mixture of the giblets, ground veal, pork, fat bacon, onion, bread crumbs, stoned olives and eggs, sautéed in lard.

In the regions where game is to be found, there are as many recipes as there are cooks to deal with the harvest of partridges *(perdizes),* pigeons *(borrachos),* quail *(codornizes),* and snipe *(galinholas).*

Almost every dish in Portugal is accompanied by either rice or fried potatoes, or both. The best-known salads are lettuce *(alface),* which is always rather green, watercress *(agrioes)* and tomato and pimento *(tomate e pimento). Chicarolas,* a type of chicory, are excellent when obtainable.

Cheeses

We have noted the scarcity of grazing land generally. However, good dairy produce can be found in the Azores because of its lush pastures, and also in the low-lying area in the neighborhood of Aveiro. Butter and matured cheeses from the islands are excellent, in the Danish tradition. Distinct from these, Portugal has also some genuine marvels for those with a nose for the good things of life. These are seasonal cheeses which should be eaten in winter and spring, like the *queijo da Serra,* which sheds generous tears of cream in the grocers' windows, and is made of ewes' milk, kneaded by hand and matured in cool cellars.

Rather more robust is the *queijo d'Azeitao,* also made with ewes' milk, or the *Serpa,* which is drier. As its name indicates, the *cabreiro* displays all the power of the goat from whose milk it is extracted. White or cottage cheese are occasionally eaten salted *(queijinhos de Tomar).* When consumed fresh, the *requeijao* or the *queijinho fresco* are silky and feathery and quite exquisite, particularly when eaten moist as they come from their little basket or tin molds. A portion of fresh cheese is often put on your table in restaurants for you to nibble at between courses.

Sweets and Desserts

Portugal has a sweet tooth. Each and every Portuguese lady jealously hides her book of original recipes, but the one universal dessert is the flan pudding (or *crème caramel*) that appears on the menu of every restaurant.

In truth the great variety of Portuguese sweets is due mostly to their intricate presentation, and to a lesser degree to imperceptible differences in flavor which the casual consumer cannot detect. The basis is egg yolk baked in sugar. In Aveiro, *ovos moles* come to you in amusing little barrels. In Caldas, *trouxas d'ovos* are soaked in thick syrup. In Abrantes, *palhas* are a golden marvel. Fifty and more specialties are just variations on a single theme. Marvelous things, yet somewhat heavier, are concocted if almonds are added to the stock recipes: to that order belong the *morgado* and the *Dom Rodrigo* from Algarve, and a host of elaborations whose names bear clerical associations; *barrigas de freiras* (nuns' "tummies") or *toucinho do ceú* (bacon from heaven). The marzipans of Alentejo and Algarve are wrought in perfect imitation of every conceivable object: animal, vegetable or mineral, decorative and exquisite. In Algarve, fantasy dictates patterns with dates and figs, chessboard and mosaics, a hen and her brood of chicks, longhaired dogs, or a turkey strutting with tail spread.

One of the glories of the ancient convents used to be quince cheese (*marmelada,* from which our word marmalade is derived), perfumed with vanilla, lemon and bergamot, the most famous being that of Odivelas. *Pasteis de Nata* are small tarts which in Belém are made with custard and cinnamon, or with cheese *(queijadas)* at Sintra and Funchal. In Torres Vedras they are filled with beans. The traditional dessert for weddings is rice pudding *(arroz doce),* made with custard and adorned with patterns traced in cinnamon.

Fruits? Fundão is famous for pears, Setúbal for oranges, Elvas for plums, Algarve for figs and almonds. Early strawberries and avocado pears are now being grown commercially in the Algarve. The small prickly red balls of fruit from the *medronha* or strawberry tree make a delicious liqueur. The fruit alone is said to be intoxicating. Apricots, large yellow peaches and nectarines *(péssegos carecas)* are the specialty of the rich lands around Alcobaça where they are also preserved and bottled.

Crystalized fruit is now expensive, but if you are passing through Elvas be sure to pick up a box of plums, they make an excellent present. Local specialties include, at Setúbal, orange *fondants* and at Coimbra, large soft *dragées* which are a feature at Easter-time. Portugal owes to its temperate climate a profusion of fresh fruit: melons of many sizes and hues, from the golden cantaloup, dripping sugar, and the big red-fleshed water melons *(melancias)* with large black seeds, to green honeydew, which is faintly peppery in taste. There are grapes, naturally, in bewildering abundance, and pineapples from the Azores, as well as sweet oranges. There are also fresh loquats or medlars *(nesperas)*. Pride of place, if only for exotic appeal, must go to the produce of the Islands, which will be to many a succulent revelation: custard apples *(anonas)* from Madeira, the flesh of which is creamy and fragrant, and the *maracujá* or passionfruit. To these should be added the better-known mangoes, avocados, and guava.

Vegetables are eaten in their season, broad beans being particularly good when simmered with coriander. Wild asparagus with its slightly bitter taste goes well with roast chicken and can be picked up on any deserted ground in the early spring.

PORTUGUESE WINE

With the exception of those classic Kings of Wines, Port and Madeira, the wines that Portugal produces are mainly honest and straightforward, unaccompanied by the snobbish mystique that shrouds French vintages. This is a country where the ordinary visitor who likes wine can enjoy an endless procession of delicious experiments for little more than the cost of a good beer. It is also possible to find wines of some age that in other countries would be very expensive, but can be enjoyed here at a very moderate cost.

Not that the history of wine in Portugal is shorter or less distinguished than the history of wine in other Continental countries. It stretches back beyond the Romans to the Phoenicians, flourished still under the teetotal Moslems, and went through a checkered time after the Moors were expelled. One of the mainstays of the wine trade's prosperity in Portugal—especially where Port was concerned—was the firm link with Britain. The trade between the two countries predates the 1386 Treaty of Windsor possibly by two centuries. After a long period of generally spasmodic development, with some regions flourishing while others, such as the Algarve, almost ceased production, the situation was taken in hand by Pombal—one of the many facets of Portuguese life that he tried to improve by diktat. In 1756 he put into operation a national plan for "demarcated" regions, geographically delineating growing areas and controlling their output and marketing, with the Port region the first to be demarcated.

Demarcation, and the attendant control of quality, really took off in the first years of this century, and there are now ten regions officially demarcated—the Algarve, Moscatel de Setúbal, Bucelas, Carcavelos, Colares, Bairrada, Dão, Douro, Vinho Verdes, and the island of Madeira.

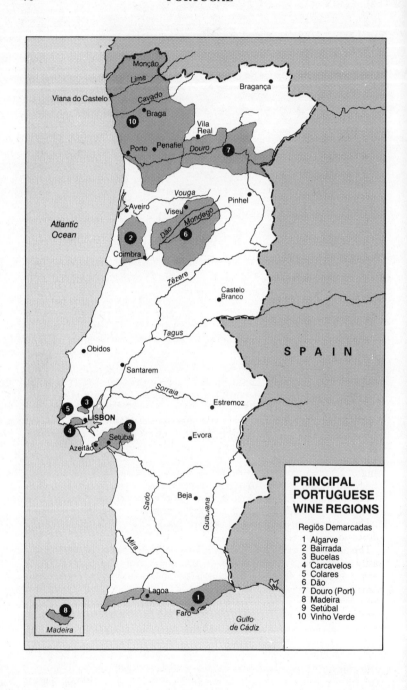

PRINCIPAL PORTUGUESE WINE REGIONS

Regiõs Demarcadas

1 Algarve
2 Bairrada
3 Bucelas
4 Carcavelos
5 Colares
6 Dão
7 Douro (Port)
8 Madeira
9 Setúbal
10 Vinho Verde

The official body that looks after wine production is the Junta Nacional do Vinho (J.N.V.), based in Lisbon. It controls all the facets of viniculture and of marketing, runs competitions, promotes cooperatives (important in the new political climate of the country), and empowers growers to use a seal of approval *(selo de origem)*, rather like the French *appelation d'origine,* which acts as a protection for the public. There are several areas which are undemarcated still, such as those around Evora, but which nonetheless produce excellent wines.

It is still too early to judge how the convoluted regulations on wine that the E.E.C. try to operate will affect Spain and Portugal, who are very recent recruits to the organization, but, as both countries represent a threat to the entrenched interests of the older members, especially France, it is certain that they will have a considerable impact in the long run.

The Algarve and the Alentejo

Starting in the south, and working our way up country, we will begin with a quick look at the wines produced in the southernmost demarcated region, the Algarve. The vast proportion of tourism to Portugal is down here, among the almond blossom, concrete hotels, and wide sandy beaches. Most of the Algarve's wine is produced in a comparatively narrow strip of land stretching between the mountains and the sea. Algarve wine is largely red, with a tiny proportion of white, and is often not unlike a good table wine, a carafe type. Among the better makes is *Lagoa.*

Higher upcountry lies the Alentejo, usually known to visitors—at least in its southern reaches—simply as a wide tract of land to get across as quickly as possible when heading for the Algarve beaches. But this view isn't really fair to the province, which can be quite lovely at certain times of year, especially in spring. The Alentejo vineyards, not yet demarcated, are almost all in the top part of the province, around Evora and over towards the Spanish border. The wines they produce even have a Spanish look and taste to them—*Redondo, Borba* (with its lovely dark color and slightly metallic flavor), *Beja,* and *Vidigueira.* They are all worth seeking out, the reds rich in color, the whites tending to be pale, with a distinct tang. All are very strong in alcohol content, so drink carefully.

The Regions Around Lisbon

There are four demarcated regions within easy reach of Lisbon—Moscatel de Setúbal, Bucelas, Carcavelos, and Colares.

The Setúbal Peninsula lies below Lisbon, across the Tagus, and is now easily reached by a through highway. It is worth exploring for many reasons, not least to discover the peace of the wooded and rocky Serra d'Arrábida. The wines produced here are well known abroad, mainly through the 150-year efforts of the House of Fonseca, based on Azeitão in the heart of the peninsula. The Moscatel which Fonseca produces, together with the small vinegrowers who make up the local cooperative in Palmela—a few miles east of Azeitão and boasting a superb pousada—is best known as a fortified dessert wine, aged and with a mouthwatering taste of honey. If you manage to find some that is, say, 25 years old, then you will find it has a liquorice color, and enjoy its sweet scent and taste. Fonseca and the cooperative produce many other wines as well as the Moscatel—fine reds (notably one called *Periquita,* or "little parrot"); rosés, of which *Lancers* and *Faisca* are much exported; and some ordinary whites, as distinct from the dessert ones, though nothing like as many as are produced elsewhere in the country.

Although Fonseca has a very old winery in Azeitão itself, there is a fascinating modern installation on the eastern edge of the little town. It is a series of great white tanks, looking for all the world like a collection of half-buried flying saucers.

The Bucelas region is situated around 30 km. (19 miles) north of the capital, in the valley of the River Trancão. Though wine from here has a considerable history, and was very popular with the British soldiers under Wellington in the Peninsular War, this is quite a small demarcated region, and all the wine it produces appears under the *Caves Velhas* label. The Bucelas wine is usually straw colored, with a distinctively full nose and a fruity taste, which can sometimes verge on the citrus. It makes an extremely good companion for the lighter kind of white meats, veal and poultry, and is especially appropriate with fish.

Carcavelos consists of just one smallish vineyard, the Quinta do Barão, sandwiched between Lisbon and Estoril along a stretch of overdeveloped and popular coastline. This is not an easy wine to find, the yearly output being quite small, but if you are interested in wines with a history, it would be worth searching out for your collection. Carcavelos is another fortified dessert wine, topaz colored, with a nutty aroma and a slightly almond taste, mostly drunk as an aperitif.

The last of the four demarcated regions around Lisbon is Colares, on the westernmost tip of Portugal, beyond Sintra. It is a fairly hostile place for vine growing, with sandy soil and exposed to the Atlantic winds. Like Carcavelos, the spread of Lisbon's commuter belt has squeezed this region which is a pity, as it has a long and distinguished history of wine production, and still yields some very individual vintages, especially red. This is a wine that definitely improves with age, of a full ruby color, an aromatic nose, and an aftertaste which is likened to blackcurrants. It can be a little astringent when young, so it is always wise to try to find one of the older years. One label to seek out might be *Colares Chita.* The Colares whites are straw colored, slightly nutty in taste, and—like the reds—improve with age. They should be drunk well chilled.

Bairrada and Dão

Higher up the Atlantic coast, and not far south of Oporto, is the region of Bairrada. It is not that long ago—1979—that Bairrada was demarcated, though, on the quality of its output, it probably should have been long before. This is a region made up mainly of smallholdings, gathered into six cooperatives. Taken all together, they turn out a fairly large quantity of wine. As there are several places of interest to the visitor—Coimbra, Conimbriga, Aveiro, and the Forest of Buçaco with its fantasy hotel—it may well be that you will easily come across the Bairrada wines. The reds are of an intense color, with a delicious nose, and a fruity, rich and lasting taste. They mellow with age, and go very well with stronger dishes, such as game, roasts, and the more pungent cheeses. There are not too many whites in this region, and most of them are slightly sparkling *(espumantes),* made often by the champagne method, though of course they cannot be called that, as the French champagne area has fought several legal battles to protect the name. Their characteristics mirror the reds, in having a slightly darkish straw color, with a heavy, rather spicy nose. They go well with fish, pasta and pâtés. One of the biggest names in the region, and one which has been largely exported, is *Aliança,* though several others such as *São Domingos,* and *Frei João* are worth tracking down. The hotel at Buçaco has its own wines, in an extensive cellar, and they add a delicious dimension to a visit to that exceptional place.

The Dão demarcated region—pronounced something like "down" with an adenoidal twang—is also a name quite well known outside Portugal. This region is just south of the Douro, in the mountainous heart of northern Portugal, crossed by the valleys of the Rivers Dão, Mondego and Alva. Because of its terrain, the climate is very capricious here, cold, wet winters, scorchingly hot summers. Unlike the sandy or clay soils to the south, the terrain is made up of granite and schist, a rock which shatters easily, with the resultant changes in the kind of grapes that are cultivated. A very high proportion of wine here is red, matured—they are known as *vinhos maduros*—in oak casks for at least 18 months before being bottled. When they are fully mature, they have an attractively dark reddish-brown color, almost the hue of garnets, a "complex" nose, and a lasting velvety taste. They are best drunk at room temperature after being allowed to breathe well, and go excellently with the favorite roasts of Portugal, lamb and pork. Some of the best names to look for are *São Domingos, Terras Altas,* and *Porta dos Cavaleiros,* or any of the labels where the word Dão precedes the name of the supplier—*Dão Aliança, Dão Caves Velhas, Dão Serra,* or *Dão Fundação.* The Dão whites are less common. They spend shorter times maturing in casks, though still six months or more, have the color of light straw, a full nose, and a dry, earthy flavor. The white *Grão Vasco* is certainly one to try, or *Meia Encosta.*

Douro and Port

The secret of Port is found, first of all in the nature of the arid, volcanic soil and the hothouse temperature of the Douro valley. Some 800 years ago, when the father of Afonso Henriques took possession of his new domain, between Douro and Minho, he planted a stock brought from Burgundy. The vine, like Count Henri, adjusted itself to the alien soil. "Eating lava and drinking sunshine," the Burgundy vines stretched, little by little, to the river's edge. They fought a bitter fight, strangling in ravines, wandering in fits and starts, to force their roots through schistous soil. Nothing but the vine could survive in this torrid pass. With tireless obstinacy, the men of the Douro broke up slate, built terraces with stone-retaining walls, struggled against drought and phylloxera, and made the lost valley the most prosperous in Portugal.

It comes alive during the grape gathering, which lasts for several weeks, since the grapes ripen according to exposure and altitude. In the vineyards sited at lower levels, the gathering is often finished long before the higher plantations are ripe, for cold winds blow down from the Serra do Marão. The region, usually drowsy—the population is scattered because of water shortage—suddenly springs into activity at the time of picking. Workers hurry in from neighboring provinces. From dawn until dusk girls are busy filling baskets, which the men carry on their backs, supporting as much as 150 pounds with the aid of a leather band looped over their foreheads. They descend in long files, towards the *lagares* at the foot of the slopes, pile the fruit in these enormous vessels, ready for treading. Over 40 varieties of grape go into the making of Port, creating the wide diversity of taste that the finished wines can have. The harvesters gather about the vats before the *must* has begun to ferment; the atmosphere is steamy, the feverish excitement of new wine induces singing and dancing. In the spring the young wine goes down by road to the lodges in Vila Nova de Gaia. Since the building of a dam across the river the age-old transportation of the wine by *rabelos,* those strange boats of Douro that look somewhat like ancient Phoenician craft, has ceased.

Port, born as it is of a soil rich in lava, is divided into two great families—vintage and blended. When a year is outstanding—as in 1945, '47, '48, '55, '58, '63, '70, '75, '77, '80 and '83—the wine is unblended and, after reinforcement and bottling, left to mature. These are the vintage wines, which will take upwards of 20 years to mature; the old bottles, dusty with cobwebs, are brought up from the cellar for weddings and christenings, and must be decanted before drinking.

By far the greater quantity of Port, though, even of good quality, is made of a carefully studied blend of new wine with old vintages, thereby obtaining a wide range of taste. For a long time, when England was the biggest market for Port, the first choice was given to full-bodied tawnies; these were served at the end of dinner, with cheese, or an apple and walnuts. However, there is a lot to be said for the white Ports, either sweet as an after-dinner drink, or dry, as an aperitif with ice and a twist of lemon.

The visitor to Oporto should definitely visit one of the Lodges to learn more about Port, taste it and, maybe, buy a bottle of one of the vintages that takes your fancy. It is quite an experience for anyone interested in wine to see these huge old cellars, and find out some of the long, fascinating history that Port has gathered, like the cobwebs, over the centuries. Language will be no problem, as there has been an alliance for more than 200 years between the English and Portuguese in the Port trade, and many of the families are totally bilingual.

Of course, not all the wine produced in the Douro demarcated region is Port. The reds here are of a deep ruby color, extremely fruity, and with a rounded taste. They go well with richer foods, variety meats, casseroles, and stews—anything that tends to be well flavored with herbs. The whites are dry, by and large, a pleasant pale yellow color, with a "full" nose. They go well with salads, hors d'oeuvres, and chicken dishes. Look for *Mesão Frio, San Marco, Quinta da Cotto,* and *Santa Marta.*

Vinho Verde

This is the largest demarcated region in the country, divided into six sub-regions: Monção, Lima, Amarante, Basto, Braga, and Penafiel. The area lies inland from the Atlantic coast, threaded by a sequence of westward-flowing rivers, and enjoying a fairly mild climate, with Portugal's highest rainfall.

Like *retsina* in Greece, vinho verde has come to mean Portuguese wine to many people. The name simply means "green wine," which refers to its delightful youth (as in Cleopatra's "salad days") and not to its color. For anyone who enjoys wine purely as a refreshing, mildly intoxicating beverage, a kind of celestial 7-Up, vinho verde is unquestionably *the* drink—gently sparkling (what the experts call *pétillant*), with a delicate fruity flavor, it embodies the coolness and fragrance of summer gardens. Vinho verde goes especially well with fish, or any kind of seafood. The reds are important to the region, but will mostly be found on their home ground, they don't travel much. They also are refreshingly thirst-quenching, sharp rather than heavy, but with a vermilion-to-purple color. Naturally, they go ideally with almost any meat dish. Try for *Alvarinho,* and *Quinta de São Claudio.*

The vineyards are particularly noticeable in the Vinho Verde district, as this is an area where they are frequently terraced, climbing up the hillsides away from the rivers, like agricultural fortifications. Also, in places, they actually arch over the roads, and often march alongside as you drive, the vines held high on colonnaded rows of pillars, reaching up to the sun. The grapes hang so high that they ripen in direct sunlight, without any rising heat from the ground.

Madeira

Like Port, Madeira—our last demarcated region—deserves a chapter all to itself. This is a volcanic island, rising up to the misty retreat of Curral das Freiras, huddled in the old crater. The soil is clearly volcanic, and the beaches, such as they are, black. The climate here is temperate, but can be humid in summer, and provides exactly the conditions in which vines can thrive although seldom seen below 300 feet above sea level, that warmer zone being taken up by bananas and sugar cane production.

The history of viniculture on Madeira is almost as long as the history of man on the island, and that started in 1419. Like Port, Madeira—the wine and its preparation—is a way of life, and a way of life in which Portuguese and British families are bound together. When Charles II married Catherine of Bragança in 1662 he, perhaps foolishly, declined to accept the island as part of her dowry.

Again like Port, the modern wine has changed a great deal from the traditional drink which was much favored by George Washington, among many other famous people. The modern light, dry versions have become popular as the public's tastes have altered. Madeira is a fortified wine, and most often blended, too. The main styles are: *Bual* and *Malmsey,* the sweeter, heavier ones, which make excellent dessert wines; *Verdelho,* not so sweet, though still a little, and useful as a light between-times drink, say as an alternative to sherry; lastly, *Sercial,* dry and light, which makes an excellent aperitif. None of these, of course, is the kind of wine you are likely to drink as accompaniment to the main course of a meal, but they are all attractive occasional wines and, when they are really aged as they often are, can provide the dedicated drinker with a rare experience.

The labels to look for—and they date back in some cases for a couple of centuries—include *Blandy, Cossart Gordon, Rutherford and Miles, Leacock,* and *Miles and Luis Gomes* (you see what we mean about British and Portuguese families). A visit to a wine lodge in Funchal is an educational and delectable way of passing a couple of hours during your vacation.

Portuguese Wine Words

Adamado	Medium Sweet
Adega	Wine vaults
Adega Cooperativa	Wine Cooperative
Aguardente	Brandy
Branco	White
Bruto	Extra dry (for sparkling wines)
Caves	Wine cellars
Colheita	Grape harvest (thus a vintage, e.g. Colh. 1980)
Doce	Sweet
Espumante	Sparkling wine
Garrafeira (or Reserva)	Fine and mature wine. Special vintage
Generoso	An aperitif or dessert wine, highly alcoholic
Meio Seco	Medium dry
Região Demarcada	Demarcated Region (see text for explanation)
Rosado	Rosé
Seco	Dry
Tinto	Red
Velho	Old
Vinho da Mesa	Table wine
Vinho da Casa	House wine

EXPLORING PORTUGAL

LISBON

Lisbon is a peculiarly beautiful city, descending from many hills to the great River Tagus to which, for centuries, she has owed her wealth and fascination. The city is a port, less busy now that international shipping has declined, but wharves, dockyards and warehouses still line the banks for some 16 km. (ten miles) from Xabregas to Belém. Terreiro do Paço or Palace Square, is the usual name for the Praça do Comércio (many of Lisbon's main thoroughfares have a second, more commonly used, designation). Surrounded on three sides by color-washed buildings above arcaded walks, in which are several Ministries, Terreiro do Paço is one of the most noble squares of Europe. The south side is lapped by the waters of the great river. Here, narrowing slightly below the Mar de Palha or Sea of Straw, the wide lagoon to the north east of the city, the river is tidal. In fact, the tides go on right up to Vila Franca de Xira, some 30 km. (18½ miles) up-river; this opening on the often turbulent waters gives a marvelous feeling of air and space to the huge square surrounding the superb 18th-century bronze equestrian statue of King José I, designed by Machado de Castro. The king, classically clad in a breastplate and plumed helmet, sits astride a splendid horse which has now weathered to a delicate green.

Many of the cross-river ferries sail from this square, as does the longer ferry route to Barreiro for the railway station, departure point of trains to the southern Alentejo and the Algarve. Although cargo boats still come up the river, the beautiful lateen-sail *fragatas,* or barges, which used to take merchandise from one bank of the river to the other, are now superseded by lorries going across the suspension bridge spanning the waters further down towards Belém. This bridge is slung high enough for the very largest liners to pass underneath even at high tide.

The center of the city is essentially 18th-century in architecture for it was rebuilt by the Marquis of Pombal, then Prime Minister, after the great earthquake in 1755. Pombal had been Portuguese Minister in London and this low part of the city, or the *Baixa,* is undoubtedly influenced by the Queen Anne architecture he had seen there. Straight rows of elegantly proportioned uniform house fronts, the surrounds of the windows and doors made of real stone (the country is rich in quarries of every kind) line the streets which are wide and straight with others crossing at right angles, so that it is a perfect example of early, and in this case very successful, town planning.

The district was to be given over to commerce and business and the streets were set apart for different trades. Thus, the Rua do Ouro, or Gold Street, still has a number of jewelers in it as well as a great many banks and the Rua dos Douradores, or Gilder's Street, is a reminder that Lisbon was noted for the fine gold leaf which was applied not only to church fittings, but also to furniture, ornaments and even the window shutters of palaces such as Queluz, which were picked out with real gold leaf.

Fortunately, the earthquake did not devastate the higher, older parts of the city—only the riverside area was totally destroyed—so visitors can still wander round the Castelo de São Jorge (Castle of St. George), whose foundations are lost in antiquity, and the medieval village which surrounds it, enclosed by great outer bastions. People still live and work here and it is a curious experience to walk along the narrow, twisting roadways between small houses alive with flowers, and gaily colored washing drying on struts above your head in the heart of the capital.

The other side of the great valley, which cleaves Lisbon from the Pombal statue at the top of the Avenida da Liberdade through the Rossio, the main square of the city, to the river, was also less affected by the earthquake. However, the ruins of the Gothic Convento do Carmo still standing above the Rossio are a perpetual reminder of what happened that morning of November 1, 1755. The splendid 17th-century Church of São Roque near the Bairro Alto, another maze of narrow streets, has survived to this day. Belém, to the west—where King José I and his court happened to be—was untouched by the earthquake, and here remains the superb Church of Jerónimos, the finest example of the late decorated Gothic style, called Manueline.

The Rossio, surrounded by austere 18th-century facades, is still the center of the city. Full of cafés and restaurants and a diminishing number of shops, it is a perpetually moving scene of dark-suited men talking together, lightly clad tourists and Lisboans scurrying about their business. Until comparatively recently, you would have seen bright yellow trams—which still run in the less busy parts of the town—bringing even more animation and color to the scene, as the flower sellers in the center of the square still do.

Today, public transport in the Baixa and up the Avenida da Liberdade is confined to motorbuses and taxis, which can be instantly recognized by their green tops. Private cars also fill up the roadways, perfect for 18th-century carriages and coaches, but not very adequate for today's automobiles. Indeed, the noble proportions of the Praça do Comércio have been much diminished by the presence of hundreds of cars parked in the large central space.

The Avenida da Liberdade, like the Champs Elysées in Paris, has been marred by apartment buildings devoted to offices and banks which are taking the place of its elegant private houses. But even so, you can still find enchanting examples of Victorian and art nouveau architecture scattered about the city on either side of the Parque Eduardo VII at the top of the Avenida da Liberdade. And just off the Rossio is one of the oddest railway stations in the world, with a Victorian-Moorish-Gothic facade: you have to go up in a lift or climb innumerable stairs to get to the trains, which are mainly suburban ones to Sintra and other surrounding towns.

With a little over 1,000,000 inhabitants, Lisbon is one of the smallest capitals in Europe. So, being cut by the great river to the south, spanned only in the last 20 years by the American-built bridge, Lisbon has always had to expand to the north, east and west. The way to the airport, for example, only a 20-minute run from the center of the city, is now built up by apartment houses; however, their color-washed facades, flower-filled balconies and natural stone embellishments give an air of solidity and a certain elegance to buildings which in other countries have so often begun to look rundown even before they have been completed.

Opening Up the World

Like all really ancient cities, the origin of Lisbon is surrounded by legends, some even saying that it was founded by Ulysses. It is an historical fact that Greeks traded along the Iberian coast and on very early maps Lisbon is called Olissibona. Later, the whole Iberian peninsula became a province of the Roman Empire. Even today, many of the roads in the country are clearly of Roman origin, and the enquiring traveler can seek out Roman bridges, some still used for their original purpose, particularly in the Alentejo. In addition, there are the well-known Roman remains at Conimbriga near Coimbra, and the Temple of Diana in Evora. The Romans were succeeded by the Visigoths who, it is believed, built the first cathedral in Lisbon.

When the Moors swept up from north Africa they not only improved the appearance of Lisbon, but also brought their sophisticated methods of irrigation to the dry lands of the peninsula, methods which are still in use today. Then came the Crusades: ships carrying English, German and Flemish crusaders to the Holy Land were driven ashore by a storm, and were persuaded by the young monarch Afonso Henriques, who had proclaimed himself king of Portugal in 1139, to stay and help him drive the Moors out of the southern part of his kingdom. So, in the summer of 1147, Lisbon was besieged and the Moors were driven southwards to the Algarve from which they were finally expelled a century later. The dedication of the Martires Church in the Rua Garrett in Lisbon recalls these foreign crusaders who fell in the battle against the Moors in Lisbon and were therefore regarded as martyrs for their faith.

In the 13th century what had been small settlements scattered over the country grew rapidly. Lisbon and Oporto in particular benefited from their position on the Atlantic coast which favored the development of maritime trade. These towns, with Braga, Coimbra and Lagos, were represented in the *Cortes,* or Parliament, which was at first held at Coimbra and then

in 1256 moved to Lisbon, which thus became the capital of Portugal. At
the end of that century the first Portuguese university was founded in Lisbon and shortly after transferred to Coimbra, thus making it one of the
earliest European universities.

Under the Aviz dynasty, which started with the election by the Cortes
of Dom João I (the previous king's illegitimate son) in 1385, Lisbon became the richest city of western Europe. Ships from all over the world
brought wealth to her harbor, and it was towards the end of this century
that a previous alliance of friendship with England was confirmed and
strengthened by the signing of the Treaty of Windsor in 1386—a treaty
which has never been abrogated and therefore remains the oldest alliance
in the world. Almost a year later King John I married Philippa of Lancaster, the daughter of England's famous John of Gaunt, Shakespeare's
"time-honored Lancaster." Their third son is known to history as Henry
the Navigator who, from Sagres in the extreme southwest of Portugal,
gathered information from seamen from all over the world and sent out
expeditions which led, after the Prince's death, to the rounding of Cape
Bojador in Africa and finally the discovery of the sea route to India by
Vasco da Gama in 1498.

These historic discoveries were equal in their day to the American moon
landing in the middle of this century. So enthralled was Manuel I that
he built palaces and churches all over Lisbon with the huge profits of the
sale of the first spices from India, giving his name to the extraordinary
flowering of late Gothic architecture which is Portugal's contribution to
European art—Manueline. The Jerónimos Church at Belém and the
Abbey of Batalha to the north of the capital are the most remarkable examples of the style. Side by side with Christian symbols are coral, ropes,
fruits, birds, fishes and exotic animals. The clergy devoted their wealth
to beautifying their churches and chapels. Lisbon cathedral, Madre de
Deus, and later São Roque, are examples of the flamboyant use to which
the new found riches were devoted. Conceição Velha, which boasts a superb Manueline facade, was founded by Queen Leonore in 1498 as part
of the Misericórdia hospice in Lisbon. Such charitable foundations, started
so long ago, still exist in all major Portuguese towns and cities. Run by
lay boards of local people, they have cared for the sick and helpless
through the centuries; now that the state has, in most places, built modern
hospitals just outside the towns, these old buildings have become homes
for local old people.

The Spanish domination, when the Portuguese crown was united to the
Spanish, lasted from 1580 to 1640. Strangely enough, the Spanish Armada
against Great Britain sailed from the Tagus in 1588. After several abortive
attempts to regain independence, a group of Portuguese nobles rose up
and turned the usurpers out of the country and founded the Braganza
dynasty. But during those 60 years Portugal declined in power, her overseas possessions were neglected by Spain, so that the Dutch were able to
annex parts of the East Indies which were formerly Portuguese.

The Earthquake and After

The great earthquake of 1755 is still such a strong folk memory that
even today few Portuguese wish to speak of that dreadful morning of All
Saints Day, November 1. The churches were crowded when, towards ten

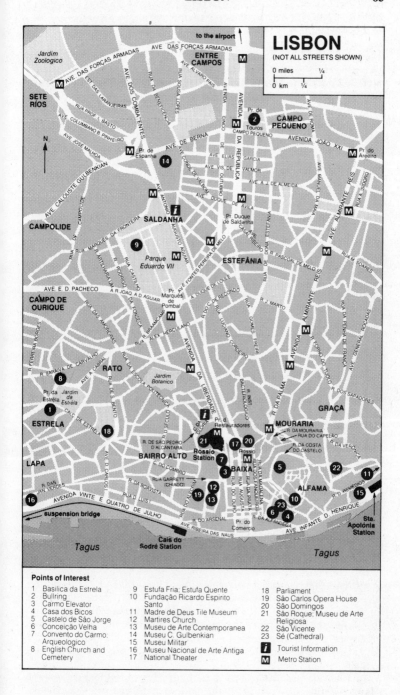

LISBON
(NOT ALL STREETS SHOWN)

0 miles   1/4
0 km   1/4

Points of Interest

1. Basilica da Estrela
2. Bullring
3. Carmo Elevator
4. Casa dos Bicos
5. Castelo de São Jorge
6. Conceição Velha
7. Convento do Carmo: Arqueologico
8. English Church and Cemetery
9. Estufa Fria; Estufa Quente
10. Fundação Ricardo Espirito Santo
11. Madre de Deus Tile Museum
12. Martires Church
13. Museu de Arte Contemporanea
14. Museu C. Gulbenkian
15. Museu Militar
16. Museu Nacional de Arte Antiga
17. National Theater
18. Parliament
19. São Carlos Opera House
20. São Domingos
21. São Roque; Museu de Arte Religiosa
22. São Vicente
23. Sé (Cathedral)

i Tourist Information
M Metro Station

o'clock, around the beginning of Mass, a hollow rumble, swelling to a roar, shook the depths of the earth, which heaved up and all about. In the swaying churches, candles set fire to the hangings and woodwork. A strong wind was blowing, fanning the blaze and scattering the sparks. From the river, the ships' crews could see the church belfries rock and fall apart, the town burst into flames. The Tagus seemed to boil, first sucked down, then spewed up, overflowing its banks and sweeping all before it. Men, women, and children were crushed by falling stone, choked to death by dust and smoke and the hot gas from the cleft earth, or drowned in the tidal wave that swept along the dead together with the rubble.

Within six minutes, the lower part of the town was destroyed, and with it countless people. Panic-stricken, the survivors fled; plunderers mingled with the troops summoned to enforce order and give first aid. In the confusion that followed the earthquake, one man stood out, to sum up the task ahead: "Close the ports, bury the dead and succor the living." That man was Pombal, Minister of José I.

The emergency powers then granted to Pombal lasted well over 20 years. Clear-sighted and forceful, he mastered the panic, set the ruined city in working order, and, while the earth was still shuddering to a standstill, drew up his plan for Lisbon, wide of street and open to the cleansing sea air. He relocated the ruined streets downtown, and what was left of the old buildings on the river's edge. Sewers were dug, streets were built wide and at right angles. Around this modern downtown section, workmen were busy repairing fine family houses as best they could, rebuilding churches, putting up whole new quarters given over to industry: a glazed earthenware factory in the Rato, a silk factory in the Amoreiras, planted with mulberry trees for the silkworms. The Rossio was left in its place, slightly off-center in the new city plan, for the monks of São Domingos had refused to yield an inch of their lands.

The 19th century gave Lisbon gaslight, a monument to Pedro IV, and the royal palace of Ajuda, unfinished at the fall of the monarchy. The fashionable walk was the Passeio Publico, a fine tree-lined space behind the national theater built by Queen Maria II. Also a fashionable meeting-place, then as now, was the uptown street of the Chiado (Rua Garrett), lined with costly shops and coffeehouses, where men gathered at all hours of the day and night to talk politics and literature.

The assassination of King Carlos I and his elder son in 1908 led to the revolution of 1910, when the young King Manuel II went into exile and from thenceforth lived in England. Dr. Teofilo Braga, the historian, was made the first President of the newly-formed Republic. In the 1914–18 War, Portuguese troops fought in France alongside their British allies but from then until the arrival from Coimbra of Dr. Salazar in 1928, there was a constant succession of governments.

In 1940, 800 years after the foundation of Portugal and 300 years after the restoration of its independence from Spain, a Portuguese World Fair at Belém, on the banks of the Tagus, was held to celebrate this anniversary. It marked the beginning of the real effort to improve the run-down parts of Lisbon and Duarte Pacheco, then Minister of Public Works, started an extensive system of road building of which the excellent results still remain.

In 1966, the suspension bridge, 2 ½ km. (1 ½ miles) long, across the Tagus was opened. Fortunately the old ferries still run and you can take a trip across the river for a modest sum. This is a delightful way of seeing the city on its many hills, particularly at dusk, when the lights gradually pierce the quickening darkness, for Lisbon is too far south to have a lingering twilight. In stormy weather porpoises come up the river to shelter and play around the myriad little vessels that use the Tagus. On the south bank, a tall statue of Christ the King, alight in the night sky, blesses the town that has kept, through long years of changing fortunes, the unfailing beauty of its wide river. A lift goes to the summit revealing an unsurpassed view of the city.

After the bloodless revolution of 1974, Lisbon's monuments were apt to be covered with political graffiti or posters, though these have largely disappeared, their equivalent today being the ubiquitous faces of would-be political leaders left over from the last elections.

Exploring Lisbon

The airport is so close to the city that the traveler is in town before he knows it, driving under the branching trees of a shady park—the Campo Grande, where lovers stroll along the leafy paths, mothers take children to play, students from the nearby university sit reading on benches and row boats can be hired by the hour on the shallow lake.

Beyond the park, and between the tallest houses, the town still looks like a garden, for the housefronts are painted in flower-colors—pink and white, yellow and green. The traffic cops shelter from the sun and rain under umbrellas striped black and white, the town colors of Lisbon. This city has kept the thousand-year-old charm of the old Olissibona of the Moors: gardens flower in hidden courtyards, behind the wrought iron of the narrowest balcony, or the plate-glass front of the marble banks. Still to be heard at times are the plaintive notes of the *Gaita de Beiços,* a kind of Pan's Pipe which the knife grinders, who also mend umbrellas, play as they wheel their curious contraptions down the street, to warn householders to come out with their blunt knives to sharpen. Some of these men will also rivet broken plates.

Those who arrive by train from France or Spain will get off at the small and elegant Victorian station of Santa Apolónia, freshly painted in pink and black and white, and banked with green shrubs. It opens onto the docks, where the brown and red sails of fishing-smacks glide between cargo boats, river barges, and steamships. Beyond the port rise the church belfries and towers, the walls and steep streets of the old town, teeming with life as in the days of King Manuel, when tattooed sailors, colored slaves, and old women peddling charms crowded the wharves of the Ribeira. Caravelles are carved in stone on the walls. You will get a passing glimpse of the Casa dos Bicos, formerly the house of the Albuquerque family, with its diamond-cut front. The fresh sea air blows through the whole town, charged with the salty tang of dried fish hanging in the grocery stores, of dripping baskets of fish on the heads of *varinas,* from the 16 km. (ten miles) of dockyards between Lisbon and Belém, and from the river, glimpsed at every turning.

The traveler who comes from Spain on the southern highway can cross the Tagus to Lisbon by the bridge at Vila Franca de Xira, or by Europe's longest suspension bridge, midway between Belém and the Terreiro do Paço in Lisbon. As for the ferry-boats, they steam slantwise below the Mar

da Palha (Sea of Straw) affording the traveler a slow, wheeling view opening full on Lisbon, much as the town appears in old etchings. A castle,
towers, and church belfries still crown the swelling hills. So boundless to
the sight is the roadstead behind the rocky spur of Cacilhas that the mouth
of the river is lost to view. Narrowing his eyes in the murky sea-mist or
the hazy sheen of heat, the traveler knows without being told that the stone
outline in the far distance is the Tower of Belém.

Modern Lisbon

Those of us who love the old Lisbon, the *Lisboa Antiga* of Amália Rodrigues' haunting *fados,* are distressed by the high square buildings of the
new quarters—sometimes painted in garish colors—at such odds with the
graceful rise and fall of the low city skyline. Yet in all fairness, this modern
Lisbon blends well with the old in a well-planned capital city of over a
million inhabitants. Every day, big buildings take the place of town houses,
decorated with turn-of-the-century stonework behind the then-fashionable
palm tree.

Built almost overnight in the mid-20th century, the new Lisbon long
kept her distance, spread out over countrified suburbs where flocks of
sheep still grazed among the weeds of the new back lots, and tall apartment
houses hemmed in small vegetable plots. There was room to spare. Fine,
wide thoroughfares branched out from squares and circles, in planned perspectives. To fill the needs of a fast-growing town, the city planners, copy-
ing Pombal, undertook the wholesale building of long, straight streets of
houses in the same pattern, keeping to the old roof tiles and the many balconies, at once filled with bird cages, flower pots, and hanging wash, that
brought to the new quarters the old way of life.

Lisbon now has many airconditioned movie houses showing the same
movies as everywhere else, shops, and restaurants, together with bowling
alleys and snack bars, gathering places of young people very different from
their elders. Experimental theaters proliferate owing to the generosity of
the Gulbenkian Foundation. Whole city blocks have gone up, with a
wealth of marble, trellised balconies and penthouses. For people of lesser
means, there are low-cost apartment houses. The surge of new building
has been roaring like a tidal wave in the direction of Estoril, crowning
successive hills with high-rise blocks. Even so, there has been an acute
housing crisis brought about by the long-term freezing of rents: with the
fall in the value of money, people have not been moving out of their rented
houses or apartments, and this has resulted in the large number of shanty
towns on the outskirts of the city. However, the rent problem has been
tackled and reasonable yearly increases are at last permitted.

Now that Lisbon has bridged the river, this modern city has spread to
the south bank, where there is a series of working-class housing estates
from which thousands of men and women commute daily.

Old Lisbon

Happily unlike most other cities, the Lisbon of the old days, the area
from the Baixa to the Rossio, from São Roque to Graça, has not been
flooded out by the new wave, but rather cleansed and embellished. The
Pombaline housefronts of the Rua Augusta, the Rua do Ouro (Aurea),

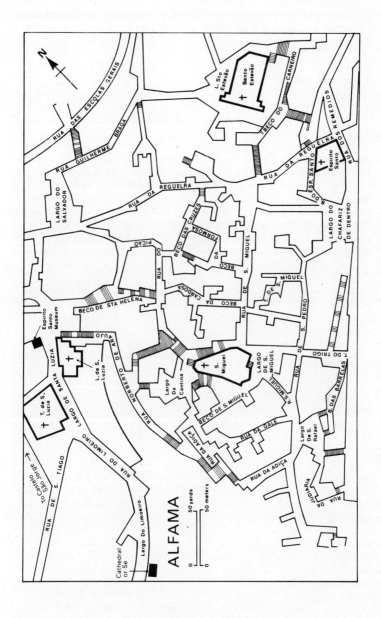

and the Rua da Prata—the Streets of Gold and Silver—have remained untouched. The pavements of black and white mosaic work are in the formal checkered patterns of old; the square of the Rossio is inlaid in a ripple of waves recalling the inrushing tidal wave of 1755; and strollers on the Avenida walk over ships in full sail. They share a family likeness with the streets of Rio de Janeiro.

The narrow pavements are always crowded by a colorful throng; the hawker of lottery tickets, the blind street singer with his guitar, the fruit peddler with his barrow and portable tin scales and many varieties of goods laid out on the ground. Beggars have returned in force since they are no longer obliged to live in special homes as they were before the revolution. Flowers are sold around the splashing fountains of Rossio. The square has been cleared of streetcars, several cafés have given way to snackbars, and within a few years fire gutted the church of São Domingos and the National Theater. They have both been rebuilt and the church now has an aluminum roof thrown over the calcined walls, making a superbly beautiful interior like a Piranesi print. The sun shines on the highest hilltop, crowned by the old Castelo de São Jorge, lit up at night with green floodlights, and overlooking the flashing neon signs of the town below.

A word of warning to the ladies—don't try to walk in town with thin-soled or high-heeled shoes, at the risk of spoiling a good pair or twisting an ankle on the pretty black and white mosaic-work of the steep streets. Wear sensible flat heels, and walk in comfort and safety.

Cats, much loved by Lisboans, flit along garden walls, clinging to the steep slope; they are of a breed which seems to be peculiar to Lisbon—striped tabbies with long, pointed faces like those of the cats from Egyptian tombs. The Portuguese people are somewhat oriental in their attitude to animals: no one is willing to put down newborn puppies or kittens, so there are a good many stray cats and dogs around; but people are kind and feed them.

A smell of coffee wafts from huge cafés to mingle with a sharp salty breeze. A crowd seethes and dawdles, at once busy and nonchalant. A play of changing sunlight throws into strong relief the strange decor, giving an impression of a city built like a theater. The Rossio, without a doubt, is the heart of Lisbon, and as the people of Lisbon seldom seem to go to bed early, the Rossio is as animated at midnight when the cafés close, as at more conventional hours of the day. The Portuguese are not early risers and many travelers are surprised when they find it difficult to get an early breakfast in *pensão* or *residência* before catching a plane or a train. But restaurants remain open until ten or eleven at night and you can always get a meal until then.

Just off the Rossio, to the right of the National Theater, the great church of São Domingos (closed lunchtime) was completely gutted in a terrible fire some 30 years ago. Instead of restoring its former flamboyant 18th-century decoration, a light aluminium roof, painted dark blue, was thrown over the wide interior, and the calcined walls were left as they were. The whole effect is of an etching by the 18th-century Italian, Piranesi.

The best shopping center has always been the Chiado, around Rua Garrett, though several city blocks in this area were devastated in the fire of August 1988. Rebuilding is underway behind those facades that were saved, but it will be a long time before the district fully regains its former position as Lisbon's shopping showcase. Despite this, idlers still sit at the marble-topped tables of the *Brasileira,* drinking black coffee and endlessly talking, as in the days of Eça de Queiroz. There are still the same crowds in the Churches of Loreto or the Incarnation, during Holy Week.

A little way to the north, in the Largo de São Roque, the church of the same name contains a wealth of good canvases and Baroque gold work, and the famous Chapel of St. John the Baptist, which was constructed in Rome by order of King João V and shipped to Lisbon. It is a symphony of lapis lazuli, agate, alabaster and mosaic. A small Museu de Arte Religiosa (Religious Art Museum) is next door.

Towards the river is the São Carlos Opera House, a lovely 18th-century building still used for its original purpose. Many of the visiting companies also give their performances at popular prices in the Coliseu, a huge circular hall accommodating 8,000 people, near the Rossio.

Throughout most of Lisbon, the rich and the poor live side by side, in an unthinking togetherness. In the flowered courtyard of a palace, children and cats play in the sun, the *varina* scrubs her fish basket at the stone fountain, the shoemaker sticks to his last under the stone coat-of-arms. Behind a peeling wall, a low door, there may well be big drawing-rooms with a wainscot of old glazed tiles, priceless East India Company china, and Germain silver, while in front of the palace of Abrantes, now the French Embassy, a former 17th-century convent shelters fishwives and dockhands in its cells and cloisters. Charcoal braziers, hanging wash, geraniums and green plants crowd the cracked stone of a fine old balcony; women gossip by a fountain as they wait in line to fill an earthenware jar with water; chickens scratch the earth, one leg tied by a string to the chair where a girl sits sewing. You will hear songs, the strumming of a guitar under the windows of a blind alley, a radio blaring in a tavern smelling of fried fish, the knife-grinder with his squeaky Pan's Pipes, the lilting cry of street peddlers—"Who wants figs?" "Sardines fresh from the sea," all the many homely village sounds that underlie the deep rumble of a big city. In the smart shopping streets you can often see elderly sable-clad men and women, the older country people who do not change into city clothes when they come up to town, but wear their usual black or dark suits and long skirts.

Strolling through Alfama

The best-known, the most beautiful, and the oldest part of the city is Alfama below the Castelo de São Jorge. The high ramparts of the Castle enclose moats in whose reedy waters swans, ducks and flamingos feed, gardens on whose tended lawns white peacocks fan open their tail feathers against the flowering bushes, and ivy-clad battlements alive with the cooing of white doves. A tall statue of Afonso Henriques in crusader's armor stands in the midst of a wide open space that overlooks the city and the river. Within the great outer walls of the Castle is a medieval village surrounding the parish church of the Holy Cross, in a tree-lined square with Michel's French Restaurant at one side. A rewarding walk can be taken through the busy, narrow lanes.

In order to reach the Castelo you'll have to clamber up through the old Alfama quarter. The streets are just about wide enough for two donkeys to pass abreast, and the visitor has to pick his way between baskets of oranges and sardines, and groups of men gossiping in front of wineshops. You will pass women carrying pitchers to the fountain and old men repairing fish nets. Sardines are usually grilled almost on the doorstep, and cats and geraniums sprawl on every balcony. Everyone seems to be busy making paper carnations for the June festivals. Old women try to sell you curious sweets and dried watermelon or sunflower seeds. There are tiny gardens no bigger than your hand, all overrun with urchins; church belfries are a-flutter with pigeons. Towards evening huge iron lanterns throw lacy shadows on the rough walls, and through narrow openings you catch a glimpse of the Tagus, busy with vast tankers and boats with red sails.

The Castelo to which you come is the Castelo de São Jorge today, but originally it bore the name of no Christian saint, for it was the Moorish Governor's palace, and his stronghold. They had picked their place well; visitors still plod up to it today for the magnificent view it affords over Lisbon and the Tagus. On the way you will arrive at the Miradouro de Santa Luzia, where a vine-shaded balcony offers an admirable view of river and rooftops. From the slopes of Alfama as far as the Tagus there arises a familiar and friendly city murmur, punctuated from time to time by the whistle of a tug-boat or the plucking of a guitar. On the walls of the little chapel here are paintings on glazed tiles: the capture of Lisbon by Afonso Henriques, and Terreiro de Paço before the earthquake.

Nearby, above Alfama, is a wide open space, filled with light from sky and water, called the Portas do Sol. All around the fine old houses of the rich stand side by side with white-washed cottages and noisy taverns. One of the finest was beautifully restored by a man of wealth and taste, the late Ricardo Espirito Santo, and furnished with his private collection of Portuguese works of art, found and brought home from all over the world. It is less a museum than a living 18th-century mansion. In a wing schools and workrooms have been installed to keep the old handicrafts alive.

Further down the slope the expertly reconstructed 12th-century Romanesque cathedral with extensive cloisters towers above the church of Santo António, built on the site where that popular saint was born. On the confines of the Alfama rises the Renaissance church and a large school, formerly a monastery, of São Vicente de Fora, whose tiled cloisters open on the chapel where all the Bragança kings, including Manuel II who died in England in 1932, are buried—no longer in glass-lidded coffins through which the embalmed bodies could be seen, but transferred to simple stone sarcophagi, except for the dynasty's founder who has been accorded Baroque pomp. King Carol II of Romania, exiled at Estoril, has been put provisionally to rest among the Portuguese monarchs. The burial chapel of Lisbon's Patriarchs nearby has room for only three more bodies.

Between the churches of São Estevão and São Miguel, antique dealers have set up shops, catering for all tastes and means. They lead downwards to the Terreiro do Trigo, and to the King's Fountain with its six outlets, one each reserved for noblemen, women, soldiers, sailors, servants and galley slaves.

The Bairro Alto and Mouraria Districts

To climb uptown to the Bairro Alto, it is best to take the Carmo elevator, built by Eiffel. Like his tower in Paris, the openwork iron structure was a thing of beauty in its time, an eyesore in later years, and now is taking on an old-fashioned charm of its own. The footbridge on top over-looks the downtown streets of the Baixa, and leads to the silent ruins of the Carmo, past the Quinta Restaurant. The cable streetcar of the Calçada da Glória, which takes off at the Restauradores, climbs up to the pretty tree-shaded terrace of São Pedro d'Alcántara, that overlooks Avenida da Liberdade below, and the Castelo São Jorge and the churches of Graça and Nossa Senhora do Monte beyond, each on its own hilltop.

In the Bairro Alto, the streets are narrow but straight, like the threads on a loom. During the day, it rings with the noise of many crafts and smells of pitch and wood shavings and printer's ink from the newspaper presses. At night, another life awakens, that of bars and *fado* houses, some elegant establishments in vaulted cellars, with still-life paintings on the white-washed walls, some pleasantly rowdy taverns, some frankly folksy for the tourist trade.

The 18th-century houses of the Mouraria on the other side of the Ros-sio, long fallen into slums, are being cleared away by the city planners, and little is left of the once charming quarter, outside of sad old songs and the small chapel of Nossa Senhora da Saude, Our Lady of Health, who saved Lisbon from the black plague of 1576. Also left standing is the renowned Rua do Capelão, haunted by the ghost of the Severa, who was loved by a nobleman but took her pleasure with *toreiros* and ruffians, the unforgettable Severa who sang the *fado* as never before, comparable only to Amália Rodrigues. And to this day all *fadistas* wear black to mourn Severa.

Adegas Tipicas and the Fado

This is as good a time as any for a slight detour on the subject of *fado* and where to hear it. *Adega tipica* is the name given to the restaurant where you listen to *fado* singers and eat Portuguese specialties. Meals, however, are never obligatory at *fado* places and you can spend your time from after dinner till the small hours of the morning on local red or white wine or whatever other drink you favor while Portuguese guitars—which have eight or twelve strings and are slightly different in shape to the Spanish guitar which has six strings—accompany the *fadistas* and when the mood is especially good, one or other of the waitresses joins in and a kind of musical dialogue ensues made up entirely on the spur of the moment. Most authentic *fado* places are situated in the Alfama or Bairro Alto, the oldest parts of Lisbon, and are known by every taxi driver should you not remem-ber the street. In case you drive your own car, anyone will be delighted to give directions. Attention though: parking space in the Bairro Alto is practically nil. There are several other *adegas tipicas* in Lisbon but those mentioned in the Practical Information section at the end of the chapter have the best *fadistas* and the most romantic atmosphere.

Even if it's only for once in your lifetime, you must not fail to hear the *fado*. It's like eating ginger for the first time, or attending a cockfight, or riding a roller coaster: *fados* are an experience to which you can't predict in advance your reactions. Nothing is likely to be more deeply disconcert-ing or perturbing. Underneath the customary external trappings—shawls, guitars, viols, gestures, posturings, melodic lines, the final great, wailing cry that is prolonged on the applause bursting forth with the last verse—*fado* can be either sublime or terrible, as replete with nuances as a rainbow.

It must be straight out of the heart's depths, stark and untamed. *Fado* makes no pretense of trying to win you. True *fado*-lovers conscientiously shun the fake atmosphere of some of the fashionable spots where an attempt is deliberately made to cultivate a loose and flashy style that is the exact opposite of the true *fado.*

If you are seeking the real thing, you will find it only in surroundings that partake more of the folk spirit. And even so, it's all a matter of good luck, proper atmosphere, right mood. It depends on who's singing, who's listening. *Fado* is an art without virtuosity: it relies on instinct, the state of the nerves, a vibration rising out of the inmost being, a call from the heart. The least gifted performer may suddenly become possessed with the spirit, while the most renowned professionals can sometimes be utterly bereft of inspiration. So, whatever your experience or knowledge of *fado*— or your lack thereof—give it a fresh approach, search out for yourself the empathy that can be achieved spontaneously in a certain place with a certain *fadista* (in Lisbon, *fado* is pre-eminently a woman's art), and you will perhaps discover some hitherto unsuspected aspect of your own responsiveness. There's no mistaking the real thing when it occurs—it's frenetically alive and soul-wrenching, harsh and utterly unforgettable.

The best time to go to a *fado* café is after 11 P.M., though they may open around 9 or 10; most stay open to 3 A.M., some until dawn. Food is not a must, but two drinks per person usually is. In some of the less touristy ones, however, a dinner, followed by a long session of *fado,* makes a really memorable evening which will not cost an arm and a leg. There is normally a minimum charge, service and tax included.

The Tagus

It is to the Tagus that Lisbon owes her wealth and beauty, which would perhaps be heightened if a fine avenue ran the length of the water's edge. But the city is a port, the wharves crowded with landings for river barges, cargo, sailing, and ferry boats, fishing-smacks and steamships, together with dockyards and warehouses that line the banks from Xabregas to Belém. But between Terreiro do Paço and Cais do Sodré there is a breach on to the river, elsewhere to be seen only from a height in the distance though it remains a constant presence.

The Cais do Sodré, while insignificant in appearance, is fascinating for its animation and its incongruous mixture of fishwives, elegant Estoril commuters, and sailors of every nationality. In the bars you'll find people drinking pale ale or gin, and speaking English. From this quay you take the electric train for the Costa do Sol (the Estoril coast). The entire quarter depends on the port and on seagoing folk for its living.

At dawn the fishermen sell their catch by auction to the *varinas,* those lusty, dark-skinned fish vendors in wide black skirts whom you see trotting about the poorer parts of the city, carrying flat baskets of dripping fish on their heads. At dusk they come back to their own little kingdom, Madragoa, just behind the French Embassy—once the royal palace of Santos. The sovereigns used to come there by boat, with courtiers and musicians, to while away hot afternoons. And since it was tranquil and remote, fishermen from the north Atlantic coast made it their home. Some of them came from the village of Ovar—hence the nickname *varina.*

The people of Madragoa cling to their simple traditions and customs. *Varinas* wear gold hoops in their ears and necklaces with a heart or cross. When they have washed their baskets and set them to dry in the sun, they sit on their doorsteps to sew or gossip. Some of these thresholds belonged to old convents, for due to 19th-century anti-clericalism the neighborhood possessed so many unused religious establishments that working people moved into them. It would be hard to find places more active—and more vocal—than the cells and refectories of these ex-convents. But one of the charms of Lisbon is the abundance of such quarters as this, which retain the rustic and intimate character of a village.

On the nights of the Santo António or São João (St. Anthony's or St. John's Day) celebrations, no one expects to sleep in the poorer quarters. There is a continual round of processions, singing, and street dancing. Sometimes the British Ambassador or the French Ambassador stands on his balcony to watch the *marcha,* a noisy lanternlit parade that passes under the windows. For Madragoa is a neighbor of Lapa, the embassy quarter, and next to it comes Estrela, with its neo-classic basilica, separated by a park from the English church and cemetery, and the Parliament building. This is a garden spot of Lisbon, full of exotic flowers, peacocks, and enchanting houses.

Madre de Deus

It is worth following the river upstream, past the go-downs and the gantries and all the fascinating paraphernalia of the docks, to Madre de Deus. This beautiful church, built in the 16th century by Queen Leonor to house the relics of one of the Eleven Thousand Virgins of Cologne, had been badly damaged by the earthquake, and further spoiled in the following century by the construction of a nearby railway. The architect entrusted with the restoration of the Manueline church front based his blueprint on the retable of St. Auta, in the Museu de Arte Antiga, which portrays the arrival of the relics, greeted with great pomp by bishops and princes on the porch of the then-brand-new Church of Madre de Deus.

The church is renowned for its paintings (among which are portraits of King João II and his wife), its carved and gilded woodwork, and blue and white glazed tile panels of the life of St. Francis. There is an amusing panel in the chancel, of an avenue of trees which seem to go into the distance away from the onlooker, wherever he is standing.

In the cloisters of the neighboring convent is the Museu do Azulejo (tiles), tiles of painted and glazed earthenware of Arab origin, formerly in great use throughout Spain (and through Spain to Holland, where they are best made at Delft); this craft is today kept alive mainly in Portugal. A rich and varied display shows the growth and change of its style, from the first simple shapes and colors of the Moorish tiles to the modern Portuguese azulejo, now undergoing a wholesale rebirth.

Also in the Manueline style, in the Rua da Alfandega, the very fine porch in interlaced stonework is all that remains of the original Church of Conceição, given by King Manuel to his sister Leonor, widow of João II. It was there that she founded the Misericórdia, a hospice that, later, moved to São Roque, and still gives food and shelter to the poor, with the money raised principally from lottery tickets and a football pool. This

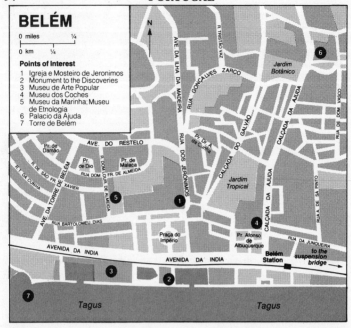

BELÉM

0 miles ¼

0 km ¼

Points of Interest
1 Igreja e Mosteiro de Jeronimos
2 Monument to the Discoveries
3 Museu de Arte Popular
4 Museu dos Coches
5 Museu da Marinha; Museu de Etnologia
6 Palacio da Ajuda
7 Torre de Belém

Misericórdia is now so extensive in its work that the buildings, hospitals, alms-houses, crêches etc. cover a large area in the center of the city.

Every town in the country has a Misericórdia, all stemming from the foundation of Queen Leonor's in 1498. In most places the hospital has been rebuilt on a more suitable site and the old buildings, usually with a lovely chapel, serve as homes for the aged.

The Museum of Ancient Art

The palace that was Pombal's keeps aloof and above the bustling port, on top of the great stone stairway that leads up from the wharves and the Avenida Vinte e Quatro de Julho. The palace houses the Museu Nacional de Arte Antiga (Museum of Ancient Art), and if at times the whole seems cramped in too narrow a space, the masterpieces are given ample room and set off by the best of lighting. The museum has on show old glazed earthenware, porcelain, sculpture, furniture, carpets, and silver and gold work, among which is the exquisite monstrance of Belém, made by the goldsmith and poet Gil Vicente out of the first gold brought back from Quiloa by Vasco da Gama. Also on display is the finest collection in the world of French silverware by the Germain brothers, whose masterly works of art were in other countries melted down or scattered as plunder during foreign and civil wars.

Most art lovers, however, go to the museum to see the paintings. The Flemish school (above all a nightmarish *Temptation of Saint Anthony* by Hieronymus Bosch with its prevision of air raids); the German school (among which a Dürer and a Cranach are outstanding); and the early Portuguese paintings. From the artless brushwork of Frei Carlos, one passes to the striking *Ecco Homo,* with the bleeding face of Jesus half hidden by his shroud. There are a few fine portraits: that of young King Sebastião, on whom coming misfortune had already cast its shadow; and that of an elegant nun in black and white, holding a coral rosary.

Above all, there is the many-paneled painting by Nuno Gonçalves (1460), one of the masterpieces of the world. Around São Vicente, patron of Lisbon, are gathered the people of Portugal, then on the threshold of her seagoing glory. There stand Henry the Navigator, King Afonso V, and the future King João II, together with their queens, among bankers and doctors, knights and captains, monks and priests, Jews, and sinners and beggars. Each man is a living portrait, and one cannot fail to be struck by the family likeness with the Portuguese of today. It is not merely a passage of time held still by Nuno Gonçalves, but the ever-renewed strain of a lasting race.

Jerónimos (Heronymites) Monastery, Belém Tower

It was a miracle that the earthquake of 1755 that rocked Portugal, and whose tremors were felt even in far Sweden, should have spared Belém, and thereby the royal family and the court.

Without the Jerónimos, without the Tower of Belém, little would be left in Lisbon of that strange, powerful, and original art form: Manueline architecture.

The Church of Santa Maria and the neighboring monastery were built on the beach of Restelo, at the very place where Vasco da Gama set sail and to which two of his three ships returned a year and a half later, half-wrecked, half the crew dead, but the holds full of spices and precious stones, and with the dream of his life come true: the discovery of the sea route to the Indies, and with it, the road to unimaginable riches.

Rarely has a monument stood so well for the spirit of its age. The fearful unknown of the high seas, the sailors' wonderstruck joy at the lushness of the tropics, the disturbing differences of race, all seem to have been worked into the stone, in a tangle of rope and shells and coral overlying the late Gothic structure. Through the south porch, facing the river, a dim watery light washes across the high nave; the noble finely decorated pillars seem so many towers of salty rock in a sea cave.

Near the tomb of Vasco da Gama is another dedicated to Camões, but the great poet died in poverty and was buried in a pauper's grave, his bones mingling with the bones of other outcasts. Nonetheless, his poetry echoes through the honey-colored arches. The royal tombs in the chancel rest on the backs of elephants, each different, with ivory tusks and wily little eyes. Be sure to see the great two-storied Manueline cloister, one of the finest in Portugal, behind the church, which can be reached from a door by the West Porch (closed at lunchtime). Stairs lead to the second story and on up to the broad walk right round the top, with lovely views over the Tagus and of the great church below. It was a Frenchman, Nicolas Chanterene, who adorned the west porch with the kneeling statues of King Manuel and his third wife Maria, daughter of a king of Spain.

Like an ivory chess piece, the Tower of Belém, rising off the river bank, is carved with openwork balconies, a loggia, and turrets topped with domes. The water lapping its stone walls recalls Venice, the surrounding palm trees are a mirage of Marrakesh, yet it is Lisbon herself. Long ago, it was the landmark that homecoming sailors strained to see from the lookout on the top mast of the sailing ship. Its beauty is a disarming front; behind the graceful stone lies hidden an armed fortress guarding the mouth of the river, with underground cells for prisoners. The terraces watched over by Our Lady of Safe Voyages have a sweeping view over the incoming and outgoing ships. Today, at the foot of the tower, the sails of pleasure craft flutter like white butterflies on the leaf-green waters of the River Tagus.

Around Belém

The monastery and the tower are reason enough to visit Belém. However, grouped around these twin witnesses of a splendid past, Belém has other points of interest, each well worth a visit.

The Monument to the Discoveries is modern, and looks, according to the angle from which it is seen, like a sword, a sail billowing in the seawind, or a *padrão,* the stone column carved with the arms of Portugal that was planted on each discovered land. It juts out into the river like the prow of a ship, and Prince Henry, caravelle in hand, sweeps seaward a whole people who for years worked with him towards the fulfilment of a country's dream: sailors and captains, soldiers and squires, priests and poets, caulkers and carpenters.

The lands and seas that Henry the Navigator caused to be discovered are mapped in many-colored marble on the star-shaped compass card that paves the open space beneath the monument.

The painted maps, the old instruments of navigation, the models of the caravelles and galleons, are all on display in the superbly arranged Museu da Marinha (Naval Museum), installed like the Museu de Etnologia (Ethnological Museum) within the precincts of the monastery. The royal barges and the cabins and fittings from the royal yacht are all fascinating.

The gold brought home from Brazil in the sailing ships was used in the gilding of the priceless carriages in the old royal riding school, now a museum, near the pink palace which is the official residence of the President of the Republic. The museum contains the largest carriage collection in the world, ranging from the leather coach of Philip II of Spain to the early 19th-century carriage that served to carry through Lisbon King Edward VII, Kaiser William and, in due course, Queen Elizabeth II. The richest, gilded and carved with mermaids and shells, trumpet-blowing allegories, and garlands of flowers, are the state coaches of the embassy which brought the Portuguese Ambassador and his suite from Rome in 1716.

The Portuguese people, fishermen, sailors, peasants and soldiers, to whom the country owed its wealth, have their Museu de Arte Popular (Museum of Folk Art) in Belém. Carvings in wood and cork by the shepherds of the Alentejo, wrought iron from the backwoods of Trás-os-Montes, *ex-votos* by the fishermen of Sesimbra, pictures of birds and flowers and boats in colored tinfoil by the fishermen of Nazaré, handmade lace and red crossstitch on shirts and bed linen, crocheted bedspreads, earthenware, rugs made of plaited rush and checkered fur, bedecked harnesses for mules, carved yokes for oxen; everything to give a touch of beauty to the hard and humdrum life of everyday. The sight of this true handicraft will go far to prevent the visitors being trapped into buying tourist trash.

Then, for the visitor who wants to make the full rounds of the Portuguese world, there are the Tropical Gardens, to the right of the monastery.

There, he will breathe in the heavy tropical odors of trees and fruit and flowers from the jungles of Brazil and Angola. And just beyond is the huge palace of Ajuda, still partly unfinished as on the day young King Manuel abdicated in 1910. The State Rooms, used for official receptions, are shown and include enchanting examples of Victorian decoration and a room furnished with Saxe porcelain, chairs, tables and mirrors. The Library contains an outstanding collection of manuscripts and incunabulae.

Edward VII Park and the Gulbenkian Foundation

So far we have spent most of our time downtown and along the banks of the Tagus. Striking up from the Rossio runs the Avenida da Liberdade, the "Champs Elysées" of Lisbon. This long tree-lined avenue repays a gentle saunter, with perhaps a stop for an ice-cream at one of the parlors on the left. The avenue isn't what it once was, for it has become the stamping ground of oil and insurance companies, houses most of the major airline offices, has several cinemas and is very noisy indeed. But the open-air cafés and the variety of statues and central trees almost make up for the din.

At the top of the Avenida da Liberdade is the square dedicated to Pombal. With one hand on the mane of a bronze lion, Pombal stands on the top of his monument, looking down over the city he re-ordered, and no doubt wondering at the swirling traffic under his nose. Behind him lie the cool, ordered, green depths of the Parque Eduardo VII, Edward VII park. This is also the area of the main hotels, from the old-established Ritz to the new Meridien. The new hotels have brought a series of shopping malls and other facilities which are a definite plus to the Lisbon scene.

In the park are the Estufa Fria and the Estufa Quente, a Cold House and a Hot House, covering several acres with exotic trees, plants and bushes under high roofs of slats and glass.

From here it is an easy walk to the Gulbenkian Foundation just off the Praça de Espanha. This complex is one of the most attractively designed museums in the world; which is not really surprising when one considers the resources and talent that were available to the builders. The Museum itself houses the priceless collection of the Armenian oil tycoon, including Catherine the Great's personal silverware, paintings and sculptures, Persian miniatures, coins and carpets and Lalique jewelry. It is not a collection that is strong in massive accumulations in any one field, but relies upon a few superb examples in each to make its impact. It is quite one of the pleasantest museums to wander through as well, since it was custom built for the collection, and most of the rooms have views out over the park that surrounds the complex. There are two halls for the annual music and ballet festivals, a large gallery for temporary exhibitions and open-air performances take place in the park in summer. The library is open for research, and there is also a handy bar and canteen. The Modern Gallery has an exceptionally good self-service restaurant. Among its cultural activities, the Foundation sends out mobile library vans to the most remote parts of the country.

Epilogue

Lisbon is neither the biggest nor the most beautiful city in Europe. However, it does have a special quality. It is a capital city that has managed to combine the features of a seaside location with an atmosphere of being out in the country, and the coolness of the hills is but a few minutes away. Resting lightly on these hills overlooking the estuary with huge tankers awaiting their turn to go into the Lisnave shipyards at Cacilhas on the south side and the great river that widens above the city into the Mar da Palha, Lisbon never conveys a feeling of heaviness. Any Sunday during the summer months May through September you can chug along by boat for two pleasant hours on the Tagus, sightseeing Lisbon and the river banks while comfortably seated. Departures are from Terreiro do Paço ferry station at 2:30 P.M.; but check times at the tourist office.

There is an infinite variety of pleasant walks to be taken. In whichever direction you may choose to go, you will come out on some new and delightfully unexpected view of the city and the river. The most ordinary-appearing street presents an unfailingly lively passing scene, and there is always something going on.

Lisbon still retains an extraordinary number of art nouveau buildings—apartments, individual houses and shop fronts. In the older parts of the city many of the facades are covered with patterned and even pictured, glazed tiles, the latter often depicting the trade carried on in the shop, such as screws and tools on an ironmongers in the Rua de São Paulo. Traffic police are kind to cars with foreign plates, but there are a large number of very reasonable car parks in the city.

In and around Lisbon there are all the pleasures of the oceanside to be enjoyed. The electric train along the Sun Coast puts the beach within ten minutes' distance from Cais do Sodré station. Sea sports are available all along the way to Cascais (plus tennis, golf, and horsebackriding). On the opposite shores of the Tagus (a ferry-boat trip always makes a nice ride), the gleaming expanse of the beaches of Caparica can be reached by ferry from Belém.

If blissful solitude is your fancy, you will find it among the dunes of Guincho beyond Cascais. And you can go fishing along the Portuguese coast at all times of the year without a license.

Should you simply want to commune with nature, a bus will whisk you off to Monsanto's wooded slopes (camping, swimming pool, outdoor restaurants, panoramic view). Thirty to 40 minutes in your car, or by train from Rossio station, will bring you to Sintra's gardens, to the Serra and its untamed fastnesses, perfect for walking, picnicking, a bit of mountain-climbing . . . or even shopping for antiques in Sintra village. From Easter-time on through the early autumn, Vila Franca do Xira (29 km., 18 miles, by motorway) stages a tauromachian spectacle, complete with processions of mounted *campinos* (cattle-herders), farriers, bullfights and bullfighters.

If time is limited and you can't possibly visit other parts of the country, the mere fact of being in Lisbon will give you a complete idea of all the diversified aspects of Portuguese life. The Portuguese genius is domestic and small-scale. People matter, so civilized living and concern for others, goodwill and politeness are the norm and not the exception.

PRACTICAL INFORMATION FOR LISBON

WHEN TO COME. Spring and fall are, naturally, the favorite times for visiting Lisbon, though the nostalgic, lingering warmth of early November is hardly less appealing. July and August are not unpleasantly hot (there is always a cooling breeze at night), but these are the peak tourist months. There are plenty of places to go in the fall and winter evenings.

Nights in Lisbon are cool. Even during the warmest months the breeze stirs towards evening, and it's advisable to take a scarf or some light wrap when you venture forth after sunset. In fact, in this city that lies like a great amphitheater under a benign sky, the wind is the reason that you see really very few outdoor terraces, although many restaurants offer splendid views from glassed-in terraces. It is a memorable experience to enjoy dinner from some vantage-point where you can watch the ruins of the Carmo gradually silhouette themselves against the sky, or see the shining lights of Rossio come on in the velvety distance; and it is safer to walk about Lisbon at night than it is in most other big cities.

TOURIST OFFICES. There are Portuguese Tourist Offices at Palácio Foz, Praça dos Restauradores (tel. 363314), at Avenida António Augusto de Aguiar 86 (tel. 575091), and at the airport (tel. 893689).

TELEPHONE CODE. The code for Lisbon is (01), but it is specifically for calling the city from the provinces, and should not be used for Lisbon or its environs when calling *from* Lisbon or its environs.

HOW TO GET AROUND. By Train. Subways, called *Metropolitano*, connect Rossio with the Zoological Gardens at Sete Rios, with Entre Campos and Alvalade. The fare is 50$00 to any point. Books of 10 tickets provide a considerable discount. Beware of pickpockets.

Frequent and excellent, one-class electric trains leave from Cais do Sodré Station, traveling along the Costa do Sol to Cascais, beyond Estoril. Fare 100$00 single to Estoril or Cascais. Trains for Sintra leave from Rossio Station. Tickets bought on the trains are subject to a huge surcharge.

By Tram. The tram service is one of the best in Europe and this is the most amusing and enjoyable way of getting about in Lisbon. Books of 20 tickets, at half the price charged on the trams or buses, can be bought at Cais do Sodré and other terminals, as can a Tourist Pass for a little over 1,000$00. You will have to produce your passport. This is good for 7 days on all trams, buses, and subways. The *Carris* (Lisbon Transport Company) produce an excellent map with all their routes for 50$00 available at the same places.

This very efficient tramway system is a fascinating survival, built by British engineers at the end of the last century. Two of the many hills are the steepest that have ever been worked by trams, anywhere in the world, without a rack or cable. These are on route 28, Graça/Prazeres and on route 12, Martim Moniz/São Tomé. If you want to see a large part of the city, take the former from the Largo da Graça to Prazeres, or route 18 from Praça do Comércio to Ajuda.

By Bus. These also provide a good city service, and Nos. 52, 53 and 54 cross the Tagus bridge.

By Cable Car. These link some of the higher, and lower, parts of Lisbon. The Gloria rises from the Restauradores to St. Pedro de Alcantara; the Lavra from the east side of the Avenida da Liberdade to the Campo Martires da Patria; and the Bica from the Calçada do Combro to the Rua da Boavista. The vertical lift of Santa Justa links the Rua do Ouro with the Carmo Square.

By Taxi. Taxis are plentiful and fairly cheap. Cabs, with green roofs, start at 76$00 and there is a 20% increase in fares at night from 10 P.M. to 6 A.M. If more than 4 passengers get into a cab, the police will stop the driver for overloading, so don't do it. There is a 50% increase for baggage weighing over 30 kg. (66 pounds). For trips out of Lisbon, the driver is entitled to the fare both ways, even if you don't return with him, and he has the privilege of quoting you a flat rate or running on the meter. Tip about 15%. For the panoramic view, it's worth taking a trip over the majestic Tagus bridge (toll out, return free). Taxi fare from airport into Lisbon is about 1,000$00.

Chauffeur-driven cars are also available, with good drivers. Inquire at car-hire firms—see under *Useful Addresses*—or from your hotel porter.

By Boat. Ferryboats for Cacilhas leave from alongside the Praça do Comércio and Cais do Sodré, the latter taking cars; for Barreiro, from the Estação do Sul e Sueste, just off the Praça do Comércio; for Trafaria, and Caparica, from the Estação Fluvial de Belém.

HOTELS. The Lisbon hotel scene within recent years has been much improved by the opening of new establishments and the modernization of others. Nevertheless, for the peak season, reservations should be made well in advance.

Deluxe

Alfa, Ave. Columbano Bordalo Pinheiro (tel. 722121). 375 rooms with bath. Restaurant *Pombalino* highly recommended. 10 minutes from center. Pool, disco, garage, good parking. AE, DC, MC, V.

Altis, Rua Castilho 11 (tel. 560071). 219 rooms with bath. International Bridge Club, garage, large car park. AE, DC, MC, V.

Avenida Palace, Rua 1° de Dezembro 123 (tel. 360151/9). 95 rooms with bath. Public rooms all gilt, crystal chandeliers and plush furnishings; very old-fashioned; breakfast only. Central, convenient for shopping. AE, DC, MC, V.

Meridien, Rua Castilho 149 (tel. 690900). 318 rooms with bath. Lisbon's latest luxury hotel, all tiles, glass and shine; rooms can be a bit on the small side. Sauna, garage, 3 restaurants. AE, DC, MC, V.

Ritz, Rua Rodrigo da Fonseca 88 (tel. 692020). 300 rooms with bath. Rooms are large and stately. Disco, garage, good parking; grill room, excellent restaurant; airconditioned. Above the Eduardo VII Park, with magnificent view over the city. AE, DC, MC, V.

Sheraton, Rua Latino Coelho 1 (tel. 575757). 388 rooms with bath. Pool, rooftop restaurant; parking difficult; airconditioned. Central location and magnificent views. A small section of the hotel, **Sheraton Towers**—28 rooms, all with bath—is set aside as an even more expensive enclave. AE, DC, MC, V.

Tivoli, Ave. da Liberdade 185 (tel. 530181). 344 rooms with bath. Topfloor restaurant with terrace and superb view; garage; central. AE, DC, MC, V.

Expensive

Diplomatico, Rua Castilho 74 (tel. 562041). 90 rooms with bath. Modern rooms; terrace with panoramic view; private parking. AE, DC, MC, V.

Dom Manuel I, Ave. Duque de Avila 189 (tel. 561410). 60 rooms with bath. Breakfast only. AE, DC, MC, V.

Eduardo VII, Ave. Fontes Pereira de Melo 5 (tel. 530141). 120 rooms with bath. Bar and roof restaurant, overlooking the city. AE, DC, MC, V.

Fenix, Praça Marques de Pombal 8 (tel. 535121). 116 rooms with bath. More suitable for families; grill room serving Spanish dishes. Strategically located at top of Av. da Liberdade. AE, DC, MC, V.

Florida, Rua Duque de Palmela 32 (tel. 576145). 108 rooms with bath. Family-type hotel; breakfast only. AE, DC, MC, V.

Lisboa Penta, Ave. dos Combatentes (tel. 7264629). 592 rooms with bath. Pool; all modern amenities. Two restaurants, garage, good parking. Located 10 minutes from center, near U.S. Embassy, and with fine view of the Tagus. AE, DC, MC, V.

Lisboa Plaza, Travessa do Salitre 7 (tel. 363922). 93 rooms with bath. Snack bar. Off Ave. da Liberdade. AE, DC, MC, V.

Mundial, Rua D. Duarte 4 (tel. 863101). 146 rooms with bath. In commercial sector. AE, DC, MC, V.

Novotel, Ave. José Malhoa (tel. 7266022). 246 rooms with bath. Pool; parking, restaurant grill. Recommended although not central. AE, DC, MC, V.

Principe Real, Rua da Alegria 53 (tel. 360116). 24 rooms with bath. Attractive rooms; pleasant, relaxed atmosphere; breakfast only. AE, DC, MC, V.

Tivoli Jardim, Rua Julio Cesar Machado 7 (tel. 539971). 119 rooms with bath. Fine annex to the Tivoli, with good restaurant, snack bar, pool, parking. AE, DC, MC, V.

Moderate

Berna, Ave. António Serpa 13 (tel. 779151). 154 rooms with bath. Breakfast only. Garage. Near the bullring and Gulbenkian Foundation. AE, DC, MC.

Botanico, Rua da Mãe de Agua 16 (tel. 320392). 30 rooms with bath. Central. Breakfast only. AE, DC, MC, V.

Britania, Rua Rodrigues Sampaio 17 (tel. 575016). 30 rooms with bath. Breakfast only. AE, DC, MC, V.

Capitol, Rua Eça de Queirós 24 (tel. 536811). 50 rooms with bath. Snack bar. Solid comfort. AE, DC, MC, V.

Da Torre, Rua dos Jerónimos 8 (tel. 630161). 52 rooms with bath. In suburbs very near Jerónimos Church, Ethnological, Coach, Folk Art and Naval Museums and Ajuda Palace. AE, DC, MC, V.

Dom Carlos, Ave. Duque de Loulé 121 (tel. 539071). 73 rooms with bath. Breakfast only, sauna, garage. AE, DC, MC, V.

Embaixador, Ave. Duque de Loulé 73 (tel. 530171). 96 rooms with bath. Disco. AE, DC, MC.

Excelsior, Rua Rodrigues Sampaio 172 (tel. 537151). 80 rooms with bath. Off Ave. Liberdade. AE, DC, MC, V.

Flamingo, Rua Castilho 41 (tel. 532191). 39 rooms with bath. Very pleasant, friendly. AE, DC, MC, V.

Impala, Rua Filipe Folque 49 (tel. 558914). 26 apartments with bath and kitchenette for up to 4 people. AE, DC, MC, V.

Infante Santo, Rua Tenente Valadim 14 (tel. 600144). 27 rooms with bath and balcony. Breakfast only; comfortable residential hotel, but not central.

Jorge V, Rua Mouzinho da Silveira 3 (tel. 562525). 49 rooms with bath. Pleasant; breakfast only; near Ave. da Liberdade. AE, DC, MC, V.

Miraparque, Ave. Sidónio Pais 12 (tel. 578070). 101 rooms with bath. Obliging staff; located beside Eduardo VII Park. Be sure to garage your car overnight, as some readers have complained of thefts when left outside.

Presidente, Rua Alexandre Herculano 13 (tel. 539501). 59 rooms with bath. Nice rooms, breakfast only; central. AE, DC, MC.

Principe, Ave. Duque d'Avila 201 (tel. 536151). 56 rooms with bath. AE, DC, MC.

Reno, Ave. Duque d'Avila 195 (tel. 548181). 51 rooms with bath. Breakfast only. AE, DC, MC, V.

Rex, Rua Castilho 169 (tel. 682161). 40 rooms with bath. Small in size, great in comfort, with first-class restaurant and easy parking. AE, DC, MC, V.

Roma, Ave. de Roma 33 (tel. 767761). 264 rooms with bath. Good value, with pool, sauna, shops, garage, snack bar, and rooftop restaurant with view over city. Not central. AE, DC, MC, V.

Senhora do Monte, Calçada do Monte 39 (tel. 862846). 27 rooms with bath and balcony. Top floor restaurant with lovely view; in old town. AE, DC, MC, V.

Inexpensive

Avenida Alameda, Ave. Sidónio Pais 4 (tel. 532186). 27 apartments, all with bath. Kitchenettes; car park.

Avenida Parque, Ave. Sidónio Pais 6 (tel. 532181). 40 rooms with bath. Breakfast only; next door to Avenida Alameda hotel.

Borges, Rua Garrett 108–110 (tel. 361951). 99 rooms with bath. Old-fashioned charm and good modern service; very popular with Portuguese and others up from the country; on main shopping street. No parking. AE, MC, V.

Dom Afonso Henriques, Rua Cristovão Falcão 8 (tel. 846574). 33 rooms with bath. Breakfast only; not central. DC, MC.

Duas Nações, Rua da Vitória 41 (tel. 320410). 66 rooms, most with bath. Breakfast only; central, in business sector.

Lis, Ave. da Liberdade 180 (tel. 563434). 63 rooms, half with bath. Breakfast only; good value and central. AE, DC, MC, V.

Metropole, Rossio 30 (tel. 369164). 50 rooms, half with bath. Breakfast only; noisy, central. AE, DC, MC, V.

Suiço Atlantico, Rua da Gloria 13 (tel. 361713). 88 rooms, most with bath. Breakfast only. Central. AE, DC, MC, V.

Vip, Rua Fernão Lopes 25 (tel. 578923). 54 rooms with bath. Breakfast only. AE, DC, MC, V.

PENSIONS. By U.S. or U.K. standards the (M) and (E) estalagems, residências and albergarias of Lisbon offer excellent value for money. There are many, and among the best are—

Albergaria Pax (E), Rua José Estevão 20 (tel. 561861). 30 rooms with bath. Breakfast only; away from center. AE, DC, MC.

York House (E), Rua das Janelas Verdes 32 (tel. 662544). 68 rooms with bath or shower; and in annex at no. 47 in same street, 12 rooms with bath. Mansion in own garden, but up long flights of steps; good simple food; highly recommended. AE, DC, MC, V.

Residência America (M), Rua Tomás Ribeiro 47 (tel. 531178). 60 rooms with bath. AE, DC, MC.

Residência Horizonte (M), Ave. António Augusto Aguiar 42 (tel. 539526). 52 rooms with bath. Breakfast only.

Residência Imperador (M), Ave. 5 de Outubro 55 (tel. 574884). 43 rooms with bath. Breakfast only.

São Mamede (M), Rua Escola Politecnica 159 (tel. 663166). 25 rooms, half with bath. Old mansion; breakfast only.

Mansão Santa Rita (M), Ave. António Augusto Aguiar 21 (tel. 547109). 15 rooms with bath.

Nazaré (M), Ave. António Augusto Aguiar 25 (tel. 542016). 32 rooms with bath. Breakfast only. AE, DC, MC, V.

Pensão Astoria (I), Rua Braamcamp 10 (tel. 521317). 67 rooms, most with bath. Central.

Residência Capital (I), Ave. Elias Garcia 87 (tel. 767330). 22 rooms with bath. Breakfast only.

Pensão Casa de Sao Francisco (I), Ave. da Republica 48B (tel. 766600). 24 rooms, most with bath. Breakfast only. Good value.

Pensão Castilho (I), Rua Castilho 57 (tel. 570822). 19 rooms with bath. Breakfast only. Good value.

Pensão Dom Sancho I (I), Ave. da Liberdade 202 (tel. 548648). 20 rooms with bath. Breakfast only; central.

Pensão Ninho das Aguias (I), Costa do Castelo 74 (tel. 860391). 16 rooms, 6 with bath. Breakfast only; superb view, no parking.

Residência Canada (I), Ave. Defensores de Chaves 35 (tel. 538159). 40 rooms with bath. Breakfast only.

CAMPING. Monsanto Parque Florestal, off the autostrada to Estoril and Cascais.

YOUTH HOSTEL. Rua Andrade Corvo 49 (tel. 532696).

RESTAURANTS. The Portuguese prefer to do most of their eating at home, whether they're *en famille* or entertaining friends, which may be a reason why every so often even really good restaurants become unpredictable; returning in pleasurable anticipation of previously excellent food, one can be faced with disappointment. In the main, however, very good meals can be had at many places. All restaurants, even the luxury establishments, have to show their price list displayed outside.

Restaurante-Cervejaria (beer-restaurants) are small, modest eateries, very inexpensive; but beware, for they cook with garlic and the heavy pungent olive oil *azeite,* and the taste and odor are not to everyone's liking.

Incidental intelligence: except in the smartest restaurants or in those with a show or dancing, you can always ask for *Vinho da Casa* and suffer no loss of face. The house wine is always easy on your palate and a bottle of red or white comes at a reasonable price. Always check your bill. Tables do not need to be reserved, except in the expensive places. Several Lisbon restaurants close on Sundays. But cafés are open.

Portuguese love children and you can take a child of any age into any restaurant—they will be very welcome and charged half price up to 8 years old and younger children can eat from your dish. Some of the inexpensive places list half portions. Two can share a dish, as portions are often too large for one.

Expensive

Alcaide do Salitre, Rua do Salitre 5A (tel. 327263). New, off Ave. da Liberdade. Small, exclusive. AE, DC, MC.

António Clara, Ave. da Republica 38 (tel. 766380). On ground floor of large, rescued, art-deco house (upstairs is a private club). Highly recommended for both atmosphere, food—some of the best in Lisbon—and an interesting wine list for anyone who wants to experiment with fine vintages at reasonable prices. Highly trained staff. Private parking. AE, DC, MC, V.

Aviz, Rua Serpa Pinto 12B (tel. 328391). Some of the best food in town, faultlessly served by knowledgeable staff who will take great pains to ensure a delightful dining experience. Decor like a set for *The Merry Widow,* with turn-of-the century atmosphere to match, and unique wash-rooms. Closed Sat. dinner, Sun. AE, DC, MC, V.

Bodegon, Praça Marquês Pombal 8 (tel. 529155). Enjoy real Spanish dishes in comfort in this, the grill room of the Spanish-owned *Hotel Fenix.* Always open. AE, DC, MC, V.

Casa da Comida, Travessa das Amoreiras 1 (tel. 685376). Imaginative cuisine in delightful setting round small, courtyard garden; attentive service; very fashionable, so book in advance. You'll have to look attentively for the door in! Closed Sat. lunch, and Sun. AE, DC, MC, V.

Casa de Leão, Castelo de São Jorge (tel. 875962). Top quality, lunches and teas only. AE, DC, MC, V.

Clara, Campo dos Martires da Patria 49 (tel. 557341). Attractively converted—and slightly out of center—townhouse; elegantly bourgeois interior; shaded patio garden for summer; helpful, professional service. Closed Sun. AE, DC, MC, V.

Cozinha d'el Rey, Rua Castilho 169 (tel. 682161). In *Rex Hotel,* first-class food in a most attractive setting. Always open. AE, DC, MC, V.

Escorial, Rua Portas de Santo Antão 47 (tel. 363758). Spanish cuisine in formal surroundings; shellfish specialties. In side street off Rossio; always open. AE, DC, MC, V.

Gambrinus, Rua Portas de Santo Antão 23 (tel. 321466). Worth the trouble to find if you enjoy shellfish and smoked things. Near Escorial above; comfortable, with entry through small bar. Always open. AE, DC, MC, V.

Gondola, Ave. Berna 64 (tel. 770426). The only place in town where you can eat under a canopy of leaves, and of course you pay for the privilege; rich Italian dishes. Opposite Gulbenkian Foundation. Closed Sat. dinner, Sun. MC, V.

Michel's, Largo de Santa Cruz do Castelo 5 (tel. 864338). Genuine French food; inside the outer walls of St. George's Castle, with easy parking. Closed Sat. lunch and Sun. AE, DC, MC, V.

Pabe, Rua Duque de Palmela 27A (tel. 535675). English-type pub with restaurant behind; near Pombal Square. Highly recommended. Always open. AE, DC, MC, V.

Sagitario, Rue de Belém 10 (tel. 645687). Near Jerónimos. Excellent food. Closed Sun.

Tagide, Largo da Academia 18–20 (tel. 320720). Tasty local specialties—like pork and clams—at top prices; recently renovated. Closed Sat. lunch, Sun. AE, DC, MC, V.

Tavares Rico, Rua Misericórdia 35 (tel. 321112). Superb cuisine and wine list, a rival of the Aviz, with turn-of-the-century setting. Closed Sat. lunch, Sun. AE, DC, MC, V.

Moderate

António, Rua Tomás Ribeiro 63 (tel. 538780). Local clientele tells its own story; usually full. AE, DC, MC, V.

Arameiro, Travessa Santo Antão 21 (tel. 367185). Always crowded, noisy and lively, and no wonder—the specialty, chicken on the spit, is truly superb. Always open.

Bistro Breque, Rua Buenos Aires 28B (tel. 607006). Up-market food and service, in Lisbon's diplomatic quarter. Closed Sun. MC.

Bonjardim, Travessa Santo Antão 11 (tel. 324389). Chicken, freshly spit roast, also excellent barbecued suckling pig turned golden brown on a spit in this modest restaurant in a narrow, short street beside the main post office in Restauradores, where there is underground parking. To get in, go earlier or later than 1 or 8 o'clock—the peak times—and this holds true for all small eating places. AE, DC, MC, V.

Caravela, Rua Paiva Andrade 8 (tel. 328811). "Tearoom" for excellent light lunches and teas, chic for Portuguese residents; the only place in town to serve real waffles. Just off the Chiado. Closed Sat. and Sun. AE, DC, MC.

Como Sequeira, Rua Gustavo Matos Sequeira 30 (tel. 677433). Near British Institute.

Fettuccine, Travessa da Trindade 10 (tel. 371547). For tasty Italian food. Just off the Rua Garrett. Open till midnight; closed Sat. and Sun.

Forno da Brites, Rua Tomás Ribeiro 73 (tel. 542724). Practical food; pretty red and white decor; staff helpful to tourists. Closed Sat. AE, DC, MC, V.

Galeto, Ave. Republica 14 (tel. 560269). Also snack bar.

Great American Disaster, Praça Marquês de Pombal 1 (tel. 521266). Hamburger joint with music. Always open. AE, DC, MC.

La Trattoria, Rua Artilharia Um 79–85 (tel. 650209). Good Italian food at reasonable rates; smart premises. Always open. AE, DC, MC.

Monte Carlo, Ave. Fontes Pereira de Melo 49 (tel. 544789). Famous, old-established restaurant. You can have the tastiest, hottest curry in the cafe-restaurant at the back. Always open.

Nanking, Rua Sousa Martins 5A (tel. 521746). Chinese food; fairly reasonable. Always open.

O Alexandre, Rue Vieira Portuense 84. Cheerful place. Near Jerónimos. Closed Sat.

O Funil, Ave. Elias Garcia 82A (tel. 766007). Plentiful portions, served in simple surroundings. Popular with office-workers.

O Manel, Parque Mayer (tel. 363167). Fine Portuguese cooking. Always open.

O Paço, Ave. Berne 44 (tel. 770642). Reasonably priced, and amusing folkloric decor. Much frequented by the Gulbenkian crowd from across the road. Always open. AE, DC, MC.

Petite Folie, Ave. António Augusto de Aguiar 74 (tel. 521948). Very acceptable French cooking. Garden terrace in summer. AE, DC, V.

A Quinta, at top of Elevador de Santa Justa (tel. 365588). Serves Portuguese, Russian and Hungarian specialties. View and pleasant ambiance. No parking. Closed Sat. dinner, Sun. AE, MC.

Rive Gauche, Rua da Rosa 253 (tel. 363622). New. In Bairro Alto.

Sancho, Travessa da Gloria 8–16 (tel. 369780). Off Ave. Liberdade. Good food and service; rustic decor. Closed Sun. AE, DC, MC.

Solmar, Rua Portas de Santo Antão 108 (tel. 360010). Fish idle about in a large tank while you make your choice; expensive for seafood. Serves wild boar, venison, game. Always open. AE, DC, MC.

Telheiro, Rua Latino Coelho 10A (tel. 534007). Enormous helpings, and no one minds if you ask for half portions. Crowded for lunch as it's near new business area, but tranquil for dinner. Always open. DC, MC.

Toni dos Bifes, Ave. Praia da Vitória 50 (tel. 536080). Small cozy bistro specializing in steaks. Closed Sun.

Inexpensive

Anarquistas, Largo da Trindade 14 (tel. 323510). Good food, though rather rough; one of Lisbon's oldest restaurants and full of atmosphere. Closed Sun. in summer.

Atinel Bar, Cais dos Cacilheiros (tel. 372419). Off Praça do Comércio. The only restaurant in Lisbon right on the Tagus—get a table by the picture windows. Outdoor eating too. Very friendly service. Always open.

Bom Apetite, Travessa da Gloria 20 (tel. 360101). Cheap, plentiful meals with friendly service. Closed Sun.

Cervejaria Trindade, Rua Nova da Trindade 20C (tel. 323506). Good-value food; with cave-style wine cellar and a garden. Always open.

Ceuta, Ave. da Republica 20C (tel. 531305). Snack bar specializing in delicious cakes which also serves meals. Always open.

China, Rua Andrade Corvo 7B (tel. 549455). Chinese cooking; near U.S. Library. Closed Tues.

Colombo, Ave. da Republica 10H (tel. 549225). Lunches, teas, dinners, plus a huge variety of good cakes. Open daily to 10 P.M.

Dionysos, Rua de Belém 124 (tel. 640632). Greek food near Jerónimos; recommended. MC.

Goa, Rua Marquês de Fronteira 80B (tel. 684847). Delicious curries and good service near Ritz hotel. AE, DC, MC.

Ladeira, Ave. Marques de Tomar 33 (tel. 772520). Serves a variety of food, with half portions if you can't manage a whole—these are enough for two. Open mid-day to 10:30 P.M. Closed Fri. dinner, Sat.

Laurentina, Ave. Conde Valbom 69 (tel. 760260). Run by Mozambiqueans, so food is somewhat exotic. Closed Sun.

Lira de Ouro, Rua Nova de São Mamede 10 (tel. 663306). Central, good food, very reasonable. Closed Sun.

Mexicana, Ave. Guerra Junqueiro 30 (tel. 886117). Just off Praça de Londres. For the best cakes in town, as well as hot and cold dishes. Air-conditioned. Always open.

Noite e Dia (Night and Day), Ave. Duque de Loulé 51A (tel. 573514). Good value and always crowded; self-service. Open 12–3, 6–10.30. Closed Sun. AE.

O Guardanapo, Rua Padre António Vieira 4A (tel. 691016). Excellent snack bar. Closed Sat., Sun.

O Rafael, Rua de Belém 106 (tel. 637420). Between Jerónimos and Coach Museum, with pretty patio for outdoor meals. Good value. Closed Mon.

Sir, Rua Braamcamp 9 (tel. 530239). Amusing modern decor, with moving stairs to first floor. Self-service. Closed Sat. dinner, Sun.

Torio, Rua Tomás Ribeiro 38 (tel. 553655). Portuguese food in snack bar and at tables. Half portions served. Closed Sat.

Venha Cá, Rua Nova da Trindade 10C (tel. 321986). Drinkable house wine and reasonable food; country decor. Closed Sun.

Xangai, Ave. Duque de Loulé 20B (tel. 557378). Like *China* Chinese cooking and is also near U.S. Library. Always open.

Snack bars and Pastelarias. These are all over town. The names may mislead you—don't expect milk shakes and sundaes, as you would at home. The following are some of the leading ones.

Apolo, Ave. Julio Diniz 10A. Large commercial center near bullring, with snackbar, plus boutique, bowling alley and cinema.

Bernards, Rua Garrett 104. For tea addicts.

Discoteca Fonomat, Ave. António Augusto Aguiar 3.

Ferrari, Rua Nova do Almada 93. Also for tea addicts.

Snack Ritz, Rua Castilbo 77. Below Ritz Hotel. Excellent light meals at counters, but expensive.

Tofa, Rua d'Ouro 177. Good coffee and tasty tidbits. Downtown.

Tascas. Pub and bistro combined. **Farta Brutos,** Travessa Espera 20, in Bairro Alto. Good food. AE.

Porto de Abrigo, Rua de Remolares 16. Smart tasca, with excellent crab and duck dishes. Closed Sun.

Sardinha Assada, Cais do Sodré 2. Very convenient, and you can eat as much as you wish for a reasonable price.

NIGHTLIFE. Lisbon nightclubs in general don't rank in the international class. New ones open, fairly new ones fold; it's unpredictable. If you are after a more atmospheric evening, you should seek out one of the Adega Tipicas (see below), both to hear *fado,* and for a less expensive time. Discos are everywhere and open and shut unexpectedly.

Ad Lib, Rua Barata da Salgueiro 28–7 (tel. 561717). Smart and respectable. AE, DC.

Banana Power, Rua de Cascais Alcantara 51 (tel. 631815). Also one of the most respectable and chic nightclubs. MC.

Barracuda, 12 Rua da Misericórdia (tel. 368649). Not exclusive; exotic but with a firm grip on reality.

Loucuras, Ave. Alvares Cabral 37 (tel. 681117). Young, fashionable spot.

Sheraton Hotel, Rua Latino Coelho 1 (tel. 575757). Top-floor restaurant with live band, dancing and stunning view. AE, DC, MC, V.

Stones, Rua do Olival 1 (tel. 664545). Chic and respectable. DC.

Whispers, in Commercial Center at Ave. Fontes Pereira de Melo 35 (tel. 575489). Also chic and respectable. AE, MC.

Port Wine Institute, Rua São Pedro de Alcantara 45. Excellent place for a pre-dinner drink, an attractive spot despite its formidable name. Open 10 A.M.–midnight. Closed Sun.

Adega tipica. This is the name for the places where you listen to *fado* singers and eat Portuguese specialties. Meals are not obligatory, you can spend your time from after dinner to the small hours in the morning supping wine or whatever other drink you fancy. The singing seldom starts before 11 P.M. Most are in the Bairro Alto.

A Severa, 51 Rua das Gáveas (tel. 364006). A bit touristy—beware souvenir-sellers. Closed Thurs. AE, DC, MC.

Cota d'Armas, Beco São Miguel 7 (tel. 868682). Parking. Closed Sun. AE, DC, MC.

Lisboa a Noite (Lisbon by Night), 69 Rua des Gáveas (tel. 368557). Don't be put off by the name, it's not *that* touristy, and the owner, Fernanda Maria, is an outstanding singer. Expensive. Closed Sun. AE, DC, MC.

Luso, Travessa de Queimada 10 (tel. 362889). One of the long-established fado places. Good value. Closed Sun. AE, DC, MC.

Machado, Rua do Norte 91 (tel. 360095). Typical bustling tourist place, where guests are invited to join the staff dancing round in a circle with the lighted candles from their tables. Closed Mon. AE, DC, MC.

Marcia Condessa, Praça da Alegria 38 (tel. 367093). With the usual dramatic trappings.

O Faia, 54 Rua da Barroca (tel. 326742). Soft, husky voices, soul-searing melodies, all the trimmings. Also folk-dancing and singing. Reasonable in price. Open to 3.30 A.M. Closed Sun.

Parreirinha de Alfama, Beco do Espirito Santo 1 (tel. 868209). Informal, with excellent food, in the oldest part of Lisbon.

Senhor Vinho, Rua do Meio-a-Lapa 18 (tel. 672681). Good parking. Smart, in diplomatic district. AE, DC, MC.

Timpanas, 24 Rua Gilberto Rola (tel. 672431). Where the real heart of Lisbon beats. Prices reasonable. Closed Mon. MC.

Dinner-dance. There are a few pleasant dinner-dance restaurants, sometimes with floorshows.

Choupana, Estrada Marginal, São João do Estoril (tel. 2683099). Newest and smartest, with live band and good food. Expensive; parking; out of Lisbon. AE, DC, MC, V.

Maxime, Praça da Alegria 58 (tel. 365365). 2 bands, 3 floorshows, including folk dancing and fados, in a *Rapsodia do Folclore Portugues*. Expensive, but not exclusive. AE, DC, MC.

Monaco, at Caxias on the road to Estoril (tel. 2432339). Looks over the sea; is expensive, and has very good food. Parking. AE, DC, MC, V.

O Porão da Nau, Rua Pinheiro Chagas 1D (tel. 571501). Has the best band to dance to. Expensive but not exclusive. Open 11 P.M.–4 A.M.

CONCERTS, OPERA AND BALLET. Opera and ballet are performed from late January through June at the São Carlos and São Luis Theaters. Concerts and recitals, as well as ballet, take place in the Estufa Fria in Edward VII Park, and at the Gulbenkian Foundation.

BULLFIGHTING. Try to attend at least one night performance of a *tourada,* or bullfight, especially if it's the kind called *antiga portuguesa,* complete with carriages, tricorns, and 18th-century embroidered costumes. In Portugal, the bull is not killed, and it's a great show whatever the quality of the actual fight, and even if you're not an ardent *aficionado.* The horses are as highly trained as polo ponies and are not touched by the bull. Starts at Easter, and continues through Oct. in the Campo Pequeno, generally on Thursdays and Sundays.

SIGHTSEEING DATA. Museums are usually open daily, except Mondays and public holidays, 10–5, but double check the times on the spot. Some close for lunch. Entrance fees are between 150$00 and 300$00.

Aquario (Aquarium), Ave. Marginal, Dafundo. Good selection of Atlantic fish; sea lions. Trams: Alges, Dafundo. Buses: 12, 23, 29, 50. Adm. free Wed. Open weekdays and holidays 12–6, Sun. 10–6; closed Mon.

Arqueologico (Archeology), Largo do Carmo. Medieval sculpture set in ruined Gothic church. Tram: Carmo. Santa Justa elevator. Closed for lunch, 12–2.

Basilica da Estrela, Praça da Estrela. Important monument; splendid view of Lisbon and the Tagus from the dome; room-sized Christmas crib is worth seeing, on payment of a small fee. Trams: Estrela, Prazeres. Buses: 9, 20, 22. Closed for lunch, 1–3:30.

Castelo de São Jorge (St. George's Castle), covering high hill to east of center. Wonderful views of city and River Tagus. Picnic facilities. Adm. free. Bus 37.

Estufa Fria (Cool House), in the grounds of Parque Eduardo VIII. Magnificent tropical plants; *Estufa Quente* (Hothouse) has superb orchids in winter. Tram: Carmo. Buses: 2, 3, 4. Adm. 100$00. Open 9–sunset.

Fundação Ricardo Espirito Santo (Museum of Decorative Arts), in an old palace at Largo das Portas do Sol. Well worth a visit: part museum, part training center for craftsmen, here you can see some of the best rugs, silver, furniture and lamps ever made in Portugal. Antiques are sent from all over the world for repair; many of the *Ritz Hotel* furnishings came from here. Tram: Graca. Bus: 37. Closed for lunch, 1–2:30.

Igreja de Madre de Deus (Church of the Mother of God). A masterpiece of Portuguese Baroque, with fine tiles and gilded woodwork. Tram: Poço do Bispo. Buses: 13, 18, 42.

Igreja e Mosteiro de Jerónimos (Jerónimos Church and Monastery), Praça do Império, Belém. The Manueline style at its best. Be sure to see the double cloisters. Trams: Algés, Dafundo. Buses: 12, 27, 28, 29, 43, 49. Closed for lunch, 12:30–3.

Jardim Botanico (Botanical Gardens), Rua Escola Politecnica. Trams: 24, 29, 30. Bus: 15. Adm. free. Closed Sat. and Sun. Sept. through Apr.

Jardim Zoologico (Zoo), Parque das Laranjeiras, Estrada de Benfica. The animals look contented in their large enclosures, only the polar bears resent the sun. Dogs and Cats Hotel, strange Pet's Cemetery, Children's Zoo with miniature houses and small animals. Picnickers are welcome; several snackbars and restaurants, and even Bingo. Buses: 15, 16, 26, 31, 34, 41, 46. Adm. 200$00, 100$00 for children 7–10 years. Open 9–sunset.

Lisbon Aqueduct. Entrance in Calçada da Quintinha, Campolide. Open July, Aug., Sept., Oct. on Sat. and Sun. 10 A.M.–5 P.M. The Mae das Aguas, the great 18th-century covered reservoir in Praça das Amoreiras, is open every afternoon except Mon.

Museu da Agua (Water Museum), Rua do Alviela 12. Closed for lunch.

Museu de Arte Contemporânea (Museum of Modern Art), Rua Serpa Pinto. 19th- and 20th-century Portuguese painting and sculpture. Tram: Prazeres. Closed for lunch, 12:30–2.

Museu de Arte Popular (Museum of Folk Art), Ave. Brasilia, Belém. Rich and eloquent presentation of provincial art and lore. Trams: Algés, Dafundo. Buses: 12, 29, 43. Closed for lunch, 12:30–2.

Museu de Arte Religiosa (Museum of Religious Art), next to São Roque Church, Largo Tríndade Coelho. Ecclesiastical vessels, goldsmiths' work, vestments. Trams: 24, 29, 30. Bus: 15.

Museu do Azulejo (Tile Museum), Rua da Madre de Deus. In the cloisters and convent of Madre de Deus. Trams: 13, 18, 42. Closed for lunch.

Museu Calouste Gulbenkian (Gulbenkian Foundation Museum), Ave. Berna. In two side-by-side sections, classical and modern. One of the world's most impressive galleries, its collection including masterpieces by world-famous painters, items bought from Leningrad's Hermitage Museum in 1929–30, a noted Middle Eastern collection, coins, bronzes, glass and carpets. The Modern Gallery has a fair amount of perishable stuff— the Gulbenkian is in the laudable business of supporting talent; but it's still worth visiting. The custom-designed rooms look out over attractive modern gardens. Good restaurant in Modern Gallery; snackbar. Buses: 30, 41, 46, 56. Adm. free weekends. Open Tues., Thurs., Fri., Sun. 10–5; Wed. and Sat. 2–7; closed Mon.

Museu da Cidade de Lisboa (City of Lisbon Museum), in magnificent Palácio Pimenta, Campo Grande. Buses: 1, 7, 33, 36, 50. Closed 1–2.

Museu dos Coches (Coach Museum), Belém. Finest collection of coaches and carriages in the world, from late 16th-century to Victorian, in beautiful 18th-century riding school. Trams: Belém, Algés, Dafundo. Buses: 12, 27, 28, 29, 43, 49.

Museu de Etnologia (Ethnological Museum), Praça do Império, Belém. Prehistoric, Greek and Roman relics. Trams: Algés, Dafundo. Closed 12–2. Buses: 29, 43.

Museu Dr. Anastácio Gonçalves, Ave. 5 de Outubro 8. Collection in private house, largely Chinese porcelain. Buses: 1, 21, 36, 38, 44, 45, 49.

Museu da Marinha (Naval Museum), Praça do Império, Belém. Fascinating for naval buffs—ship models, royal uniforms, barges. Next to Planetarium. Trams: Algés, Dafundo. Buses: 29, 43. Adm. free Wed. Open 10–5.

Museu das Marionetas (Marionette Museum), Largo Rodrigues de Freitas 20. Bus: 37.

Museu Militar (Military Museum), Largo dos Caminhos de Ferro. Armor and weapons from 15th-century to present. Tram: Poco do Bispo. Buses: 9, 13, 17, 35. Open 10–4.

Museu Nacional de Arte Antiga (Ancient Art), Rua das Janelas Verdes. One of Europe's great collections of paintings, ceramics, silver and tapestries. Fine Portuguese primitives; famous 15th-century polyptych by Nuno Gonçalves, *Triumph of St. Vincent;* works by Hieronymus Bosch, Frans Hals, Holbein, Dürer, and many other Dutch, Spanish and Italian painters. Germain brothers' silver table service made for King João V and gold church vessels. Tram: Alcantara. Buses: 27, 40, 49 or 54. Snack bar with pies, sandwiches, etc.

Museu Nacional do Trajo (Costume Museum), Largo São João Baptista 2, Lumiar. In lovely 18th-century Palmela Palace, with superb gardens. Restaurant (expensive). Buses: 1, 7, 36. A way out in the suburbs, but possible to use a taxi and get it to wait (as long as you aren't having a meal too). Closed for lunch 1–2:30.

Museu do Teatro (Theater Museum), beside Costume Museum, see above. Fascinating if slightly provincial theatrical exhibits, very well displayed in restored old palace. Same transport and times as the Costume Museum.

Palácio de Ajuda (Ajuda Palace), Largo da Ajuda. Early 19th-century palace with fine rooms, good furniture and paintings, etc. Tram: Ajuda. Buses: 14, 40, 42.

Planetarium, Praça do Império, Belém. Shows, mostly at weekends, announced on board outside. Buses 29, 43.

São Vicente (St. Vincent's Church), Largo de São Vicente. Impressive building with exquisite wall tiles in the cloisters. The Braganza royal Pantheon is off the cloisters. Tram: Graça. Closed for lunch, 1–3.

Sé (Cathedral), Largo da Sé. Rebuilt 13th-century structure with a notable iron grill in the cloister. Tram: Graça. Bus: 37. Closed for lunch, 12–2:30

Torre de Belém (Belém Tower), Ave. da India. Marks the place from which the tiny caravelles sailed to unknown shores. Collection of arms and armor. Buses: 29, 43.

TOURS AND EXCURSIONS. Among the Lisbon travel agents offering every kind of travel assistance including tours are: *Capistranos,* Ave. Duque de Loulé 47A (tel. 542973), whose coaches pick up passengers at several hotels for day and overnight tours; *Citirama,* Ave. Praia da Vitória 12B (tel. 575564), who operate daily sightseeing tours with taped commentaries in eight languages; *Marcus and Harting,* Rossio 50 (tel. 369271).

SPECIAL EVENTS. Easter. Clam-hunt—on Maundy Thursday and Good Friday crowds are to be seen on the beaches north of Sintra, digging and scraping clams off the rocks, to be put into a tasty clam soup at the end of the day. By all means join in, although the tradition is fading nowadays. Just remember to use a knife or some other strong blunt instrument.

June. International Fair at Belém. The *Feira Popular,* a fun fair, is open in summer near Entrecampos. 13, 24 and 29: merry noisy festivities in old Alfama, to honor the *Santos Populares,* Saints Anthony, native son of Lisbon, John, Peter and Paul. The costumed evening parade held yearly on the eve of June 13, each *bairro* in fierce, enthusiastic competition with the others, lasts well after midnight, and is followed by celebrations till dawn. Small taverns are packed, people jostle, dance and shout in the streets, whilst the unmistakable odor of grilling sardines wafts under paper lanterns swinging over winding alleyways.

SHOPPING. Shopping in Lisbon can be both rewarding and fun as there are still large numbers of individual shops and very few big stores. The smartest are in and around the Rua Garrett, or the Chiado, as it is always called—although the fire of August 1988 devastated part of this area—and the Baixa, the area between the Rossio and the River Tagus, but there are also excellent shops in the new residential districts towards the airport. All handmade goods, such as leather handbags, shoes, gloves, embroidery, basketwork and fine book-binding are to be found at very reasonable prices. Most Lisbon shops are open from 9–1 and 3–7, and shut at 1 P.M. on Saturday.

Jewelry and Antiques. It is easy to get old clocks and watches and antique jewelry well repaired: the former at *António Couto,* Rua Sampaio Pina 52, near the Ritz Hotel, while jewelry can be reset as well as mended at *António da Silva,* Praça Luis de Camões 40. The last-named shop and *Barreto & Gonçalves,* Rua das Portas de Santo Antão 17, have the widest selection of antique jewels and silver for sale. There are many modern jewelers' shops in the Baixa, and *Sarmento,* Rua do Ouro 251, has an exceptional collection of the gold and silver filigree work which is so characteristic of Portuguese craftsmanship.

It is exceedingly rare to find a bargain in Lisbon antique shops, which are concentrated in the Rua Escola Politecnica, Rua Dom Pedro V, Rua da Misericórdia and the Rua do Alecrim (really one street although it has four different names). The flea market, the *Feira da Ladra* in the Campo de Sta. Clara is behind the Church of São Vicente. It is held all day on Tuesdays and Saturdays.

Leather Goods. Shoe shops are all over the city but, as Portuguese have very small feet, it is often difficult to find the larger sizes ready-made. However, all the better shoe shops will undertake to have shoes made to measure. Beautiful handbags and fine luggage can be found at *Galeão,* Rua Augusta 196, and *Casa Canada* at 232 in the same street also has a large selection. Gloves are usually sold or made to order in specialist shops in the Rua do Carmo and the Rua do Ouro. *Coelho,* Rua da Conceição 85, is excellent for leather belts and will make up your own material into leather-backed belts. This street, one of the cross roads in the Baixa, is famous for buttons, wools, cottons and all sewing materials.

Porcelain, Pottery and Tiles. *Vista Alegre,* in the Largo do Chiado 18, produces the finest porcelain in the country. Their factory near Aveiro was founded in 1824 and you can buy perfect reproductions of the original table services and ornaments as well as modern designs. They also sell fine glass. Portugal is full of clay, and local craftsmen turn out delightful bowls and plates for daily use, as well as the glazed pictorial tiles for which the country is famous. *Viúva Lamego,* Largo do Intendente 25, has the largest selection of tiles in Lisbon. Not only are their prices very competitive, but the staffs are most helpful, and their stock vast. The green pottery cabbage leaves, plates and tureens from Caldas da Rainha are to be found in all the handicraft shops.

Embroidery and Basketwork. Being light in weight, both embroidered goods and baskets make wonderful gifts for airborn travelers. The *Casa Regional da Ilha Verde,* Rua Paiva de Andrade 4, just off Rua Garrett, has beautifully embroidered table linen and blouses from the Azores. *Tito Cunha* at numbers 179 and 246 Rua do Ouro, specializes in the same type of goods from Madeira. Arraiolos carpets, hand-embroidered in wool in traditional or modern patterns, are to be found at *Quintão,* Rua Ivens 30. Baskets and basketwork of every kind can be bought in the markets which are all over Lisbon, selling fruit, vegetables, fish, meat and poultry, but are only open until 2 P.M. One of the best specialist shops for baskets is *Cestos,* Ave. Duque d'Avila 8B, which is at the top of the city off the Ave. da Republica.

Food and Wine. The major exports of Portugal are port wine and cork. The latter, from the great cork forests in the Alentejo, does not make attractive presents, though you will find small boxes and zinc-lined buckets called *tarros,* with fitting lids which will keep ice frozen for hours. The *Grandela* department store, already mentioned, has a large selection. Port wine comes from the vineyards of the Douro river above Oporto, and can be bought at any of the good wine shops and grocers around the city. One of the best is next to *Vista Alegre* in the Largo do Chiado, and if you want to sample several varieties go to the *Solar do Vinho do Porto,* Rua São Pedro de Alcantara 45, which is run by the trade and where you can sample over 100 varieties of Port.

Martins & Costa, Rua do Carmo 41, has the largest selection of fine foods, including the delicious regional cheeses as well as a big range of wines. Those from the different regions are particularly good, not only *Dao,* which is well known, and *Setúbal,* a generous wine from south of Lisbon, but also *Redondo, Borba, Evel* and *Vidigueira* from the Alentejo, *Lagoa* from the Algarve, *Nabantino* from Estremadura, *Cartaxo* from the Ribatejo, *Bairrada* and the *Vinhos Verdes,* or green wines, which are slightly sparkling, from the north.

The best fresh chocolates are to be found at *Benard's* at the top of the Rua Garrett. They also stock the many varieties of dried and crystallized fruits including Elvas plums, which are a feature of the country, and serve light lunches and teas.

All these firms are reliable for sending goods abroad and the *Centro de Turismo e Artesanato,* Rua Castilho 61, not only stocks a wide variety of typically Portuguese products, but they will also despatch goods abroad by air or sea freight even if bought elsewhere.

A Final Round-up. *Ramiro Leão,* Rua Garrett 83, is an excellent store for all household goods, materials, baby clothes, etc.

There are good hairdressers and barbers all over town, the smartest being *Bruna,* Largo de São Carlos 8 (tel. 363821). *Adelina* at Rua Garrett 61 (tel. 321982) is also very up-to-date as is *Hair,* Galerias Ritz, Rua Castilho 77A, Shop 5 (tel. 577855), *Tabot,* Ave. António Augusto de Aguiar 19-CV-D (tel. 532755), is smart and very reasonable in price. They all do facials and beauty treatments. Only the leading hairdressers make appointments—in the others clients wait their turn.

For books in English go to the *Livraria Britanica,* Rua de São Marçal 170, at the side of the British Institute, with a very large stock of paperbacks and hardbacks. *Bertrands, Sá e Costa* and the *Diario de Noticias* bookshops are all in the Rua Garrett and have foreign as well as Portuguese books. If you break your glasses or lose your prescription, *Ramos e Silva,* Rua Garrett 63, are excellent and quick for repair work or filling new orders.

SPORTS. For further details of sports facilities ask at Tourist Offices. **Tennis:** courts near Campo Grande or at Cruz Quebrada can be reserved at the Club Internacional de Ténis, Rua Professor Sousa Camara 193 (tel. 682084). There are also tennis courts, as well as a **swimming** pool and a 9-hole **golf** course in a picturesque natural setting at the Lisbon Sports Club, Carragueira, near Belas, 15 minutes' drive from Lisbon.

Clay-pigeon shooting at the beautiful Monsanto Club, 10 minutes' drive from town. **Horse-riding** rates are reasonable.

Skindiving: divers interested in the Portuguese underwater flora and fauna, or those who feel up to coping with a live lobster, should contact the Centro Portuguese de Actividades Subaquáticas, Rua do Alto do Duque 45 (tel. 616961), which organizes tourist expeditions to the coast at Sesimbra, Arrábida, Algarve, in which non-members can also participate.

Fishing is done from the shore by hired rowboat or by specially equipped large boats for big game fishing (swordfish, tuna, or big-eyed tuna off Madeira). There is fresh-water fishing, for trout, rainbow trout and large-mouthed bass, which was imported a few years ago from America.

NEWSPAPERS. Lisbon has a large number of weekly and daily newspapers, of which the *Diario de Noticias* is the most comprehensive. The *Anglo-Portuguese News* is an English-language weekly covering local and general news.

USEFUL ADDRESSES. Embassies. *American,* Ave. das Forces Armadas (tel. 7266600); *British,* Rua São Domingos à Lapa 37 (tel. 661191); *Canadian,* Rua Rosa Araújo 2 (tel. 563821). **Travel Agents.** *American Express,* Star Travel Service, Ave. Sidónio Pais 4A (tel. 539841/50/71), and at Praça dos Restauradores 14 (tel. 362501); *Wagons Lits/Cooks,* Ave. da Liberdade 103 (tel. 361521), and at the Ritz Hotel, Ave. Rodrigo Fonseca 88 (tel. 680632); *Wasteels Expresso,* Ave. António Agusto de Aguiar 88 (tel. 579180).

Car Hire. Most international firms have offices at the airport: *Avis,* Praça dos Restauradores 47 (tel. 361171); *Europcar,* Ave. António Augusto Aguiar 24 (tel. 535115); *Hertz,* Ave. 5 de Outubro 10 (tel. 579027); *In-*

terRent, Praça dos Restauradores 74 (tel. 366751); *Travelcar,* Ave. Fontes Pereira de Melo 6 (tel. 578006).

Chauffeur Driven Cars. *Auto Estrela,* Ave. João Crisóstomo 65 (tel. 534331); *Castanheira,* Ave. João Crisóstomo 87 (tel. 540744); *Olivauto,* Ave. João XXI, 12D/E (tel. 880178); *Turigal,* Rua Fialho Almeida 36E (tel. 542846).

Automobile Clubs. *Automobile Club of Portugal,* Rua Rosa Araujo 24 (tel. 563931); *Touring Club of Portugal,* Ave. da Liberdade 258 (tel. 561011).

Pharmacies. See any paper for the day's list of pharmacies open that night or Sat. P.M. or Sun.; if closed the pharmacy has a notice giving the nearest that are open.

Hospital. *British Hospital,* Rua Saraiva de Carvalho 49 (tel. 602020), (night tel. 603785), with English-speaking staff, for both in- and out-patients.

Lost Property. Should you lose or mislay sunglasses, cameras, gloves or whatnot, try checking at the municipal *Governo Civil,* right next to the São Carlos Opera House, where found objects are generally deposited. Those found in public transport are deposited at the top of the Santa Justa lift, off the Carmo Square.

Chambers of Commerce. *American Chamber of Commerce,* Rua Dona Estefania 155 (tel. 572561); *British-Portuguese Chamber of Commerce,* Rua Estrela 8 (tel. 661351).

Libraries. *American Library,* Ave. Duque de Loulé 22B (tel. 570102), afternoons only; *British Institute,* Rua Luis Fernandes 3 (tel. 369208), with library and reading room (closed for lunch, 12:30–2, and Wed. A.M.).

Bank. Lloyds Bank plc., Ave. da Liberdade 222 (tel. 535171) and Rua do Ouro 40 (tel. 361211).

Churches. St. George's Church (Anglican), Rua São Jorge (tel. 663010), set in historical English cemetery; Corpo Santo Church (R.C.), Largo do Corpo Santo (tel. 323208), served by Irish Dominican Fathers.

THE ENVIRONS OF LISBON

Unlike the suburbs of many capital cities, those of Lisbon are attractive. However, there are still some shanty towns, particularly toward the airport.

The sea road out to Estoril and Cascais (N6) really starts after Belém, at Algés, with the great estuary of the Tagus to the left, and sandy beaches guarded by forts built to protect the sea approaches to Lisbon in the 17th century by King João IV, father of Catherine of Bragança who married King Charles II of England. This Estrada Marginal is bordered on the land side by private houses, many set in large gardens filled with brightly colored geraniums, bougainvilleas, bignonias, wisteria, cannas, roses and arum lilies, flowering in their different seasons, with the geraniums and bougainvilleas apparently in flower for most of the year. Constant electric trains also follow the sea from Cais do Sodré station in Lisbon to Cascais.

Estoril, Cascais and the Mouth of Hell

Inland, a four-lane motorway leads up from the Pombal statue at the top of the Avenida de Liberdade in Lisbon, through Monsanto Park until it joins the coast road between Cruz Quebrada and Caxias. The Estrada Marginal carries on through Paço d'Arcos, Oeiras, Carcavelos and Parede, which all have long, sandy beaches, to Cascais.

At Porto Salvo, behind Paço d'Arcos, there is an interesting museum which contains recently discovered terracotta urns and flat dishes of the era of the Emperor Diocletian. Nearby are freshly unearthed Roman ruins.

In Oeiras stands the small, 18th-century pink palace built by the Marquis of Pombal before he fell into disgrace. It is a delightful sight, with curved eaves to the pagoda-like roofs of the low, spreading buildings. In the grounds, now given over to horticultural research, are a charming Fishing Pavilion beside a great water tank backed by large blue and white azulejo panels, as well as other architectural features near the palace.

The town limits of Estoril are ill-defined and lost in greenery and building developments, but its center is the casino, where hopefuls throng the gaming tables and slot machines. The casino has a restaurant, cinema, exhibition space and a pretty winter garden. Wide avenues leading to the sea are lined with palm trees and first-rate hotels. This is a holiday world of suntan oil, of tennis-balls bouncing on well-kept courts.

Some of the beaches are hemmed in by low cliffs and submerged rocks. The best and longest beach is at Monte Estoril, which joins on to that of Estoril, where there are shops, snackbars, changing rooms, and beach chairs for hire. The houses climb the hill toward the golf course, their delightful shapes and colors half-hidden by the hibiscus bushes, the mimosa trees, the trailers of plumbago, as pale a blue as the sun-bleached sky. In late May and June the jacaranda trees are a mass of violet blue blossom, so thick that the new leaves are entirely hidden.

Within walking distance along the sea wall, and across the bay, lies Cascais, rival of Estoril. Between the two resorts rises the huge pile of the Hotel Estoril-Sol, 14 stories high, with its swimming-pool, flowered terraces, and elegant shops.

Cascais is rich in history and tradition, and proud of her past. Here, the governor of the town was beheaded on the public square for opposing the forces of the Spanish Duke of Alba. Before the royal family went into exile in 1910 they came to Cascais with their court for the summer holidays, walking at ease through the town—then small—and greeting passers-by. A cove below the elegant Hotel Albatroz still bears the name of Queen's Beach.

For many years Cascais remained a fishing village, the boats being dragged up on to the sand, and the catch sold by Dutch auction nearby. Nowadays, the crates of newly caught fish are auctioned in a large covered space near the fishermen's beach, opposite the Hotel Baia.

In the 1930s, percipient painters and writers, some from overseas, rented the cottages above the rocky shore, worked when they felt like it, and drank endless cups of coffee in the cafés and endless glasses of wine in the taverns. But after World War II, more and more foreigners were attracted by the fishermen's houses, by the small squares filled with fishing nets hung out to dry in the sun, and the cobbled streets and steps leading down from the upper levels, so that now Cascais is filled with smart shops, particularly in the pedestrian Rua Frederico Arouca, with numerous restaurants and bars, plus a few hotels, residencias and pensions.

It was a fisherman of Cascais, according to local legend, who was first to discover America, ten years before Christopher Columbus. He was called Afonso Sanches, and during a voyage to the East Indies his boat was carried off to the coast of America. He managed to reach Madeira with two or three companions, exhausted like himself, who died soon after their arrival. Afonso Sanches was lodged by his friend, Columbus, a Genoese navigator, who had settled on the island after marrying the daughter of the Governor of Porto Santo. It was thanks to these men's ship's log that Columbus landed in the New World.

Marshal Carmona, President of the Republic for 22 years (1928–1950), whose favorite residence was, for a long time, the citadel, loved this time-worn shore, the old ramparts baked in the sun, and the people of the port, serious and industrious, who each day, no matter what the weather, put out to sea in their small boats to fish in open waters. On calm days you can see pork bladders painted bright red or yellow, and floated on the surface of the green water to indicate shoals of fish. Sometimes boats, in pairs, sails and masts lowered, rest side by side, connected by a great net, like those of the fishermen on the Lake of Tiberias.

The parish church of Cascais, at the top of the town, has some good paintings in it including a series by Josefa of Obidos and an elegant golden altar. Opposite the church is one of the entrances to delightful Castro Guimarães park, in which is a shallow lake with a café at one end, a small zoo, and tables and chairs set out under the trees for picknickers; to the west, on the road to Guincho, is the Museum. In a former private house bequeathed to the town by the owners, this museum has great charm, with beautiful objects alongside Edwardian splendor. At one end is a small archeological section with objects excavated from the neolithic tombs at Alapraia, near São João do Estoril. A library nearby has open shelves with quite a large English section, comfortable armchairs in which to read and, in the winter, a large fire burns in the hearth.

A greater attraction to travelers, the Boca do Inferno, or Mouth of Hell, is an awesome chasm in the rocks, where the inrushing sea is sucked down in a cream-colored whirlpool of water. Dozens of stalls selling local crafts line the road above. Soon the windswept coastline becomes rocky, and the cliffs crumble slowly into sea-wracked shingle.

The road passes a noble early 19th-century lighthouse, the Farol da Guia, and a number of small restaurants, each with its seawater tank occupied by swimming lobsters, crabs and crayfish for the future delectation of customers. To the right are two clubs, open to temporary members: the Dom Carlos has a fine swimming pool, tennis courts, riding facilities and a restaurant; the Quinta da Marinha has, in addition, a golf course designed by Robert Trent Jones.

After passing another, small 17th-century fortress on the low cliffs, a turning to the right, signposted Oitavos, leads up to the old semaphor station from which the arrival of ships was signaled before the invention of the telegraph. The building has been enlarged and is now a restaurant, from where you can look over a sea of umbrella pines to the Atlantic Ocean. Further west, as the trees fall back, dunes take over, and past another (later) lighthouse, at Cabo Raso, you come on to the superb Praia do Guincho. To the right is the long serrated line of the Sintra hills, dappled when the sun is shining, and to the left the grand profile of Cabo da Roca, the westernmost point of the continent of Europe. The beach is so long that the great rollers from the Atlantic pound unrelentingly on the sand even on calm days, so that swimming can be very dangerous. However, both wind- and boardsurfers find themselves in their element.

The strong pull of the tides throws up a wall of high waves which threaten to take the old fortress—now a superbly converted hotel—by storm, and to sweep the clapboard restaurants away to sea. People drive out from town to eat grilled lobster, stuffed crabs, and *percebes* (barnacles), which fill the mouth with the taste of the sea. The strong salt wind burns all that grows, save the hardy mesembryanthemum with pink and yellow flowers, whose fleshy leaves cover the autumn dunes with carpets of purple and rust. In late summer the sands above high tide are pierced with a lovely species of strongly scented white lily, *pancratium maritimum.*

The road (N247) then goes inland through a forest of pine and eucalyptus trees until Malveira da Serra, with its elegant houses, where it joins the road to Sintra (N9–1). Below the upward-winding road are amazing views of the Guincho and of the bare, stony country rolling away to the end of the Sintra range to your right. Several of the little villages above the sea are being gradually developed by people wanting to escape the trammels of town life. At the road's highest point, a left turning leads down to Cabo da Roca, passing through the village of Azoia with several good restaurants.

The Cape has an early lighthouse, built in 1772, which is surrounded by the now deserted but charming little houses of the lighthouse keepers who tended the great lamps before they were mechanized. There is plenty of parking space and even a small restaurant at this strange outpost, where the visitor feels the immensity of the ocean stretching away to the coast of the New World.

On the land side, a small building straddles the westernmost point of the Serra de Sintra. This is Peninha, in early times a hermitage when—as in so many early hermitages around the coasts of Europe—a light would presumably have burned at night to warn ships of the long headland below. The small chapel, even its ceiling, is entirely lined with blue and white tiled panels of New Testament scenes.

Monsanto Park

Some 50 years ago Lisbon was surrounded by thorny wastes, but in the intervening years the City Fathers have planted vast tracts of land with pine, eucalyptus and hardwoods, so that now Monsanto Park is a green thicket of trees, their scent blending with the sea breeze to freshen the air that blows through the city.

The vale of Alcantara is spanned by the lovely archways of the early 18th-century stone aqueduct, so solidly built that the earthquake of 1755 barely affected it. The central arches are enormously high, and the whole great ensemble is best seen from the motorway already mentioned, running from the Pombal statue to the coast. After this the highway speeds on between the trees, mingled with mimosa or yellow gorse, heather or rose laurel, according to the time of year.

If you have time, drive off the highway and up a road to the Alto da Serafina, where you will be rewarded by a bird's-eye view of the city and the river. From the heights of Serafina you will have a night view of an enchanted city, streets and river and bridge twinkling with lights, beneath the statue of Christ the King.

Lisbon's camping ground here, with its green spaces, shady trees, big swimming pool, post office, shops, hairdresser, laundry and cafeteria, is a model of its kind.

Queluz

The most attractive of the royal residences is the Rococo palace of
Queluz on the way to Sintra (N17). The estate has always been the endow-
ment of the royal princes, or rather, the younger sons of the king. It was
there that, in 1667, Pedro, second living son of João IV, went into retirement, to plan the bold move that was to give him both the throne and
the wife of his older brother, Afonso VI.

In 1758, the future Pedro III entrusted two architects, the Portuguese
Mateus Vicente de Oliveira and the Frenchman Jean Baptiste Robillon,
with the construction of his miniature Versailles in place of the house he
had inherited. Finished in 1794, the elegant pink palace turns its best front
to the formal gardens, where statues and azulejos frame pools and fountains. A stately Throne Room and graceful Music Room, decked out with
fresco scrolls and flower garlands, painted ceilings and gilt mirrors, enclose elegant 18th-century furniture. One room, lined with chinoiserie
tiles, has charming bamboo armchairs.

Pedro IV was born and died in Don Quixote's Room, but Queluz was
put at times to more sinister use than chamber music concerts by candlelight and courtly gatherings in the gilded ballroom. Plots against Pombal
were whispered in its corners; and Queen Carlota Joaquina, Spanish wife
of João VI, banished from Lisbon, here held her opposition court. Outside
there are a few strange touches: the stone sphinxes with ruffs and ribbons
above their women's breasts, looking blindly down the leafy alleys; the
great theatrical stairway over the cages, behind whose bars the wild beasts
once paced imprisoned; the slow stream down which boats drifted to the
sound of music between the walls of azulejos, while men and girls played
a sophisticated hide and seek in the boxwood maze, long since destroyed.

Queen Elizabeth II of Great Britain stayed in the charming Pavilion
of Queen Maria, residence of visiting heads of state. Other parts still in
use are the chapel, often the scene of smart weddings, and Cozinha Velha,
the old palace kitchen, now a luxurious restaurant and tearoom serving
the old royal recipes. The palace is closed on Tuesdays.

Not far from Queluz, at São Domingos de Benfica, the Fronteira Palace
stands in superb formal gardens with statuary and a long water tank
backed by iridescent tiles of heroic-sized prancing horsemen, each different. Visitors can wander in the lovely demense and visit the palace (see
Places of Interest at end of this chapter).

Sintra and its Palaces

Whereas in Estoril and on the Sun Coast the sea breeze blows the clouds
away from a clear sky, even in winter, the hills or *serra* of Sintra gather
the sea mists and, even in summer, stay fresh and cool. No sun can dry
the water that wells up from the rich earth, patched blue with periwinkles.
When the heat snaps the pine twigs and bursts open the sweet-smelling
eucalyptus buds, the walls stay green with moss along the road that winds
from Pena Palace to Colares through the silent forest of Sintra. The diminutive cells of the abandoned monastery of Capuchos are lined with cork
to keep out the damp.

The road passes by some of the finest country houses in Portugal, belonging to the classes privileged by birth or money, talent or taste. They

house collections of old weapons or china, ivories or music scores, and in the gardens there are stone basins shaded by lemon trees, tree ferns, roses and wild lavender.

A few live in Sintra the year round, most in summer only. Some have noble houses, with a private chapel and stables. Others have simple dwellings, taking pride in a giant magnolia or a magnificent view. All are under the spell of Sintra, from which there is no release.

Like all enchanted places, Sintra can disappoint the newcomer. Never go there in low spirits, or in bad weather. The local saying goes that if the Sintra hills are hidden by cloud, or if the donkeys are braying, better stay away.

The lovers of Sintra take pleasure in this white weather, when mists catch and tear on the spurs of rock and the tops of tall trees, when the glazed tiles sweat with water, and wisps of cloud drift soundlessly through the broken ramparts of the old Moorish castle. At times, the fog is so dense that the peak-top Palace of Pena disappears from view. Cars move slowly, in a yellow blur of headlights. Frogs splash in the stone basins, among the floating camellia petals. Distance is within touch, the world is small and cold, and you feel the need of a fireside and hot tea. Meanwhile, the hapless traveler, walled in by the white silence, is lost in the unknown.

A shift in the wind will all at once blow the mists away, revealing the stone cross on the hilltop, bringing back sight and sound. Lizards dart through the undergrowth, the air smells strongly of moss, wet bark, and magnolias. The roof of the Pena shines in the sun, the light falls bright on the tangle of greenery. Horse-drawn carriages trot slowly up the steep and winding ways that lead to the monastery of the Capuchos or to the Cruz Alta, and fireflies flit through the warm evening air in May.

The Castelo dos Mouros

The castle of the Moors dates back to the 7th century. Its stone walls rise from a natural rampart of rocks, making it safe from enemy attack. The sentry path has a sweeping view over the plain and down to the sea. The fortress was safeguarded against all dangers, whether enemy soldiers, thirst, or hunger, by lookouts, deep cisterns, and underground vaults. And yet it fell, as did the castles in Lisbon and Palmela, taken by storm by Afonso Henriques and his men-at-arms in 1147.

Abandoned, the old Moorish castle is overrun by brambles; the stone steps crumble underfoot, birds nest in the battlements, and on wintry days the wind sighs through the empty cisterns. It is a wild, still place, a haunt of loneliness, unrelieved in its gloom.

The Paço da Vila

If the Arabs had built a fortress on the hilltop, it was to keep watch over the valley, but the Palace was built far below, in a bower of cypress and palm trees.

Most of the kings of Portugal have loved Sintra, and left their mark on her. What Windsor is to the history of England, St. Germain-en-Laye to the history of France, the Paço da Vila in Sintra is to the history of Portugal.

Dinis, the poet king, of whom an old song tells that "he did all that he pleased," resided in this palace. But it was the Aviz dynasty that built the Paço da Vila and King John I planned here the expedition to Ceuta in 1415, and it was also here that he betrothed his daughter Isabela to the powerful Philip of Burgundy. To bring back his bride, the duke had sent a token court of chosen envoys, among whom was the renowned painter Van Eyck, whose style so strongly influenced Nuno Gonçalves. In memory of the wedding, the king ordered a ceiling in the palace to be painted with swans, emblem both of the princess and of her husband's capital city, Bruges. This is a particularly lovely and unusual room, long and narrow, with splendid Chinese porcelain bird tureens on the tables. State banquets sometimes take place here.

In Sintra, too, King João was caught kissing a lady-in-waiting of his English queen, Philippa of Lancaster, daughter of John of Gaunt, one of England's great warriors. The king swore that the kiss was *por bem,* without consequence, and his wife believed him; but the incident gave rise to such gossip that the king, exasperated, ordered a ceiling in the palace to be painted with as many magpies as there were chattering court ladies. Each bird is different and has in its claw the red rose of Lancaster, and, by its beak, the words: POR BEM, to cry the king's blamelessness throughout the ages.

Perhaps, on taking her husband's word, Queen Philippa was thinking of her grandfather, King Edward III of England, who, also married to a Philippa, and caught with a lady's garter in his hand, created the Order of the Garter, bearing the words HONI SOIT QUI MAL Y PENSE: Shame be to him who evil thinks.

Afonso V, nicknamed the African, seldom lived within his kingdom; but he was born and died in Sintra, in the same bed-chamber.

It was to Manuel I, however, that the Paço owed its crowning glory. The Fortunate King, as he was known, undertook to enlarge and embellish the old palace in a Moorish style that is not, as is often supposed, the work of its Arab builders, but the result of a taste brought back from Manuel's travels in Spain, where he had seen and admired the horseshoe windows, the multicolored azulejos, and the flowered patios murmuring with water. It is to his love of Andalusian artistry that we owe the tall chimneys, the sunlit fountains in the orange-scented courtyards, and the ceiling painted with the coats-of-arms of the noble families in his kingdom. In this hall, he received with royal pomp ambassadors and poets, among them Gil Vicente. Here, too, he held his courts of love, gave banquets, and watched his Moorish dancing girls.

In the sunset of a dying dynasty, sitting on the bench of glazed tiles in the Patio of the Negress, young King Sebastião listened to Camões reading his *Lusiad.* Fired by the epic of his forebears' glory, the foolhardy boy led an army to conquer Morocco, but was doomed to total defeat and death.

Sintra was to be a prison for a yet more unfortunate king. Afonso VI, bereft of his throne and his wife by his ambitious younger brother, betrayed, half mad, lived the nine years until his death locked up in a palace room, wearing out the flagstones with his ceaseless pacing.

The earthquake of 1755 shook the old walls, cracked the tiles, split the painted wood and crumbled the plaster arabesques. However, while the royal residences in Lisbon, in Evora, in Santarém and in Almeirim were destroyed or damaged beyond repair, the old Paço in Sintra stood steadfast, surviving both the havoc of nature and clumsy restoration.

There are the kitchens, with vast conical chimneys in Moorish style, the great echoing rooms with their polished floors, their decorated ceilings: the Swan Room, the Mermaids' Room, and the Escutcheon Room. Near the palace windows, seats of azulejos remind one of countless queens and princesses who must have sat there with their embroidery, waiting for their husbands to come back from hunting expeditions or the wars. There are even Edwardian rooms, to the right of the entrance hall, charmingly decorated for King Carlos, who was assassinated in 1908, and his wife Queen Amélia. If the guide does not take you in to these elegant rooms, ask him to do so as they are worth seeing for the price of a tip.

The Palácio da Pena

The 19th century did not find the old Paço to its taste. Queen Maria's second husband, Ferdinand of Coburg, anticipated the building mania of his mad relative, Ludwig of Bavaria. In 1840 he began to transform the monastery built by Manuel I between 1503 and 1511 on the topmost hill of Sintra into a pseudo-medieval palace, a sample patchwork of every style of architecture, with Arab minarets and Gothic turrets, Renaissance cupolas and gazebos, together with a few fantasies of his own. The resulting jumble is something of a curiosity, saved by the natural beauty of its setting. The gardens and rocky woods and its height above the surrounding countryside all combine to give a strange feeling of unreality.

The years have passed. The Portuguese kings are dead. The Pena's ill-matched styles, all equally bygone, are bound together by time. Indoors, the Victorian furnishings—deer antlers, Saxe porcelains, plush chairs and antimacassars—unfashionable for so long, have now come back into favor.

At a lower level lies a botanical park, in which nothing is missing: stone ponds with gliding swans; fountains with different tasting waters, all spring-cold and refreshing; clusters of camellias, streams and Japanese bridges, rock gardens, summer houses and grottos; even a gigantic stone man in armor, among the umbrella pines. (Baron Von Eschweg, the architect of Pena.) There are hothouses, tree ferns, dwarf cedars, gulches, and a barren stretch of under-brush, over which the sparrow-hawks wheel unceasingly. For a slight extra charge automobiles or taxis can drive through the narrow winding roads of this great estate. The Palácio da Vila is closed on Wednesdays, the Pena on Mondays.

Sintra

If, being a tourist, you cannot hope for an invitation to one of the wonderful *quintas,* or country houses, in Sintra, you can always offer yourself the luxury of going to the palace of Seteais, now a hotel.

At the end of the 18th century it was built by a Dutch consul who made a fortune in Brazilian diamonds, and who there received, in great style, King João VI and his queen. To honor the event, he built a second identical wing to his house, joining it to the first by an arch of triumph which frames the overhanging Palácio da Pena on one side, and on the other the valley of Colares. On an outcropping of rock in the garden, Byron sat to write enthusiastically about Sintra in the shade of laurel leaves, as befits a poet.

Today, the house, still in harmony with an age of elegance and leisure, stays renowned for its good fare as a luxury hotel, set in lawns, boxwood and roses, the evening air scented with sun-warmed heliotrope. The hotel's name comes from *sete ais,* seven sighs—of relief by the Portuguese, after the signing of the Treaty of Sintra in 1807, by which Junot pledged himself and his French troops to leave Portugal, though they were back again in 1808!

The 18th-century Palace of Ramalhão, on the direct road between Estoril and Sintra, has lovely wall-paintings; once a royal palace, it is now a school and convent, and not open to the public. Also regrettably closed to the public are the 16th-century Palace of Ribafrias and the neo-Manueline Manor of Regaleira—an extraordinary example of late-Victorian fantasy just before Seteais. More accessible are the Library-Museum with its pictures and prints in the Palace of Valenças, the Gothic Churches of Santa Maria and São Pedro, the latter with great tiled panels, the Church of São Martinho in the town, and the circular chapel at Janas, towards the sea, scene of a big *romaria* and fair on August 17, when people bring their animals to be blessed.

In São Pedro de Sintra, a fair is held on the second and fourth Sundays of each month. Livestock is sold, and harness and seeds and boots, together with flowers, fruit, and vegetables. But you will also find old prints, pewter tankards, glass, fob watches and gilt wood, all jumbled together with rusty lanterns and artless earthenware pottery, beside an old woman in a black shawl selling *queijadas,* the sweet cheese tartlets that are a specialty in Sintra.

A very strange property, Monserrate, on the way to Colares, was built at the whim of a rich Englishman, Sir Francis Cook, an early 19th-century merchant from the City of London. A Turkish harem in marble, Etruscan tombs, a fretwork chalet, form an incongruous yet impressive whole. But the beauty of Monserrate lies in its gardens, laid out at a time when travel was long and difficult; the seedlings that survived the journey were planted outdoors in alien weather, to take root and grow beside the simple plane tree and the hardy palm. There you will find the greatest variety of ferns in the world, together with giant daturas, strawberry trees, bamboos, and plants that have elsewhere lost popularity long ago, like the Chinese gingko and the monkey puzzle.

On the road running north from Sintra to Ericeira lies Odrinhas. The Archeological Museum of São Miguel de Odrinhas here is of great interest, containing pieces from the first century B.C. In the well-kept garden surrounding the museum are traces of a Paleo-Christian temple and some lovely mosaics.

Colares and the Sea

Colares is a region of countryfolk and vine-growers, of good wine to be drunk with hearty food at tables under the trees, overlooking a stone bridge and a slow-flowing stream half choked with grasses and wild flowers. The village of Colares, up the hill, is still unspoilt with charming color-washed houses and cottages. The road goes on up to Penedo, another delightful group of pretty houses.

Between Colares and the sea, the road is lined with holiday homes, partly hidden by the pinewoods of Banzão. The pines go down to the sands of Praia das Maçãs, a beach with a swimming pool and camping ground.

Nearby is Praia Grande, a yet longer sandy beach with thundering break-ers.

Farther still, the coastline grows wilder, the cliffs pitted with mussel-studded coves. A mile or so away lies Azenhas do Mar, a white village on a high ledge of rock. Far below, the tide-mills that gave the place its name have become swimming pools, washed by the waves of the incoming sea.

The woods and pastures on either side of the road abound in wild flow-ers in early spring, before the torrid sun has dried the soil to a hard red crust on which only cistus, heather and low heaths can survive the long summer months.

The farther you go, the wilder the seascape; until you see, jutting for-ward like the prow of a ship, the headland of Cabo da Roca, Europe's westernmost point, where the Serra of Sintra drops to the sea.

The Northern Suburbs

At the other end of the Campo Grande is Lumiar, a once delightful vil-lage now dominated by the motorways cutting through it. Lumiar has two entertaining museums: a Costume Museum set in the lovely gardens of the Duke of Palmela's *Quinta,* with a good, expensive restaurant, and a Theater Museum in the equally lovely Palace of Monteiro Mor next door.

You can catch a glimpse beyond of a curious fountain whose colored tiles tell—somewhat like cartoon-strips—how the Odivelas church was desecrated in 1671 by a thief, and how he was subsequently punished. Now submerged into the almost nameless city suburbs, the history of Odivelas is a long one. King Dinis asked to be buried here under the fine old trees in the square together with his royal spouse, Isabel, the "Beggar Queen." But later the Saint-Queen's body was moved to Coimbra, the whole church being perfumed with the scent of roses when her remains were transferred to a solid silver tomb. Here, too, in 1415, Queen Philippa died of the plague, after solemnly bestowing on her sons, who were on their way to Ceuta, the swords emblematic of their knighthood.

In the 18th century, the convent resembled a finishing school for well-born young ladies, renowned for their soirées of poetry readings and recep-tions with music, with which the nuns entertained callers. A goodly num-ber of these charming girls did not lack for romantic adventure: the best-known story that has come down to us concerns the long and passionate romance of King João V and Madre Paula.

At Loures is the fine country house of Correio Mor built by a Postmas-ter General in the late 18th century. A road leads due west out of Loures, through Caneças and past the headwaters of the Lisbon aqueduct, with its splendid stone conduits and small water towers, striding off across a still largely deserted countryside to Queluz.

South of the Tagus

The bridge over the Tagus opens the road to the south, but no pedestri-ans are allowed on it. However, one can still cross the river from Caes de Sodré and Praça do Comércio by ferry boat, which docks in Cacilhas (the former ferry took cars). Cacilhas is backed by the low-price suburb of Almada, where tall buildings are fast reaching out towards the Costa da Caparica. The 34 km. (21 miles) of fine sand can be dangerous for the unwary swimmer, as is the equally exposed coast beyond Sintra, where huge breakers often close the beaches. Several new resorts near Caparica are just on the verge of becoming popular but in the lonely sand dunes of the southern end you may still escape from the world.

The motorway to the south is lined with pinewoods, studded with summer cottages and drive-in restaurants; and even though there are many signs of growing industrial involvement and spreading suburban sprawl, there are still also long unspoiled stretches of trees and rice paddies, silent under the sun but for the strong beating of wings as the storks swoop down on the croaking frogs.

A village at a crossroads on the old highway, Azeitão is well worth a stopover. There is a remarkable fountain in carved stone, an old church, and fine old houses. The shops sell a good muscatel wine and a renowned ewes' milk cheese.

Along the road to Setúbal, a strange science-fiction area of white domes visible on the left is in fact a modern winery which produces a delicious wine, famous for centuries, under up-to-the-minute conditions. Visitors are welcome. Another fine old dwelling, the Quinta das Torres, is now a guesthouse and restaurant. Overlooking a large ornamental water tank with a miniature temple rising from the waters and a leafy park, the rooms are full of antique furniture and paintings, polished brass and firearms, sunlight and green shadows. In winter, it is alight with the glow and scent of woodfires.

Bacalhoa, one of the earliest inhabited houses in the country, is a beautiful late 16th-century L-shaped building, its corners adorned with canteloupe-melon cupolas. Arched terraces overlook the box-hedged gardens, and the air is filled with the heady scent of orange trees. The great water tank washes a pavilion with pyramidal towers which houses the earliest dated tile panel in the country, that of Susannah and the Elders, 1565. The house, with full staff, can now be rented by the week.

Fork left for Palmela, with a huge Templar's Castle crowning the hilltop above a network of cobbled streets between low white-washed houses. The Castle, with a luxury pousada installed in the 18th-century buildings at one end, is fascinating, with superb views towards Lisbon and the "Sea of Straw," bathed in a filmy light. To the south lies Setúbal and the river Sado with its still waters and rice paddies beyond groves of the orange trees for which the district is famous.

Branching to the right, in Azeitão, the road leads to Sesimbra, now surrounded by high-rise apartment houses, but by the sea and still a lively fishing village where many Lisboans have a summer house. Perched on a hilltop, the five towers of an old castle overlook the port on the rounded beach, guarded by a fortress, and littered with boats, coils of rope, and anchors. On the return of the fleet at day's end, fish are sold at the water's edge to the highest bidder. Sardines are plentiful, and deep-sea fishing is rewarded by the catch of swordfish, weighing as much as 200 pounds.

Traveling west along the excellent road, you will be rewarded by the view from Cape Espichel, a salt-encrusted headland on which 18th-century arcaded pilgrim houses border a huge open space. At one end is a great forsaken pilgrimage church in this lonely land's end given over to silence and seagulls. Behind the church the turf above the low cliffs is alive with wild flowers in the spring, though the scene is somewhat marred by strange modernistic sculptures placed at random and looking very much out of place in this calm 18th-century atmosphere. To the north, unsullied beaches extend up to Caparica, for no roads lead to these remote sands which take the full force of the Atlantic gales. Big romarias are held here on August 15 and on the last Sunday in September.

The Serra d'Arrábida

It is loneliness and silence, and the boundless seascape, that the monks were seeking in the barren range of Arrábida, where they built a monastery on a southern slope of the hills. A striking statue by Frei Martinho greets the traveler: arms outstretched in a cross stands a monk with heart and mouth shut by a padlock. The white walls of the monastery cling to the hillside, falling away into the brilliant sea.

The hills are covered by a scratchy underbrush of thorn bushes, stunted lentisk and juniper trees, gnarled oaks and prickly pears, survivors of the primeval forest of the peninsula; here and there, the green distaff of a cypress tree springs skywards from the stony ground that crumbles down to the sheltered beach of Portinho d'Arrábida, lying like a shell among the jutting rocks. The old fortress has been turned into an Estalagem, where outdoor tables under a vine trellis look over and down into the glass-clear water. On summer Sundays, Mass is said in the grotto of Santa Margarida, visited by Hans Christian Andersen when he was in Portugal in 1866. Far away, the sun shines on the sands of Troia, the long peninsula at the mouth of the river Sado, which is now becoming a popular resort.

Two roads along the hills lead to the old, but industrialized, town of Setúbal, at the foot of the Castelo de São Filipe, inside the walls of which there is a pousada. The sheltered harbor, the nearby stretches of salt-pans, the plentiful catch of sardines, have given rise to a rich canning industry. The town is also renowned for red mullet, and muscatel wine, the last in great favor at the table of Louis XIV. It prides itself on being the birthplace of the poet Bocage, and on the fine Manueline church of Jesus, with strange twisted columns and handsome porch of Arrábida marble.

Alongside is the Municipal Museum, containing a series of lovely Portuguese paintings in Baroque frames which were taken out of the Church of Jesus some years ago.

Ferry boats taking cars connect Setúbal with the beautiful beach of Troia and the sunken ruins of the old Roman city of Cetóbriga, engulfed in the year 412. Large-scale development is taking place, and the whole atmosphere of the area is rapidly changing.

An 18-hole par 72 golf course designed by Robert Trent Jones stretches alongside the River Sado at Troia, with natural water hazards cleverly incorporated in some of the fairways. Tennis courts are also available, at a reasonable price.

PRACTICAL INFORMATION FOR
THE ENVIRONS OF LISBON

TOURIST OFFICES. There are local tourist offices in the following towns: **Almada,** Rua Conde Ferreira 8; **Cabo da Roca,** Cabo da Roca; **Cascais,** Ave. D. Carlos 1; **Costa da Caparica,** Praça da Liberdade; **Ericeira,** Rua Eduardo Burnay 33A; **Estoril,** Arcadas do Parque; **Palmela,** Largo do Chafariz; **Sesimbra,** Ave. dos Naufragios; **Setúbal,** Rua do Corpo Santo; **Sintra,** Praça da Republica.

HOTELS AND RESTAURANTS

Alcabideche (Lisbon), on the road from Estoril to Sintra. *Sintra Estoril* (E), tel. 2690720. 187 rooms with bath. Indoor pool, tennis, sauna, garage, 9-hole golf course and autodrome nearby. AE, DC, MC, V.

Azeitão (Setúbal), south of Lisbon. *Estalagem Quinta das Torres* (M), tel. 2080001. 10 rooms with bath. Former private residence with charming old-world atmosphere and set in real country, ideal for walkers. Good food; in summer, dine in the garden by the pool, or indoors by candlelight. Two independent cottages in grounds.
Restaurant. *São Lourenço* (M), tel. 2080164. Good café-restaurant at entrance to village. MC.

Bacalhoa. Superb 16th-century country house. 5 double, 2 single rooms with bath. Full staff. Pool. Minimum booking one week for up to 8 people. Apply, Thomas Scoville, 3637 Veazey St. N.W., Washington DC, 20008.

Bucelas. Home of the wine drunk by Wellington's officers.
Restaurants. *Barrete Saloio* (M), (tel. 9854004). Good home cooking. Closed Tues. *Casarão* (M), (tel. 9854511). Closed Mon.

Cacilhas (Setúbal). **Restaurants.** Several restaurants on river wall, with price lists displayed outside. Get a table by the window and see the lights of Lisbon come up over the Tagus as you eat, or watch the porpoises playing, in rough weather.

Carcavelos (Lisbon). *Praia Mar* (E), tel. 2473131. 158 rooms with bath. Modern hotel with sea view and pool, disco, shops; almost on the huge sandy beach. AE, DC, MC, V. *Albergaria Narciso* (M), tel. 2470157. 17 rooms with bath. Breakfast only; actually on the beach.
Restaurants. There are several beach restaurants.

Cascais (Lisbon), a short train ride from Lisbon. *Albatroz* (L), Rua Frederico Arouca 100 (tel. 282921). 40 rooms with bath. On low rocks above the sea, an attractive old house, now extended and modernized, but retaining its character. Charming bedrooms, dining room with picture windows looking on to the sea, terrace bar, pool, garage. Especially good for summer. AE, DC, MC, V. *Estoril-Sol* (L), on the Estrada Marginal (tel. 282831). 310 rooms with bath and balcony. Restaurant and bar on 9th floor with panoramic view; warm seawater pool, sauna, Health Club Soleil, disco, shops, garage. AE, DC, MC, V.

Cidadela (E), Ave. 25 de Abril (tel. 282921). 115 rooms with bath, plus 15 self-contained apartments overlooking garden and swimming pool, shops, garage, restaurant. Pleasant but noisy. AE, DC, MC, V. *Nossa Senhora das Preces* (E), Rua Visconde de Gandarinha 43 (tel. 280376). 15 rooms with bath. Secluded country house in wooded outskirts; pool, tennis; restaurant with good local cooking. AE, DC, MC, V.

Baia (M), Ave. Marginal (tel. 281033). 85 rooms with bath. Noisy, but lovely view over Fishermen's Beach. Handy restaurant terrace. AE, DC, MC, V. *Equador* (M), Alto da Pampilheira (tel. 2840524). 117 service apartments with bath and kitchenette. Pool, sauna, supermarket, etc. Very good value; not in center. AE, DC, MC. *Estalagem da Guia* (M), Estrada do Guincho (tel. 289239). 29 rooms with bath. Pool. AE, DC, MC, V. *Nau* (M), Rua Dra. Iracy Doyle 2 (tel. 282861). 54 rooms with bath. AE, DC, MC, V. *Valbom* (M), Ave. Valbom 14 (tel. 2865801). 40 rooms with bath. Simple and a bit basic; breakfast only; garage. In heart of town. AE, DC, MC, V.

Restaurants. *Adega do Morgado* (E), Ave. Marechal Carmona 1 (tel. 2867198). Country decor; parking. Closed Mon. in winter. AE, DC, MC. *Baluarte* (E), Ave. D. Carlos 1 (tel. 2865471). Picture windows overlooking the bay. Always open. AE, DC, MC. *Batel* (E), Travessa das Flores (tel. 280215). Excellent seafood, prompt service, quiet decor. Always open. AE, DC, MC. *Dom Leitão* (E), Ave. Vasco da Gama 36 (tel. 2865487). Roast sucking pig; a specialty—but a distinctly tourist-orientated place, with occasionally cavalier service. Closed Wed. AE, DC, MC. *João Padeiro* (E), Rua Visconde da Luz 12 (tel. 280232). Best sole on the coast, served in atmospheric decor (ancient leather-lined walls). Closed Sun. dinner. AE, DC, MC. *John Bull* (E), Praça Costa Pinto 31 (tel. 283319). On main street, with fireplace, easy chairs, prints on the wall—small and crowded restaurant with pub downstairs. Always open. AE, DC, MC. *Pescador* (E), Rua das Flores 10 (tel. 282054). Good seafood. Very folksy with low, cluttered ceiling. Always open. AE, DC, MC. *Pimentão* (E), Rua das Flores 16 (tel. 2840994). Comfortable, stylish place with good food and attractive downstairs bar. Always open. AE, DC, MC. *Reijos* (E), Rua Frederico Arouca 35 (tel. 280311). Small, American-owned and with real hamburgers. Always open. *Visconde da Luz* (E), Jardim Visconde da Luz (tel. 2866848). Good food and obliging staff; don't be put off by woodland exterior. Closed Tues. AE, DC, MC.

Alho Porro (M), Rua Alexandre Herculano 13 (tel. 2868660). Excellent fish and grills. Closed Mon. AE, DC, MC. *Burladero* (M), Praça dos Touros (tel. 2868751). Recommended. Closed Tues., also Wed. lunch. AE, DC, MC. *O Caixote* (M), Rua Carlos Ribeiro 3 (tel. 2845001). Friendly place, Austrian-run. Happy hour from 6–7 in the evening. Special tourist menu. Very near station. *Frango Real* (M), Ave. 25 de Abril 17C (tel. 2868186). Specializes in chicken. Closed Wed. AE, DC, MC. *Gil Vicente* (M), Rua dos Novagantes 22 (tel. 282032). Excellent cooking. AE, DC, MC, V.

Casa do Largo (I). Very attractively designed bar close to the fort (just along from the Ceramica). Simple food, and pleasant clientele. *Duke of*

Wellington Bar (I), Rua Frederico Arouca 32 (tel. 280394). Busy bar, canned music, cheerful atmosphere and indifferent food. Always open. *Galego* (I), Ave. Valbom 1 (tel. 282586). Real country tasca. Always open. *Pigalo* (I), Travessa Frederico Arouca 12 (tel. 282802). Small, intimate, very good value; near station. Closed Wed. *Santini* (I), Ave. Valbom 28F (tel. 283709). For the best ices on the coast. Open summer only; closed Mon. *Victor* (I), Rua Visconde da Luz 43A (tel. 282344). Closed Mon. Very good value.

Nightlife. *Forte Dom Rodrigo,* Casa Santa Isabel, Estrada de Birre (tel. 2851373). The smartest place to hear fados. *Kopus Bar,* Largo das Grutas 3 (tel. 2845201). For fados. Open daily 9 P.M.–3 A.M. *Van Gogo,* Travessa Alfarrobeira 9 (tel. 283378). Dancing. Open daily 11 P.M.–4 A.M. AE, DC, MC.

Caxias. Restaurants. *Monaco* (E), Estrada Marginal (tel. 2432339). Picture windows on to sea; dancing, live music; parking. AE, DC, MC, V. *Trigal* (I), Mercado 7–8 (tel. 2433249). Good local food and wine.

Colares (Lisbon). *Estalagem do Conde* (E), Quinta do Conde (tel. 9291652). 11 rooms with bath. An interesting find: beautiful views, several orchard-set cottages. Pleasant but remote (car essential). DC, MC. *Miramonte* (I), Pinhal da Nazaré, Banzão (tel. 9291230). 72 rooms with bath. English-owned; good value; garden. On road to Praia das Maças.

Costa Da Caparica (Setúbal). Across the river from Lisbon and only a short drive by bus from Cacilhas, 34 km. (21 miles) of long sandy beach beloved by Lisboans, many of whom own small cottages along the beach. Much frequented by painters and writers. A small train takes you along the dunes if you don't want to walk. There are many small pensions. *Estalagem Colibri* (E), Ave. 1 de Maio (tel. 2900573). 25 rooms with bath. *Praia do Sol* (I), Rua dos Pescadores 12 (tel. 2900012). 54 rooms with bath. Breakfast only. AE, DC, MC.

Restaurants. Several small restaurants, mostly (I). *Carolina do Aires* (M), Ave. General Humberto Delgado (tel. 2900124). Parking. AE, DC, MC.

Estoril (Lisbon). A short electric train-ride from Lisbon. (See also Monte Estoril.) Casino. There are several pensions. *Palácio* (L), Casino Gardens (tel. 2680400). 200 rooms and suites with bath. Front rooms have nice view; park, heated pool, Health Club Soleil; good food. Considered the most elegant. AE, DC, MC, V.

Anka (E), Estrada Marginal (tel. 2681811). 89 rooms with bath. Magnificent view over bay; seascape from the top-floor terrace-restaurant is picturesque by day and bewitching by night. AE, DC, MC, V. *Estalagem Belvedere* (E), Rua Dr. António Martins 8 (tel. 2689163). 16 rooms with bath. Excellent food. AE, DC, MC. *Estalagem do Fundador* (E), Ave. D. Afonso Henriques 11 (tel. 2682221). 12 rooms. Jolly bar; mainly English-speaking guests. *Lennox Country Club* (E), Rua Eng. Alv. P. Sousa 5 (tel. 2680424). 32 rooms with bath. Very comfortable; a favorite with golfers, who can have all-in terms including golf and transport to the course. Small pool; good food. Garage. AE, DC, MC, V.

Apartementos Alvorada (M), tel. 2680070. 51 rooms with bath. Pleasant and good value; breakfast only; facing Casino. AE, DC, MC. *Casa da Rocheira*

(M), Ave. de Belgica 5 (tel. 2681094). 6 double rooms with bath. Country
House; pool; dinner available. *Estalagem Pica Pau* (M), Ave. D. Afonso
Henriques 48 (tel. 2680556). 48 rooms with bath. Night club. AE, DC, MC.
Lido (M), Rua Alentejo 12 (tel. 2684098). 62 rooms with bath. In quiet
street, not close to beach; pool; good food and good value. AE, DC, MC, V.
Paris (M), Estrada Marginal (tel. 2680018). 78 rooms with bath. Pool,
disco. Rather noisy. AE, DC, MC, V.

Inglaterra (I), Rua do Porto (tel. 2684461). 49 rooms with bath. Good
family hotel, with pool. Breakfast only.

Restaurants. *Casino* (E), (tel. 2680176). Dinner with floor show; dancing. You will need your passport to get into the gaming rooms. AE, DC,
MC, V. *Choupana* (E), Estrada Marginal (tel. 2683099). Right on the sea on
the approach to Estoril. The smartest place along the coast, and the food
is rightly famous: the bill is high, but you get what you want plus the view.
Band, dancing, parking. Always open. AE, DC, MC, V. *Four Seasons* (E), in
Hotel Palácio, Casino Gardens (tel. 2680400). Parking. Closed for lunch
out of season. AE, DC, MC, V. *Frolic* (E), Ave. Clothilde (tel. 2681219). Under
the Palácio, you dine well in gilded splendor; spacious dance floor; enjoyable bar. Always open. AE, DC, MC, V.

Deck Bar (M), Arcadas do Parque (tel. 2680366). Under the arcades
near the Tourist Bureau. Noisy, never a dull moment. Closed Mon. *Garrett*
(M), Ave. Nice (tel. 2680365). Tearoom just past the Post Office going
up Avenida Nice, serving lunches *à la carte,* on covered terrace or inside.
Quiet and restful. Closed Tues. *Golf Club* (M), Ave. da Republica (tel.
2680176). Restaurant open to public. Lunch only. DC, MC. *Pickwick Club*
(M), Ave. Biarritz 3G (tel. 2686726). AE, DC, MC. *Tamariz* (M), tel.
2683512. Snackbar on the beach. Open in summer only. AE, DC, MC.

Curry House (I), Ave. Marginal 60 (tel. 2680393). Delicious Goan food.
Also has 14 good rooms with breakfast. Parking.

Guincho (Lisbon). A beautiful stretch of sandy beach (beware the
heavy undertow) beyond Cascais. A car is essential if you stay, although
there are buses in and out of Cascais. For a quiet sun-and-sea rest with
really good food and comfortable rooms you can hardly do better than
to take en pension terms at one of the hotels listed below.

Estalagem do Forte Muchaxo (L), tel. 2850221. 24 rooms with bath. Sea-
water pool. Started life as a simple hut where fishermen could buy drinks
and coffee; the hut remains but the estalagem is an attractive building on
the beach with splendid views from the rooms—price depends on the view!
If you don't come for a room, certainly come for the food, especially the
seafood. AE, DC, MC, V. *Hotel do Guincho* (L), tel. 2850491. 36 rooms with
bath. One of the most attractive hotels in Portugal—an old fort converted
with superb craftsmanship; on the beach. A romantic setting, whether for
a stay, dinner or just for drinks. Topnotch restaurant with excellent service. Guests can use the pool at the *Estoril-Sol* hotel, Cascais. Check availability, as seems to be closed often without warning. AE, DC, MC, V. *Quinta
da Marinha* (L), tel. 289881. 40 self-service villas. Restaurant, pool, 18-
hole golf course, tennis, riding.

Estalagem Mar do Guincho (E), tel. 2850251. 13 rooms with bath. Also
known by its original restaurant name of *Mestre Zé;* pleasant rooms with
stunning view. Shellfish a specialty, but expensive; other seafoods more
moderate. AE, DC, MC.

Restaurants. As might be expected, the restaurants in the area are particularly good for seafood. To find a restaurant overlooking the entire coast, drive along the Cascais–Guincho road, look for the sign to Oitavos, and there drive up the short steep road to the old semaphore station. *Abano* (E), tel. 2850221. On the cliffs above an enchanting tiny beach at Praia do Abano, reached over a bumpy road signposted on the left about 200 meters along the road from Guincho towards Malveira da Serra. Closed Tues. AE, DC, MC. *Faroleiro* (E), tel. 2850225. The first restaurant to be opened in the Guincho, located on the far side of the road out of sight of the sea, but the food is very good and, of course, lobster is always available, at a price, prepared in several ways. Always open. AE, DC, MC. *Furnas Lagosteiras* (E), Estrada do Guincho (tel. 289243). One of several right on the sea. There are a few tables out in the sun, and on windy days spray floats towards you like bubbles, or else you sit behind the large picture windows. If you prefer to choose your own lobster, you climb down a steep ladder to their wave-fed grotto. Always open. AE, DC, MC.

Loures (Lisbon). **Restaurant.** *Horta* (M), Rua dos Bombeiros Voluntarios 2 (tel. 9833804). 6 km. (4 miles) north of Lisbon, specializing in roast kid, also duck; *tipico* ambience. Delightful. Kitchen in view. Closed Wed.

Monte Estoril (Lisbon). Between Estoril proper and Cascais; as its name implies, it's hilly. *Estoril Eden* (E), Ave. Saboia (tel. 2670573). 162 studio apartments. On sea above Estrada Marginal. 2 restaurants, 2 heated pools, health club, garage. AE, DC, MC, V. *Aparthotel Touring Estoril* (M), Rua do Viveiro (tel. 2683385). A complex of buildings with a large number of fully-furnished independent and service apartments. Between Monte Estoril and Estoril, 15 minutes' walk from the beach. Pool, bar, good restaurant. AE, DC, MC. *Atlantico* (M), Estrada Marginal (tel. 2680270). 175 rooms with bath. Huge pool; the electric train runs between hotel and sea. AE, DC, MC, V. *Grande* (M), Ave. Saboia (tel. 2684609). 72 rooms with bath and balcony. A good oldtimer with restaurant, bar, and heated pool. Good value. AE, DC, MC, V. *Londres* (M), Ave. Fausto Figueiredo 17 (tel. 2684245). 68 rooms with bath. Pool. AE, DC, MC, V. *Zenith* (M), Rua Belmonte (tel. 2680202). 48 rooms with bath and balcony. Glorious view from top floor; pleasant bar, rather shallow pool, friendly. AE, DC, MC.

Restaurants. *English Bar* (E), Estrada Marginal (tel. 2680413). On the Estoril–Cascais road; serves first-class food in a relaxed atmosphere. Parking. Closed Sun. AE, DC, MC. *A Maré* (E), next to Hotel Atlantico, Estrada Marginal (tel. 2685570). Good food; open every day. AE, DC, MC, V. *Casa Pizza* (M), Rua do Viveiro. Good Italian food. *Ferra Mulinhas* (M), Rua do Viveiro 5 (tel. 2680005). Closed Tues. AE, DC, MC, V. *Maggie's Coffee Lounge* (M), Ave. São Pedro 1. Tea, coffee, snacks. Friendly. Closed Mon. *Ray's Bar* (M), Ave. de Saboia 25 (tel. 2680106). No food. Always open from 6 P.M. *Cozinha do Mar* (I), Ave. São Pedro 9 (tel. 2689317). Friendly; two can share a dish. Closed Tues. DC, MC, V. *O Sinaleiro* (I), Ave. de Saboia 35 (tel. 2685439). Excellent food, very reasonable; try their chicken. Closed Mon.

Oeiras (Lisbon). Superb beach. *Catalezete Youth Hostel.*
Restaurant. *Adega Tipica* (I), Rua Marques de Pombal 18–22. Good country food; own wine. Recommended. Closed Sept.

Palmela (Setúbal). *Pousada do Castelo de Palmela* (L), tel. 2351226. 29 rooms with bath. One of Portugal's best, in splendid Templars' castle on high hill at end of the Arrábida range, overlooking Setúbal and River Sado to the south, Lisbon and the Tagus to the north. Pool. Don't leave anything in your car. AE, DC, MC, V.

Portinho D'Arrábida (Setúbal). *Residência Santa Maria da Arrábida* (M), tel. 065 2080527. 33 rooms with bath. Breakfast only. Very safe, sandy beach. Open June through Sept.
Restaurants. *Beira Mar* (I–M) and *Galeão* (I–M). Both on superb beach.

Praia Grande (Lisbon). *Hotel da Piscina* (M), tel. 2992145. 23 rooms with bath. Over the Olympic swimming pool. *Hotel das Arribas* (I), (tel. 9292145). 20 rooms with bath. AE, DC, MC, V.

Queluz (Lisbon). **Restaurants.** *Cozinha Velha* (L), Palácio Nacional (tel. 950740). One of the best restaurants in the Lisbon region. The original kitchen of the Queluz Palace, it has retained its old fittings, including the spits for roasting oxen whole. Worth the expense. AE, DC, MC, V. *Quadriga* (I), Ave. Elias Garcia 114 (tel. 951611). Well-cooked, simple food. Closed Thurs.

Rio De Mouro (Lisbon). *Quinta da Fonte Nova* (E), Serradas (tel. 9260021). 5 double rooms with bath, pool, riding, tennis, dinner by request. A Country House.

Santo Amaro De Oeiras (Lisbon). **Restaurant.** *Saisa* (M), tel. 2430634. Right on the beach. Real Spanish *paella* and *sangria* to quench your hunger and thirst. Closed Mon. AE, DC, MC.

São Pedro De Sintra (Lisbon), about 1 km. from Sintra. **Restaurants.** *Galeria Real* (E), tel. 9231661. Very popular for wedding receptions; surrounded by antique shops. Closed Tues. AE, DC, MC. *O Cantinho* (M), Largo da Feira (tel. 9230267). French cooking, exceptional house wine. Parking. Closed Mon. and dinner Thurs. AE, DC, MC. *Solar São Pedro* (M), Largo da Feira 12 (tel. 9231860). Very good cooking and wine. Parking. Closed Wed. Avoid 2nd and 4th Sundays, which are Fair Days, as there is no parking available. AE, DC, MC.

Sesimbra (Setúbal). *Hotel do Mar* (E), tel. 2233326. 120 rooms with bath and balcony. Sea view, pool, disco, intriguing architecture. Fills up, so make sure your booking is firm. AE, DC, MC. *Espadarte* (I), tel. 2233189. 80 rooms with bath. On the esplanade, rather noisy. Good food. DC, MC.
Restaurants. *Ribamar* (M), Largo do Fortaleza (tel. 2233107). Always open. AE, DC, MC. *Gary's Bar* (I–M). On the waterfront; fun, mostly for drinks but also for coffee and snacks.

Setúbal (provincial capital). *Pousada de São Filipe* (L), tel. 065 23844. 15 rooms with bath. In ancient castle out of town, with splendid view over River Sado. Don't leave anything in your car. AE, DC, MC, V. *Esperança* (M), Ave. Luisa Todi 220 (tel. 065 25151). 76 rooms with bath. AE, DC, MC. *Pensão Bocage* (M), Rua São Cristovão 14 (tel. 065 21809). 20 rooms with bath.

14 more in annex. Breakfast only. *Pensão Mar e Sol* (M), Ave. Luisa Todi 606 (tel. 065 33016). 31 rooms with bath. Breakfast only.

Restaurants. There are several good *tascas* or small (I) restaurants near the ferry station for Troia, as well as reasonable eating houses all over town. *A Roda* (E), Travessa Postijo do Cais 7 (tel. 065 29264). Elegant. Closed Mon. AE, DC, MC. *Bocage* (M), Rua Marquês do Faial 5 (tel. 065 22513). Good Portuguese food: try muscatel brandy and the sweet, fortified muscatel wine, both from the region. Closed Mon. dinner and Tues. AE, DC, MC. *Cactus* (M), Rua Vasco da Gama 83 (tel. 065 34687). AE, DC, MC. *O Tunel* (M), Praça Bocage 62 (tel. 065 22732). A brash restaurant, excellent for a reasonable meal. *O Retiro* (I). A shack under the trees, for grilled sardines and barbecued chicken *al fresco. Rio Azul* (I), Rua Guilherme Fernandes 44 (tel. 065 22828). Local spot with good steaks and seafood; good value, quite near pousada. Closed Wed. AE.

Sintra (Lisbon). *Palácio de Seteais* (L), tel. 9233200. 18 rooms with bath. Superb 18th-century palace with glorious view; delicious food. A mile out of Sintra, and ideal for lunch when visiting the Sintra area. Set meal with plenty of choice. AE, DC, MC, V. *Quinta da Capela* (E), Monserrate (tel. 9290170). 11 rooms with bath. Lovely country house in beautiful setting. Small pool, gym, sauna. No restaurant, but several in nearby Colares. Closed Dec. to Feb. MC. *Quinta de São Thiago* (E), Monserrate (tel. 9232923). All rooms with bath. English owners take guests into their lovely 16th-century house. Pool. Meals. *Tivoli Sintra* (E), Praça da Republica (tel. 9233505). 75 rooms with bath; 5 suites. Good food and very reasonable winter terms. AE, DC, MC, V. *Central* (M), Praça da Republica 35 (tel. 9230963). 11 rooms with bath. In main square overlooking palace; large terrace; comfortable. *Pensão Sintra* (M), Travessa dos Avelares (tel. 9230738). 10 rooms with bath. *Pensão Nova Sintra* (I), Largo Afonso de Albuquerque 25 (tel. 9230220). 13 rooms. In pleasant villa. Up flight of steps to lovely terrace. Very reasonable, friendly.

Restaurants. There are several small restaurants. *Apeadeira* (I), Ave. Miguel Bombarda 3. Good food and wine. Closed Thurs. *Tulhas Bar* (I), Rua Gil Vicente 4. With good food and house wine. Closed Wed. AE, DC.

Troia (Setúbal). 12 minutes by car ferry from Setúbal. *Aparthotel Rosa Mar* (E), tel. 06544151. 138 independent apartments. Kindergarten, baby-sitting service; open-air theater; cafeteria and reasonably priced restaurants. Long, attractive beaches; golf course designed by Robert Trent Jones. Part of the huge, super-modern Torralta Complex. AE, DC, MC. *Apartamentos Torralta* (M), tel. 06544221. 377 apartments. Pool. Also part of the Torralta Complex, with above facilities. AE, DC, MC.

CAMPING. There are campsites at the following places: Cascais (Guincho/Orbitur); Costa da Caparica (6 different sites); Lagoa de Albufeira (2 sites); Lisbon (Monsanto); Oeiras; Palmela; Praia Grande (Colares); Sesimbra (3 sites); Setúbal (1 site); Sintra (Capuchos); Troia (Torralta); Vila Fresca de Azeitão.

POLLUTION REPORT. Unfortunately this area has a serious pollution problem because its sewage system is inadequate. The water off nine of the beaches between Lisbon, Estoril and Cascais has levels of pollution far above those permitted by the E.E.C. The problem is a long-standing one brought about by the development of the area, and there have been outbreaks of gastric disorders and skin infections for many years. At long last, a sewage treatment plant is to be built in Cascais, and the treated water will be carried far out to sea in an underwater pipe. Meanwhile, we strongly advise you not to use any beach in the area unless it has been officially declared safe.

PLACES OF INTEREST. Museums are usually open daily, except Mondays and public holidays, 10–5, but double check the times on the spot. Some close for lunch. Entrance fees are between 150$00 and 300$00.

Almada. Municipal Museum, Convento do Capuchos. Arabic archeology and tiles, 18th-century tiled panel depicting St. Francis of Assisi, paintings.

Alverca. Museu do Ar (Museum of Aviation). Full-size and scale model planes, helicopters and gliders.

Azeitão. Bacalhoa, Vila Fresca de Azeitão. Gardens open Mon. to Sat. 1–5; closed Sun. and Bank Holidays. Tip 200$00. Ring at gate along narrow entry overhung with bushes, opposite bus station.

Caparica. Municipal Museum, Convento de Madre de Deus (Convent of the Mother of God). 15th- and 16th-century ceramics, 17th- and 19th-century glass and local craftsmanship displayed in convent built in the 16th century by Franciscan monks and rebuilt in the 18th century.

Cascais. Museum and Library Condes dos Castro Guimarães, Furniture, paintings and books. Ethnographic and Cultural Section with agricultural utensils, regional costumes, earthenware, tiles, coins, and archeological remains. Library has English section.
Boca do Inferno. Deep chasm in the rocks with a whirlpool in rough weather.

Moita. Igreja da Nossa Senhora da Boa Viagem (Church of Our Lady of the Safe Journey). Rebuilt at the end of the 17th century, and containing several fine paintings on wood, gilded altars and 18th-century tiles.

Monserrate. Eccentric buildings and famous gardens. Between Sintra and Colares. Open daily 10–6.

Montijo. Igreja do Espirito Santo (Church of the Holy Spirit). 14th-century church with two beautiful classic portals of the early 17th century, 17th-century tiles, and gilded altars.
Igreja da Nossa Senhora da Atalaia. Pilgrimage church with 18th-century tiles; ex-votos. Romaria late June.

Odrinhas. Archeological Museum. Roman and Early Christian remains in the open air. Closed for lunch 12–2. Adm. free.

Palmela. Templar's Castle. Crowning high hill, partly a pousada.

Porto Salvo, Paço d'Arcos. Small archeological collections from Roman ruins nearby.

Queluz. Royal Palace. Mid-18th century palace with decorative art and furniture, *Arraiolos* carpets, Chinoiserie glazed tiles, and royal portraits. Lovely gardens. Closed Tues.

Rinchoa. Museu Leal da Camara (Leal da Camara Museum). Paintings and drawings of regional farmers, as well as paintings of Paris, by Leal da Camara.

Santa Susana, near Odrinhas. Small museum of pottery figures of country folk by artisan, Snr. Eduardo Azenha, who also sells his work.

São Domingos De Benfica. Palácio de Fronteira. Lovely formal gardens and notable private house. Open Sat. 1–5, Mon. 10–12 and 2:30–5. First Sun. of the month, 2:30–5. Entrance to gardens only, 300$00. Gardens and house 1,000$00. Bus No. 46.

Seixal. Church. With lovely 17th-century panels and *azulejos*.
Ecomuseu Municipal. See the tidal water mill now working again.

Sesimbra. Municipal Museum. Archeology, numismatics, ethnographics and sacred art.

Setúbal. Archeology and Ethnography Museum. With section devoted to fishing traditions of the region and miniatures of ships.
Convento de Jesus. Contains examples of 15th-, 16th- and 17th-century architecture, paintings and examples of the goldsmith's art, as well as 14th-century documents and a library of 12,000 volumes including 16th-century first editions and valuable collection of autographs.
Oceanography and Fishing Museum. A valuable collection of marine species.

Sintra. Library and Historical Archives, Palace of Valenças. Collection of Romantic engravings of the 19th century, general literature and manuscripts.
Museum Anjos Teixeira. Statues, bronzes and other sculpture.
Museum Ferreira de Castro. Collection of this well-known Portuguese author's writings and his library.
Palácio Nacional (National Palace). In the town center, built on the site of a Moorish palace; with architectural features from the Arab to the Edwardian eras; lovely painted ceilings and beautiful furniture. Closed Wed.
Palácio da Pena (Palace of Pena). Unique example of 19th-century Portuguese Romantic architecture, with good decorative art, especially porcelain and furniture. Superb park with rare trees and shrubs. Closed Mon.
Regional Museum. Archeological and ethnographical exhibits.

ESTORIL CASINO. The Estoril Casino (tel. 2684521) is designed round a central patio, has deep upholstered sofas and chairs, not unlike a comfortable modern hotel lounge. There is also a red-and-gold nightclub with floorshows, a restaurant, comfortable cinema with afternoon and evening films, and in August a concert and ballet season. There are also frequent exhibitions by modern artists.

In the gambling rooms (note: take your passport) you can play roulette, boule, baccarat and craps. There is a special salon for slot machines, and one for bingo. Not smart; ample parking. Open 3 P.M.–3 A.M. AE, DC, MC.

SPECIAL EVENTS. The following are some of the many events taking place in this area. Check dates with Tourist Offices. **February.** During the 3 days of carnival before Ash Wednesday, gala balls are held nightly at the Estoril Casino. **May.** At Penha Longa, between Estoril and Sintra, a Country Fair is held on the Monday after Pentecost; music and dancing go on into the night. **June.** The annual fair of São Pedro takes place on June 29 at São Pedro de Sintra (where large fairs are also held on the 2nd and 4th Sundays of each month).

July. The *Feira do Artesanato* is held at Estoril (continuing into August)—an excellent occasion to enjoy regional specialties like the naïve colorful pottery from Portugal's northern provinces. Taste regional fare and wines at the many restaurants or just sample country bread hot from an old-fashioned kiln. Music and ballet festival in Casino. The *Feira de Sant'Iago* at Setúbal, end of month, includes various exhibitions of the region's agro-industrial activities, a funfair, folklore dancing and other attractions.

August. At Alcochete, in the 2nd week of Aug. are the festivals of the *Barrete Verde* (green cap) and the *Salinas,* with bullfights and outdoor celebrations. (Take the ferry to Montijo, then the bus.) On Aug. 17 at Janas (about 15 minutes' drive from Sintra) the day of the patron saint, São Mamede, is celebrated: animals are blessed after their three tours round the unique, pre-Roman circular chapel; pottery and fairings are laid out on the grass.

September. The *Festa das Vindimas* (Feast of the Grape Harvest) takes place at Palmela, with symbolic treading of the grapes and the blessing of the must, dancing, folklore, fireworks, winetasting and, on the last night, the castle of Palmela is burnt in effigy; end of month.

SHOPPING. The area around Lisbon can provide a wide range of shopping opportunities, from the smart boutiques of Cascais to the simple crafts deep in the heart of the countryside. **Crafts.** Estoril offers good quality merchandise: for reasonably priced country goods and embroideries, try *Regionalia,* 27 Arcadas do Parque; for filigree jewelry, *M. Fernandes,* Hotel Palácio. In Cascais, the *Cestaria de Cascais,* Rua Visconde da Luz 5, is devoted to baskets and basket work of all kinds—a fascinating display; *Bagatelle,* Ave. 25 de Abril, is an excellent little shop for pretty gifts in porcelain and silver plate.

On the road between Sintra and Mafra, the visitor passes through the town of Pero Pinheiro. On both sides of the road large slabs of marble are stacked. At *Pardal Monteiro Ltd.,* visitors are welcome to watch the fascinating work of cutting and polishing. Marble objects, such as ashtrays, bought or ordered at the source are amazingly inexpensive.

Fashion. In Cascais, hosts of small boutiques have sprung up, particularly in the smart pedestrian Rua Frederico Arouca. Look out for *Gloria's* at No. 55 for good clothes, *Perfumaria Katinka* at No. 37 for scents, face creams, etc., and *Peacock,* opposite, for belts and handbags. Near the market, at Ave. 25 de Abril 10A, is *Tara,* a teenager's heaven for ready-made dresses and slacks.

Flowers. Flowers for gifts to others or for yourself can be bought from the shop in the western Arcade in Estoril, or on the Estrada Marginal 2 in Cascais. The most reasonable flower shop is in the Pão de Açucar supermarket on the Estrada Marginal at the entrance to Cascais. But naturally, flowers are cheaper in the Cascais market, open till 2 every afternoon except Sundays.

Food. The best days to visit Cascais market are Wednesday and Saturday, when the country people come in and mounds of newly gathered fruit and vegetables are piled on the ground. Bargaining is expected, the final price being often three quarters of that originally asked.

Among the many supermarkets, perhaps the best is *Espaçial,* Ave. Biarritz 12, Estoril. Prices are lowest at the huge *Pão de Açucar,* Estrada Marginal 6, Cascais, which also has 2 cinemas and a number of smart shops on the 1st floor.

SPORTS. The area is full of opportunities for the sports enthusiast. There are many specialist clubs and some have facilities for several sports. The *Quinta da Marinha* club (tel. 289881), past Cascais on the Guincho road, has a new 18-hole golf course designed by Robert Trent Jones, as well as two pools, tennis, equestrian center, and restaurant. On the same road, available to visitors as well as members, is the *Clube de Campo D. Carlos I* (tel. 2852362), a pine-covered property offering a very pleasant heated swimming pool, sauna, tennis courts, and riding.

Golf. *Lisbon Sports Club,* Belas (tel. 960077); *Quinta da Marinha* (see above); *Clube de Golfe do Estoril* (tel. 2680176), which rents all equipment and has a restaurant and pool (turn off at signpost on Ave. Sintra); a new nine-hole course at Linhó (tel. 9232461), between Estoril and Sintra; *Troia Golf Club,* Troia (tel. 065 44151), 18-hole course in splendid country on River Sado.

Riding. *Centro Hipico de Cascais,* Quinta da Guia (tel. 2843563). *Centro Hipico da Costa do Estoril,* Charneca, Cascais (tel. 2852064). *Centro Hipico da Quinta da Marinha,* Cascais (tel. 289282). *Centro Hipico de Campo D. Carlos I,* Quinta da Marinha, Cascais (tel. 2851403). *Escola de Equitacão da Areia,* Cascais (tel. 289284). *Pony Club,* Quinta da Bicuda, Torre, Cascais (tel. 2843058).

Tennis. *Lisbon Sports Club,* Belas (tel. 960077); *Clube de Campo D. Carlos* (see above); *Grupo Desportivo de Pescadores,* Costa da Caparica (tel. 2904110); *Clu-be de Ténis do Jamor,* Estadio Nacional, Cruz Quebrada (tel. 2112147); *Hotel de Turismo de Ericeira,* Ericeira (tel. 061 63545); *Clube de Ténis do Estoril,* Ave. Amaral, Estoril (tel. 2681675); *Grande Hotel,* Estoril (tel. 2684609); *Hotel Sintra Estoril,* on road to Sintra (tel. 2690721); *Clube Montijense de Desportos,* Montijo; *Clube Escola de Ténis de Oeiras,* Oeiras (tel. 2436699); *Clube de Ténis de Setúbal,* Setúbal (tel. 065 27038); Parque das Merendas, Sintra (tel. 9232800); *Apartamentos Turisticos Torralta,* Troia (tel. 065 44151).

Sailing. *Clube Naval Barreirense,* Barreiro (tel. 2073779); *Club Naval de Cascais,* Cascais (tel. 280125); *Associação Naval de Lisboa,* Lisbon (tel. 600488); *Clube Naval de Lisboa,* Lisbon (tel. 369354); *Clube Naval de Se-*

simbra, Sesimbra (tel. 2233451); *Clube Naval Setubalense,* Setúbal (tel. 065 22756).

Windsurfing. *Escola de Carcavelos de Windsurfing,* Carcavelos (tel. 2470113); *Clube Naval de Cascais,* Cascais (tel. 280125); *Windsurfing Center Cascais,* Cascais (tel. 2841736); *International Windsurfing School,* Estoril (tel. 2681665); Praia de Santa Cruz, tel. 061 23094.

TOURS AND EXCURSIONS. *Tip Tours,* Avc. Costa Pinto 91A, Cascais (tel. 283821), have bus excursions to Lisbon, Fatima, Alcobaça, Batalha, and other places, picking up passengers at hotels. They also hire out bicycles and arrange deep-sea fishing expeditions.

USEFUL ADDRESSES. Travel Agents. *American Express,* Star Travel Service, Ave. de Nice 4, Estoril (tel. 2680839 and 2681945); *Wagons Lits/Cooks,* Aracadas do Parque, Estoril (tel. 2680225); *Agencia Abreu,* Galerias Estoril-Sol Cascais (tel. 280861).

Car Hire. *Avis,* Tamariz, Estoril (tel. 2685728); *Rent-a-Car Guérin,* Cruzeiro, Estoril (tel. 2680066).

Villa Hire. *Cicerone,* Ave. Bombeiros Voluntarios 6, Estoril (tel. 2680389).

Bank. Lloyds Bank plc., Ave. de São Pedro 1, Monte Estoril, Estoril (tel. 2670536).

Club. *American Women of Lisbon Club,* Ave. de Sintra 3, Cascais (tel. 280252). Friendly group including other nationalities; numerous activities, library, meals. Also has a few rooms with bath.

Churches. St. Paul's Anglican Church, Ave. Bombeiros Voluntarios 1C, Estoril (tel. 2683570); Corpo Santo Parish Center (R.C.), Rua do Murtal 368, São Pedro do Estoril (tel. 2681676); Mass is also said on Sun. midday in St. Sebastian's Chapel, Parque de Castro Guimarães, Cascais.

THE ALGARVE

The Algarve is only 300 km. (200 miles) due south of Lisbon and yet it
might be in a different country. A mere 40 km. (20 miles) deep, it is bounded on the south by the Atlantic flowing towards Gibraltar and the southern coast of Spain, and on the north by high hills which stretch from the
ocean to the River Guadiana, its eastern boundary with Spain. Owing to
this south-facing aspect and the protection of the hills the Algarve is much
warmer than the rest of the country: the vegetation is far more luxuriant
and the bathing is superb.

Here the advantages of the civilized life can be enjoyed amid great natural beauty. There is not only sun and perfect bathing but excellent golf,
water sports of all kinds, smart shops and even casinos (at Alvor, Vilamoura and Monte Gordo). Rare wild flowers grow and many migratory
birds pass through, making the province a paradise for bird watchers. Although many of the beaches have been overbuilt, most of the developments
in the Algarve are of architectural interest, and there are still lovely
stretches of lonely sand to be discovered.

For some years, indeed a couple of decades or so, the Algarve has been
the dream destination for people from northern Europe looking for property in the sun to retire to—especially the British. Many Algarve towns
now have a solid suburban fringe that might have been transported from
a British town—except for the architecture and the swimming pools. The
latest lure to the unwary investor is that of time-sharing developments.
But along with the undoubted attractions of the area has come a whole
cadre of dubious businessmen, who have managed to fleece unwary dream-
ers unmercifully. We give a few tips in the *Practical Information* at the
end of this chapter on the current situation.

For centuries the province was almost completely secluded. Kings of Portugal were proclaimed Kings of Portugal *and* the Algarves. It was the last of the provinces to be wrested from the Moors, and their 500 years of occupation have left their beneficent mark to the present day. They irrigated the land by digging innumerable wells, planted orange groves and fig trees and also perfected intricate art forms in pottery and weaving, and even in chimney design (putting up delicately pierced chimneys above blank walls). Villages stand out white amid the orchards, bearing names like Odeceixe, Ameixial, or Alvor.

Other parts of Portugal bear testimony to the Reconquest: Romanesque chapels in Trás-os-Montes and Minho, Gothic cathedrals in Estremadura, and, on the Atlantic side, Manueline monuments springing full-blown from the ardent fervor of the Discoveries. Not so the Algarve, which can lay claim only to almost supernatural sea-grottoes hewn out by fierce waters, to Moslem-domed village churches with weathered whitewashed walls and Moorish thick-walled houses with terracotta tile roofs.

A Garden by the Sea

The hilly barriers of Monchique and Caldeirão are just a brushcovered area barely 1,000 meters (3,000 ft.) high; rising from the vast wheatlands south of the Tagus, they form a wall that seals off the Algarve from the north, so that the entire province faces the sea, which was the source of its early prosperity and prestige as well as of the dangers that threatened it. The Phoenicians set up enclaves in the Bay of Lagos and the Faro marshes that became important trading posts for ivory and amber. Centuries after the Christian cross had replaced the Moslem crescent in Tavira and in Silves (the "Xelb" of the Moors), barbarian galleys continued to put in at inlets along the chrome cliffs and to ply their trade with fishermen from Olhão and Albufeira. The cream of the Genoese and Majorcan navigators pitted their skill against the knowledge of Henry the Navigator's cohort of armigers, who were the first to launch the caravelles from Belixe (Beliche). In the taverns, spies from Venice and Alexandria mingled with men from the sardine and tuna fishing fleets. Out at sea, French, Dutch, British, and Spanish ships tangled with one another in naval battles which reached their climax in the last century in civil war between the liberal and absolutist forces.

Although its seamen rank among Portugal's finest, the Algarve's true vocation is with the land. The highway that takes you from Sagres to Vila Real de Santo António—in the process threading through the main Algarve towns—was originally traced out for market gardeners' produce wagons, passing between orange groves and farmlands. The road touches in at the estuaries of the coastal streams, glances off at fishing ports, and, to reach the ocean, zigzags in and out amid bamboo canes and gnarled fig trees. Behind the high protecting cliffs and fig plantations, the coastal region manages to hold firm in its innermost recesses.

A Realm of Daylight

From January through December, sun-starved tourists tanning themselves on hotel terraces are no longer a sight to surprise the locals, who calmly continue to insulate themselves against the sun's rays by wearing protective head-coverings and retreating behind their Moorish walls and sheltering screens. When they venture forth in their carts, they drive under the shade of a parasol. Fishermen siesta in the shade of their boats. Nothing shakes the inveterate—and well-founded—local belief in the demonic power of the sun.

In midsummer, the coast seems to glow with amber cliffs, varicolored rocks, and yellow sand bordering the indigo sea. If we are to believe the calendar, winter officially begins on December 22. Yet in the Algarve it is a bare five weeks until the spring first appears. By February, blossoming bean fields look as if swarms of delicate butterflies were hovering over them. Flowering narcissus spring up on the banks of the streams. In the orange groves the fruit glows like lamps and the flowers scent the air with their pungent sweetness. And most breath-taking of all is the spectacle of the almond blossoms.

Legend tells that, once upon a time, a handsome and ardent Moorish chief wooed and won a lovely princess from the northern countries, and brought her here to live. Despite the love and gifts that he lavished upon her, the lady was obviously pining away. When at length she shyly confessed to homesickness for the snows of her native land, the Moor's love found a way; he ordered his entire domain to be planted as far as the eye could see with almond trees that bloom during February, carpeting the slopes with snowy blossoms.

The same miracle recurs annually. No matter how well you are prepared in your mind for it, you are invariably thrilled and delighted. No sooner have your eyes discerned what you think is a single early-flowering branch than you suddenly discover in some sheltered dell whole trees that have burst forth literally overnight with shell-like petals.

Two months later, in April, the giant white cistus flowers in all its glory so that the land looks as if lightly powdered with snowflakes and in this month too the wild lavender covers the verges of every lane with swathes of deep purple.

Discovering the Algarve

There are several ways of reaching the Algarve (see *Practical Information* at the end of this chapter). By road, the *autostrada* from the Tagus Bridge to Setúbal gives you a choice of taking the car ferry to Tróia, the shortest route to Lagos and the western end of the province (but beware the queues in spring and summer), or you can follow the Sado river to Alcácer do Sal and Grandola. Here a superb new road south cuts through the Serra do Caldeirão to São Bartolomeu de Messines (you can lunch at the excellent restaurants en route at Canal Caveira, still in the Alentejo), from where roads go south to Albufeira, east to Loulé and Faro and west to Silves, Portimão and Lagos. Another but longer route goes from Grandola through Aljustrel and Castro Verde to São Brás de Alportel with a good *pousada*.

It is here—at São Brás adrift on the sea of almond-blossoms, at Loulé, and at Silves, the erstwhile paradise of Moorish poets—that you penetrate the very heart of the Algarve. Distant villages are seen as white patches, but as you draw near you will find unsuspected delights. First you will notice the intricately wrought patterns of the chimney tops; hand-fashioned ornamental embellishments grace the facades of the most modest dwellings. Your overall impression is that of a monumental piece of embroidery set off against a background of blue sky and green trees. Gaudily painted mule-drawn waggons, driven by peasants who stand as they guide the reins, career along the highway in the midst of modern traffic. The local inhabitants braid esparto grass and hammer copper articles for the artisans' fairs that are held at Loulé and Faro. The great variety of fruits are carefully packed for the market: citrus fruits, figs and almonds form the basis of wonderful candies, including marzipan mosaics and the tinfoil-wrapped *Dom Rodrigos.*

The city of Loulé has managed to preserve an Oriental flavor, its white houses topped by the typical chimneys. Remnants of the 12th-century walls are still visible and the castle is not on a hill but in the center of the town. The Gothic parish church is charming, and the ruined Convent of Graça has some interesting features; while a visit to Nossa Senhora da Piedade through the forested countryside is worth making.

Silves lies beneath a Moorish castle, carpetted with blue Jacaranda blossoms in May, whose cisterns continue to supply water to this day. The parapets give wide views over the countryside. The Gothic cathedral was built in the 13th century. On the way out of the town toward São Bartolomeu de Messines, notice the 16th-century Cross of Portugal. The colorful village of Alte should not be missed, nor the nearby caves of stalactites, especially Buraco dos Mouros.

A short road north from the main Silves–Messines road (N124) leads to the beautiful Arade dam which is the source of irrigation for this part of the Algarve, as the Bravura dam behind Lagos is for the western end.

A perfectly viable dirt road west from the Arade leads to a beautiful, wild, deserted part of the country, alive with birds and carpeted with flowers in the spring. There are water sports and fishing on both these lakes.

Lagoa on the east–west highway, N125, is still untouched by tourism; the center of the vine growing district, it gives its name to one of the best of the local wines. Estombar, just off the main road three km. (nearly two miles) to the west, is an attractive town. Sparkling white houses lead up the hill to a huge church with a Manueline portal.

Then, too, there are the mountains. Looming somberly under their uninviting scrubby cover in the Serra do Caldeirão—they are transformed into something verdant at Foia near Monchique. Majestic chestnut trees mingle in lush profusion side by side with mimosa trees. The scarlet and yellow berries of the arbutus produce a liqueur *Medronho,* that easily rivals in quality another of the Algarve's specialties, *brandymel.* Footpaths guide you up to observation points from which on a clear day you can contemplate half of southern Portugal.

Faro

Faro, the provincial capital of the Algarve, is a beautiful city, though now somewhat marred by highrise buildings on the outskirts. A yacht basin reaches out into the central square of the town, on which are the main hotels, the Maritime Museum, and at one side the beautiful Renaissance Arco da Vila, which cuts through the ramparts of the old city to the cathedral, lovely squares and the other museums. When you are visiting the large Renaissance cathedral containing fine Baroque additions, note particularly the red Chinoiserie organ to one side of the nave. Two good museums are located behind the cathedral: the Infante Dom Henrique and the Ferreira d'Almeida collections, both containing paintings, furniture and sculpture. The former Jesuit College has been restored and contains a small, untouched 18th-century opera house, built by the Bivar family after the Jesuits had been suppressed in Portugal in the middle of the 18th century. The Bishop's library, pillaged by the Earl of Essex, became the nucleus of the Bodleian Library in Oxford.

The city is filled with pretty Baroque churches, of which the best is São Francisco, its plain facade giving no hint of the golden interior. São Pedro, in the town center, has a Rococo chapel surrounded by blue and white azulejos of the life of St. Peter. The huge Carmo church, a couple of hundred yards away is, however, disappointing, with a fussy and formless interior.

The Praia de Faro is long and sandy, located on an island off the city, reached by bridge or by ferry from the Porta Nova Quay. The view from here of the white houses and the belfries of the town is lovely. The beach has all amenities, with restaurants, bars and the Estalagem Aeromar hotel. The other islets off Faro are long and lonely, though on the Ilha da Barreta there is a lighthouse and a small village.

The Ria Formosa Nature Reserve extends all along this coast, with numerous islets going right up to Cacela Velha. The birds include every variety of duck and wader as well as flamingos, royal terns and eagles.

The Algarve is an important staging post for migratory birds including hoopoes, bee-eaters, azure-winged magpies, golden orioles, and Alpine swifts. Both European and African butterflies are to be found in the right season.

Inland from Faro (ten km., six miles, on N2) at Estoi, is the charming late-18th century country mansion with formal gardens. Flights of steps with pools and statuary lead up to the terrace on which stands the elegant pink facade of the house. A short way to the west, out of the village of Estoi, lie the Roman remains of the ancient city of Milreu. Just off the road, but fenced in, are the apse of a third-century church, polychrome mosaics, and shattered columns. Many of the remains are in the museum in Faro, and further excavations are being undertaken by a German team. The whole setting in lovely country is enchanting.

The Cliffs of Barlavento

West of Faro the country is very beautiful. Fine sand beaches are intersected more and more by tall cliffs etched by brine and seafoam. Everyone has his own favorite spot among those tiny inlets fringed with their varicolored backdrops. The best beaches are being rapidly developed; Alvor has sprouted large tourist complexes, while others have been taken up by the big hotels at Albufeira, at Armação de Pera and Praia da Rocha. On many of the smaller beaches the day's catch is auctioned when the fishing boats come in.

A short distance west of Faro is the Quinta do Lago, an elegant resort with a 27-hole golf course and another course nearby at Vale do Lobo. Vilamoura is a huge, rather arid, complex of houses, apartments and hotels, boasting a casino and two more golf courses. Nearby is the Praia da Falesia with a long and beautiful beach.

On the road to Albufeira (N125) at Almansil, the church of São Louren-ço is entirely lined with 18th-century blue tiled panels on the life of the saint. An Arts Center has been opened by the church. Almansil also has a Water Pleasure Park, a tourist attraction with many water-based amusements.

In Albufeira you must pass under a tunnel to reach a splendid beach that is connected by a series of terraces to an international luxury hotel. However, the original charm of the village remains intact, with its steep narrow streets, the asymmetric overlapping of the eternally white houses, and its churches with their Moorish cupolas. The central part is now a pedestrian precinct. Oddly shaped rock formations and strange, deep caverns dot this area of the coast, which can be explored by boat. Amateur photographers will find abundant inspiration in the Moorish silhouettes of Albufeira as seen from the new upper heights of the city, or from the Bem Parece mirador. The fish market is open every morning and on Saturday mornings there is a country market with people coming in from the surrounding districts to sell their own produce.

By the main road (N125) at Porches, the Olaria Pottery produces hand-made objects of all kinds. They also run a bar, but are closed on Sundays.

Long before it was discovered by the new-wave tourists, Praia da Rocha had already become famous as a winter resort. Then, visitors lounged under the tall palm trees above the wide golden beach strewn by ruin-like rocks, but with the extra precaution of either a light wool wrap or a parasol. Nowadays a row of hotels lines the avenue parallel to the shore. You can ride in a horse-drawn carriage with flowered curtains that will take you to the attractive fishing port of Portimão, a lovely town with exceptionally good shops, three km. (two miles) away up the estuary of the Arade. Try the grilled fresh sardines at one of the little places by the bridge. Portimão and Vilamoura both have Big Game Fishing Centers with special boats. Ferragudo on the other side of the estuary, which only a short time ago was a kind of fisherfolk's suburb atop a peak overlooking the turbid river, now attracts nocturnal wanderers bent on enjoying the soft music in the small bars of old buildings. The beach just beyond the village is now the main center in the Algarve for sailboarding, surfboarding and windsurfing.

Between Portimão and Lagos (18 km., 11 miles) there are numerous inlets of the sea and long beaches which have not been developed at all. The well known Penina Hotel golf course (with two nine-hole courses in addition to the 18-hole one) lies just off the main road.

Lagos

Lagos was for centuries the most famous of the coastal settlements. It was from here that the 16th-century caravelles, which charted many of the sea routes to India, set out on their long voyages. Around the square, over which presides the statue of Henry the Navigator facing the ocean that he conquered, you can still see arcades of what was the only slave market in Portugal. In the church of Santa Maria there is the Manueline window from which young King Sebastião exhorted the troops who were doomed to perish with him at Alcacér Quebir. The dun-colored walls of the former governor's residence line the avenue up to the Gateway to the Sea. A fort reminiscent of Vauban protects the little strand on which the

fishing smacks are beached, near the fish market. The chapel of Sto. António is the showpiece of Lagos. The church, in fact it is a good deal larger
than a chapel, is entirely lined with superb gold Rococo boiseries and set
in this golden cave are charming canvasses of the miracles of St. Anthony
of Padua, who was actually born in Lisbon. On the altar is a statue of the
saint with, across his chest, the red sash of a British General of the Peninsular War period.

The Regional Museum next door contains an extraordinary mixture of
exhibits: fishing nets, model ships, shells, paintings, church vessels, books
and a portable altar of St. Anthony, used for the troops when Napoleon
invaded Portugal at the beginning of the last century.

North of Lagos the Bravura dam, already mentioned, is another great
sheet of water which irrigates this western part of the Algarve, enabling
melons, tomatoes, maize and other fruits and vegetables to be ripened
early.

A short distance from Lagos the coast begins to shatter and shred under
the constant pounding of the surf. Purple-dyed rocks slither down into
technicolor-green depths that are alternately mirror-smooth and furiously
churning. The waves moan as they dash themselves against the seaweed-
draped grottoes, where boats move as if through an aquarium struck with
shafts of sunlight. One mile south of Lagos, Ponta da Piedade is worth
an excursion from the Praia de Dona Ana, to see the sea foaming in and
around the lacy-patterned rocks. Six km. (four miles) to the west is Praia
da Luz, a beach with an elegant tourist complex, complete with Club
House and villas to let for short periods.

Palmares, the most easterly of the splendid golf courses with which the
Algarve is endowed, is across the river from Lagos and five of the 18 holes
are played over sand dunes, as were the original links at St. Andrews in
Scotland.

Sagres

A different world awaits you beyond Lagos. The few beaches have been
little developed. Salema, Burgão and Porto de Mos retain their unsophisti-
cated air: fishermen lounge by their boats and there are not many hotels
and restaurants. Inland, off the main N125, is Vila do Bispo, a charming
village with a superb azulejo-lined church. As you drive towards Sagres
on N268 you may notice how bare the land is—red soil which is slowly
plowed by oxen in the early months of the year—and how powerful the
wind is, how the almond trees and reeds have been bent by it and how
the fig trees crouch low, almost as if to thrust their ash-colored branches
back into the ground. On your right you will notice the little Romanesque
chapel of Nossa Senhora de Guadalupe in which Prince Henry the Navigator, who was known as the Infante of Sagres, prayed for the success of
his ventures.

All this was his realm. It has a kind of wild grandeur. The Tôrre de
Aspa (over 150 meters, 500 ft., high) is the tallest cliff of the Algarve coast.
Rocks claw at the surface of the soil, ripping the carpet of grass and flowers. Soon you see only the sturdy geraniums that resist both drought and
fog, then a few asphodels, and finally the saber-leaved aloes. Squalls rage
relentlessly over this forked promontory which, like an antenna of Europe,
gropes out uneasily toward infinity.

For the ancient mariners, the Cape of St. Vincent represented the World's End. The only vessels that sailed around it were Phoenician and Greek galleys, presumably under the protection of the gods: the latter, according to legend, repaired there to recuperate from their long day's work and to watch the sun sink with a hiss into the sea. Long after the Mediterranean had been explored, charted and tamed, this cape continued to define the beginning of the unknown.

On a rock-bound cape, at the remotest point where the known world was assumed to end, a group of Christian followers had buried St. Vincent's body after he had been put to death at Valencia. Four ravens are said to have kept a vigil over the grave until the first King of Portugal, Afonso Henriques, was finally able to secure a truce with the Moors and get the remains transferred to Lisbon, where ravens are incorporated into the city's coat of arms.

The place remained uninhabited over a long period of time. Shipwrecked seafarers, together with the flotsam and jetsam of their vessels, were cast ashore there. In order to be able to question these survivors and to unearth the secrets of those far-off places that were reputed full of marvels, a prince took up his residence in this remote fastness, specifically at Sagres. For 40 years he waited, ever on the alert for the Great Unknown, a clear-headed visionary who was both watchful and patient. Around him were gathered the boldest and most progressive minds of the time: geographers and astrologers, navigators, shipbuilders and adventurers. This motley group, hailing from the islands of the Mediterranean, the ghettoes of Bohemia, from Dalmatian, Flemish, and Genoese ports, pooled their resources and knowledge in an effort to resolve the burning question of the day: how to find the sea route to the East, the lands of spices and of gold.

At the time of his death in 1460, the Infante Henrique, third son of João of Aviz, was still beset by misgivings. Thirty-eight more years were to elapse before first Bartholomeu Dias and then Vasco da Gama rounded the Cape and the latter reached port at Calicut, India, in 1498, after a voyage which owed its success to Prince Henry's years of unremitting efforts and research.

Little if any now remains of the Infante's austere dwelling-place, but his giant, reflective shadow haunts the great paved courtyard and chapel of the old fort. There is no admission fee and cars can be driven in through the ever-open tunnel-like entrance. The size of the enclosure is huge, with a lighthouse at the extreme tip of the promontory. A stone compass dial was discovered under the short turf many years ago and is now uncovered, but it seems impossible that this dates from the time of Prince Henry, though many of the original encircling walls do still stand. There is a Youth Hostel and Tourist Office in part of the old buildings and a film depicting the Prince's life and the Voyages of Discovery under the cross of the Order of Christ, whose Grand Master he was, is shown in English, French and German every afternoon. You may have to brace yourself firmly against the parapet to resist the strong gusts of wind that swoop down over the ramparts and around the lighthouse on Cape St. Vincent, five km. (three miles) away. However, the terraces of the pousada in Sagres and of the hotels and inns around the calm waters of the bay are drenched in sunshine. There has, alas, been indiscriminate building, but so far no highrise apartments have been permitted.

Sagres is the Mecca for travelers who long for grandiose horizons, spectacular sunsets, the briny tang of sea winds, real deep-sea fishing, snipe and quail-hunting in the marshes up the coast. It is in fact one of the very last refuges where man can draw inner strength from the very core of the earth, where you will find both rough-and-ready fellowship and true solitude combined with comfort.

The West Coast

On the way north from Lagos on N120 or Sagres on N268, you will come to Aljezur with an unrestored castle crowning a hill. For long riddled with malaria, but now dry and healthy, Aljezur is a charming small country town with a river running between the old part and the late 18th-century "new town." West of Aljezur there are two splendid beaches. The Arrifana beach lies below high cliffs and a very steep cobbled road leads down to it. As always on the Atlantic coast, bathing is dangerous in rough weather. There are a few houses and small restaurants by the sea. Monte Clérigo, very wide and sandy, is reached by a lovely road winding along a valley.

Continuing up the coast, Odeceixe, 17 km. (10½ miles) on N120, on the border with Baixo Alentejo (southern Alentejo), still has an exotic Moorish air, with little houses climbing up the hillside. Lovely deserted beaches stretch along the low coastline to Zambujeira, which is surrounded by weird rock formations. One huge block, called the Palheirão, rises vertically from the sea.

Odemira, the one-time Wadi Emir of the Arabs, on the River Mira, is still an Algarve town, though fully into the Alentejo. 42 km. (26 miles) further north, a road leads to the new bridge over the estuary of the Mira at Vila Nova de Milfontes, where Hannibal took shelter with his ships. The small fort-like castle built by Dom João IV in defense against pirates from Morocco still stands solitary guard at Milfontes, and is a superb guest house. The rocky cliffside behind the Praia das Grutas is honeycombed by countless mysterious grottoes. In winter, when the sea suddenly turns menacing, the large bell standing at the estuary of the Mira issues a warning to boats to hurry back to safety.

From the Spanish Border to Faro

The Sotavento, to the east of Faro, is accessible from southern Spain either by one of the winding roads into the eastern Algarve or by ferry (which takes cars) across the beautiful broad estuary of the Guadiana (the international border) shortly to be spanned by a bridge. You will find well-appointed hotels complete with swimming pools, terraces and sea views, nightclubs and—by the endless beach of Monte Gordo—a casino. In the evening, after a relaxing day of sunbathing, you will enjoy going to Vila Real de Santo António, a completely 18th-century town, built in five months by the Marquis de Pombal in 1774. Street lamps glimmer softly over the great black-and-white mosaic square in which is the small Manuel Cabanas Museum, and the air is scented with orange blossoms. There is an atmosphere of the Spanish *rambla* on the streets specially traffic-free for strolling.

You can also take a carriage ride to the ancient castle at Castro Marim, first headquarters of the fighting monastic Order of Christ in the 14th century, after the dissolution of the Knights Templar.

Vila Real is the site of the great central fish market set up by Pombal. Tuna fishing takes place in the summer and provides work at the Sotavento cannery. From April to July, shoals of the huge fish leave the calm Algarve waters to make their way to their spawning banks some hundreds of miles west of Gibraltar. These succulent, firm-fleshed tuna are the most sought-after of the species. Later on, by the end of August, when they have returned to the warm estuaries of the Algarve, their meat has lost some of its quality and is more dry.

If it is excitement that you crave, tuna fishing, for all its inevitable cruelty, provides a thrilling spectacle. The fish are captured alive in huge nets that are then hauled to the surface of the sea, at which point the *copejo,* or combat, begins. The tuna must first be gaffed before it is hoisted on deck. Some of these fish weigh as much as 180 kg. (400 pounds) and have sufficient strength in their powerful tails to lash out and break a man's back if he is caught off guard. Such accidents happen when it becomes necessary for the men to join their adversary in the water for close-combat fighting, in the case of the more violent specimens. From the boat deck where the already landed fish are heaving in their final death-throes, the men sing and shout encouragement to their fellow fishermen thrashing about in the water with the wounded tuna in a frenzied flurry of foam and blood. (If you are interested in witnessing or filming these expeditions, you should apply to the Comissão do Turismo in Tavira or Faro or to the Big Game Fishing Center in Portimão or Vilamoura).

The tuna-processing industry provides Sotavento with one of its main sources of income. Not a single shred of the animal is discarded. The choicest fillets are canned in their natural flavor, with oil or tomato sauce. The less desirable portions are dried and sold for food to the poorer classes of the population. By-products are processed to make a fertilizer with a high phosphorus content.

Tavira—Olhão

Between Monte Gordo and Tavira there is a lush expanse of farmland, where fig and citrus trees flourish, along with the magnificent centuries-old carob: its beans are used not only as cattle feed but also to make fine cosmetics.

Tavira is one of the most attractive towns in the Algarve. Once a bustling port—its harbor is now unfortunately sanded up—it is clearly still prosperous and astonishingly unspoilt, with delightful small public gardens and exceptionally fine churches. In the castle with its steep stairways, a terraced garden perfumes the air and overlooks a rusty-tiled expanse of Moorish rooftops that seem to bubble up into the sky. Buildings reflect their Renaissance facades in the still waters of the Gilão, spanned by a seven-arch Roman bridge. A porcelain-blue tiled church lends piquancy to a narrow little street lined with the intricately patterned tracery of lattice-work doors.

At the end of the 18th century Olhão, east along N125, was only an obscure and unprepossessing fishing port. The blockades that accompanied the Napoleonic wars provided its inhabitants with a chance to deal in profitable smuggling with Cádiz. The wealth thus acquired enabled them to replace their fishing shacks with real houses, always stark white, often with ridges accented in blue and of course the typical Moorish-style chimneys. Alas, as so often happens, here too progress acted to the detriment of picturesqueness. Modern constructions replaced many of the most attractive aspects of this small city formerly so reminiscent of a North African kasbah of dazzling white houses, with narrow stairways climbing steeply to the flat, terraced roofs. Formerly so beloved by painters, even known as the "Cubist" city because of the distinctive nature of its perspective, Olhão by now has lost a great deal of its former charms. Incidentally, the big covered markets on the seafront are the best in the Algarve. Having become one of the main canning centers, factories spread out over the surrounding areas rendering them uninteresting and characterless. Nonetheless, ascending to the top of the church, you may perhaps recapture some aspect of pre-progress charm: at least the sight of the famed Algarvian chimneys can still gladden the eye.

PRACTICAL INFORMATION FOR THE ALGARVE

TOURIST OFFICES. There are local tourist offices in the following towns: **Albufeira,** Rua 5 de Outubro; **Aljezur,** Largo do Mercado; **Armaçao de Pera** (Alcantarilha), Ave. Marginal; **Carvoeiro** (Lagoa), Largo Praia do Carvoeiro; **Faro,** Rua de Misericórdia 8–12, Rua Ataíde de Oliveira 100, and Airport. **Lagos,** Largo Marquês do Pombal; **Loulé,** Edifício do Castelo; **Monte Gordo,** Ave. Marginal; **Olhão,** Largo da Lagoa; **Portimão,** Largo 1° de Dezembro; **Praia da Rocha** (Portimão), Rua Tomás Cabreira; **Quarteira** (Loulé), Ave. Infante Sagres; **Sagres,** Promontary; **Silves,** Rua 25 de Abril; **Tavira,** Praça da Republica; **Vila Real de Sto. António,** Praça Marquês de Pombal.

INFORMATION. The *Algarve News,* and the *Algarve Magazine,* with a full guide to what is going on, are monthly publications given free at Faro airport and other centers.

WHEN TO COME. The Algarve climate is pleasantly mild in winter, with temperatures seldom less than 10°C (50°F) except when rare storms or high winds occur. The ocean water may be even warmer than the air itself, and the number of sunny hours it enjoys each year is never less than 3,000. Late January and early February the almond trees in blossom are a sight not to be missed.

GETTING TO THE ALGARVE. By Plane. *TAP* and *British Airways* both fly four times a week between London and Faro, the former also direct from New York, Paris, Amsterdam, Frankfurt and other European cities. Planes also fly regularly from Lisbon and Oporto.

By Train and Bus. There are *rail* services from Lisbon to Lagos and Faro, also several *bus* services (see *Facts At Your Fingertips* section).

By Car. The car is a better way to reach the Algarve, especially during the busy tourist season when public transport is packed. The most scenic route from Lisbon is the Lisbon–Lagos road, N120. However, if you wish to go direct to Faro, take the N259 where the routes diverge at Grândola, south of Alcácer do Sal, a lovely town, which is alive with storks in the spring, and then N2.

HOTELS AND RESTAURANTS

Albufeira (Faro). *Balaia* (L), tel. 089 52681. 193 rooms with bath. Rooms have balconies and are airconditioned. Now belongs to Clube Mediterranée; located 4 km. (2 miles) east on cliff top, with independent villas in grounds, two heated pools, yachting, water-skiing, tennis, shops, etc. AE, DC, MC, V. *Boavista* (E), tel. 089 52175. 51 rooms with bath. Restaurant-grill, pool, gymnasium, sauna. AE, DC, MC, V. *Apartamento Auramar* (M), Areias de São João (tel. 089 533337). 282 rooms with bath. Pool and other amenities. Just outside town. Closed Nov. through Mar. DC, MC. *Residêncial Vila Recife* (M), Rua Miguel Bombarda 6 (tel. 089 52047). 29 rooms with bath. Breakfast only. Pool, garden, bar with fados, live music, sandwiches and light refreshments. AE, DC, MC, V. *Rocamar* (M), tel. 089 52611. 91 rooms with bath. AE, DC, MC, V. *Sol e Mar* (M), tel. 089 52121. 74 rooms with bath. Central, overlooking beach, with restaurant, pool, nightclub. AE, DC, MC. *Baltum* (I), tel. 089 52106. 26 rooms with bath, plus annex with 23 rooms. Noisy, near beach. DC, MC.

At **Cerro da Piedade**, *Estalagem Mar a Vista* (E), tel. 089 52154. 29 rooms with bath. On hillside. DC.

Restaurants. There are a great many small eating houses, mostly in the Inexpensive price category, including some good places just out of town at Olhos de Agua, Olhos da Balaia, Castelo do Bispo, Quinta da Saudade and Borda de Agua. *A Ruina* (M). Unusual setting; good seafood from fish market next door. *Cabaz da Praia* (M), Praça Miguel Bombarda. Lovely sea view. Closed Sat. and Sun. *Sir Harry's Bar* (M). English pub off the main square; an international rendezvous with a friendly owner.

Discos. *Splash, Kiss,* and *Summertime.*

Almansil (Faro). *Residêncial Sta. Teresa* (I), tel. 089 95525. 24 rooms with bath. Comfortable rooms, breakfast only. Just along turning off the main road.

Restaurant. *Casa da Torre Ermitage* (E), (tel. 089 94329). Delicious French food. Dinner only. Closed Wed. Booking essential. AE, DC, MC. *Pituxa* (I). Very good small restaurant almost opposite the Residêncial Sta. Teresa, serving lunches and dinners efficiently and in pleasant surroundings.

Alvor (Faro). Casino here. *Alvor Praia* (L), tel. 082 24020. 236 rooms with bath. Pool, tennis; fine views. Conference facilities. AE, DC, MC, V. *Penina Golf* (L), tel. 082 22051. 202 rooms with bath and balcony. On road between Portimão and Lagos. Olympic-sized pool, beauty parlor, shops, excellent restaurant, grill-room. Tennis, disco. Lovely grounds. Sports International Championship 27-hole golf course designed by Henry Cotton; small state-run airport for private planes, planes also for hire. AE, DC, MC, V. *Delfim* (E), tel. 082 27171. 312 rooms with bath. Pools, tennis. AE,

DC, MC, V. *Dom João II* (E), tel. 082 20135. 219 rooms with bath. Overlooking magnificent beach; pool and other facilities. AE, DC, MC, V. *Apartmentos Torralta* (M), tel. 082 20211. Large apartment complexes—including some in (I) category—near beach. Daily maid service, restaurants, pools, riding, tennis, discos, shops, sailing. Very good value; recommended. AE, DC, MC, V.

Restaurants. *Al-Vila* (E), Sitio das Amoreiras. Recommended. Also has villas to rent. Closed Mon. AE, DC. *Barca de Alvor* (E). Nightclub on beach. DC.

Armação da Pera (Faro). *Garbe* (M), tel. 082 32187. 109 rooms with bath. Restaurant overlooking sea; pool. AE, DC, MC, V. *Levante* (E), tel. 082 32322. 41 rooms with bath. Beautiful situation above sandy beach a mile west of town. Terrace, pools for adults and children, restaurant. AE, DC, MC, V. *Apartamento Rosa Mar* (M), tel. 082 32377. 42 units.

At **Alporchinchos,** *Vila Lara* (L), tel. 082 32333. 87 apartments. Superb complex set in beautiful gardens overlooking large beach. Restaurant, heated sea-water pool, water-skiing, windsurfing, sailing, riding, 6 tennis courts, 4 lit up at night. AE, DC, MC, V.

Restaurants. *A Santola* (E), Largo 25 de Abril. Picture windows onto beach. Closed Sun. lunch. AE, DC, MC. *Caique* (M), Rua Dr. José António dos Santos. Pleasant ambience and good food. Closed Wed. *Grelha* (M), Rua do Alentejo 2. Good seafood. Closed Mon. DC, MC.

Burgau (Faro). Pleasant small beach. *Holiday Apartments* (M), tel. 082 65234.

Restaurant. *Ancora* (E). Dinner only. Closed Mon., Tues. also in winter, and all Dec. AE, DC, MC.

Faro (provincial capital). *Eva* (E), tel. 089 24054. 150 rooms with bath. Rooms are airconditioned and have panoramic views. On main square, opposite yacht basin, with nightclub, pool, shops, restaurant and snack bar. AE, DC, MC, V. *Casa Lumena* (M), Praça Alexandre Herculano 27 (tel. 089 22028). 12 rooms with bath. Former ducal residence, English owned. DC, MC. *Faro* (M), tel. 089 22076. 52 rooms with bath. On main square; restaurant. AE, DC, MC, V. *Albacor* (I), Rua Brites de Almeida 23 (tel. 089 22093). 38 rooms with bath. Breakfast only. DC, MC. Several pensions can also be found here.

At **Praia de Faro,** the local beach reached by road or ferry. *Estalagem Aeromar* (E), tel. 089 23189. 19 rooms with bath. AE, DC.

Restaurants. There are dozens of small restaurants, also several beach restaurants and bars at Praia de Faro. *Cidade Velha* (E), Largo da Sé 19. Highly recommended. Closed Sat. lunch, Sun. AE, DC, MC. *Alfagher* (M), Rua Tenente Valadim 30. In old Portuguese residence with attractive dining room and pleasant terrace. Food is good. DC, MC. *Caracoles* (M), Terreiro do Bispo 26–28. Attractive rustic ambience; regional dishes. *Kappra* (M), Rua Pé-da-Cruz 37. Closed Sun. AE. *Lady Susan* (M), Rua 1° de Dezembro 28. English-owned. Closed Sat., Sun. DC, MC, V. *A Doca* (I). Excellent Portuguese food with good wine and elegant tables; on main square. *La Roque* (I). Good local food on the beach at Praia de Faro. Closed Wed. *Porto Fino* (I). Amusing decor and excellent food. Dozens of other small restaurants.

Bars. *Caravel* and *Paddy's Bar* are both friendly places for a drink.

Ferragudo (Faro). Across the river from Portimão. **Restaurant.** *A Lanterna* (E). Specialty duck, and fish soup. Closed Sun. v.

Foia/Monchique (Faro). *Mons Circus* (E), Estrada da Foia (tel. 082 92650). Delightful large rooms with bath, terraces and superb views. Pretty restaurant, good bar and public rooms. Big pool and paddling pool, 2 tennis courts. AE, DC, MC, V. *Abrigo da Montanha* (M), tel. 082 92131. 6 rooms with bath. Beautiful garden with camelias and magnolias. Pleasant service in restaurant. AE, DC, MC, V.
Restaurants. *Paraiso da Montanha* (I), Estrada da Foia. Good chicken. One of several Inexpensive restaurants on this road. Closed Thurs. *Terezinha* (I), Estrada da Foia. Tables on outdoor terrace. First restaurant going up. Closed Mon.

Lagoa (Faro). *Motel Alagoas* (M), Estrada Nacional 125 (tel. 082 52243). 22 rooms with bath. Pool, disco. AE, DC, MC.
Restaurant. *O Braseiro* (M), Praça da Republica 15. A cheerful, German-run restaurant. Closed Sun. *O Lotus* (M), Rua Marquês de Pombal 11. Closed Sat. winter, Mon. summer. MC.

Lagos. Accommodations include numerous pensions. *Golfinho* (E), tel. 082 62081. 262 rooms with bath. Pool and all facilities. Above the Praia de Dona Ana beach—reached by long flight of steps; boats for hire to see the caves and grottoes. AE, DC, MC, V. *Lagos* (E), Rua Nova da Aldeia (tel. 082 62011). 273 rooms with bath. Central; spacious, with heated pool, disco. AE, DC, MC, V. *Motel Marsol* (M), Estrada Nacional 125 (tel. 082 62032). 20 self-service villas for 4. Fine view; recommended. *Motel Ancora* (M), Estrada de Porto de Mos (tel. 082 62033). 60 units with bath. Disco, snack bar. *Residência Sol e Praia* (M), tel. 082 62026. 43 rooms with bath. Breakfast only. Also above the Praia de Dona Ana. *Rio Mar* (M), Rua Candido dos Reis 81 (tel. 082 63091). 40 rooms with bath. Pleasant modern hotel in town center; terraces; good value. DC. *São Cristovão* (M), Rossio de São João (tel. 082 63051). 77 rooms with bath. Excellent, modern and well equipped; on edge of town. AE, DC, MC, V.
Restaurants. As well as those listed here there are several small, reasonable restaurants. *Dom Sebastão* (E), Rua 25 de Abril 20. Closed Sun. in winter. AE, DC, MC. *Mandarim* (E), at Colicas. Chinese and international food. Dinner only. MC. *Muralha* (E), Rua Atalaia 15. Dinner only; open 8 P.M.–3.30 A.M. Fados and live music. Closed Nov. through Jan. AE, DC, MC.

Loulé (Faro). *Pensão Iberica* (M), Ave. Marçelo Pacheco 157 (tel. 089 62027). 18 rooms with bath. Breakfast only. Recommended. *Pensão Cavaco* (I), Rua Candido Guerreiro 32 (tel. 089 63455). 14 rooms with bath. Breakfast only.
Restaurants. *Avenida* (M), Ave. José Mealha 13. Closed Sun. AE, DC, MC.

Meia Praia (Faro). On way to Palmares Golf Club across the river from Lagos. *Meia Praia* (M), tel. 082 62001. 66 rooms with bath. Heated seawater pool. Closed Nov. through Mar. AE, DC, MC, V. *Meia Praia Beach Club Apartments* (M), tel. 082 60234. 83 apartments. Two pools, restaurant. Quiet; discount at Palmares Golf Club. Like the Meia Praia, has an uninterrupted view of the sea and is not too far from a splendid sandy beach. AE.

Montechoro (Faro). Just north of main road N125 between Alcantarilha and Almansil. Self-service apartments are also available. *Montechoro* (E), tel. 089 52651. 362 rooms with bath. Rooms are large and have terraces. Two pools, shops, tennis, disco, sauna; bus to beach at Albufeira. AE, DC, MC, V.

Restaurants. *Michael's* (E). Dinner with floorshow. Closed Mon. *O Pimpão* (E). Steak house; dinner only. Fados. AE, DC, MC.

Monte Gordo (Faro). Casino on town beach. *Alcazar* (E), Rua de Ceuta (tel. 081 42184). 95 rooms with bath. Disco. Pool; near to beach. Pleasant atmosphere and good service. AE, DC, MC, V. *Vasco da Gama* (E), Ave. Infante D. Henrique (tel. 081 44321). 165 rooms with bath. On sea, with pools, nightclub, tennis. AE, DC, MC, V. *Albergaria Monte Gordo* (M), tel. 081 42124. 25 rooms with bath. On sea. AE. *Caravelas* (M), Rua Diogo Cão (tel. 081 44458). 87 rooms with bath. In pinewoods. AE. *Navegadores* (M), Rua Gonçalo Velho (tel. 081 42490). 344 rooms with bath. Pool. Near beach. DC, MC. *Aparthotel Guadiana* (I), tel. 081 42269. 174 apartments. Highrise building on sea, with 3 bars serving snacks. *Apartamentos Monte Sol* (I), tel. 081 42136. 40 apartments. MC, V.

Restaurants. *Casino* (L). Live floor show. Dinner only. AE, DC, MC, V. *Mota* (M), on beach. Live music. Kitchen in view.

Olhos D'Agua (Faro). Near Albufeira. **Restaurant.** *La Cigale* (E), (tel. 089 54637). One of the best restaurants in the Algarve. Dinner only in Oct., Nov. Closed Dec., Jan., Feb. AE, DC, MC.

Olhão (Faro). There are several small pensions. *Hotel Rio Sol* (I), Rua General Humberto Delgado 37 (tel. 089 72167). 53 rooms with bath. Breakfast only. MC, V.

Restaurants. *Don Quixote* (M), Rua da Lavadeiras 18. *Ilido* (I), Bairro dos Pescadores.

Portimão (Faro). Accommodations include many simple pensions. *Albergaria Miradouro* (M), Rua Machado dos Santos 13 (tel. 082 23011). 25 rooms with bath. Breakfast only. *Globo* (M), Rua 5 de Outubro 26 (tel. 082 22151). 71 rooms with bath. In town; set meals in top-floor restaurant with lovely view. AE, DC, MC, V. *Residência Nelinanda* (M), Rua Vincente das Vacas 22 (tel. 082 23156). 32 rooms with bath. *Pensão Pacheco* (I), Rua Diogo Gonçalves 2 (tel. 082 22912). 20 rooms with bath. Breakfast only. Very good value.

Restaurants. *Alfredo's* (E), Rua da Pé da Cruz 10. Dinner only. Closed Tues. AE, DC, MC. *O Gato* (E), Quintinha 10. Recommended. *Porto de Abrigo* (M), Vale de França. Closed Tues. AE, DC, MC. *Brumar* (I), Rua Diogo Gonçalves 8. Good food in pleasant surroundings. *Carvi-Marisqueira* (I), Rua Direita 34-A. Recommended. *Lucio* (I), Largo Francisco Mauricio. Specialty is shellfish. One of several simple places near bridge, serving grilled sardines. Closed Mon.

Praia Da Falesia (Faro). *Alfamar* (E), tel. 089 66351. 263 rooms with bath. Villas, bungalows and apartments also to let. Terraces; one indoor and one outdoor pool; 18 tennis courts, 7 squash courts; watersports; very long and beautiful beach. Beware of high "sleeping policemen" in drive— mind your car springs! *Aldeia das Acoteias* (I), tel. 089 66267. 416 villas and apartments. Large vacation center with sports complex, pools, disco, riding for disabled and other facilities. Very good beach; restaurant; nice personnel. AE, DC, V.

Praia Da Galé (Faro). Near Albufeira. *Vila Joya* (L), tel. 089 54795. 14 rooms with bath. Spacious and luxurious accommodations. Price includes breakfast and four-course candlelit dinner, lunch à la carte—all excellent. Heated pool; direct access to beach. Restaurant open to public but reservations essential. AE, DC, MC.

Praia Da Luz (Faro). *Luz Bay Club* (E), near Lagos (tel. 082 69640). Villas for hire over short or long periods in new village which merges into the old village so well that it seems part of it. All villas near beach; daily cleaning. 3 swimming pools, 3 restaurants, bar, good shops in village. One of the earliest and best developments in the Algarve. AE, DC, MC, V.
Restaurants. There are several small restaurants as well as those listed. *O Trovador* (E). Extensive menu. *Bar 53* (M). English-run bar-restaurant with garden at the back. *Barroca* (M). Very pleasant. Arrangements can be made for a night on a sardine boat. *Os Arcos* (M). Country pub atmosphere, with good food. Disco. *Privé.*

Praia Da Quarteira (Faro). Hotels are on main street. *Atis* (M), tel. 089 34333. 40 service apartments. *Beira Mar* (M), tel. 089 34030. 51 rooms with bath. Breakfast only; right on beach. AE, DC, MC, V. *Dom José* (M), tel. 089 34310. 134 rooms with bath. Disco. Pool. AE, DC, MC, V. *Quarteirasol* (M), tel. 089 34421. 110 rooms with bath. Apartments too. Good modern hotel with excellent service; nightclub, pool, shops. AE, DC, MC. *Pensão Mario* (I), tel. 089 33242. 36 rooms. Breakfast only. One of several reasonable pensions.
Restaurants. *Alphonso's* (E). AE, DC, MC. *Belo Horizonte* (M). Closed Sun. AE, DC, MC. *Cataplana* (M). Closed Wed. in winter. AE, DC, MC.

Praia Da Rocha (Faro). Well-developed resort with all hotels and apartment complexes above the beach, which is beautiful and has strange rocks and caves. *Algarve* (L), tel. 082 24001. 220 rooms with bath. Rooms have balconies facing the sea. Pool, cliff-top nightclub, shops, sauna. AE, DC, MC, V. *Jupiter* (E), tel. 082 22041. 144 rooms with bath. Pool, shops, disco, restaurant and other amenities. AE, DC, MC, V. *Tarik* (E), tel. 082 22161. 296 apartments with bath. Disco, shops. AE, DC, MC, V. *Rocha* (M), tel. 082 24081. 77 rooms with bath; annex of 71 rooms with bath. *Solar Pinguim* (M), tel. 082 24308. 14 rooms with bath. Breakfast in rooms. Charming old house directly above beach, with terrace and steps down to it. English run, central, and with very reasonable winter terms. *Alcala* (I), tel. 082 24062. 22 rooms with bath.

Outside Praia da Rocha, on the road to Praia de Alvor, there are several good new developments. *Torre Três Castelos* (E), tel. 082 23136. Apartments. Restaurant, pool, tennis. *Apartamentos de Santa Catarina* (M), tel. 082 23318. 26 apartments. Restaurant. AE, DC, MC, V. *Rocha Vau* (M), tel. 082 26111. 56 rooms. Breakfast only. Pool, coffee shop and other amenities. AE, DC, MC, V. *Rocha Vaumar* (M), tel. 082 26958. 144 apartments. Two pools, restaurant, etc. AE, DC, MC, V.

Restaurants. *Titanic* (E), Edificio Columbia. Always open. Kitchen in view. AE, DC, MC. *A Falesia* (M). Pretty first-floor restaurant with attentive service. AE, DC, MC. *Safari* (M), Rua António Feio. An African touch to the food. DC, MC. *Fortaleza Santa Catarina* (I). On esplanade in old fort. Good menu and picture windows on to beach. **Disco.** *Hugo's.*

Praia Da Salema (Faro). *Beach Villas* (E), tel. 082 65252. 150 houses and apartments. Tourist complex with attractive low buildings, pool, shops, restaurant. Near very pleasant beach and village with several small restaurants. *Estalagem Infante do Mar* (E), tel. 082 65137. 30 rooms with bath. Pool, charming restaurant.

Praia Do Carvoeiro (Faro). *Club Solferias* (E), tel. 082 57401. 61 apartments. One of three large apartment and villa complexes on low hills around Carvoeiro. Off main road to beach; spacious, beautifully laid out, with pools and restaurants. AE, DC, MC, V. *Monte Carvoeiro* (E), tel. 082 57813. Apartment and villa complex well signposted up steep, narrow road to the west of beach. Restaurants, pools, shopping centers, other amenities. AE, DC, MC, V. *Quinta do Paraiso* (E), tel. 082 57378. Next to Monte Carvoeiro and with same facilities. AE, DC, MC, V. *Dom Sancho* (M), tel. 082 57301. 47 rooms. Breakfast only. Overlooks small agreeable beach. AE, DC, MC, V.

Restaurants. *Castelo* (E), Casa São José. Closed Thurs. AE, DC. *4 Dauphins* (E). Well-known restaurant in the Monte Carvoeiro complex. DC. *Encontro* (E), Carvoeiro Tennis Club. Dinner only in restaurant; buffet lunches in summer by pool. Closed Sun. AE, DC, MC.

Disco. *Bote.*

Praia Do Vau (Faro). Lovely, almost deserted beach between Alvor and Praia da Rocha. *Jardim do Vau* (M), tel. 082 82086. Attractive self-service apartments. Restaurants, pool, and other facilities. Elegant, low, white building—the only development on this beach. AE, DC, MC, V.

Quinta Do Lago (Faro), near Almansil. *Four Seasons Country Club* (E), tel. 089 94271. Studio apartments and villas to let. Huge, heavily wooded estate descending to three km. (two miles) of sandy beach. One of the Algarve's most luxurious clubs—open to non-members—with pools, tennis, squash, sauna, gymnasium, 27-hole golf course, restaurant.

Sagres. (Faro). Accommodations include several pensions as well as a youth hostel inside the fortress. *Pousada do Infante* (L), tel. 082 64222. 15 rooms with bath. Beautifully appointed rooms overlooking rugged seascape. By the promontory. Riding. AE, DC, MC, V. *Baleeira* (M), tel. 082 64212. 108 rooms with bath. Beautiful location near small sandy beach; pool, tennis, disco, shops. Recommended. DC, V. *Gambozinos* (M), Praia do Martinhal (tel. 082 64318). 17 apartments. DC, MC. *Residência Dom Henrique* (M), tel. 082 64133. 15 rooms with bath. Fine view of sea and way down to beach. MC.

Restaurant. *Forteleza do Beliche* (E), tel. 082 64124. 5 km (3 miles) southeast out of town on the road to Cape St. Vincent. Excellent food in a converted fortress above the sea. There are also 4 rooms.

Santa Bárbara De Nexe (Faro). *La Réserve* (L), tel. 089 91234. 20 suites with bath. Suites are airconditioned and luxurious, with kitchenette and T.V. Two pools, tennis in large estate. Restaurant (E) serves delicious French cuisine (closed Tues.). Dinner only. Booking necessary. The only Portuguese member of Relais et Châteaux and Swiss International Hotels.

Restaurant. *The Outside Inn* (E), (tel. 089 91443). Closed Tues. Booking recommended. Dinner only.

Santa Luzia, Tavira (Faro). *Pedras da Rainha* (I), tel. 081 22181. 800 villas and apartments. Restaurants, attractive bars with live music; pools, yacht basin, good beach with self-service restaurant. *Pedras D'El Rei* (I), tel. 081 22176. 245 apartments and villas. Pools, 6 tennis courts, disco, restaurant.

São Bartolomeu De Messines (Faro). *Apartamentos Turisticos Larga Vista* (M), tel. 082 45387. Apartments in lovely country setting. Pool.

São Bras De Alportel (Faro). About 24 km. (15 miles) north of Faro on the national highway. *Pousada de São Bras* (E), tel. 089 42305. 29 rooms with bath. Delightful hotel with splendid view from terrace. AE, DC, MC, V.

Senhora Da Rocha (Faro). *Viking* (E), tel. 082 32336. 185 rooms with bath and balcony. Very comfortable. Pools, disco, shops, sauna, restaurant. AE, DC, MC, V. *Vila Senhora da Rocha* (E), tel. 082 32394. 65 apartments, 160 villas. Restaurant, supermarket, 4 pools. AE, DC, MC, V.

Tavira (Faro). *Aldeia Turistica das Oliveiras* (M), tel. 081 22107. 60 apartments and villas. Self-service accommodations; pool, restaurant in summer. Two km. (just over a mile) from town and beach. *Eurotel* (I), Quinta das Oliveiras (tel. 081 22041). 80 rooms with bath. 4 pools, tennis. Two km. from town and beach. AE, DC, MC, V. *Pensão Lagoas* (I), Rua Candido dos Reis 24 (tel. 081 22252). 17 rooms, most with bath. Breakfast only. In town.

Restaurants. There are several good tascas on the river; try chicken with clams. *Imperial* (I), Rua José Padinha. Closed Wed. in winter.

Vale Do Lobo (Faro). *Dona Filipa* (L), tel. 089 94141. 135 rooms with bath. Rooms are airconditioned and also have balconies. Pool, restaurant, tennis, shops, on beach and near an 18-hole golf course which is one of Portugal's best and newest. Bring confirmation of your booking—you may need it! New Dutch owner is improving all facilities. AE, DC, MC, V. *Vale do Lobo Tourist Complex* (L), tel. 089 94145. 500 units. Set in well-landscaped, undulating land, with restaurant, disco, 3 pools, Roger Taylor tennis center, and other facilities.

Restaurants. *Caprice* (E). Closed Thurs. AE, DC, MC. *Chez Antoine* (E). Dinner only. Closed Mon. AE, DC, MC. *Pink Panther* (E). Super disco; drinks and snacks. *Rotunda* (E). Friendly. DC, MC. *Bistro da Praça* (M). Good food. *Olimpia II* (M). Closed Wed. AE, DC, MC. *Floresta* (I). Closed Sat.

Vilamoura (Faro). Huge, flat area with casino, tourist complexes, hotels, bungalows, swimming pools, yacht marina and two 18-hole golf courses. *Atlantis* (E), tel. 089 32535. 109 rooms with bath. Terraces; pools; tennis; shops. AE, DC, MC, V. *Marina* (E). 406 rooms with bath, 2 pools, tennis. *Dom Pedro* (M), tel. 089 35450. 109 rooms with bath and balcony. 3 pools. Tennis, shops. AE, DC, MC, V.

Restaurants. *Au Petit Port* (E). Dinner only. AE, DC, MC. *O Vapor* (E), on boat in the marina. Open summer only. AE, DC, MC. *Mayflower* (M). Kitchen in view. AE, DC, MC.

Vila Real De Santo António (Faro). *Apolo* (I), tel. 081 44448. 42 rooms with bath. Breakfast only. New building at entrance to town. AE, DC, V.

Restaurants. The town has many pleasant restaurants. *Caves do Guadiana* (M), Ave. da Republica 90. Overlooking estuary and the Spanish town of Ayamonte. Well cooked food in nice surroundings. Closed Thurs. *Don Jota* (M), Praçeta de Sto. António. AE, DC, MC. *Joaquim Gomes* (I), Rua 5 de Outubro. Closed Wed. in winter.

CAMPING. There are excellent, large campsites with amenities all along the coast, at: Albufeira; Alvor; Armação de Pera (2 sites); Espiche; Faro; Ferragudo; Lagos (2 sites); Monte Gordo (2 sites); Olhão (2 sites); Portimão; Praia da Salema; Praia de Luz; Praia Verde; Quarteira; Raposeira; Tavira; Vila Nova de Caçela.

PLACES OF INTEREST. Museums are usually open daily, except Mondays and public holidays, 10–5, but double check the times on the spot. Some close for lunch. Entrance fees are between 150$00 and 300$00.

Castro Marim. Castle. First headquarters of Order of Christ in 14th century. Small archeological museum.

Estoi. Gardens of 18th-century mansion. Recently bought by Faro City Council. Open to visitors on request: ring heavy bell at large gates by village church. Tip 200$00.

Milreu. Roman remains. Open daily 10–7. Tip 100$00 to 200$00 to the guardian.

Faro. Ferreira d'Almeida Collection. Next door to the Convent of Nossa Senhora da Assunção. Paintings, sculpture, furniture, jewels, metalwork, coins. Open Mon. to Fri. 9–12, 2–5; closed public holidays.

Igreja do São Francisco (Church of St. Francis). Open 7:30 A.M.–1:30, 4:30–7 P.M. Small collection of life-size statues of saints shown on request.

Infante Dom Henrique Museum, Convent of Nossa Senhora da Assunção. Behind the cathedral. Archeological remains, many from Milreu, military memorabilia, some pleasant religious paintings and church furnishings. Elegant double cloister. Open Mon. to Sat. 9:30–12, 2–7; closed public holidays.

Maritime Museum. By yacht basin next to Hotel Eva. Model ships, fishing nets, navigational aids, etc. Open Mon. to Fri. 9:30–12:30, 2–5:30; Sat. 9:30–1.

Regional Ethnographic Museum, Praça da Liberdade. Paintings, ships and local craftsmanship. Open Mon. to Fri. 9:30–12:30, 2–5; closed public holidays.

Lagos. Regional Museum. Next to Church of Sto. António. Amusing mixture of exhibits: ships, books, pictures, statues. (The church alongside is a fine example of 17th-century Baroque.) Open Tues. to Sun. 9:30–12:30, 2–5; closed Mon. and public holidays.

Moncarapacho. Archeological, sacred art and numismatic collection made by local parish priest, who will show it on request.

Silves. Large castle. One of the most remarkable Moorish remains in the country. Gothic cathedral.

Tavira. Alvaro de Campos Museum. In private house of this Portuguese man of letters.

Vila Real De Sto. António. Manuel Cabanas Museum, Praça Marques de Pombal. Paintings, engravings, regional artefacts. Open Tues. to Sun., summer, 2–8, 9 P.M.–11 P.M.; winter, 11:30–12:30, 2–7. Closed Mon. and public holidays.

SHOPPING. Crafts. Little woven sisal baskets and hampers make good souvenirs and welcome gifts—available everywhere in the Algarve. You will see women weaving the sisal fibres while sitting in the doorways of their houses, or following their donkeys. The center for reasonably priced hand-knitted sweaters is Sagres. Modern pictures can be bought in *Galerias Portimão,* Rua Sta. Isabel, Portimão, and in the same street are shoe shops and *Vista Alegre's* showrooms where you can rest your eyes on the cool beauty of the varied porcelain objects on display. There are temptations galore at *Abracadabra* in Albufeira. Local marble (if you are not flying!) and copper, brass and pewter are all hand-worked in the Algarve. The *Olaria Pottery,* 3 km. (2 miles) west of Porches, has become famous for its fine traditional and original ware (closed Sun.). In Faro, the Rua de Santo António is a pedestrian precinct with attractive shops below fine 18th-century houses.

Confectionery. The local confectioners' sugary sweet-meats betray their Moorish heritage, consisting of elaborate combinations of ground almonds, eggs, and figs. Each village concocts its own specialty. Tavira makes delicious caramels, Lagos produces its *Dom Rodrigos.* Some of the almond confections take on amusing shapes of flowers, birds and fishes.

Wine. The Algarve has the fortunate reputation of producing excellent grapes, along with fine local wines, particularly those from Lagoa and Lagos. The local liqueurs *Medronho,* made from the arbutos berry, and *Amendoa Amarga,* from bitter almonds, are worth trying.

COUNTRY FAIRS. Albufeira: Feb. 4, Aug. 15, Nov. 29. **Almansil:** Oct. 6. **Armação da Pera:** July 4. **Castro Marim:** Aug. 15. **Estoi:** Sept. 10–11. **Faro:** Feira do Carmo July 15–26. Feira de Sta. Iria Oct. 20–26. **Lagoa:** São João June 23–25, Sept. 5–10. **Lagos:** Aug. 16–17, Oct. 12–13, Nov. 20–22. **Loulé:** Aug. 29, Oct. 28, Dec. 9. **Montecarapacho:** Aug. 15. **Olhão:** Apr. 30, Sept. 25–30. **Portimão:** Aug. 6, Nov. 11. **Quarteira:** Sept. 24. **Sta. Bárbara de Nexe:** Apr. 22. **São Bartolomeu de Messines:** 4th Mon. of May, Sept. 19–21, Oct. 3–4. **São Bras de Alportel:** Feb. 2–3, Sept. 2. **Silves:** May 3–4, Oct. 31–Nov. 2, Dec. 21. **Tavira:** Aug. 1–2, Oct. 4–6. **Vila do Bispo:** Sept. 20. **Vila Real de Sto. António:** Oct. 10–15.

Market Days. Albufeira: every Sat. Lagos: 1st Sat. of each month. Loulé: every Sat. Portimão: 1st Mon. of each month. Quarteira: every 2nd Wed. Silves: 3rd Mon. of each month. All the main towns have weekly vegetable markets.

REAL ESTATE. The Algarve is a marvelous place to consider if you are thinking of buying property for a holiday home or retirement. However, property has greatly increased in value, so bargains are no longer available. We would also warn you to be very careful indeed when faced with pushy salesmen. The real estate waters of the Algarve are shark infested, and many an innocent swimmer has lost an arm and a leg. Remember that buying property in Portugal requires the same common sense as buying it at home. You may well be approached in the street by someone who has property to sell and will offer all sorts of blandishments to entrap you. You wouldn't think of dealing with him if he approached you in your home town, so don't be a sucker here in the sun. If you are really interested in buying property, or a part of a time-sharing development, then go about it seriously through a reputable real estate agent.

SPORTS. For further details of sports facilities ask at local Tourist Offices. **Golf.** *Quinta do Lago Club,* Almansil (tel. 089 94529), 27-hole course designed by William Mitchell; *Palmares Club,* Meia Praia, Lagos (tel. 082 62961), 18-hole course designed by Frank Pennink; *Penina Club,* Montes de Alvor, Portimão (tel. 082 22051), 18-hole course plus two 9-hole courses designed by Henry Cotton; *Vale do Lobo Club,* Vale do Lobo, Almansil (tel. 089 94145), 27-hole course designed by Henry Cotton; *Dom Pedro Club,* Vilamoura (tel. 089 35562), 18 hole-course designed by Frank Pennink; *Vilamoura Club,* Vilamoura (tel. 089 33652). 18-hole course designed by Frank Pennink. *Parque da Floresta,* Budens. 18 holes designed by Pepé Gancedo. All of these courses have clubhouses with full facilities.
Tennis. Can be played in every resort.
Horse Riding. Burgau, tel. 082 65290; Quinta da Balaia, (tel. 089 55787); Quinta do Lago, (tel. 089 94369); Quinta dos Amigos, (tel. 089 95636); Vilamoura, (tel. 089 66271). Carvoeiro, Casa Pegasus (tel. 082 52051); Guia, Quinta da Saudade, (tel. 089 56182).
Sailing. All along the coast. Main centers are at Ferragudo and Praia Grande.
Squash. Hotel Montechoro, (tel. 089 52651). Carvoeiro Club (tel. 082 57847). Quinta da Balaia, (tel. 089 55787).
Big Game Fishing. Praça da Republica 24A, Portimão (tel. 082 25866). There is also a Big Game Fishing Center at Vilamoura.

Windsurfing. Equipment can be hired and lessons are available at Albufeira, Alvor, Armação de Pera, Burgau, Faro Island, Ferragudo, Lagos, Praia da Luz, Praia Grande, Quinta do Lago and Vilamoura.

Water Skiing. Equipment and lessons available at Albufeira, Alvor, Armação de Pera, Burgau, Ferragudo, Praia da Luz, Praia da Oura and Praia Grande.

EXCURSIONS. Boat trips up the River Guadiana operate regularly in summer. Details from the Ferry Station in Vila Real de Santo António.

WATER PLEASURE PARKS. Alcantarilha, Almansil and Estombar have Water Pleasure Parks. At Almansil, for example, for 1,500$00 adults, children up to 10 half price. you can spend the entire day enjoying huge water slides, rapids, surf pools and many other water-based amusements. Half day, adults 750$00, children 450$00. All the parks have restaurants and snack bars.

USEFUL ADDRESSES. Consulate. *British,* Rua Sta. Isabel, 21–1° Esq., Portimão (tel. 082 27057).

Travel Agents. *American Express,* Star Travel Service, Rua Conselheiro Bivar 36, Faro (tel. 089 25126), and Rua Judice Bikar 26A, Portimão (tel. 082 25031).

Car Hire. All these and other leading car firms have offices at Faro airport as well as other main centers of the region. *Avis:* Estrada do Aeroporto. *Europcar:* Rua Diogo Leote, Albufeira; Rua Aboim Ascenção 111, Faro; Estrada Nacional 120, Lagos; Ave. 2, Portimão; Ave. Tomás Cabreira, Praia da Rocha. *Hertz:* Hotel Albufeira Jardim, Albufeira; Hotel Viking, Armação da Pera; Rua 1 de Maio 9, Faro; Vila Magna, Montechoro; Rua Tomás Cabreira, Praia da Rocha; Aldeia do Mar, Vilamoura.

Villa Hire. Mrs. Rosemary Reynolds, Quinta da Nora, Figueira 8500, Portimão, is a reliable local agent for renting houses or apartments, with or without self-drive cars.

THE ALENTEJO

The Alentejo is Portugal's largest province, stretching south of the River Sado from the Atlantic to the Spanish border. It is rolling country with great wheat fields, cork forests, olive groves, and the occasional castle-topped town or village. The only real mountains are those on the frontier and the long range dividing the Alentejo from the southernmost province, the Algarve.

Although Portugal is a small country, its provinces are highly individual, not only in their configuration but also in the people who inhabit them. The Alentejanos are independent, self-sufficient and fanatically clean. They whitewash their houses and cottages every year, which gives a delightful appearance to the scattered hamlets and *montes* (farmhouses), locally so called as they are almost always built on a low hill, or *monte*.

For hundreds of years the Alentejo was a battlefield: here the Portuguese fought first against the Moors and then against the Spanish. The border with Spain is long, defined by the low mountains running southwards from Portalegre in the north, then from near Elvas by the River Guadiana which marks the frontier for some 80 km. (50 miles). The Guadiana then meanders through the plains around Moura and Serpa, flows below Mertola—with its Christian church superimposed on a mosque—and turns east again to the frontier at Pomerão, from where it flows south for some 50 km. (30 miles) until it reaches the broad estuary between Vila Real de Santo António in the Algarve and Ayamonte in Spain.

As a result of invasion threats the Alentejo has a wealth of castles, great fortresses with high keeps (for example, Beja and Estremoz) and walled cities (Evora, Serpa, Elvas). There are many reminders of battles long ago, not only in the castles but, for instance, in the coat of arms of Evora to which two severed heads were added in honor of the deeds of a certain knight, Geraldo Sem Pavor (the Fearless). Warrior monks had monasteries here: the Order of São Bento de Aviz and the Hospitalers of St. John of Jerusalem at Flor da Rosa near Crato, where the Prior of Crato became a claimant to the Portuguese throne in 1589.

In the Middle Ages and right on until the beginning of the 19th century many attempts were made to come to terms with the Spaniards, whom the Portuguese have always regarded as their natural enemies. To this end a number of royal weddings took place, and it was in the Alentejo that the future couples would meet. King João V even built a palace at Vendas Novas in 1729 for the reception of the royal parties for the double marriage of his daughter to the elder son of Philip V of Spain and of that king's daughter to his own heir-apparent.

Almost until this century the Alentejo was the least peopled and most impoverished of all the provinces. In his classic book, *The Bible in Spain,* George Borrow, who crossed the Alentejo at the beginning of the last century, describes the landscape as one of extraordinary desolation inhabited by gypsies and ragged grazing flocks. Since the bloodless revolution of 1974, which ended 40 years of dictatorship, the countryside is slowly again becoming the granary of Portugal, aided by the construction of dams and irrigation projects. Much of the land is given over to large plantations of cork oak, known as cork forests even though the trees are set wide apart. Each tree is numbered, as by law the bark is allowed to be stripped only every nine years.

Under the trees sparse crops are sometimes grown or sheep grazed. Herds of razor-backed black pigs, now a rare sight, used to root for acorns beneath the cork trees, watched by a solitary swineherd in a brown, furred, tiered cape. However, the province is still famous for its excellent smoked pork products as well as for its local wines.

Second to the cork trees in number are the olive trees, which yield the oil used in all Portuguese and, indeed, Spanish cooking. Rice is grown in the paddy fields up the River Sado. Around Borba, to the east, there are enormous deposits of marble, so that in the local towns every doorstep and window surround is made of it.

The Big Farms

"The Alentejo has no shade" is an old saying, but although the sun strikes straight down for six months of the year, the winters can be exceptionally cold. A part of the harsh Iberian *meseta,* the Alentejo has the bare nobility of its landscape, its qualities of space and endurance.

Properties in the province are often very large. In the old days owners would visit them infrequently, for the cork stripping or at harvest-time, and many of the laborers were employed only for the plowing, seeding and harvesting periods. It was, then, not surprising that after the revolution it was a common occurrence for farm workers to take over the properties; this led to a sharp drop in production as the workers lacked the necessary expertise. In the last few years the government has been dividing the larger properties into smaller ones in order to spread ownership, and many of the original owners have been given back at least part of their lands.

It is not only the cottages, with their curious fretwork chimneys, that are special to the Alentejo, but even the farm carts, which have rounded, almost wagon-like tops to protect the driver and his produce from the burning sun or the icy winds and rain. These carts, painted in bright colors, are drawn by exceptionally large and handsome mules which are bred on most of the larger farms. They are dark brown in color, with blue eyes and black eyelashes.

Springtime in the Alentejo

The wide open spaces, castle-crowned hill towns and the wild flowers which carpet the ground in the spring, as well as some memorable buildings and works of art in several of the cities and towns, make this province the most beautiful in the minds of many travelers. But go in the spring or fall rather than in the height of summer, though even at this season the land has a noble beauty in its tawny, lion-colored spaces, barely shaded by the small leaves of the cork oak and the olive.

Spring is the time when the eucalyptus scent the air, storks build their untidy nests on church towers or trees and shepherds in long sheepskin coats carry newborn lambs. Much of the farm work is done by women and girls who sing as they work—almost polyphonically around Beja— and a man's felt hat, with an ear of wheat or a wild flower stuck in the ribbon, worn over a spotted headscarf protects them from the sun. The men sometimes stick a flower behind an ear, giving them a delightful rakish look.

In the oak groves, the workmen strip the cork from the bleeding tree trunks which smell of fresh sap, as do the cartloads of cork drawn by slow oxen to the warehouses. At noon, women walk beside the way, carrying water in earthenware jars—it is time for the midday meal. Soup is eaten from the *tarro,* a cork bucket that keeps food hot in winter and in summer keeps cold the soup of bread soaked in water and olive oil, with chopped raw onion, garlic and herbs. Here, you should taste the hearty herb-flavored soups, the salty smoked sausage, the fresh ewe cheese.

Discovering the Alentejo

Many travelers who fly into Lisbon and drive rapidly through the western part of the Alentejo en route to the Algarve are unaware that there are beautiful places on the way south.

Alcaçer do Sal is the first real Alentejano town. In the spring storks nest on every tower and belfry and make a strange clacking noise with their red beaks as they fly overhead. It is a charming town, tumbling down to the River Sado, and boasts a ruined castle and a small archeological museum (next to the municipal offices).

Avoid Sines on the coast, marred by the huge half-finished oil terminal and refinery started some 20 years ago with the idea of providing work. The few beaches on this long stretch of the Atlantic coast are beautiful but unsafe for bathing owing to the great force of the waves and the strong undertow. However, Vila Nova de Milfontes is safe (see *The Algarve* chapter), being on the estuary of the River Mira, and has delightful places in which to stay.

You may like to cut straight through the wheat fields from Alaçer do Sal towards Beja. At harvest-time the June countryside is whitened by the blur of chaff rising from the threshed grain. Work begins at sunrise, and goes on late into the evening. At midday, eucalyptus trees by the roadside seem to writhe in the burning sun.

In Beja, a museum is now housed in the convent behind whose walls Mariana Alcoforado, who lost her heart to the handsome Chevalier de Chamilly, wrote him the most moving of love letters. The wrought-iron window, behind which the Portuguese nun looked so long and so vainly for her lover's return, is shown to visitors. The turret still stands, and whoever has the strength to climb the steep stairs winding to the top will be rewarded by a breathtaking view of the outlying countryside. The castle, complete with towering keep, has Roman foundations.

Southwest of Beja—57 km. (35 miles) on N18 and N2—is Castro Verde, which has a particularly fine parish church with huge blue and white 18th-century pictorial glazed tiles of the Battle of Ourique above a tiled dado of dragons and vases of flowers. Not far away is one of the most delightful pousadas, that of Sta. Clara, overlooking a superb man-made lake; the lake is used for irrigation, so there are no ugly power complexes.

Near to the invisible line dividing the Alentejo from the Algarve—42 km. (26 miles) east of Castro Verde on N123—is Mertola, rising up from the lovely, wide, slow-moving River Guadiana to a castle with a fine keep built in 1292. The parish church was clearly once a mosque; it has an unmistakable *mihrab* at one side of the five aisles. Also in this town there is a charming little museum in the old Misericórdia; in a small workroom 17th- and 18th-century statues from churches round about are carefully restored. There are archeological remains, church ornaments, and paintings, including a pair of large naive paintings of Our Lady with St. George and the Dragon below.

This southeastern part of the Alentejo is particularly beautiful. The land is gently rolling, well cultivated, and in the spring covered with the giant white cistus, and wild lavender. Hoopoes dart about and rare birds of prey hover overhead.

Serpa—28 km. (17 miles) east of Beja on N260—is a castellated city guarded by two big round watchtowers, the Portas de Moura and the Portas de Beja. A couple of miles outside the town and overlooking the plain is the Pousada de São Gens, well-installed just below the Chapel of Our Lady of Guadaloupe. This ancient edifice stands high above the age-old olive trees that are said to have borne fruit when Serpa was wrested from the Moors 800 years ago.

Moura—28 km. (17 miles) northeast of Serpa—is another remote and delightful castellated city with the air of tranquillity that many of these distant Alentejo towns have.

North of Beja is Viana do Alentejo—49 km. (30 miles) by N18, N258–1, and N257—where the church, built against the castle walls, has a magnificent Manueline doorway; a few miles away is Agua de Peixes, country house of the Espirito Santos, the great banking family. Alvito is a picturesque place with white ancient houses, the Marquis of Alvito's 15th-century castle, and a 16th-century church.

Arraiolos

The small town of Arraiolos, due east of Lisbon on N4, has been known since the Middle Ages for its handsome hand embroidered carpets (visitors are welcome in the workshops) and its smoked loin of pork, or *paio*. The ruined castle, built by King Dinis around 1310, overlooks the whole countryside.

Nearby, it is worth going out of one's way to see the Quinta dos Loios, formerly a 15th-century convent (the fortified church is completely lined with 17th-century pictorial azulejos, including one of Edward the Confessor), and the manor house of Sempre Noiva, on the road to Evora. In spite of clumsy 19th-century repairs, it remains a splendid example of Moorish-Manueline domestic architecture.

Evora

Southeast of Arraiolos is Evora, a town in which it is a pleasure to get lost! The very names of the streets are a delight—street of the Countess's Tailor, of the Cardinal's Nurses, square of Our Lady of Poverty or of Our Lord of Earthquakes, alley of the Unshaved Man or of the Sulking Child. Fine avenues of plane trees lead to the gateways of palaces, so crowded together that long trailers of jasmine bind one to the other. There are 31 conventual buildings within the town walls.

The best stopover for the night is at the Pousada dos Loios. This unique hotel is installed in the former Convent of Loios, which dates from the early 16th century. During the reign of Manuel the Fortunate, Arruda, master builder of the Tower of Belém, embellished the chapter house with a horseshoe archway, and pillars topped with stone turbans. Under João II, a parlor was added, with Pompeii-style frescos. Now, the restaurant is installed behind the glassed-in arches of the cloister, halls are converted to magnificent lounges and the rooms (the former nuns' cells or bedrooms) are furnished with antique pieces.

Just outside the entrance stands the Temple of Diana, by far the finest remains of the Alentejo's Roman past. Built during the second century, much worn and for long marred by brick walls (it was a slaughterhouse until 1870), its fluted pillars now rise magnificently against the timeless sky. It is a pity, but no doubt practical in this close-built town, that cars are allowed to park around its base. The formal garden in front of the temple gives out onto a fine view over the countryside.

With her stark white walls, her archways, her wrought-iron balconies, her paved courtyards, her winding cobbled streets, Evora is still a Moorish town. The Largo das Portas de Moura is a setting for the Arabian nights, where ghosts of veiled women sit on the floor of the arched open gallery of the Cordovil Palace, or bend over the still waters of the stone basins.

The History of Evora

On a moonless night in the 12th century, Geraldo Sem Pavor climbed into the sleeping town and took it unawares; the Moors fought like lions to keep the town they loved, but it was a losing battle; the soldier brigand opened the gates to Afonso Henriques, and passed out of history.

In itself, the town meant nothing to the Burgundian kings, who preferred Coimbra or Leiria to the emptied shell stranded on a lonely sunburnt plain. It took the 14th century to bring it back to life, when the king left Lisbon to hold court in Evora, which fast became a hotbed of plots and counterplots, ending in bloodshed and prison.

Though taken up with the kingdom's rising sea power, the Aviz dynasty stayed very much attached to Evora. The Infanta Isabel, who was to become Grand Duchess of the Western World, was born there. Manuel I built himself a palace, and there gave Vasco da Gama the command of the first fleet to reach India. Gil Vicente, goldsmith and poet, welcomed in verse the birth of a prince, later João III, who was to make of Evora a center of learning. The University of the Holy Spirit produced some of the foremost scholars of the day.

Little is left of the royal palace, beyond its handsome windows in a public garden; but the old university, now again in use, is in good repair, with courtyards, galleries, carved woodwork and painted ceilings. Held forever in a painted life, smiling gentlemen greet you at the door; a wainscot of glazed tiles, with hunting scenes, banquets, and feastings, lines the corridors, stairways and classrooms.

Of her royal past and renowned scholarship, Evora has kept the riches of her museums, her libraries, and the treasures of her churches. The Sé, a rugged and squat cathedral with battlements, spiked tower, and a Romanesque belfry, has a carven row of stern apostles over its porch. In the Treasury is a Gothic Virgin who holds open her cloak to show the nine outstanding happenings of her life, carved in ivory. Religious art in Evora takes strange forms. Strapping young men, stone brothers to Michelangelo's, recline on the Baroque facade of the church of Graça. The museum, in a palace between the Cathedral and the Temple of Diana, has some splendid early canvasses including many by Frei Carlos, a monk who worked in Evora in the 16th century. But the most macabre sight is in the church of São Francisco. Here you will find the Ossuary Chapel, with its walls and pillars lined with the bones of about 5000 people.

In the old town, the living walk unheeding beside the unseen ghosts of the dead. Students and priests pass under the stone archways, mingling with peasants in brown woolen capes, up from the country to sell the oil from their olive trees, to bargain for a mule harness, or to buy a jalopy for the farm. In the narrow winding streets, bric-à-brac shops offer a medley of wares, with sometimes a find among the jumble of dusty junk. However, the best old pewter and earthenware are not for sale; they have been bought up by Snr. Gião, innkeeper and art lover.

The new sports center, a short distance away outside the walls, is set among green lawns, with paddling pools for children, a fine swimming pool from whose diving board you can glimpse the age-old walls and sky-stabbing church belfries of the ancient city.

Off the beaten track near the Spanish frontier at São Leonardo on N256, is Monsaraz, some ten km. (six miles) from Reguengos. A fortified town, unspoilt since the Middle Ages, it overlooks the wide valley of the Guadiana where that river flows into Portugal. Nearer to the border is Mourão, another castellated city which was also once a key stronghold.

Evoramonte and Estremoz

On the road between Evora and Estremoz (N18) is the perfect walled village of Evoramonte on a high hill with a great square castle overlooking the wide plains. See the smallest Misericórdia in the country and rare frescoes in the parish church.

As old and noble a town as Evora, Estremoz, dazzling in its whiteness, raises its hilltop castle against the sky, cut in blue stripes by the archers' loopholes on the proud battlements. It is hemmed in by a network of narrow winding streets, lined with fine Gothic or Manueline houses. The lower town is guarded by fortified gateways, bastions with oubliettes, and moats. The Rossio is a wide open space, surrounded by convents, a hospice, and the town hall. In it is held, on Saturdays, a bustling market, where everything is for sale, from livestock to wooden spoons, and a wide range of pottery. Nearby is the potters' street, its cobbled steps flowering with geraniums, red and pink and white. It was to Estremoz that Saint Queen Isabella came to die, as did her son Pedro, lover of Inês de Castro, in 1367. In their palace by the keep of the great castle is now a superb pousada.

Opposite, the old Hospital de Caridade houses a charming museum with lovely examples of the local pottery and a workshop below, where copies of the traditional pots and jars can be bought, as well as modern figurines and ornaments.

In another museum on the Rossio is a small and fascinating collection of handicrafts from all parts of the Alentejo, with household objects carved in cork and reed and willow wood by shepherds during the long dark winter evenings in the *montes* or farmhouses.

In Estremoz, as in the nearby village of Borba, the window frames and portals of even the poorest houses are made in marble, often whitewashed to cover the weather stains. The very streets of Borba are paved in marble, and the village is renowned for its wrought-iron balconies as well as for the array of antique shops along the main street. Borbo, Redondo and Vidigueira produce much of the best wine of the Alentejo.

Fronteira, Avis, and Brotas

A big swing round from Estremoz north, west, then southwest, starting on N245, will bring you first to Fronteira, which prides itself on its 17th-century town hall and houses.

Aviz—23 km. (14 miles) west on N243—overlooking a series of narrow lakes, is the cradle of the Military Order of Aviz created in 1211 by Afonso II. There are the remains of old walls, some churches, and outside the parish church an interesting marble pillory surmounted by an eagle with widespread wings.

Southwest of Aviz, along a good road, N370, is the cheerful town of Pavia, remarkable for a huge dolmen in the main square. The Alentejo is noted for its large number of dolmens and other Megalithic remains, usually out in the country. Pavia's dolmen encloses a tiny chapel dedicated to St. Denis. In the same square is a museum (open only in the afternoon). At the top of the town the parish church of St. Paul has the typical Alentejo pepperpot-topped buttresses at either side. The vaulted roof is supported by very early columns crowned by anthropomorphic capitols.

The nearby village of Brotas has a charming pilgrimage church, now a national monument, in its center. Carpet azulejos line the walls and the ivory Virgin on the altar is carved from an elephant's tooth.

Four km. (two miles) from Brotas, along a difficult track through the cork and olive groves, is a strange, early 16th-century building standing some 18 meters (60 ft.) high amid low cottages and farm sheds. This is the Torre das Aguias (Eagle's Tower), built as a country house for the Condes de Atalaia in 1520, and seems to be unique. The noble stone walls are pierced by Gothic windows and the parapet is topped by the usual Alentejo cylindrical pyramids.

Many of the churches in the Alentejo have whole chapels and rooms covered by *ex votos*. These touchingly naive paintings, some dating from the 18th century, portray the happy recipients of cures of various ills, and are a fascinating record not only of faith but also of furnishings and clothing.

Vila Viçosa

The rich Duke of Bragança, who occupied the throne of Portugal in 1640, after 60 years of Spanish occupation, missed his newly finished palace, the concerts given in his chapel, and his library filled with old musical scores. Vila Viçosa, indeed, has the very feel of happiness and peace. Nevertheless, the strong walls and ramparts of the old town are grim reminders of the dangers that threatened the place throughout the Middle Ages. Vila Viçosa has many legends of unhappy loves, and it was there that King Carlos spent his last night before his assassination in Lisbon, in 1908.

The classic proportions of the big square, or Terreiro do Paço, where João IV forever rides a bronze horse; the strong scent of orange blossom in the spring; the simple dignity of the house fronts; the silence of the stark white streets, all give the small town an old-fashioned charm that slows the most restless of wanderers to a standstill. Geraniums and rambling roses grow up the walls to the rooftops, fall from balconies, and fill the courtyards. Sad ghosts haunt the splendid ducal palace, in whose big wardrobes hang the fading clothes of the last ill-starred monarchs. The dressing-room of Queen Maria Pia still holds her wrapper, her silver-backed brushes, her scent bottles. The unexpectedly gifted watercolors of her son Carlos, the hideous dining room with chandeliers made out of antlers, and the table set with cut glass silver and china, evoke the tranquil hours of the royal family before death and banishment overcame them. The palace is beautifully kept but as a museum it is somewhat disappointing, despite the fine Brussels tapestries, Empire clocks and superb porcelain. However, the photographs of royal junketings at the beginning of this century are delightful, and the coach museum, armory, and the kitchen with an array of polished copper pans are all worth seeing.

Elvas

The town of Elvas is almost on the frontier. The Vauban-style fortifications hold within their bastions a chalk-white town, busy as a beehive. The Manueline cathedral, the museum, the noble houses, all recall a royal past. The octagonal 16th-century church of the Freiras de São Domingos is most unusual. The eight Tuscan columns supporting the roof are painted with formal flowers and arabesques and the walls are lined with carpet tiles. In the streets, in the squares, under the archways, the jingling of mule harness mingles gaily with the church bells. The five tiered arches of a handsome 15th-century aqueduct cut a row of eyelets in the deep blue sky. The modern pousada, just outside the walls, is noted for its excellent restaurant.

North to Portalegre

Driving north from Estremoz on N18 into the Serra da Boa Viagem, you will come upon a different Alentejo—one of rolling hills, rushing streams, and flowering acacia trees.

Portalegre is renowned for its 17th-century houses, the convent of St. Bernard, and the cathedral. The cathedral has fine retables, and at its side an unusual Baroque cloister with oval windows set in frames above the pediments of the classical arches. In the library of the bishop's palace alongside, rare vestments, embroidered by nuns in England before the 16th-century Reformation, are shown on request. Nearby is a delightful regional museum filled with furniture, antique pottery, silver snuffboxes and lovely porcelain. The church of Bomfin, at the end of the town on the road to Castelo de Vide, is a jeweled box of Baroque goldwork. Also open to visitors is Portalegre's famous tapestry factory, where 5,000 shades of wool are used to copy the cartoons of the French artist Lurçat and other master tapestry-designers, Portuguese artists such as Almada Negreiros and Carlos Botelho, Manuel Lapa and Camarinha.

Yet another colorful border town is Marvão—north of Portalegre, 15 km. (nine miles) by N359—its fortified walls standing high on a rocky spur, like an eagle's nest, affording a vast panorama. Blue-tailed kestrels hover above the castle walls, and flowers hang from every window. The pousada will tempt you to stay there.

Castelo de Vide, a little northwest, is a joy. As aloof from the world as Monsaraz, it has none of its harshness; the white town is a bower of roses in the soft green-filtered sun. The town's narrow little streets, lined with houses ornamented by Gothic and Manueline doorways, meander up to the castle, past the Jewish quarter with its tiny 16th-century synagogue. Inside the castle walls there is a whole village, also ablaze with flowers and alive with people chatting. You may eagerly be shown a small house, the home of an artisan who makes and carves fascinating figures, unfortunately not for sale.

To the west of Portalegre by N119, lie two old strongholds of the Knights of Malta—the 14th-century fortified monastery of Flor da Rosa, and Crato, seat of the Prior of the Order since 1350. At the time when Philip II of Spain occupied Portugal, the Prior of Crato was António, illegitimate son of King Pedro, and in 1589, aided by the British Admiral Sir Francis Drake and Sir John Norris with 12,000 men, he led the Portuguese nationalists.

PRACTICAL INFORMATION FOR THE ALENTEJO

TOURIST OFFICES. There are local tourist offices in the following towns: **Alcaçer do Sal,** Largo Pedro Nunes; **Alter do Chão,** Largo do Pelourinho; **Arronches,** Rua Dr. Eduardo Corvelo; **Beja,** Rua Capitão João Francisco de Sousa 25; **Castelo de Vide,** Rua Bartolomeu Alvares da Santa; **Elvas,** Praça da Republica; **Evora,** Praça do Giraldo 73 and Ave. São Sebastião; **Grandola,** Rua Dr. José Pereira Barradas; **Marvão,** Rua

Dr. Matos Magalhães; **Monsaraz,** Rua Direita; **Moura,** Praça Sacadura Cabral; **Nisa,** Rossio; **Portalegre,** Rua 19 de Junho 40–42; **Santarém,** Rua Capelo Ivens; **Santiago do Cacèm,** Ave. D. Nuno Álvares Pereira; **Serpa,** Largo D. Jorge de Melo 2–3; **Sines,** Largo Ramos da Costa; **Vila Viçosa,** Praça da Republica.

HOTELS AND RESTAURANTS

Alcaçer Do Sal (Setúbal). *Estalagem Herdade da Barrosinha* (M), Estrada Nacional 5 (tel. 065 62363). 10 rooms with bath. Pleasant rooms and excellent cuisine. Fishing. A restful stopover about a mile off the Lisbon–Algarve highway. DC, MC, V.

Beja (provincial capital). *Pensão Cristina* (E), Rua de Mertola 71 (tel. 084 23036). 31 rooms with bath. AE, DC, MC. *Pensão Santa Barbara* (E), Rua de Mertola 56 (tel. 084 22028). 26 rooms with bath. DC, MC. *Bejense* (M), Rua Capitão Francisco Sousa 57 (tel. 084 25001). 24 rooms with bath. *Residência Coelho* (M), Praça da Republica 15 (tel. 084 24031). 26 rooms with bath. All serve breakfast only.
Restaurants. There is a large number of café-restaurants as well as the following. *Aficionado* (M), Rua dos Açoutados 38. Good parking. Closed Tues. AE, DC, MC. *Central* (M), Praça da Republica 23. *Luis da Rocha* (M), Rua Capitão Francisco Sousa 63. MC. *Tipico Bar Dancing* (M), Rua da Branca 5.

Canal Caveira (Setúbal). Three excellent restaurants in a row on main highway to Algarve. All (I) with kitchens on view. Two can share a dish.

Castelo De Vide (Portalegre). Spa. *Albergaria Jardim* (E), Rua Sequeira Sameiro 6 (tel. 045 91217). 20 rooms with bath. *Pensão Casa do Parque* (M), Ave. da Aramanha (tel. 045 91250). 23 rooms with bath. Breakfast only. *Sol e Serra* (M), tel. 045 91301. 51 rooms with bath. Pool. Excellent food. AE, DC.
Restaurants. *Dom Pedro V* (M), Praça D. Pedro V 10. MC. *Parque* (I), Ave. Aramanha. Good parking. MC.

Elvas (Portalegre). *Estalagem Dom Sancho II* (E), Praça da Republica 20 (tel. 068 62684). 24 rooms with bath. Good food. DC, MC. *Pousada de Santa Luzia* (E), tel. 068 62194. 11 rooms with bath. Just outside the walls; light, pleasant flower-filled rooms in summer, blazing fire in winter. Excellent food. Cellar full of antiques for sale. AE, DC, MC, V. *Dom Luis* (M), Ave. de Badajoz (tel. 068 62756). 46 rooms with bath. Pool. AE, DC, MC. *Pensão O Lidador* (M), Rua de Alcamin 33 (tel. 068 62601). 19 rooms. With annex; breakfast only.
Restaurants. *Aqueduto* (M), Ave. da Piedade. *Don Quixote* (M), Pedras Negras 4. MC. *Cidade Nova* (M), Praça Dr. João Varela. *Sagres* (M), Praça 25 de Abril 12. *El Cristo* (I), Parque de Piedade. Closed Mon. AE, DC, MC.

Estremoz (Evora). *Pousada da Rainha Santa Isabel* (L), tel. 068 22618. 23 rooms with bath. In a splendid castle; rooms are airconditioned and fittings luxurious and in perfect style. Wonderful seafood specialties. AE, DC, MC, V. *Alentejano* (I), Rossio 50 (tel. 068 22717). 22 rooms. Right on the huge main square. Breakfast only. AE, DC, MC, V. *Pensão Restaurante Estremoz* (I), Rossio 15 (tel. 068 22843). 9 rooms. *Residência Carvalho* (I), Largo da Republica 27 (tel. 068 22712). 15 rooms with bath. Breakfast only. Recommended.

Restaurants. *Aguias de Ouro* (M). On the main square. AE, DC, MC. *Alentejano* (M). Also for good food on the main square. AE, DC, MC. *Arco-Iris* (I), Rua Brito Capelo. Good food and wine. Closed Mon.

Evora (provincial capital). Choice of accommodations includes several pensions and a youth hostel. *Pousada dos Loios* (L), tel. 066 24051. 28 rooms with bath. Lovely 16th-century monastery beside Diana's Temple, museum and cathedral. Dine in the glassed-in cloisters. AE, DC, MC, V. *Albergaria Vitoria* (E), Rua Diana de Lis (tel. 066 27174). 48 rooms with bath. Breakfast only. AE, DC. *Monte dos Pensamentos* (E), (tel. 068 22375). 3 rooms with bath, 2 sitting rooms, pool, riding. Meals available. Country House Tourism. *Planicie* (M), Rua Miguel Bombarda 40 (tel. 066 24026). 33 rooms with bath. Ask for a quiet room at the back. AE, MC. *Santa Clara* (M), Travessa da Milheira 19 (tel. 066 24141). 30 rooms with bath. AE, DC, MC. *Solar O Eborense* (M), Largo da Misericórdia 1 (tel. 066 22031). 29 rooms with bath. Pleasant and quiet; breakfast only. AE, DC, MC.

Restaurants. *Cozinha de Santo Humberto* (E), Rua da Moeda 39. Rustic decor. Closed Thurs. AE, DC, MC. *Fialho* (E), Travessa das Mascarehnhas 14. Recommended. Closed Mon. AE, DC, MC. *Abadia* (M), Rua Pedro Simão 8. *O Gião* (M), Rua da Republica 81. Good but folksy; owner-managed. Closed Mon. AE, DC, MC.

Ferreira do Alentejo (Beja). *Estalagem Eva* (E), Estrada Nacional (tel. 084 72251). 8 rooms with bath. Restaurant serving regional specialties. *Pensão Santo António* (M), Estrada Nacional 2 (tel. 084 72320). 14 rooms with bath. Breakfast only.

Restaurant. *Planicie Verde* (M), Rua de Lisboa.

Marvão (Portalegre). *Pousada de Santa Maria* (E), tel. 045 93201. 9 rooms with bath. Enchanting situation in medieval hilltop town. Pleasant rooms and good food. AE, DC, MC, V. *Estalagem D. Dinis* (M), Rua Matos Magalhães (tel. 045 93236). 8 rooms with bath. In nice house on medieval street; restaurant. AE, DC, MC.

Mansaraz (Evora). *Estalagem de Monsaraz* (E), Largo de São Bartolomeu (tel. 066 55112). 7 rooms with bath. Recommended. AE, DC, MC.

Montemor-O-Novo (Evora). *Pensão Monte Alentejo* (M), Ave. Gago Coutinho 8 (tel. 066 82141). 10 rooms with bath. Breakfast only.

Restaurants. Several café-restaurants, including *Catita* (I), Largo Humberto Delgado. Good simple food with excellent wine.

Moura (Beja). *Hotel de Moura* (I), Praça Gago Coutinho 1 (tel. 984 22494). 37 rooms with bath. Breakfast only.

Restaurants. *Mourense* (I), Rua da Republica. *O Cantinho* (I), Rua da Republica.

Portalegre (provincial capital). Accommodation choices include a youth hostel. *Dom João III* (M), Ave. da Liberdade (tel. 045 21192). 56 rooms with bath. MC. *Mansão Alto Alentejo* (M), Rua 19 de Junho 59 (tel. 045 22290). 15 rooms. Breakfast only. Central. *Pensão Nova* (M), Rua 31 de Janeiro 28 (tel. 045 21605). 12 rooms with bath. *Quinta da Saude* (M), tel. 045 22324. 11 rooms with bath. MC. *São Pedro* (M), Rua da Mouraria 14 (tel. 045 21190). 14 rooms with bath. Breakfast only. *Residência Facha* (I), Largo António José Lourinho 5 (tel. 045 23161). 23 rooms with bath. New, good value, central; breakfast only.

Restaurants. *O Alpendre* (M), Rua 31 de Janeiro 19. MC. Closed Mon. *O Tarro* (M), Ave. Movimento das Forças Armadas. Bar lounge; good food and Vale de Rocha wine from Portalegre in pleasant restaurant. Closed Mon. MC.

Redondo (Evora). **Restaurant.** *Casa dos Frangos* (I). Excellent food and Redondo wine.

Santa Clara-A-Velha (Beja). *Pousada de Santa Clara* (E), tel. 083 52250. 6 rooms with bath. Remote, in wonderful country about 30 km. (20 miles) from Odemira, overlooking splendid lake. Garden, pool, boating, water sports. Excellent food. AE, DC, MC, V.

Santiago do Cacèm (Setúbal). *Pousada de São Tiago* (E), tel. 069 22459. 7 rooms with bath. Near Roman ruins of Mirobriga. AE, DC, MC, V. *Albergaria D. Nuno* (M), Ave. D. Nuno Alvares Pereira 88 (tel. 069 23325). 75 rooms with bath. Breakfast only. AE. *Pensão Esperança* (M), Largo 25 de Abril 20 (tel. 069 22193). 40 rooms with bath.

Restaurants. There are several cafe restaurants.

Serpa (Beja). 32 km. (20 miles) from the Spanish border. *Pousada de São Gens* (E), Alto de São Gens (tel. 084 90327). 17 rooms with bath. Pleasant rooms, very comfortable with good food. About 2 km. out of town, in lovely country. AE, DC, MC, V.

Restaurant. *Café Alentejano* (M), Praça da Republica.

Sines (Setúbal). *Pensão Malhada* (E), Rua Deputado António Santos Silva 2 (tel. 069 634055). 27 rooms with bath. With annexes; rather noisy. Breakfast only. MC. *Pensão Buzio* (M), Ave. 25 de Abril (tel. 069 632114). 40 rooms with bath. With annex. Breakfast only. AE, DC, MC.

Restaurants. *Buzio* (M), Ave. 25 de Abril. Closed Mon. AE, DC, MC. *Varanda do Oceano* (M), Rua Rampa. Closed Sat. AE, DC, MC.

Torrão (Setúbal). *Pousada de Vale do Gaio*, tel. 065 66100. 7 rooms with bath. By huge artificial lake in lovely country, 25 km. (15 miles) from Alcaçer do Sal. Fishing, shooting. AE, DC, MC, V.

Vila Nova de Milfontes (Beja). *O Castelo* (L), tel. 083 96108. 12 rooms with bath. Visitors entertained as guests in this beautiful house overlooking the Mira estuary—an experience not to be missed. No casual visitors for meals. *Duna Parque* (M), tel. 083 96451. 27 apartments and 11 bungalows. AE, DC, MC, V. *Moinho da Asneira* (M), tel. 083 96182. Rooms and villas for short and long stays. Pool, water sports, restaurant; under same management as Duna Parque. AE, DC.

Restaurants. *Mil Reis* (M). Good for seafood. *Chave d'Ouro* (I). Budget fish dishes.

Vila Viçosa (Evora). *Casa dos Arcos* (E), Praça Martim Afonso de Sousa 16 (tel. 068 42518). 8 rooms with bath. Lovely old palace. Breakfast only. AE, DC.

Restaurant. *Ouro Branco* (M), Campo da Restauração 43. Closed Mon. MC.

CAMPING. There are campsites at: Beja; Evora; Melides (Praia de Galé and Lagoa de Melides); Portalegre; Sines; Sto. André; Vila Nove de Milfontes (Centro de Férias and Parque de Milfontes).

PLACES OF INTEREST. Museums are usually open daily, except Mondays and public holidays, 10–5, but double check the times on the spot. Some close for lunch. Entrance fees are between 150$00 and 300$00. Most towns have churches with some interesting features, worth dropping in to if you are passing through.

Alcaçer do Sal. Municipal Museum, Igreja do Espirito Santo (Church of the Holy Spirit). Archeology of the district displayed in 14th-century church (greatly modified in 18th century).

Alter. Estação Zootecnica (National Stud), 3 km. (2 miles) from Alter do Chão. Originally the royal stud, now the national horse-breeding center and experimental farm.

Arraiolos. Castle. Workshops for hand-embroidered carpets.

Beja. Museu de Rainha D. Leonor (Queen Leonor Museum), Convento da Conceição. Collections of paintings, liturgical silver, azulejos, local costumes. Closed for lunch.

Military Museum, in castle. Closed for lunch.

Roman Villa, at Pisôes nearby. Ruins and small museum exhibiting tiles, jewelry, and so on.

Castelo de Vide. Megalithic Monuments and **Roman Ruins.**
Medieval Jewish Quarter. With tiny synagogue.

Crato. Municipal Museum. Containing a collection of images of the Child Jesus.
Templars' Monastery of Flor da Rosa.

Elvas. Municipal Museum. Amusing collection.

Estremoz. Craft Museum, beside Misericórdia in the Rossio.
Municipal Museum. In former Hospital de Caridade, near the castle, with pottery workshop below. Open P.M. only.

Evora. Cathedral Treasury. Up long flight of stairs to the choir and galleries of the cathedral. Remarkable church vessels, statues and fittings.
Igreja das Merces (Church of Mercy). Decorative art. Open Thurs. and Sun. only.
Municipal Museum, in former Archbishop's Palace. Fine collection of Portuguese Primitive paintings, furniture and archeological remains.

Mertola. Sacred Art Museum, in former Misericórdia chapel. Open P.M. only.

Pavia. Local Museum. In main square, opposite Chapel of St. Denis in dolmen. Open P.M. only.

Portalegre. Bishop's Palace, by the Cathedral. English medieval embroidered vestments shown on request. Tapestry workshops. **House of José Régio.** Folk art. Closed Tues.
Municipal Museum. By the cathedral, with good furniture and porcelain.

Santiago do Cacèm. Castle. Of Arab origin, rebuilt by Christians in 13th century.
Municipal Museum. Archeological and ethnographical exhibits. The nearby Roman city of Miróbirga is being excavated.

Sines. Municipal Museum. Archeological and ethnographical exhibits.
Natural History Museum. Collections of marine and land flora and fauna.

Vila Viçosa. Palácio Ducal (Ducal Palace). Splendid rooms and contents of a royal palace. Also coaches and carriages. Open Tues. to Sun. 10–5; closed for lunch.

SPECIAL EVENTS. For further details and exact dates, consult local tourist offices. **February.** Huge annual fair at Evora, Feb. 2. **May.** Romaria at Convento de São Paulo, Serra da Ossa, on Ascension Thursday (annual opportunity to visit Convent of St. Paul the Hermit, with fine 18th-century buildings and azulejos). May Fair at Vila Viçosa, held in the streets between medieval castle and ducal palace, end of month. **June.** Huge annual fair at Evora, June 29. **August.** Feira de São Lourenço at Castelo de Vide, Aug. 10: popular fair in medieval streets, agricultural produce and local handicrafts sold. **September.** Important cattle fair at Moura, mid-month, agricultural produce, locally made woven baskets and earthenware pottery. *Romaria do Jesus da Piedade* at Elvas, gathering of country people for big cattle fair, Sept. 20–25. Fair and festival of Nossa Senhora de Aires at Viana do Alentejo, with regional agricultural produce and local artisan work, last weekend of Sept.

SPORTS. For further details of sports facilities ask at local Tourist Offices. **Horse Riding.** *Sociedade Hipica e Lebreira de Elvas,* Elvas (tel. 068 63734); *Sitio da Lameira,* Reguengos de Monsaraz (tel. 066 52465).
Tennis. Jardim Municipal, Elvas (tel. 068 62314); *Clube de Futebol de Estremoz,* Estremoz (tel. 068 22163); *Juventud Sport Club,* Evora (tel. 066

22426); Estalagem Monte das Flores (tel. 066 25490); *Ténis Clube de Portalegre,* Portalegre (tel. 045 22698); *Clube de Ténis de Santo André,* Santiago de Cacèm (tel. 069 23185); Camara Municipal, Sines (tel. 069 633181); *Ténis Clube Vila Viçosa,* Vila Viçosa (tel. 068 42305).

Sailing. *Barragem do Caia,* Campo Maior (tel. 068 68432); *Clube Nautico de Sines,* Sines (tel. 069 63377).

Windsurfing. *Barragem do Caia,* Campo Maior (tel. 068 68432).

RIBATEJO

Reached by the northern autostrada, Al, Vila Franca de Xira is the Portuguese bullfighting capital. Its only monument is the bullring. The bridge that spans the River Tagus connects it directly with the vast, humid plains where fighting bulls and horses are raised side by side. Both are magnificent.

From ancient times, the bull has always been a symbol of force and fertility. The Romans were therefore surprised to find, in the Iberian Peninsula, men who liked to measure their strength against bulls that were particularly aggressive and spirited, and which in Lusitania they confronted on horseback or sometimes even on foot.

In the early days, various phases of the hunt were imitated, the horseman being armed with a lance; later the pursuit became a kind of ritual dance with death. During the reign of King Manuel, people diverted themselves by pitting bulls against tigers, rhinoceroses or black slaves armed with daggers, even as Nero had done, and soon afterwards young nobles in turn entered the arena, assisted by their attendants.

By the 18th century, the cavaliers began the technique of highschool training for the superb stallions, that were already used in Portugal for the bullfights. The heirs of the most illustrious families of the kingdom wanted to display their banners and affirm their prowess in the *touradas* that were organized at any and every pretext. The royal family never failed to attend these events, for which nearly everyone got into debt, as this form of entertainment has always been fantastically expensive. Only adult bulls and thoroughbreds were presented. The constantly perfected rules of the game required intense and prolonged training. The infatuation and enthusiasm of the public drove the *toureiros* to recklessness: that of the Portuguese Count of Arcos in Salvaterra de Magos (1799) was fatal to him. He was killed before the eyes of the entire court. It was at this time that the King, a severe critic of these costly amusements, declared: "Portugal is too weak to risk the life of a man against that of a bull."

From this day on, putting the bull to death was prohibited, the horns of the animal were protected by a ball placed at the tip of each horn, held in place by a leather sheath (the bull is *embolado*). The Portuguese *toureiros* continued to refine their technique and fashioned Portuguese bullfighting into a performance that does not have the violence of the Spanish *corrida*, though it surpasses it in elegance and virtuosity. Even today, many Portuguese aristocrats become *cavaleiros*—fighters of the bull on horseback.

The bulls are all the more pugnacious in that they are of unimpaired vigor. The best fighting animals are raised in rich, vast pastures where the young bulls can roam freely.

The River Tagus and Festa Brava

When it reaches Ribatejo, the River Tagus, weary of its long and often turbulent journey across the harsh plateau of Castile and the rough ridges of the Portuguese Beiras, spreads out and takes its ease in the plain as soon as it has been joined by the Zêzere, which shifts its course toward the south. The railroad to Lisbon follows the river and gives a splendid view of this fascinating part of the country.

The river then becomes so big—especially when swollen by the mountain snows at winter's end—that it spreads out across the Santarém basin, flooding the surrounding countryside, the *lezirias* (low-lying land). In the spring, it calms down, the waters recede, leaving on its soft banks a thick, fertile sediment. The humid meadows then become covered with succulent grass and the islets encircled by the myriad arms of the now drowsy Tagus yield abundant harvests. These green or gold islands are the *mochoes* which, seen from the air, look like rafts floating on the waters of the majestic river. There is just time to sow the wheat, and the rice in the paddy fields at the water's edge, to reap and store them before the return of winter with its floods and the exodus of man and beast. Only the shad fishermen stay at their posts, their white houses mounted on piles. Some of them even live all year round in their boats among the osier groves and the weeping willow beds along the banks. Much of this strange world is a bird sanctuary and not only rare ducks and waders but even the occasional flamingo can be seen.

Black bulls gallop across the pasture, where the grass is so thick it appears blue. The distant landscape is hazy, the horizons immense. The cattle-raising farms are thinly scattered and vast, the living quarters often of an exquisite charm, rose walls ennobled by the glorious purple of huge bougainvillaea, distaff-shaped yews and clipped boxwood. However, the most luxurious part of these big houses is found in the stables and stalls. Breeding is carefully planned and the young animals, foals or bulls, are placed under observation from birth. Only the most exceptional will know the exhausting glory of the arena.

The bullfighting season opens on Easter Sunday. It is a spectacle that, despite the competition of football matches, continues to fascinate Portuguese of all ages. Although the *corrida,* properly speaking, is the glorious finale of the festivities, it is given additional flavor and excitement by the varied preliminaries and the extension of the epilogue and in order to savor a *festa brava* in all its colorful diversity, one must go to the Ribatejo.

The bulls are brought in on the eve of the fight; one sees them passing through the streets, proudly led by mounted *campinos* who have donned their white stockings, starched shirts fastened at the collar and wrist by silver buttons, and the sash of red flannel well-tightened about the waist. Loose, scarlet vests provide ample elbow room and, pushed down to the eyes, the green bonnets with their red pompons flap in the breeze raised by the gallop. This is called the *espera,* or the wait for the bulls.

The bulls will parade through the festive, bedecked towns, which are thronged with curious onlookers lining the streets. The weight and gloss of the animals are discussed, bets are placed, and the daring amuse themselves by goading the bulls. There is always one that becomes detached from the group and finds himself isolated. This is a foreseen diversion. This young bull, irascible but not ferocious, will never know the arena. He is destined for the recreation of amateurs who dare to brave him, ready to scale balconies and lamp posts to evade him. Occasionally, when one of these encounters has been heated, there are torn shirts, some broken bones, quite a few scratches. One or two *campinos* are on duty to see that this never goes any further.

During this time, the real fighting bulls are assembled in the *curral,* where they will rest in the shade until it is time to enter the lists. Bullfighting in Portugal, when it is performed in the old-fashioned style, in full gala dress, is a dazzling sight. Heralded by the sound of bugles, the kettledrummers in 18th-century costume enter, followed by golden carriages from which the matadors descend and mount their thoroughbreds. The splendor of their trappings is surpassed only by the costumes of the matadors, silk vests embroidered with gold, satin jackets, tricorns with ostrich plumes. At the throat, the black tie of mourning. After that come the *moços de forcado* on foot. The *Peao de Brega* carries the lances and the beribboned darts or *bandarilhas* and the capes which are unfurled. All those who are to participate in the combat are lined up in the vast arena under the heat of the sun or the spotlights. They salute the audience before leaving.

Then the horsemen begin the *cortesias,* parading around the enclosure and guiding their stallions through the most elegant and complicated equestrian maneuvers. A second blare of bugles announces the arrival of the bull. The gate is opened, and he charges like a huge black torpedo into the sunlight. The bullfight unfolds with the placing of a certain number of *bandarilhas* in order to fatigue the bull and lead him to that moment of truth which permits the mortal thrust, but in Portugal this final thrust is always feigned.

The laws that govern bullfighting are very strict. The animal must never be attacked by treachery, or when he is immobile. The *bandarilhas* must not be placed at random but in a narrowly limited region of the upper back known as the *morillo.* Of course, the bull must never even graze the horse. The darts become shorter and shorter, the engagement more and more close between the bull and his adversary. The parries, the close calls, are of lightning rapidity and amazing suppleness, the fallible precision required to execute these movements is reminiscent of a ballet. The danger is always present, and provides the solemn counterpoint to all the lightness and grace. But the danger, too, is hidden.

The "Pegas"

A highly developed exercise in style, the Portuguese bullfight ends with the placement of the final *bandarilha*. The horseman then leaves amid acclamation from the crowd after having directed a final salute to the public, and another spectacle begins, that of a more rugged tone, *as pegas*. And this is a bullfighting exercise that is practiced only in Portugal. The *pegas*, imported from Greece, are the famous "dances of the sacred bull" which one sees on Cretan vases. The practise has been lost there while it lives on in Portugal in all its astonishing audacity. On foot, bare-handed, eight men advance in single file to meet the bull. Their leader detaches himself from the group and challenges the beast, hands on hips, offering himself as a target to the furious charge. And when the bull accosts him, he throws himself at its head, does a hand spring on its horns while his companions grapple with the animal and subdue it. There are various kinds of *pegas* depending on whether the animal is attacked head on, from the side or even in backing away. It is always awesome.

The bullfight ended, the oxen come in to fetch the bull. Depending upon the virtues he has exhibited in combat, he will be slaughtered or brought back to Ribatejo for the reproduction of other animals as valiant as he. A bull can never be put into the arena twice; familiarized with all the tactics, he would be too dangerous.

After the last bull has gone back to the *curral,* the crowd leaves the Praça de Touros, and then begin suppers that last until dawn. The plaintive clamor of the *fado* pulsates in the darkness. The folklore festivals of Ribatejo are noisy, colorful, earthy—well-earned relaxation following weeks of hard work, hours of feverish anxiety. They take place all through the summer in towns and villages of the plain. The blessing of the flocks, large fairs and more modest suppers in the inns of Salvaterra de Magos or Vila Franca combine with, if one desires, a minor experience in the *redondel* facing a bull calf.

Discovering Ribatejo—Santarém

The best time to visit Ribatejo is while the bullfight season is on at Vila Franca or Salvaterra (beginning with the Easter holidays), or better still during a local festival, such as the *colete encarnado* (red vest) at Vila Franca de Xira in the first or second week of July, or the *barrete verde* at Alcochete on the second Sunday in August. Each year there are the *feiras,* or great cattle fairs, the *pegas* and *tentas,* accompanied by Pantagruelic repasts of fish from the Tagus, whole sides of beef roasted on spits, and much red wine. All this merrymaking is an exciting and unforgettable experience.

Ribatejo is synonymous with bullfighting. But it does not stop there. Santarém is a beautiful city built on a rocky spur that dominates the river. From the *mirador* of the Portas do Sol, one readily imagines oneself at the prow of a ship cleaving the immense plain. This impression becomes even more powerful in January if the floods have drowned the fields, the vines and even the villages. It is the ringing of the tocsin of the old Torre das Cabaças that, when the flood threatens, gives the warning. When the poet Tennyson visited the Portas do Sol in 1859, he said that he considered this view "to be one of the great panoramic landscapes of Europe."

The main agricultural cènter of this province, Santarém retains some beautiful vestiges of its ancient grandeur: tombs and Flamboyant church portals, ramparts, and Gothic fountains. It was in Santarém, during his reign, that the only son of King João II was killed while galloping along the banks of the Tagus with one of his pages. The body of the young prince was carried back in a fisherman's net and it is for this reason that Queen Leonor took as her emblem this net, which can be seen on numerous Manueline monuments in, among other places, the church of Madre de Deus (Lisbon) and in Batalha.

The city, which is most attractive, has an archeological museum in the early church of São João de Alporão, the Braamcamp Freire Museum with a good library, furniture and paintings, as well as several fine churches. That of Marvila is lofty, its interior covered with patterned azulejos like Persian carpets, gradually increasing in size until they reach the roof. The Gothic church of Graça was built in 1380 and contains several carved tombs. Almost at the entrance to the city, in the Praça Sá da Bandeira, is an 18th-century seminary, with a particularly agreeable Baroque facade and looking not unlike a palace, with the church in the center. By a large public garden nearby, the local market is a charming Edwardian building faced with amusing blue and white tiled panels of local places of interest. Over the Tagus is Alpiarça, with a fascinating museum in the Casa dos Patudos which José Relvas, a politician, left with its contents to his native town. Also near Santarém lies the ruined convent of the Bernardine nuns at Almoster.

Some 32 km. (20 miles) north of Santarém on N365, Golegã is noted for horse breeding. The horse-fair on November 11 is the largest and most famous in Portugal. The parish church has a huge Manueline portal, with all the usual decorations of twisted columns and rope decorations.

Almourol to Ourem

Going on up the Tagus, almost to its junction with the Zêzere, one discovers in the middle of the river a genuine fairytale castle, Almourol. Periwinkles and tamarisk bloom at the foot of the high walls which have never undergone an assault though they have nurtured many a legend.

With its ten round towers, fortified walls and crenels, Almourol was a castle of the Templars, monk-soldiers who played such an important role in the "reconquest." It was in reward for services rendered, in particular during the capture of Santarém, that King Afonso Henriques granted them this territory which they enriched and fortified. Their Grand Master, Gualdim Pais, solidly entrenched them not only in Almourol in 1171, on the site of a Roman fort, but also in Castro Marim, on the Algarve frontier with Spain, and finally in Tomar.

The Castelo de Bode dam on the Zêzere not far from Almourol contains a long and beautiful lake, a delightful spot for boating. Castelo de Bode is one of the first modern achievements of Portugal in the domain of irrigation, so vital to the development of its agriculture and hydroelectric power. The imposing dam blends harmoniously in a green landscape, and the surroundings of the huge artificial lake that it has created are so agreeable that a pousada has been built there, as well as an estalagem on an island.

The Tagus flows into Ribatejo by way of Abrantes, a historic town that has always been the key to the defense of the north. It was there that General Junot received from Napoleon (1807) the title of Duke of Abrantes, but this pretty little town is above all famous because of its castle, the origins of which date back to the reign of King Dinis. In the chapel, since transformed into a museum, one can see the tombs of the Almeidas, Counts of Abrantes.

The N2 leads north from Abrantes to Sardoal. This lovely town is noted for the series of paintings by the 16th-century Master of Sardoal, that are found in the parish church. The terrace outside overlooks the verdant plain to the Tagus, the Misericórdia below, lined with 18th-century *azulejos,* and the many colored tiled roofs of the elegant houses, which make this one of the most charming and unspoilt towns within easy reach of Lisbon.

Traveling west, now, on N3, you will come to Constância, a town in the form of an amphitheater, to which the great poet Camões was exiled for having compromised a young girl of the court, Catarina d'Ataide. She is, from all evidence, the "Natercia" of his most beautiful love poems and it was to her that he dedicated his famous sonnet *Amor é fogo que arde sem se ver,* "Love is a flame which burns without being seen."

Starting from Torres Novas (ruined 14th-century castle and three beautiful churches, including the Misericórdia with exquisite *azulejos*), about 22 km. (14 miles) to the north, one reaches the loftily perched medieval village of Ourem, which is adorned with the castle of the Counts of Ourem and from which the view is magnificent. This superb 15th-century castle (lying one-and-a-half km. (one mile) outside Vila Nova de Ourem), merging with the ruins of a Renaissance palace, represents 200 years of imaginative fortification, entered through two massive gates. As noted in the *Practical Information* section at the end of this chapter, an American couple stage fascinating banquets and reconstructions of Portuguese history in a palace hall.

Tomar

The most interesting city in Ribatejo, Tomar contains the extraordinary complex of the Knights Templar Convent of Christ. Delightfully situated on the banks of the River Nabão, Tomar has spacious public parks and gardens, and a pleasing Victorian railroad station adorned with tubs of flowering plants. This station is in the center of the town, and is conveniently served by several trains daily from Lisbon's Santa Apolonia station.

The Knights Templar, with their flowing white capes marked with an open, blood-red cross, fought in the vanguard of the interminable struggle against the Moslem. In the fever of this holy war, they did not lose, as often alleged, the high moral values of the law of St. Benedict. Thus, when King Dinis agreed to dissolve their order and confiscate their property upon the insistence of Philippe-le-Bel (who in France had outlawed them and burned their great leader), it was to found immediately the Order of Christ, which inherited their prerogatives. The *infantes,* then the kings, were the Masters of this order. The immense resources of its domain per-

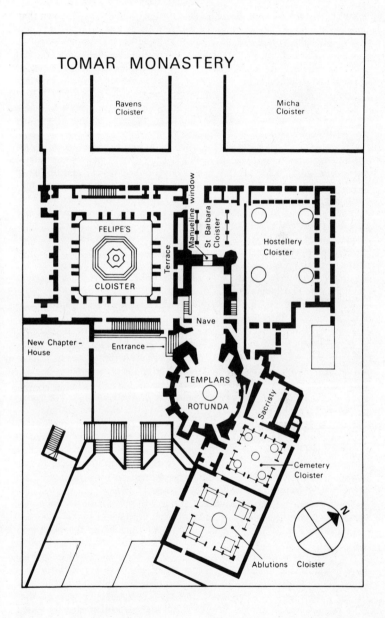

TOMAR MONASTERY

Ravens Cloister

Micha Cloister

FELIPE'S CLOISTER

Manueline window

St Barbara Cloister

Hostellery Cloister

Terrace

Nave

New Chapter - House

Entrance

TEMPLARS ROTUNDA

Sacristy

Cemetery Cloister

Ablutions   Cloister

N

mitted Henry the Navigator to maintain, without weakening it, the exhausting effort of his famous "plan" which, almost 40 years after his death, would open the sea route to India. Is it not just, then, that the caravelles of the Discoveries spread, in all the winds of the world, white sails so like the capes of the Templars and marked with the same Cross of Christ? Is it not natural that, anxious to fix in stone, with its seashells, its coral and its treasures, the great tide which broke upon his kingdom, Manuel I wanted above all to adorn Tomar? With the instinct that is bestowed by certain moments in the life of exceptional people, he opened the sacred circle of the Charola (or Sanctuary) of Tomar and made of it the heart of a vast shrine which he built around it. From it the faith then spread and radiated over half the world.

Crowning a hill just outside the town, this huge complex of buildings, the Convent of Christ, contains no fewer than seven cloisters, ranging in date from the 12th to the 17th centuries. It is a glorious treasure house of carving in wood and stone, of color and imagination. Gold was no longer confined to the church. King Manuel I wanted Tomar to express visibly the power of triumphant Christianity. In the church an octagonal baldacchino was built over the altar, Moorish curves intertwined with Byzantine lines, prolonging them. The monastery served less for contemplation and prayers than for planning conquests and celebrating their victories. The architects, Diogo de Arruda and especially João de Castilho, abandoned themselves to the excesses of an impetuous inspiration related to the heroic and brilliant times in which they lived.

The window of the Casa do Capitulo (Chapter House) is a pictorial history of the early 16th century; one can see the coats of arms that tell the tale of the Discoveries. It was necessary, in order to admire it properly, to remove the roof of the little Cloister of Santa Barbara. On either side are the cork oak and the English oak, of which the wood served to construct the caravelles. Grouped and interlaced in the center are ropes, nets, seaweed, chains, floaters—among which the outlines of sails are etched. Even the Order of the Garter, conferred on Prince Henry the Navigator by King Henry VI of England, is incorporated in the wild ensemble.

João III, less brilliant than his father, wanted Tomar to become a monastery again. The long corridors of brick and colored tiles, the Christ in bonds behind his dark barred cell, two Renaissance cloisters, one Palladian and one of glacial dignity, were added to the five other cloisters in this extraordinary complex. At the end of the passages spreads a Tuscan landscape: vales, graceful and delicate cypresses. The visitor is overwhelmed by the vastness, the superabundance, the superb position of the buildings, parts of which now house a seminary and a military hospital.

The small Renaissance Church of Conceição passed on the way up to the convent is much admired by architectural experts, but its very perfection is curiously cold, or seems so as it is no longer used as a place of worship. The town is not large, its center being laid out on a gridiron plan with narrow streets lined with pretty late-17th and 18th-century houses. In this part is an interesting early 15th-century synagogue with a Luso-Hebraic museum. Below the Templars' hill the beautiful square, the Praça da Republica, is bounded by elegant municipal buildings, and on one side by the parish Church of St. John the Baptist. This church is Flamboyant Gothic in style, with Manueline features, including an unusual belfry; inside are several fine primitive paintings.

Every second year, early in July, Tomar is the scene of the very ancient Tabuleiros festival. This procession is believed to have originated at the time of the Roman occupation of the peninsula, and it is known that its present form has been practically unchanged since the 16th century. Young girls clad in white walk through the streets of the town to the Praça da Republica, but what makes this festival singular is that each girl—and there may be a hundred or more—balances on her head circular baskets from which rise pyramids of canes threaded through rolls of new bread, decorated with paper flowers and topped by a paper crown. Each girl is attended by a young man in a white shirt and black trousers who is at hand to steady the contraption, which may be almost as tall as the bearer. Following, and this is where the Roman origins can be seen, are a number of oxen with gilded horns preceded by black-robed men carrying crowns on cushions. A brass band takes up the rear. When they all finally arrive in front of the Church of St. John the Baptist, the bread is given to anyone who asks for it and to charitable organizations in the town. The oxen are taken away to the municipal slaughterhouse and the meat given to those in need.

The huge aqueduct of Pegões Altos, off the road to Fátima, is an astonishing sight. Built at the end of the 16th century to take water to the Convent of Christ, 180 great stone arches straddle a remote valley with no human habitation to detract from the grandeur of this monumental work.

PRACTICAL INFORMATION FOR RIBATEJO

TOURIST OFFICES. There are local tourist offices in the following towns: **Abrantes,** Largo da Feira; **Santarém,** Rua Capelo Ivens 63; **Tomar,** Ave. Dr. Candido Madureira; **Vila Nova de Ourem,** Ave. Nuno Álvares Pereira.

HOTELS AND RESTAURANTS

Abrantes (Santarém). There are also several pensions. *Turismo* (M), Largo de Santo António (tel. 041 21261). 41 rooms with bath. Wonderful view from terrace. AE, DC, MC.

Restaurants. *Cristina* (I), Rio de Moinhos. Closed Mon. DC. *Pelicano* (I), Rua Nossa Senhora da Conceiçao. Closed Thurs.

Alpiarça (Santarém). **Restaurant.** *Olívio* (M), Rua Dr. Bernardino Machado 12. Good grills. Closed Mon. *Restaurante O Chico* (I), Rua José Relvas 128.

Belver. Restaurant. *O Castelo* (I), with some simple rooms.

Cartaxo. Restaurant. *Torricado* (M), Rua Serpa Pinto 3. Good regional food in upstairs dining-room.

Castelo de Bode (Santarém). *Estalagem da Ilha do Lombo* (E), tel. 049 37128. 15 rooms with bath. Pool. On an island in the great lake. Boat trips on the lake. AE, DC, MC, V. *Pousada de São Pedro* (E), tel. 049 38159. 16 rooms with bath. On lakeside near the hydro-electric dam, ten km. (six miles) from Tomar. AE, DC, MC, V.

Constancia (Santarém). *Palácio de Constancia* (E), tel. 049 93371. 3 double rooms with bath. Dinner available. Beautiful old house on the banks of the River Tagus. Country House.

Golegã (Santarém). *Pensão/Restaurante Central* (I), Largo Nossa Senhora da Conceição (tel. 049 72187). Good country food; very popular with locals.

Ourem (Santarém). **Restaurant.** *The Banquet of the Kings* (M), with live show of medieval Portuguese history staged for parties of 14 to 110 people, though individuals or smaller parties are accepted if places are available. Reservations are essential and should be made to Joseph H. Braun, Castelos de Portugal, Ourem (tel. 049 42870) or, in the States, to *Fatima Travel Inc.*, Washington, N.J. 07882 (tel. 201–689–4600).

Rossio Ao Sul do Tejo (Santarém). On the south side of the Tagus, crossed by a bridge at Abrantes. *Residência Vera Cruz* (I), tel. 041 31250. 18 rooms with bath. Comfortable rooms and good restaurant. Recommended.

Salvaterra de Magos (Santarém). **Restaurant.** *Ribatejano* (M), Largo Combatentes G. Guerra (tel. 063 54314). Large regional restaurant.

Santarém (provincial capital). *Abidis* (M), Rua Guilherme de Azevedo 4 (tel. 043 22017). 27 rooms, 6 with bath. *Central* (I), Rua Guilherme de Azevedo 24 (tel. 043 22028). 23 rooms. Breakfast only.
Restaurants. In **Almeirim**, a nearby village. *O Touçinho* (M), Rua Timor 20. A charming, friendly country spot, serving the typical *stone soup*. Closed Thurs. *Retiro do Campino* (I). Recommended.

Sardoal. Restaurant. *Tres Naus* (M), Rua 5 de Outubro. Closed Thurs.

Tomar (Santarém). *Hotel dos Templarios* (E), Largo Candido dos Reis 1 (tel. 049 33121). 84 rooms with bath. Pleasant rooms; pool, tennis, disco, shops. AE, DC, MC. *Pensão Trovador* (M), Largo da Rodoviaria Nacional (tel. 049 31567). 30 rooms with bath. Breakfast only. DC. *Pensão Nuno Álvares* (I), Ave. D. Nuno Álvares Pereira 3 (tel. 049 32873). 12 rooms. Good food; try the local Nabantino wine. *Pensão Restaurante Luanda* (I), Ave. Marques de Tomar (tel. 049 32929). 14 rooms, 6 with bath.
Restaurants. There are several pleasant and Inexpensive restaurants by the River Nabão, including the *Bela Vista* (M), by the bridge, for very good food. *Chez Nous* (M), Rua Dr. Joãquim Jacinta 31. French cooking. Recommended. Closed Tues.

Torres Novas (Santarém). *Pensão Solar de São José* (I), Ave. Dr. Jorge Martins Azevedo 43 (tel. 049 22362). 10 rooms. Breakfast only.

Restaurants. *Zé Manel* (M). Good Portuguese regional cooking. Closed Mon. AE, DC, MC. *Adega Regional* (I). Good country food. Closed Sun. *O Vintém* (I), Ave. Miguel Arnide 73. Recommended.

Vila Franca de Xira (Lisbon). *Estalagem São Jorge* (E), Quinta da Santo André, Estrada Monte Gordo (tel. 063 22776). 8 rooms with bath. Pool, riding school. Ranch-style hostelry in fine country. *Estalagem da Lezíria* (M), Rua Alves Redol (tel. 063 22129). 15 rooms. Right in town. *Pensão Restaurante Flora* (M), Rua Noel Perdigão 12 (tel. 063 23127). 21 rooms, most with bath. DC, MC.

Restaurant. *Redondel* (E), Praça dos Touros. Easy parking. Closed Mon. AE, DC, MC.

Camping. There are campsites at the following places: Castelo de Bode, by the dam; Golegã; Salvaterra de Magos; Tomar (2 sites).

PLACES OF INTEREST. Museums are usually open daily, except Mondays and public holidays, 10–5, but double check the times on the spot. Some close for lunch. Entrance fees are between 150$00 and 300$00. Keep an eye open as you pass through towns for interesting churches. They usually reward exploration.

Abrantes. Lopo de Almeida Museum, in Church of Sta. Maria do Castelo. Early tombs and sculpture.

Alcochete. Municipal Museum. Roman ceramics, fragments of Hispano-Arabic tiles, 15th-century polychrome statues, agricultural and navigational instruments.

Nature Reserve, on the River Tagus. Flamingo breeding ground.

Almourol. Templar's Castle, on island in Tagus. Call the boatman to row you across.

Alpiarça. Casa dos Patudos. A large private house with interesting contents, left to the town by José Rélvas, a local politician. May be closed owing to recent burglary.

Belver. Fine **castle** overlooking river Tagus.

Cartaxo. Wine and Regional Museum. Quinta das Pratas.

Santarém. Anselmo Braamcamp Freire Museum. With remarkable library, paintings, furniture and a coach and carriage museum in an adjoining building.

Archeological Museum. In the Romanesque-Gothic Church of São João de Alporão.

Museulógica (Railway Museum). In local station on the banks of the Tagus. Steam locomotives and the wedding coach given to D. Maria Pia by her father King Victor Emanuel of Italy on the occasion of her marriage to King Luis of Portugal in 1862. Admission on request to the Station Master.

Sardoal. São Tiago e São Mateus, rare 16th-century primitive paintings kept in this church. 10 km. (6 miles) northeast of Abrantes, just off N244–3.

Tomar. Abraham Zacuto Museum, Rua Joãquim Jacinto 73. Housed in 14th-century synagogue.

Convento do Cristo. Knights Templars' astonishing complex of buildings including seven cloisters.

Museu, Ave. Dr. Candido Madureira. Small museum above Tourist Office.

SPECIAL EVENTS. For further details and exact dates, consult local tourist offices. **June.** *Feira Nacional de Agricultura* at Santarém, 2nd week: at this famous agricultural fair cattle, horses and other farm animals, and machinery are exhibited, and many European countries also exhibit. *Festa de São Pedro* at Montijo, June 28–29, when the fishing boats are blessed and sardines traditionally grilled in the open. **July.** *Festival of the Tabuleiros* at Tomar, held every two years, early in the month: very ancient and colorful procession through the streets of the town; enquire at Tourist Office. *Festas do Colete Encarnado* (Feast of the Red Waistcoat) at Vila Franca de Xira, 1st weekend: a colorful event with the loosing of young bulls in the streets, a fair and other activities; the red waistcoat is worn on feast days by the *campinos* or herdsmen of the fighting bulls. The *Barrete Verde* at Alcochete, 2nd Sun.: cattle fair, with bullfights, etc. **November.** *Feira de São Martinho* at Golegã, Nov. 11: the national horse fair, where every kind of horse is shown, from saddle horses to bullfighting and carriage horses; chestnuts are roasted on charcoal braziers in the streets.

SPORTS. For further details of sports facilities ask at local Tourist Offices. **Horse Riding.** *Clube de Santarém,* Santarém (tel. 043 22030). **Tennis.** *Camara Municipal,* Abrantes (tel. 041 22326); *Hotel dos Templarios,* Tomar (tel. 049 33121); *Clube Desportivo de Torres Novas,* Torres Novas (tel. 049 22430). **Sailing.** On the River Tagus and on the Castelo de Bode Lake.

ESTREMADURA

This province, stretching northward from Lisbon to Leiria, can be reached from the Lisbon area by several roads going through lovely country, as well as by the Autostrada, A1, (toll payable) through Vila Franca, technically in the Ribatejo. This motorway may be the fastest route but it misses some of the country's outstanding sights. Longer but more rewarding are the two roads north from Sintra, one going through Ericeira (N247), the other via Mafra to Torres Vedras (N9) and then on by a very winding but superbly beautiful route (N8) to Obidos, Caldas da Rainha and Alcobaça and Batalha—where are two of Portugal's most famous buildings—to Leiria.

A third road (N8) into Estremadura worth following starts at the end of the Campo Grande in Lisbon and takes you on an autoroute to Loures and on to Malveira, scene of a big country fair every Thursday, and then to Turçifal. This village has been by-passed, but is worth driving through to see the elegant 18th-century country houses lining the main street, and the great church on a terrace, constructed with stone left over from the building of the Palace of Mafra. For many miles along this road you will see on your right an unusual rounded hill with a tiny white chapel on the top. This is the scene, on August 5, of one of the biggest *romarias* in the region, when the country people go up to the small Chapel of Our Lady of Help. The chapel has interesting Gothic-Manueline features and is surrounded by small houses used in former times by pilgrims in need of a night's rest after walking many miles.

The Market Gardens and Mafra

Soon after leaving Lisbon on any of the secondary roads north you will see on both sides of the highway the *terras saloias,* the rich market gardens which provide the capital with fresh fruit and vegetables. The land is carefully tended by hand and kept irrigated by water from donkey-powered wheel-cranked wells. Pumpkins are lined up along the eaves of the houses, and fruit trees grow in every spare corner. On the hilltops windmills twirl, while the terracotta whistles tucked in their sails pour forth music into the wind, telling the miller when to adjust the sails.

In the midst of all this rustic simplicity stands the imposing Mafra Monastery, covering an area of some 27,000 square meters (290,000 square ft.) and comprising, beside the austere wing of the Franciscan friars, a splendid marble basilica with remarkable sculptures and a vast palace. Begun in 1717 by Dom João V in fulfilment of a vow on being granted an heir, 45,000 workers toiled till 1730 following the plans of Frederico Ludovice who intended to provide his royal patron with his own Escorial. He partly succeeded in outdoing his Spanish model by installing, it is said, 4,500 doors and windows. The pair of carillons in the church towers are often played on Sunday afternoons and the strange tinkling sound can be heard for miles around. Behind the long lichen-covered facade are endless Royal Suites furnished with Directoire and Empire pieces.

After a long walk through the huge edifice the visitor comes to the beautiful library, very long and narrow and washed in a silvery light, for the decoration is in grisaille, a moonlight gray. One of the loveliest libraries in Europe, it is understated compared with that other fine Portuguese library, the high Baroque library of the University of Coimbra.

On the way up to the Royal Suites there is a museum of religious art containing church fittings and statues. But visitors with little time to spare can insist on going straight to the apartments above. The basilica, in the center of the curiously satisfying plain facade, lightly covered with lichen, is austerely grandiose within, but in the atrium are superb 18th-century carved figures of the Apostles. Heroic in size, their marble garments billowing in the wind, they will give pleasure to all lovers of 18th-century sculpture.

Behind the palace, whose facade rises directly from the square in front as do most Portuguese palaces and country houses, there is a large enclosure surrounded by a wall 20 km. (12 miles) in length. Called the Mafra Chase, this great area is strictly protected and is the home of deer, civet cats and even wild boar. A gate at the very back of the Chase, reached by the road to Murgeira and Gradil, gives access to a collection of very pretty late-Victorian and Edwardian carriages, including pony traps and dog carts, one of which, made entirely of wickerwork, belonged to Queen Amelia, the last Queen of Portugal. There is also the Museu da Caça (Hunting Museum) with a large number of stuffed animals shot in long-forgotten hunts in the park. The iron gates are closed, but a caretaker appears when the bell is rung, and visitors are asked to produce some form of identification such as a passport, and their temporary address, before a car is allowed inside.

Ericeira, Peniche, and the Berlengas

A road (N116) leads due west from Mafra for nine km. (5½ miles) to Ericeira, a popular beach resort and still a busy center for deep-sea fishing. From the little chapel of Santo António, where old people sit on stone benches and gaze pensively out on the water, you can look down on the fishermen's beach and watch the men shoving their boats up the stone ramp. The northern part of this small town is charming, with narrow winding streets going up to the Misericórdia Church and a small museum alongside. On a big open space is the circular hermitage of São Sebastião, dating from the early 17th-century, its interior entirely covered with patterned azulejos.

The road on to the north first winds over low cliffs and deserted beaches until, after a few miles, it turns inland through vineyards which cover the rolling hills as far as the eye can see. At Roliça and Vimeiro, the latter a popular spa with a golf course, General Junot encountered the first reverses in the Peninsular War, and the third French invasion was halted before the lines of Torres Vedras. Wellington's victories are commemorated by a monument in the town square in front of the convent of Graça, whose cloisters are lined with splendid pictorial azulejos. This by no means exhausts Torres Vedras' attractions, as there is also a 12th-century castle, a prehistoric monument at Zambugal, the first of the redoubts of the Lines of Torres Vedras, sensitively restored, and a small museum with agreeable pictures, statues and interesting tiled panels.

Northwards on N8–2, through Lourinhã, the road reaches Peniche, with a great 16th-century citadel above Cabo Carvoeiro, a crazy pile of cinder-black rocks, where the high tide furiously pounds, hollowing deep grottoes and widening the gaps with its sledge-hammer blows.

In calm weather, a ferryboat leaves Peniche in the morning for the Berlenga Isles, one hour's distance. Propped on the water like so many ocean birds, these barren russet-hued islands are often enshrouded by mist. Wild black rabbits roam over them through salt-petrified brush, and seagulls and eiders nest in the rock's inaccessible crevices. Here, also, is a realm of fishermen. From the old rust-brick fortress jutting out into the sea, now used by campers, expeditions are launched early in the morning or at sundown. The diminutive fleet of boats belonging to the "boss" and his fellow fishermen (some of whom come from France with their boats and gear) is tied up at the float. The biggest events of each day are the departure and arrival of the fishing boats. When each man's catches have been spread out over the flat stones of the jetty, it is really a marvelous sight. A mere beginner easily brings in 9 kg. (20 pounds) of blue mackerel or sardines. Champion fishermen hold out for only the big fish, and display mullet over 60 cm. (two ft.) long, or swordfish weighing more than a 45 kg. (100 pounds). Hire a boatman to take you round the sea grottoes with their blue transparent water.

Obidos

Inland from Peniche—21 km. (13 miles) on N141—and rising most majestically above the beautiful Gaeiras vineyards, the fine medieval town of Obidos is silhouetted against the sky, with its rust-colored walls, its square castle and great weather-beaten towers making it loom up like a ship grounded on the shores over which it stood watch in the time of the Moors. Afonso Henriques had to subdue it by force. A century and a half later, Dom Dinis, passing through with his young bride, made her a present of the town because she had admired the ramparts twining like a ribbon around a bouquet of shining white houses. From then on, Obidos was the wedding present given to Portugal's queens. One of them was married there at the age of eight to a cousin barely older that she, Afonso V. A coat of arms marks the house in which Maria I dwelt.

Sheltered within its walls, the city has not noticed the passage of time, despite the traffic problem in the narrow lanes. There should be a sign at the city gate requesting travelers to leave their cars outside. The *pousada,* located in what used to be the governor's castle, is a bare 450 meters (500 yards) distant, and there are interesting things all along the way. Underneath the fortified archway, a lamp is burning in front of the little shrine to Our Lady of Grace, built in memory of a 22-year-old girl who died for love.

Once within the gate you will see a scene reminiscent of those ingenuous yet artful illustrations that adorn the margins of Books of Hours. Slightly crumbling stairways, sprouting clumps of wild flowers on each step, will take you up to the wide, old lookout path which goes right round the top of the walls. Two streets go zigzagging in between the white facades of houses. Vine branches make the rooftops touch over your head, and growing green plants fill the windowsills. Nothing is quite in a straight line, yet somehow everything is in its right place, and any change would disrupt the marvelous balance of it all. The Renaissance doorway, the Manueline window, the ogival arch—they are all in their proper order. You see churches on all sides, with walls of colored tiles and painted ceilings, and they give off that reassuring fragrance of candle tallow and altar incense. The oldest is the Gothic chapel of São Martinho and the handsomest, that of Santa Maria, with a tombstone sculptured by Jean de Rouen and paintings by Josefa of Obidos. Her 17th-century contemporaries admired this painter as much for her intelligence and culture as for her talent—a talent that, like Zurbarán's, is at its best in depicting, rather than religious subjects, the wondrous beauty of everyday objects: pewter's dull gleam, the rich brown crust on a loaf of bread, the glow of velvety-skinned grapes. The church also has the walls lined with most unusual blue and white *azulejos* in swirling patterns, while the ceiling is painted with arabesques, flowers, luxuriant foliage and negro figures. Outside the walls, on the road to Caldas da Rainha is the strange hexagonal church of Senhor da Pedra, scene of a *romaria* on May 3.

The Museum, in the same square as the Church of Santa Maria, was set up with the co-operation of the Gulbenkian Foundation. There are some lovely things in it, including 17th- and 18th-century polychrome statues, and in a special Gallery exhibits relating to the Peninsular War from the Pinto Basto collection at Gaeiras, nearby. Also in this square is a pottery works in the Solar da Praça de Santa Maria, in which you can see young people learning this fascinating craft and producing interesting things.

One of the enchantments of Obidos is the walk along the wide top of the walls, reached by many sets of steps, which give a delightful view of not only the many-colored roofs of the town below, but of the lovely countryside, over the Lagoa de Obidos, to the sea.

Between Obidos and the sea, close by to the northwest, lies the Lagoa de Obidos, a lagoon separated from the sea by a wide sandbank at Foz do Arelho. The bank is opened every so often to let in the tides to clean out the lake-lagoon which, despite its great size, is easily polluted. In its depths live eels as thick as a man's arm. In autumn there are wild duck and other wildfowl for the hunter. Portugal's kings, from João V to Luis I, enjoyed feasting here in the open. If the visitor is lucky he may find a fisherman to row him in a flat-bottomed boat across the calm waters to the beautiful moors on the other side. A winding road hereabouts leads to the beach of Praia do Rei Cortiço, with its seemingly endless, calm sands.

Caldas da Rainha

The green statue standing in the park here represents the lady of the place, Leonor, who was twice a queen. She had been the wife of João II, and, although Manuel, his successor, had three wives, it was mostly Leonor, his sister, who reigned by his side. The story goes that, while on her way from Obidos to Batalha for the funeral of her father-in-law, Afonso V, she came across people bathing near the roadside in a foul-smelling pool. They assured her that the water could cure all sorts of ills. Leonor herself then proceeded to bathe in the pool, thereby obtaining such relief that she immediately decided to build a hospital at this site, and donated her own laces and jewels to the cause. In its first year (1485), she personally directed the hospital, and the locality was known as *Caldas da Rainha,* the Queen's Thermal Baths. The calcium sulphide waters of Caldas da Rainha are indeed effective against respiratory ailments and rheumatism.

In the last century, by a quirk of fashion, Caldas became the most popular hot springs resort in Portugal. The ladies played croquet under the elms, and prominent writers of the day, such as Eça de Queiroz and Ramalho Ortigão, pitted their wits against those of caricaturist Rafael Bordalo Pinheiro, who had just launched an art pottery workshop there. (Local clay was in abundant supply and the museum owns vases going back to the 15th century). Bordalo Pinheiro founded a school and created a style: glazed ceramic reproductions of fruits, vegetables, and animals. Although some of these ceramics are in magnificently bad taste, the Caldas pottery works also produces, in addition to the traditional ware, various cleverly conceived and attractively executed items. Ceramics are for sale in all the streets, especially in those that lead from the hospice to the market place. Ceramic lizards and snakes disport themselves on the house fronts, while a gigantic lobster adorns the beautifully laid-out park. Also in the park is a delightful museum of Portuguese landscape paintings, mainly of the latter half of the last century, and something of a revelation. Alongside the park and near the Spa stands the Manueline Church of Nossa Senhora do Populo with a rare belfry of the same period, lovely 16th-century carpet tiles right up to the vaulted ceiling, and a superb Portuguese primitive triptych depicting the Crucifixion.

At Alfeizerão the road divides, the eastern branch—N8—leading through the hills to Alcobaça, the western—N242—to the up-and-coming fishing village of São Martinho do Porto on a shallow beach ideal for children, in a bright, sunny, rounded cove, protected by dunes, where the sea comes in to warm itself at high tide. From the dramatic Facho cliff you have a sweeping view over the landscape before continuing for 13 km. (eight miles) through the coastal pine forest to Nazaré.

Alcobaça

While King Afonso Henriques was marching against Santarém, an especially well-defended Moorish stronghold, he began to be assailed by misgivings. Months earlier, he had persuaded foreign crusaders to join forces with him instead of continuing on their way to the Holy Land. Had he really the right to do so, even for the purpose of wresting out a Christian kingdom? He vowed that, if God blessed his expedition, he would build a monastery dedicated to St. Bernard, the crusaders' preacher. Upon victory, he selected a site at the junction of two streams, the Alcoa and the Baça. The royal abbey of Santa Maria was founded in 1153 and the Cistercian monks settled here in 1178.

The surrounding fields were marshy but fertile. The monks set to work, planting orchards that continue today to yield the choicest fruit in Portugal. Succeeding donations added to the wealth of the abbey, which became one of the most powerful in the kingdom. Functioning simultaneously as a sanctuary, a school, and a hospice, the monastery of the white Cistercians was also a domain containing 13 market towns and three seaports, over which the abbot had judicial authority. During King Sebastião's reign the Pope recognized Alcobaça as the rightful seat of the Cistercian order.

Under Spanish domination the monastery declined so drastically that its walls were threatened with ruin. Pombal restored it, endowing it with a library, a cloister, and new arable land. The English writer, William Beckford, a voluntary exile in Portugal whose diaries are a fascinating record of the period, was a guest at the monastery in the 18th century, and describes in extravagant terms the monks' wealth and the feast that was served. He also pays due tribute to the learning and culture of these men of God, who for over six centuries defended the Christian faith.

The long, light Baroque facades of the monastery buildings contrast dramatically with the Abbey Church between them. Strangely enough, the somewhat over-ornamented church facade surrounds a perfect Gothic portal and rose window above. The largest church in Portugal, it was started in 1178 and has an interior which is wonderfully impressive in its austere beauty. Honey-colored columns lead up to the carved tombs of Dona Inês and Dom Pedro on either side of the chancel. Dom Pedro's serious face is framed by a curly beard and long hair, on his head is his crown, in his hands a sword and on his feet spurs. It was in the bare solitude of this church that hapless King Pedro wished to sleep his last sleep beside his adored Inês. The story is well known, in all its awesome and tragic beauty. The prince, married for reasons of state, fell madly in love with one of the Infanta's ladies-in-waiting, a young Galician girl named Inês de Castro. When he became a widower, he married her secretly, keeping her hidden in a *quinta* on the banks of the Mondego. Two children were born of this love. But malicious courtiers warned the old king against the peril of having a foreigner so close to the throne, and having convinced him, three of them took advantage of the prince's absence one night to murder the gentle Inês. When the old king died, and Pedro reigned in his stead, the murderers sought refuge in Spain and Italy. Pedro had the two who had escaped to Spain delivered to him and killed, tearing out their hearts in an orgy of stormy revenge. The third reached sanctuary in Italy.

Then, in great ceremony, he had Inês brought out of her tomb, placed her on the throne beside him, and forced the courtiers to kiss her fleshless hand. She was carried, amid torches and mournful chants, in an interminable funeral procession to the Alcobaça monastery. There he placed her in a handsomely carved and decorated tomb, which he himself had designed. Opposite he placed his own tomb, so that on the Day of Judgment they would rise facing each other. The rather clumsy replastering job on her broken nose and dented chin attests to the desecration committed during one of the Napoleonic invasions by the Count d'Erlon's troops, who broke open the tombs in the hope of finding jewels.

This was the final tragic touch in the destiny of this gentle loving soul. In the church that is bathed in filtered silvery light, the uncrowned queen reposes on her stony pillow, smiling serenely and profoundly while the guides explain the long rebus that winds around her tomb. It is still a common sight to see a child's bunch of wild flowers laid beside her rounded cheek.

In the south transept is a lovely group of 17th-century polychrome terracotta figures illustrating the death of St. Bernard, much damaged, alas, in the Peninsular War. Also on this side of the church is the highly convoluted Manueline doorway to the sacristy, beyond which is a most unusual circular relic chapel, its walls entirely lined with golden Baroque carvings enclosing busts and statues of various saints.

On the other side of the church a door leads to King Diniz's beautiful and aptly named Cloister of Silence. The Chapter House off this cloister is filled with huge terracotta statues of saints and angels, the latter most elegant in kilt-like garments. At the side, a stairway leads up to the enormous dormitory, its lovely vaulted roof supported on numberless columns. The windows of this vast chamber look out on to another cloister in which, on fine days, elderly gentlemen are to be seen enjoying the warmth of the sun, for part of the huge monastic complex is now a home for the aged. The great kitchen has a brook flowing through it for the monks to keep live river fish in. There is a high centrally-placed fireplace and long marble tables once used for preparing meals for great numbers of monks. The refectory is next door and has a stone pulpit to one side.

While you are inside the monastery you may hear the muffled sounds of the market outside beneath the monastery walls. The big, firm peaches and pears in the marketwomen's baskets are from trees whose forebears were brought from France by the monks.

At the other end of the cloister a doorway leads in to the Sala dos Reis, an 18th-century room in which statues of the kings of Portugal stand high on the walls, in dramatic poses. At one end is a manuscript azulejo panel telling the story of the monastery's foundation. Such manuscript azulejos are exceedingly rare, one of the few others being in the Church of Milagres, near Leiria.

In the shops on the spacious sunny esplanade, you will find only some rather unattractive blue pottery ware "Souvenirs of Alcobaça" mixed in with grimy pieces of copperware and painted wooden figurines of saints. It is wiser to buy the sealed glass jars of fruit preserved in clear syrup, or the fragrant bright-pink Morello cherry liqueur called *ginginha*. In the town itself and in its immediate surroundings there are numerous churches and monasteries, as well as castle ruins.

Nazaré

The name "Nazaré" on a signpost is irresistible. Only ten km. (six miles) on N8–4 from either Alcobaça or 12 km. (eight miles) on N242 from São Martinho, with the possibility of continuing across the long stretch of coastal pines all the way to Marinha Grande and Leiria. In the concave corner below the Pederneira cliff the ocean has left a long, sandy beach: Nazaré was born out of the furious struggle that, day after day, relentlessly hurls the waves against the strand along this empty stretch of earth.

You should first discover Nazaré from Sitio, the dazzling white village on the cliff top to which the fisherfolk have withdrawn, crowded out by the ever-increasing masses of tourists who have taken possession of "the most picturesque town in Portugal." Nazaré has been painted, filmed, photographed a thousand times over, to succumb at last to its own fame: at least in summer, when parking becomes a nightmare and the seafront is a seething mass of pedestrians and cars. Better to escape by cable car to the comparative peace and quiet of Sitio, to admire the superb view from the vast plaza in front of the church that commemorates a miracle credited with saving the life of Fuas Roupinho, the *alcaide* of Porto de Mós and companion in arms of Afonso Henriques. He was pursuing a white deer, when one of the district's typical sea mists caused him to lose his bearings. Our Lady appeared through the mist and halted his horse in its tracks— you can still see its hoof-print. The huntsman dismounted to kneel to the apparition and, as the mist lifted, he found himself on the extreme brink of the cliff. More than 90 meters (300 ft.) below, the foam-fringed beach stretches away into the distance beyond the boom town which has swallowed up the village.

Off shore, the best—and most dangerous—fishing in all of Portugal is carried on. When the look-outs spot a shoal of fish, the fishermen run to the jetty to push their boats out into the water. The boats are sturdy, round-bottomed vessels with high, narrow bows which slice into the curve of a wave. The fishermen row off to cross the barrier reef, which has a difficult swell that must be tackled again on the homeward trip: it is so powerful that boats with their entire crews are sometimes scattered and lost there, swallowed up under the gaze of their womenfolk, who have been waiting, squatting motionless, for hours on the beach. Then you hear the women weeping and wailing, shouting curses upon the heavens, before they finally draw away to cover themselves with heavy black mourning shawls.

Danger is the daily ration of Nazaré menfolk. It is also their pride. They live on the fringe of the world. They have their own code of honor, their traditions and their standards. The members of a crew form a more closely-knit unit than any family. Practically all the fishermen have their own homes, gear, and share in the catch. After their boats have been hauled up on the beach by tractors instead of by oxen as in the old days, the men abandon boats and contents to the others. It is the women, children, and old people who unload the catch, sort out the fish and sell it, or dry it on racks in the sun; it is they who haul in the nets, repair them and roll them up.

The summer vacationers set up their beach tents, towels, and air mattresses on sand that has been trampled under by a full year's labors and is tide-swept clean each new day. They take photographs of the old fishermen, buy model ships, lobsters, plaid fabrics for shirts. They fill the hotels and pensions. They admire the returning fishing boats, the sunsets, the storm mists. Then they all go away, and Nazaré slowly regains its normal appearance.

Baroque enthusiasts should see the superb, unknown Bernardine Church at Coz, a few miles to the north of the road between Alcobaça and Nazaré. The golden woodwork and 17th-century statues are untouched, and the nuns' choir is lined with early 18th-century azulejos.

Batalha

In the chapel of São Jorge on the plains of Aljubarrota, a few miles north of Alcobaça, a pitcher of daily-fresh water has been placed in a niche since a hot August day in the year 1385 when the fate of Portugal was decided, after its invasion by the King of Castile and his troops, with whom many Portuguese noblemen had joined forces, either through divided loyalty or personal ambition. The outcome of this Lusitanian Battle of Yorktown was the confirmation in power of João I, who fought alongside his crossbow men and his valiant captain Nun' Álvares Pereira who, like his king, was 20 years old. Suffering an agonizing thirst during the battle, the latter vowed that from then on there should always be fresh water by the roadside for travelers. The king, realizing that a miracle had made him victorious, swore to build the most beautiful church imaginable to the Virgin—it happened to be August 15, Assumption Day. According to the story, he hurled his lance into the air, and on the spot where it landed there now stands Santa Maria da Vitória, better known as Batalha. We can only conclude that the "King of the Good Memory" was a real superman, because the sanctuary lies nearly five km. (three miles) from the actual battlefield!

The church was naturally to be in the Gothic style. A fine limestone was selected, to be gilded by the sun's rays. Afonso Domingues, the masterbuilder, drew up plans modeled after Alcobaça. However, the king had just married Philippa of Lancaster, daughter of the famous John of Gaunt, who encouraged the Angevin architect Huguette to introduce a perpendicular Gothic style that was indeed quite English. After King João's death, his son Duarte, aware of the grandeur of his dynasty, undertook to build the Pantheon of the House of Aviz in Batalha. His aim was to keep it simple in style, adorned solely with the proud motto of his royal brothers, "Talan de bien fayre," "Good deeds are our pleasure." He could not have foreseen that the kingdom was to become an empire flung to the four corners of the earth, nor that, on Batalha's austere walls, there would blossom forth the coral reefs and riggings, the arabesques and symbols of the Manueline style.

King João I and his queen rest in the Founder's Chapel, surrounded by their sons. In connection with this founder of the Aviz lineage, the monument that commemorates his most famous—if not his greatest—victory also relates the strange and significant history of his family in all its brilliance and tragedy, a résumé of Portuguese history.

The royal cloister was designed for meditation and prayers of thanksgiving. In its midst, Manuel planted luxuriant carved vegetation, which im-

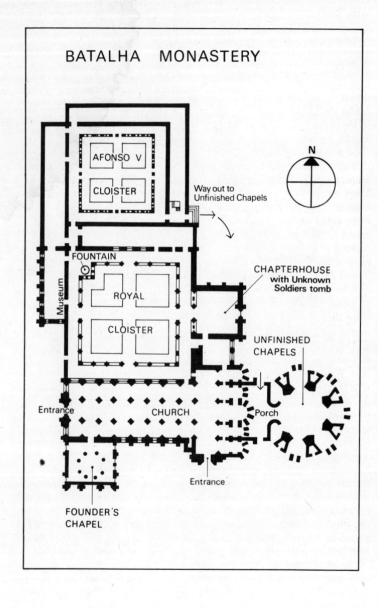

BATALHA MONASTERY

mediately found its way up the columns and across the ogival arches, filtering the daylight through a maze of foliage: lotus, clover, laurels, thistles, with here and there the Cross and the Armillary Sphere, visible symbols of power and faith that were asserted to the very ends of the earth.

The Chapter House defies all known laws of gravity and equilibrium. Afonso Domingues, old and blind, had his computations challenged and criticized by architects who were in greater favor at court; he found it difficult to persuade the workmen to remove the scaffoldings. Staking his life on his accumulated experience as a great builder, he spent the night alone under the vaulting. His portrait carved in stone is to be seen in one corner of the great hall, where a soldier stands on guard, keeping watch over Portugal's two Unknown Soldiers, killed during World War I, one from Europe and the other from Africa.

You will find Batalha's dazzling splendor most striking in the Capelas Imperfeitas (Unfinished Chapels). Haunted by their great dream, the Aviz kings succeeded one another. None of them forgot Duarte's plans for a funeral chapel, in which the remains of João I and his descendants were to be reunited. But Afonso V, after his African and Spanish campaigns, found himself in such straitened circumstances that he was reduced to melting down the gold and silver plate from the churches, yet still outfitted caravelles to discover the Azores and Cape Verde Islands. Manuel acquired both wealth and glory, but was obliged to honor his oath of gratitude to the Virgin of Belém. Still, he did manage to erect the chapel's flying buttresses, and, impelled by a desire to outstrip the magnificence of everything that makes Belém and Tomar sumptuous, he built an entrance doorway that is undoubtedly the jewel of that so precious and so greatly diversified Manueline art. The stone is as delicately undercut, carved, and fretted as a piece of ivory. Its reliefs and transparencies make it resemble pillow lace. Worked into the delicate tracery is the motto of Dom Duarte I: "Leaute faray, ta yaserey." The last two words, " . . . ta yaserey," are repeated 200 times, like a persistent echo; but the dynasty was dying out. João III, who was more a friar than a knight errant, was building the great Renaissance cloister of the Filipes at Tomar, which was later modified by Queen Catherine of Bragança, widow of King Charles II of England, when she was Regent of Portugal. Funds were short. The pillars that were to support the dome of the Capelas Imperfeitas remained only half-completed. The vegetation that was already entwining itself around them became the ivy of abandonment. The last of Batalha's architects renounced his rule and compass, went off to Morocco with Sebastião in 1578, and was killed by the Moors. Batalha was never finished, and the magnificent doorway whose carvings rivaled in richness the Hindu temples and the undersea architecture of madreporarian coral leads only to a roofless octagon.

The wide open area beside the great church used to be crowded close with small old houses and little craft shops. But progress dictated that these should be swept away and replaced by a characterless shopping precinct, which still contains craft shops, restaurants, and the pleasant modern pousada, but which introduces a note of low-grade modern commercialism right beside one of the great triumphs of Portuguese, and indeed European, architecture. In the center of the wide parade ground stands a huge equestrian statue of Nuno Álvares Pereira.

At Porto de Mós, on the Santarém road, ten km. (six miles) south, the much restored crenelated ramparts and green-tiled towers of the fairytale castle dominate the white town, which straddles the River Lena.

Leiria

Some 12 km. (seven miles) north of Batalha by the highway is the castle of Leiria, the most impressive in Portugal. The splendid 12th-century keep and battlemented towers surmount a high rock between the old city and the by-pass. The town, between the Rivers Lena and Lis, is delightful, with an arcaded square where you can sit and drink coffee. There is a fine Renaissance cathedral, a museum by the Town Hall and, opposite the castle hill is another, lower, eminence on which is the sanctuary of Nossa Senhora da Encarnação, approached by a very long flight of steps. The castle is easily reached by a signposted road from a maze of small streets in the town, and the adventurous are rewarded not only by a thrilling view, but also by the extensive and well-restored remains of the royal palace. This palace was the favorite dwelling place of Dom Diniz and his wife, St. Elizabeth of Portugal. It was he who, in the late 13th century, established the great pine forest between Leiria and the sea in order to anchor the sand dunes. Called the Pinhal do Rei, this great pine forest is one of the oldest deliberately planted forests in the world, and stretches for mile after mile from the beach resort of São Pedro de Muel northwards beyond Praia de Vieira.

Halfway between Leiria and São Pedro de Muel west on N242, at Marinha Grande, is a glass factory established in 1748 by an Englishman named John Beare. Twenty years later it was bought by two brothers called Stephens, and became famous all over Europe, although now it is having a hard struggle to survive.

Due north of Leiria is the small village of Milagres, dominated by a large early-18th-century Baroque church. Beautiful in its elaborate way, it is an extraordinary building to find in such a tiny place.

Fátima

East of Batalha—20 km. (12½ miles) on N356—the cultivated plains and hills gradually give way to a sterner, loftier landscape given over to sheep and goats.

In such a solitary and desolate setting, on May 13, 1917, three young shepherds suddenly saw a light shining from above the low branches of a holm oak. The Virgin then appeared to them and asked them to pray for the peace of the world. She promised to appear again on the 13th day of every month until October. The children were at the subsequent rendezvous, accompanied each time by an ever-increasing crowd. Some 70,000 witnessed at noon the sun rotating, casting a strange, vivid light on their upturned faces, at the sixth and final apparition.

The cult of Our Lady of Fátima quickly spread throughout a wartorn world. Pilgrims thronged. Miraculous cures occurred. For a long time, the faithful camped out on the barren plain, under a broiling sun or amid autumnal storms. A basilica was built, which houses two of the shepherds' graves. The beatification of Francisco and Jacinto Marto is now in progress. The third, Lucia, is a Carmelite nun in a convent in Coimbra.

During the pilgrimage season, from May to October, and towards the 13th of every month, on all the highways of Portugal the people of entire villages can be seen on their way to Fátima, some in buses, others in carts and wagons, many of them on foot, camping along the roadside or in barns and singing hymns as they trudge along following their parish priests.

Although Fátima has become one of the foremost shrines of pilgrimage, it remains relatively isolated. Aside from the inevitable vendors of religious objects peddling medals, figurines and sacred images, you will see only religious houses and hostelries large and small, opened for the accommodation of pilgrims and sick persons. Fátima impresses less by any architectural feature of the basilica with its 65-meter (213-ft.) high tower surmounted by a bronze crown weighing 7 tons and a great crystal cross, lighted during the night services, than by the grandiose conception of its tremendous square surrounded by white marble colonnades connecting with the hospital and retreat houses and esplanade. This huge square has seen congregations of up to a million pilgrims when, for example, a pope is making a visit.

Below Fátima, in the Serra do Aire, about 30 km. (19 miles) by N360, there is a plethora of caverns—the Mira de Aire Caves, the São Mamede Caves, the Alvados Caves, and the Santo António Caves, all reached by elevators, and with fascinating underground treasures to reveal, lakes, stalagtite and stalagmite formations, strange colors, opalescent rocks, many of them beautifully lit, and normally open year round. Most of them have been discovered only since World War II, some as late as the early '70s.

PRACTICAL INFORMATION FOR ESTREMADURA

TOURIST OFFICES. There are local tourist offices in the following towns: **Alcobaça,** Praça 25 de Abril; **Batalha,** Largo Paulo VI; **Caldas da Rainha,** Praça da Republica; **Ericeira,** Rua Eduardo Burnay 33A; **Fátima,** Ave. D. José Correia da Silva; **Leiria,** Largo Goa, Damão e Diu; **Mafra,** Ave. 25 de Abril; **Monte Real,** Jardim Publico; **Nazaré,** Rua Mouzinho de Albuquerque 72; **Obidos,** Largo São Pedro and Rua Direita; **Peniche,** Rua Alexandre Herculano; **Pombal,** Camara Municipal; **Porto de Mós,** Jardim Municipal; **Praia da Areia Branca,** Lourinha; **Praia de Santa Cruz,** Ave. 5 de Outubro; **Praia da Vieira,** Marinha Grande; **São Martinho do Porto,** Ave. 25 de Abril; **São Pedro de Moel,** Ave. Sá e Melo; **Torres Vedras,** Rua 9 de Abril; **Vila Nova de Ourem,** Ave. Nuno Álvares Pereira.

HOTELS AND RESTAURANTS

Alcobaça (Leiria). *Pensão-Restaurante Corações Unidos* (M), Rua Frei António Brandão 39 (tel. 062 42142). 16 rooms, 8 with bath. Good food and wine. MC. *Pensão Mosteiro* (I), Rua Frei Estevão Martins 5 (tel. 062 42183). 13 rooms. *Hotel Santa Maria* (I), Rua Dr. Zagalo (tel. 062 43295). 31 rooms with bath. Breakfast only. Overlooking the great monastery. MC.

Restaurant. *Trindade* (M), Praça D. Afonso Henriques 22. Closed Sat. in winter. MC.

Aljubarrota (Leiria). *Casa da Padiera* (E), tel. 062 48272. 8 double rooms with bath. Pleasant modern house; dinner available. Country House.

Batalha (Leiria). *Pousada do Mestre Afonso Domingues* (E), tel. 044 96260. 22 rooms with bath. Comfortable, modern ranch-style pousada by the great abbey. Good food. AE, DC, MC, V. *Motel São Jorge* (M), Estrada Nacional 1 (tel. 044 96186). 10 rooms with bath. Pool. Outside, on the road to Fátima.

Berlenga Islands (Leiria). *Pensão Restaurant Mar e Sol* (I). A few rooms. Quite good meals.

Caldas Da Rainha (Leiria). Spa. All hotels and pensions serve breakfast only. *Malhoa* (M), Rua António Sergio 31 (tel. 062 26444). 113 rooms with bath. AE, DC, MC. *Pensão D. Carlos* (M), Rua Camões 39 (tel. 062 22551). 16 rooms with bath. *Pensão Portugal* (M), Ave. Almirante Candido dos Reis 24 (tel. 062 22180). 28 rooms, most with bath. MC. *Central* (I), Largo Dr. José Barbosa 22 (tel. 062 22078). 29 rooms, 7 with bath. *Pensão Estremadura* (I), Largo Dr. José Barbosa 23 (tel. 062 22313). 23 rooms, a few with bath. *Pensão Olhos Pretos* (I), Rua do Rosario 10–12 (tel. 062 22188). 36 rooms, most with bath. MC.
Restaurants. *Convivio* (M), Praça da Republica 1. *Lareira* (M), Ave. Almirante Candido dos Reis 30. Closed Tues. MC. *Páteo da Rainha* (M), Rua de Camões 39. Live music. AE, DC, MC.

Ericeira (Lisbon). *Estalagem Morais* (E), Rua Dr. Miguel Bombarda 5 (tel. 061 62611). 40 rooms with bath. Pool. AE, DC, MC. *Estalagem Pedro O Pescador* (E), Rua Eduardo Burnay 22 (tel. 061 62504). 25 rooms with bath. *Turismo* (M), Rua Rezés (tel. 061 63146). 154 rooms with bath. On seafront, with terrace, bar, regional decor, disco, shops, 2 pools, tennis. AE, DC, MC.
At **Talefe**. *Albergaria Dom Fernando* (E), Quinta da Caluda (tel. 061 55204). Pool, riding. With excellent restaurant. Advance booking essential. AE, DC, MC.
Restaurants. *Parreirinha* (M), Rua Dr. Miguel Bombarda 12. Closed Tues. in winter. AE, DC, MC. *Mar a Vista* (I), Rua Santo António 16. Closed Wed. in winter.

Fátima (Santarém). *Dom Gonçalo* (E), Rua Jacinta Marto (tel. 049 52262). 42 rooms with bath. A friendly Estalagem and great value, with garden, and top food at budget prices. AE, DC, MC. *Beato Nuno* (M), Ave. Beato Nuno (tel. 049 51222). 87 rooms, all with bath. Carmelite Friars' guest house. *Exercito Azul* (M), Rua São Vicente de Paulo (tel. 049 51020). 59 rooms with bath. Operated by the Blue Army, American priest often in charge. AE, DC. *Pensão das Irmãs Dominicanas* (M), Rua Francisco Marto (tel. 049 52317). 86 rooms, most with bath. Good food. *Regina* (M), Rua Conego Dr. Manuel Formigão (tel. 049 52303). 77 rooms with bath. AE, DC, MC. *Santa Maria* (M), Rua de Santo António (tel. 049 51015). 59 rooms with bath. AE, DC, MC. *Tres Pastorinhos* (M), Cova da Iria (tel. 049 52429). 92 rooms with bath. Modern, aseptic, but tidy and new. AE, DC, MC. All the religious houses take guests.

Restaurant. *Grelha* (M), Rua Jacinto Marta 76. Closed Thurs. AE, DC, MC.

Foz do Arelho (Leiria). *Facho* (I), tel. 062 97110. 40 rooms, 20 with bath. Old-fashioned, on sea front; near the Lagoa de Obidos with good coarse fishing. AE, DC, MC.

Leiria (provincial capital). Choice of accommodations includes several pensions and a youth hostel. *Dom João III* (M), Ave. Heróis de Angola 2 (tel. 044 33902). 64 rooms with bath. AE, DC, MC, V. *Euro-Sol* (M), Rua D. José Correia da Silva (tel. 044 24101). 54 rooms with bath. Pool, disco. AE, DC, MC. *Lis* (I), Largo Alexandre Herculano 10 (tel. 044 22108). 42 rooms with bath. Breakfast only. Old-fashioned, in town center by River Liz. AE, DC, MC.
Restaurant. There are also several cafés and tascas. *Regional Verde Pinho* (E), Rua Comandante Almeida Henriques. With good country fare.

Mafra (Lisbon). *Albergaria Castelão* (E), Ave. 25 de Abril (tel. 061 52320). 19 rooms with bath. AE, DC, MC.
Restaurants. The town has several small restaurants.

Marinha Grande (Leiria). *Albergaria Nobre* (E), Rua Alexandre Her-culano 21 (tel. 044 52226). 25 rooms with bath. Good restaurant. MC.

Nazaré (Leiria). There are several pensions. *Nazaré* (M), Largo Afonso Zuquete (tel. 044 51311). 50 rooms with bath. DC, MC. *Praia* (M), Ave. da Vieira Guimarães 39 (tel. 044 51423). 40 rooms with bath. AE, DC, MC. *Pens-ão Madeira* (I), Praça Sousa Oliveira 71 (tel. 044 51180). 29 rooms, most with bath. AE, DC. *Pensão Maré* (I), Rua Mousinho de Albuquerque 8 (tel. 044 51750). 28 rooms. Breakfast only. AE, DC, MC.
Restaurants. There are also several Inexpensive restaurants. *Arte Xave-ga* (E), Calçada do Sitio. *Mar Bravo* (E), Praça Sousa Oliveira. Lovely view. AE, DC, MC.

Obidos (Leiria). *Pousada do Castelo* (L), tel. 062 95105. 9 rooms with bath. *The* place to eat and stay if you can get in: the romantic, ancient—and restored—Governor's castle of Obidos. Try the local Gaeiras wine. AE, DC, MC, V. *Albergaria Josefa d'Obidos* (E), Rua D. João de Ornelas (tel. 062 95228). 14 rooms with bath. Breakfast only. AE, DC. *Estalagem do Con-vento* (E), Rua Dr. João de Ornelas (tel. 062 95217). 13 rooms with bath. Charming inn along the road just below the walled city. Cheerful rooms. DC, MC.
Restaurants. *Alcaide* (M), Rua Direita. Closed Tues. AE, DC, MC. *João V* (I), Largo da Igreja do Senhor da Pedra. Highly recommended. Outside town on the Caldas da Rainha road. Closed Mon. MC.

Peniche (Leiria). *Praia Norte* (M), tel. 062 71660. 92 rooms with bath. Pool, disco. AE, DC.
Restaurant. *Nau dos Corvos* (E), Cabo Carvoeiro. AE, DC, MC.

Porto de Mos (Leiria). *Quinta do Rio Alcaide* (M), tel. 044 42124. 9 rooms with bath. Rooms in 4 different houses, each with a kitchen. Beautiful country property; dinner provided. Country House.

Praia da Areia Branca (Lisbon). There is also a youth hostel. *Estalagem da Areia Branca* (E), tel. 061 43757. 29 rooms with bath.

São Martinho do Porto (Leiria). Excellent safe sandy beach for children. Accommodations include several pensions and a youth hostel. *Estalagem da Concha* (E), Largo Vitorino Frois (tel. 062 98220). 27 rooms with bath. DC, MC. *Apartamentos Turisticos São Martinho* (M), tel. 062 98335. 160 units. Pool, restaurant. AE, DC, MC. *Parque* (I), Ave. Marechal Carmona (tel. 062 98506). 44 rooms, most with bath. Breakfast only; tennis, disco. AE, DC, MC.

São Pedro de Muel (Leiria). *Hotel Mar e Sol* (M), Ave. Sá e Melo (tel. 044 59182/3). 43 rooms with bath. DC, V. *Hotel São Pedro* (M), Rua Dr. Adolfo Leitão (tel. 044 591 20). 53 rooms with bath. *Pensão D. Dinis* (I), Rua Dr. Fernando 1 (tel. 044 59156). 18 rooms, 3 with bath. *Pensão Miramar* (I), Rua dos Servicos Florestais (tel. 044 59141). 11 rooms with bath. Saltwater pool by beach. *Youth hostel* (tel. 044 59236), open May through Sept.

Sobral de Monte Agraço (Lisbon). *Quinta de São José* (E), Ereiria (tel. 061 94133). 7 double rooms with bath. Pool, restaurant. Country House.

Termas dos Cucos (Lisbon). Spa. Near Torres Vedras. *Termas dos Cucos* (I), tel. 061 23127. 35 rooms, some with bath. In charming Edwardian setting with Natural Hot Mud Baths. Open May through Sept.

Torres Vedras (Lisbon). *Pensão Moderna* (M), Ave. Tenente Valadim (tel. 061 23146). 35 rooms, 14 with bath. Breakfast only. *Residêncial dos Arcos* (M), Bairro Arenas (tel. 061 32489). 28 rooms with bath. Garage. Breakfast only, but restaurant next door.
At **Santa Cruz** beach nearby. *Santa Cruz* (M), Rua José Pedro Lopes (tel. 061 97199). 31 rooms with bath; disco. AE, DC, MC. *Pensão Miramar* (I), Rua José Pedro Lopes (tel. 061 97216). 27 rooms. Breakfast only.

Vimeiro (Lisbon). Spa with nine-hole golf course at Porto Novo. *Termas* (I), tel. 061 98104. 88 rooms, 49 with bath. Pool, tennis, disco. Open July through Sept.
At **Porto Novo**. *Golf Mar* (M), tel. 061 98157. 284 rooms with bath. On beach, with pool, tennis, shops, disco. AE, DC, MC.

CAMPING. There are campsites at the following places: Alcobaça, Parque Municipal; Berlenga Islands, in old fort jutting out to sea; Caldas da Rainha, Orbitur; Ericeira; Lourinhá; Mafra, Parque do Sobreiro; Nazaré, Parque do Valado/Orbitur, Vale Paraiso; Peniche, Parque Municipal; Praia da Areia Branca, Parque Municipal; Praia da Vieira; Praia de Pedrogão; Parque Municipal; Praia de Santa Cruz, Parque de Campismo;

São Martinho do Porto, Parque de Campismo; São Pedro de Muel, Orbitur (2 sites).

PLACES OF INTEREST. Museums are usually open daily, except Mondays and public holidays, 10–5, but double check the times on the spot. Some close for lunch. Entrance fees are between 150$00 and 300$00.

Alcobaça. Abbey of Santa Maria, 12th-century Abbey Church, the largest in Portugal, with later decorated Gothic cloister.

Batalha. Abbey Church. Gothic Abbey Church with Manueline features and cloisters. Military museum off cloisters.

Caldas da Rainha. José Malhoa Museum. Paintings, sculptures, ceramics. In the park.

Fátima. Shrine. One of Europe's main places of pilgrimage.

Leiria. Municipal Museum. By the Town Hall.

Mafra. Ethnographical Museum, Rua José Elias Garcia. Closed for lunch, Sat. morning, and Sun.
Museu da Caça (Hunting Museum) and collection of Victorian and Edwardian carriages, in Mafra Chase. Ring bell at iron gates, show identification; tip 200$00.
Palace. With superb library and royal reception rooms, and Religious Art Museum.

Mira de Aire. Caves. Europe's deepest cave with underground lakes and beautifully lit caverns. Two elevators.

Nazaré. Museu Joaquim Manso. House and library of well-known journalist.

Obidos. Municipal Museum. Interesting Peninsular War collection; paintings and sculptures.

Torres Vedras. Municipal Museum. Tiles, pictures and sculptures. **Peninsular War redoubt.**

SPECIAL EVENTS. For further details and exact dates, consult local tourist offices. **May.** Big romaria, *Senhor da Pedra,* held near Obidos on May 3. At Fátima, the first of the two great annual pilgrimages to the shrine takes place May 12–13; impressive ceremonies are also held here on 12th and 13th of each month until the second main pilgrimage in Oct. **July.** Annual Fair of St. James held at Ericeira on July 25. **August.** At Turçifal, huge romaria to chapel of Our Lady of Help on high hill, Aug. 5. At Peniche, Festival of *Nossa Senhora da Boa Viagem,* patroness of fishermen, first weekend. **September.** Festival of *Senhor dos Milagres* in village of Milagres, 8 km. (5 miles) north of Leiria, on Sept. 13. At Nazaré, religious celebrations, big fair, bullfights, colorful procession in local costumes, mid-September. **October.** Second great annual pilgrimage at Fátima, Oct. 12–13. **December.** At Carvoeira between Mafra and Ericeira. Romaria of *Nossa Senhora do O* to the chapel of S. Julião by the stream. Early in the month.

SPORTS. For further details of sports facilities ask at local Tourist Offices. **Golf.** *Vimeiro Golf Club,* Vimeiro (tel. 061 98157).

Horse Riding. *Centro de Educaçao Fisica,* Equitação e Desportos, Mafra (tel. 061 52005).

Tennis. *Campo de Ténis,* Alcobaça (tel. 062 42377); *Clube de Ténis,* Caldas da Rainha (tel. 062 22400); *Ténis da Camara Municipal,* Peniche (tel. 062 72271); *Aero-Clube de Torres Vedras,* Parque Municipal de Santa Cruz (tel. 061 97299).

Sailing. *Clube Naval de Ericeira,* Ericeira (tel. 061 63122); *Clube Naval de Peniche,* Peniche (tel. 062 72271).

Windsurfing. *Apartamentos Turisticos Ivoteis,* São Martinho do Porto (tel. 062 98335).

THE THREE BEIRAS

The three Beiras, Beira Alta, Beira Báixa, and Beira Litoral—Upper Beira, Lower Beira, and Coastal Beira—stretch right across Portugal, from the bare uplands by the Spanish frontier, north of Castelo Branco, through the Estrela mountains to the sea west of Leiria.

The province is watered by the Mondego, which rises near Trancoso, flows through lovely green countryside to Coimbra, one of the oldest universities in Europe, and waters the rice fields at Montemor-o-Velho before entering the sea at Figueira da Foz, a popular seaside resort.

The winters are glacial here, and the summers usually fearfully hot. The few crops struggle against both the rocky soil and the difficult climate—small wonder that this province is one of the poorest regions of Portugal. But it *is* wonderful country for goats. Fine herds of 40 or 50 long-horned, silkily-coated, brown or beige animals guarded by a goatherd, wander in the scrub, delicately picking at short herbage, which is covered with brilliantly colored wild flowers in the spring. Jays and hoopoes preen their feathers in the road, and flocks of magpies fly around.

In Coastal Beira, one is never sure which will emerge victorious, the land or the sea, they are so closely wedded. The sea thrusts inland through innumerable lagoons, and the shore stretches out until it is lost from sight.

Discovering the Three Beiras

The route to Portugal from Castilian Spain, via Burgos and Salamanca (the frontier post is at Vilar Formoso), brings you into the country through its highest gate—a gate that is barred by the city of Guarda. This is the city that a Portuguese saying describes as *forte, feia, fria e farta*—strong, ugly, cold, and rich—the highest city in Portugal, with an altitude of just over 1,000 meters (3,400 feet). The air is so brisk that King Ferdinand of León came here to treat his ailing lungs; it snows often in winter, and spring comes late, when the flowering broom turns the country into a sea of gold. The cherries don't ripen until July, but when they do little girls make bouquets of them, offering them to passing motorists at every turn of the road.

This city of granite presents an austere setting for the beauty of its 14th-century Gothic cathedral, which was patterned after Batalha. Surmounted by battlements and enveloped in a network of stone, this cathedral possesses a sumptuous Renaissance altarpiece and a lofty nave which seems to be suspended in mid-air at the summit of its clustered columns and the twisted Manueline pillars which support the chancel arch. There is a magnificent view from the 12th-century Torre dos Ferreiros over the Serra da Estrela.

A side road running north from Vila Formoso, N332, would take you to Almeida, a more remote, though still large, frontier town completely enclosed in double Vauban-type fortifications. It was successively captured and defended in the Peninsular War by British and Portuguese forces under Wellington, and the French commanded by Masséna.

The Serra da Estrela

The region around Guarda is very wild. Ancient avalanches deposited piles of stone and rubble on the flanks of the mountains and their coarse heather coverage provides rough pasture for goats. Nevertheless, among these gigantic pinnacles there are small stone walls which enclose tiny fields of rye, and even a few fragile vineyards near picturesque, formerly fortified towns, a scattering of which are dotted in a wide circle around Guarda. Three of these lie in a rough triangle north of the city. Pinhel (north along N221) is filled with noble 17th- and 18th-century houses beneath a greensward on which are two high towers, all that remain of the castle. The impressive walls of Trancoso (off N221 on N340 and then N226), and Celorico da Beira's spreading castle (just off the N16 highway northwest), recall romantic, heroic legends from the pages of history—but the country is poor and the earth unyielding; in spite of strong family ties, the people leave to work in France or Germany, but when they have saved enough they return to their *terra,* their native land, and build themselves houses. This is the reason why you see so many horrendous new villas around these historic towns.

To the north of Trancoso (27 km., 18 miles, on N102) is the strange lost village of Marialva. The castle surrounded by ruined houses, some as recent as the 18th century, is set within long walls which also enclose the parish church and two Renaissance chapels. The new settlement below is of little interest. Slightly to the northeast but with no direct road, the tall heart-shaped castle of Penedono rears up from the living rock beside the village street. Camões, the famous epic poet, tells that the Knight of Penedono was one of the 12 legendary knights of Portugal, who went to England to joust for the honor of 12 fair ladies.

Westward from Trancoso (N226 and N229) lies Aguiar da Beira, at a fair altitude. The town has strange Gothic architecture, a square keep with toothed battlements, an elegant Manueline pillory and a low battlemented building—the medieval council chamber—open to the sky, built above the town spring.

Running southwest from Guarda, the Serra da Estrela prolongs the rough backbone—the *cordilheira*—of the Iberian Peninsula. Its bare ridges, bristling with rocky outcroppings resembling human forms, sometimes give the impression of a lunar landscape. Its peaks are often covered with snow. Wandering shepherds lead their sheep and goats into the valleys for the summer, sleeping in the open air among their flocks and taking shelter from the rain beneath their cloaks of straw. There is some skiing during the winter on the high plateau of Torre, near the summits of Penhas da Saude. The Ski Club of Portugal has built shelters and cleared trails, and a good hotel has been opened there.

From the Plateau de Torre you can see vast areas of Portugal and Spain. The Serra's enchantment, however, does not depend on the season. As soon as the spring sun has melted the last snow, the countryside is thick with flowers, and the scent of narcissus floats over a hundred bubbling springs.

Summer is exquisite in the mountains of Serra da Estrela. While the sun is scorching plains and beaches everywhere else, there is cool shade under the black pines of Lake Escura. The Penhas Douradas cast their brilliant reflection in the lake's still waters and the meadows are covered with purple lavender and white cistus.

On the northwestern slopes of the Serra are several places of great interest. Due west of Celorico on N16, a major through highway here, is Mangualde, where the 17th-century Palácio Anadia is open to the public. Off route N17 southwest from Celorico, Linhares has a restored medieval castle, old manor houses, and astonishing primitive paintings in the two churches. A little further on is Seia, near which is held one of the popular *romarias*. This shepherds' pilgrimage occurs in early fall to Nossa Senhora do Espinheiro, and is dedicated to a small figure of the Child Jesus. Dressed in uniform, it is called the Little Captain. Further on again along N17 is Lourosa, with a rare tenth-century pre-Romanesque church.

Harsh and poor, the Serra is a silent refuge. Life goes on here according to ancient customs. They still bleed a pig on the feast of Santa Lucia, make famous cheese (*queijo da Serra*) from ewes' milk in wooden troughs, and offer passers-by roasted chestnuts watered down with *geropiga,* a sweet liqueur.

Beira Baixa

On the road south from Guarda to Castelo Branco, along the western edge of the Serra da Estrela—N18—the first place of interest is Belmonte, with a partially preserved medieval castle. Nearby is a chapel with tombs of the family of Cabral, discoverer of Brazil, and a statue of the Virgin brought from Brazil in the 16th century. About half a mile away is the watch tower of *Centum Celas,* dating from Roman times. To the east, alongside roads and N233, the walled towns of Sortelha and Sabugal are both dominated by high castles. The latter's five-sided keep is as unusual as the castle of Penedono.

The towns on the road south—N18—from Belmonte are industrious places. At Covilhã (a winter sports resort) and Fundão, waterfalls power textile mills, and the roads are bordered by lengths of fabric and skeins of multi-colored wool stretched out in the sun to dry. The sheltered valleys between the mountains are so balmy that you can find almond trees blossoming in February, and the orchards of Fundão are famous, especially for their pears. Fundão, in its setting of forests and groves, is a departure point for trips into the Serra da Guardunha. A few miles south are the remains of a Roman road at Alpedrinha.

The lowlands now descend towards the River Tagus, the best region of Portugal for the production of olive oil, made from olives gathered in December. Here the houses seem to blend in with the rocky landscape in which they nestle. Monsanto—about 48 km. (30 miles) eastward from Fundão on N239—is the best known of these isolated places. Its houses huddle below a ruined castle, most bearing heraldic insignia, on a site where the surroundings and traditions are equally picturesque. Although it was subjected to more than 20 sieges by both the Moors and the Spaniards, it was never taken. Defended by the steepness of the rocks and surrounded by a triple fortification of walls, the city was impregnable. During one siege, when Monsanto's inhabitants were close to starvation, the mayor had a fatted calf thrown down from the walls in defiance of the besieging forces: taken in by this trick, the enemy believed continued waiting would be fruitless, and gave the siege up as unsuccessful. This event is commemorated every year on May 3—young girls dressed in white climb to the top of the walls and throw jars filled with flowers down from the heights. On top of the church tower, where a huge clock has been striking the hour for centuries, a silver cock is installed—emblematic of the fact that many years ago Monsanto was chosen as "the most Portuguese village in Portugal," though, in fact, it is unlike any other village in the country! The houses built among the rocks are reached by rough steps and there seems to be no level place in the whole extraordinary conglomeration. Although life is hard here, the area breeds centenarians.

Castelo Branco, prosperous and busy, has retained little of its ancient splendor. The museum displays beautiful Arras tapestries in the original setting of this former Episcopal Palace. The statues in the unusual gardens represent the Apostles, the virtues and the signs of the zodiac below the Stairway of the Kings of Portugal, decorated with 17th-century sculptures, wherein the scorn of the Portuguese for the Spanish dynasty is shown by the much smaller scale of Philip I and II. Castelo Branco is famous for its hand-embroidered linen bedspreads (*colchas*), which the young girls make in preparation for their wedding night. They also embroider magnificent spreads in silk, modeled on ancient Persian designs, in exquisite nuances of jade, pearl-gray and lavender, with highlights of purple and gold. A school for this embroidery is attached to the museum.

The Mondego—West of the Serra da Estrela

The railway line followed by the *Sud* Express to Paris travels below the mountain range and runs north of the delightful valley of the Mondego River (the road along here is the N234). The Mondego is the most Portuguese of all the country's rivers, because it rises, flows, and empties into the sea without having contained a single drop of Spanish water. The view from the train provides you with wide and beautiful panoramas inaccessible to the motorist on the highway.

And the trip westward from Guarda becomes even more entrancing once you have descended to the wide valley of the river; Nelas, with its lovely shaded palaces, and Santa Comba Dão, not far from the road-bridge at the confluence of the Dão and Mondego rivers. The nearby village of Vimieiro, with its terraced vineyards, was the birthplace of Oliveira Salazar, and he chose to be buried there. This is vineyard country, where the wines, especially the reds, are famous. Finally you arrive at Luso and the entry to the Forest of Buçaco. Alternatively, you can reach Luso by turning off the main north/south motorway, Al, at Mealhada, and taking the N234.

Buçaco

Buçaco is sheltered within its long wall constructed by the barefooted Carmelites, who built it in the 17th century in order to mark off the area where they strove to find, through labor and meditation, the mystic union preached by their master, St. John of the Cross. A modest church embellished with many-colored pebble mosaics and a convent with cork partitions to give protection against the cold mountain air testify to the self-discipline of these Carmelites. Patiently they enriched this slope of the Serra, creating a treasure which the passing of the centuries has served only to enrich—for the rules of their order commanded them to plant every year a certain number of trees, which they chose from among the most beautiful available: beeches, oaks, sycamores and cypresses, which grow to a height of more than 150 feet. The *Cupressus lusitanicus* are famous the world over. Now there are 700 varieties—a silviculturist's paradise. Beneath this thick foliage, scores of shade-growing flowers sprang up: ferns, belladonna, hydrangea and lilies-of-the-valley, which flourish along the green moss-covered paths surrounding the silent pools.

At the beginning of the last century, this marvelous kingdom of silence was the scene of a great and bloody battle. The troops of Napoleon commanded by Masséna, persisted in an assault on the heights of Buçaco, where the Portuguese and English forces under Wellington had entrenched themselves. September 27, 1810 was a costly day for both sides, and marked the beginning of the end of four disastrous French invasions. A small military museum near the Porta da Rainha (Queen's Gate) helps you to reconstruct the battle on the scene of its actual occurrence.

After the last Carmelites had been expelled as a result of the Liberal Wars when the religious orders were proscribed, King-Consort Ferdinand, builder of the Palácio da Pena at Sintra, commissioned Luigi Manini, scene painter of Lisbon's opera, to turn the austere monastery into a royal residence. The Manueline extravaganza with a 12-arched loggia and rotunda of lacy arches was not finished until 1909. The 20-year-old Manuel II, last king of Portugal, used this palace only when he was passing by to commemorate the famous battle or to keep a rendezvous with the beautiful Gaby Deslys.

In 1910 the monarchy was overthrown and Manuel went into exile in England, where he died in 1932. This neo-Gothic piece of confectionery became a hotel, which has successfully preserved a regal stateliness in the great hall where the Battle of Buçaco is reproduced in blue-and-white azulejos, in the tiled arcades, the frescoed dining room and the enormous staircase. An atmosphere of calm and peace reigns here, helped by the silent depths of the forest and the crystaline purity of the air. This is a good place to pause for a while to relax—or better still, to use as a base while exploring the beauty and variety of the surrounding country.

From here you can return through the forest, passing the Fonte Fria, with a cascade, and the hermitages where the monks lived while in retreat. Just outside the forest, on a hill, stands the Obelisk, erected to commemorate the battle, where you can admire the magnificent view from the surrounding terrace, or go on to Cruz Alta, with another good view, right over to the Atlantic.

Viseu and Caramulo

Northwest of Buçaco by N234 and N2, across the fertile farmlands of A Terra Chã, is Viseu. (Alternatively, it lies due west of Mangualde, 22 km. (14 miles) on N16.)

They are still debating whether the Cava de Viriato, situated at the entrance to the city, was in reality the camp of Viriato, rebel hero of the Lusitanian resistance against the Legions of Rome. But Viseu has other, undebatable claims to glory. Its 13th-century cathedral is remarkable for the later Manueline vaulting of knotted cables supported on the columns along the nave. The sacristy ceiling is a painted riot of satyrs, monkeys and wild boars among tropical flowers and foliage. From the cathedral's upper choir you can get into the small but rewarding Treasury with early ivories, Limoges enamels, and polychrome statues.

The space in front of the cathedral is bordered by noble houses and the Episcopal Palace, now the Grão Vasco Museum. Opposite is the superb wide Baroque facade of the Misericórdia Church, making this great square one of the most original and beautiful in the country. The Grão Vasco Museum unites the masterworks of this early Portuguese painter, who inspired his own 16th-century school. The paintings of St. Peter and the Crucifixion are the two most noteworthy of his canvasses on display. Among the works of his followers is a representation of the *Adoration of the Magi,* in which Balthazar is depicted as a Tupi Indian (a tribe which the Portuguese explorers had just encountered in Brazil).

The Almeida Moreira Museum is in the house of its namesake who left his residence and its contents to the city he loved. It is a charming collection of furniture, Chinese porcelain, miniatures and paintings.

All around the walled nucleus of the city (brightened only by the Baroque facades of many of the churches) a new city has sprung up, complete with modern hotels and promenades. There's an abundance of secondhand stores and antique shops, also an entire industry devoted to the reproduction of fine copies of antique furniture.

Parallel to the Serra da Estrela range, the Serra do Caramulo is a chain of granite mountains which stands out in stark relief. These hills have such a favorable exposure that they are carpeted with purple heather, you can pick all the mimosa and pink laurel you want, and orchids grow wild on the ground. A center for the prevention and treatment of diseases of the lungs has been established here, but don't imagine that Caramulo is a sad sanatorium—on the contrary, people come for the sheer pleasure of the place, and to visit a museum which is perhaps unique in the world. Founded by an art-loving doctor, the museum derives its treasures solely from gifts offered by private collectors, or from works contributed by the painters and sculptors themselves. On display there you'll find Tournai tapestries, enamel work, jewels, ceramics and an invaluable collection of paintings—from Jordaens to Salvador Dali, from Grão Vasco to Picasso. At the Escola de Artesanato, you'll find Arraiolos rugs and the like for sale, while nearby there's an amusing Veteran Automobile Museum, with a large number of vehicles in perfect running condition, the oldest a 1902 Darracq.

Coimbra

Since the days of Camões, Portugal's finest poet, who studied at Coimbra and used to sit beneath the poplars and pen his odes to Leonor, the city has been celebrated in countless poems and songs. Built in tiers above the river's lazy current and dominated by the square tower of the university, Coimbra appears at its best approached from the south beyond the Mondego.

The tangled streets and alleys are so steep that one of the narrowest is aptly called Quebra Costas (the "rib-cracker"). The *couraças*—circular boulevards which follow the course of the ancient walls—surround the closely-packed center of the city. To get the best possible impression of Coimbra you should go directly to the university. You'll be greeted by the statue of King Dinis, who founded this Portuguese University in 1290. Some 250 years later, King João III gave his own palace to the students. The prodigal King João V donated in 1724 one of the most beautiful libraries in the world.

At Coimbra the student is king. He has his own code of behavior, drawn up in "kitchen Latin." It is full of many complicated rules which he piously respects. For a long time the only authority to which the student submitted was the university, which had its own tribunals and its own jails. The students wear romantic black capes, encircling their black frock coats—stifling garb for a city which is among the hottest in Portugal. Each rip you see in these capes marks a happy affair of the heart—like notches on a gun. Although the student never wears a hat, he is rarely without his guitar. When you see the students of today passing by the Mondego River, they are as likely to be on their way to the swimming pool or the stadium as to be courting the girls or the muses in the Choupal—but they have not yet given up their capes, or the *fado:* very different from the *fado* of Lisbon—a melancholy song sung in strident tones normally by a female voice—the *fado* of Coimbra is rather a sentimental ballad, more likely to be sung by a tenor. The tender and plaintive accents of these songs fill the numerous courtyards, gardens and squares of Coimbra.

Apart from Camões, others who studied here were Saint Anthony of Padua, who was actually born in Lisbon; the philosopher Antero de Quental; the novelist Eça de Queiroz; the former Portuguese prime minister Oliveira Salazar and his successor, Marcello Caetano; and several other eminent personalities of present-day Portugal.

The urbanization of the upper section of the city, an area traditionally reserved for the students, was regarded as a sacrilege by many Portuguese. But the modern buildings of the Faculties of Sciences and Letters form an elegant frame for the ancient Renaissance palace, which you enter via the Porta Ferrea. A double staircase mounts to the Via Latina, an attractive arcaded gallery where Latin was once the only language allowed to

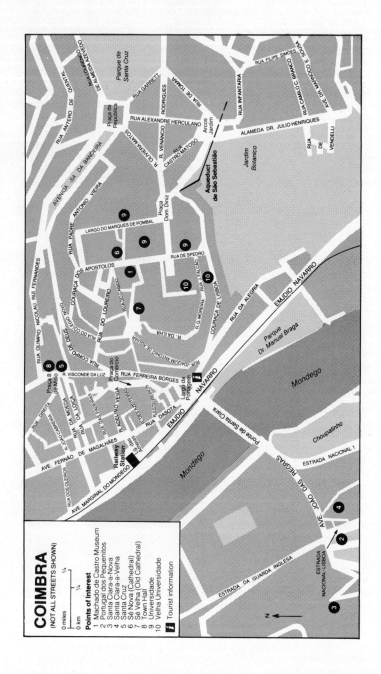

COIMBRA
(NOT ALL STREETS SHOWN)

0 miles   ¼   ½

0 km   ¼   ½

Points of Interest
1 Machado de Castro Museum
2 Portugal dos Pequenitos
3 Santa Clara-a-Nova
4 Santa Clara-a-Velha
5 Santa Cruz
6 Sé Nova (Cathedral)
7 Sé Velha (Old Cathedral)
8 Town Hall
9 Universidade
10 Velha Universidade

ℹ️ Tourist information

be spoken. The clock tower, nicknamed Cabra, "the Goat," by the students, regulates the rhythm of academic life. You can visit the Sala dos Capelos where the diplomas are presented, and which is decorated with portraits of the kings of Portugal.

Beyond, the Sala dos Bispos is lined with lovely 17th-century tiled panels of blue flowers in tall vases. Outside, a catwalk balcony round the top of the building gives stupendous views of the city and the river. Below you is the Machado de Castro Museum, with its graceful columns, courtyard, and loggia. There you can see some of the magnificent sculptures which have made Coimbra the capital of this art in Portugal: among them are statues of the Virgin in wood and polychrome stone, and also the famous Apostles in lifesize painted terracotta by the Frenchman Philippe Houdart, who was working in Coimbra in the middle of the 16th century, as well as lovely canvases and superb religious vessels in gold and silver.

This esplanade is the heart of the academic complex, closed on three sides by the university buildings and open on the fourth to the splendid view. To one side stands the library, whose glorious interior is rivaled only by the National Library in Vienna. Sadly, its architect is unknown, but he was an artistic genius. The interior is rich and rare. Brazilian ebony, imitation Oriental lacquer, theatrically carved curtains held aside by *putti*, all combine to create a lovely Baroque effect. The books are no less valuable, having been assembled over the centuries, the collection being reinforced, after 1834, by the libraries of secularized religious houses. Next to the library is the Manueline chapel, decorated with 17th-century carpet azulejos, with a small adjacent museum.

If you abandon yourself to the steep descent of the stairways and alleys, you'll end up, among the many ancient and slightly mildewed facades, before the severe battlements of the Romanesque Sé Velha (Old Cathedral), built in 1170. The Renaissance Porta de Santa Clara is extraordinarily beautiful. The somber beauty of the interior is brightened by the highly decorated Gothic altarpiece of Olivier of Ghent. The first university press was set up in the cloisters to the side of the cathedral.

Steep winding lanes descend to the Town Hall and the Manueline splendor of the Santa Cruz monastery which contains the tombs of Afonso Henriques and Sancho I, Portugal's first two kings. Be sure to see the sacristy, chapter house, the lovely two-storied Cloister of Silence, and upper choir; in the last named are the finest 16th-century stalls in the country, with the voyage of Vasco da Gama depicted in gold in high relief.

The school year finishes in May at Coimbra. In a frenzy of joy the students burn the colored ribbons which decorated their black gowns (red for Law, yellow for Medicine, blue for Letters, etc.). It's the Queima das Fitas, which comes after final examinations. During the summer, courses for foreigners draw many visitors to the university area and the small hotels of the upper city. The Portuguese students delight in initiating their friends to the ways of Coimbra, sharing their feasts of roast suckling pig or grilled sardines, or teaching them their repertoire of lyric songs and bawdy ballads in the intimacy of their lodgings where groups of students, called *republicas,* live together on a low budget, dividing their time among studies and politics, poetry and the amours of an evening.

The 50-acre Botanical Gardens, designed by William Elsden, have lovely 18th-century architectural features with stone stairways and statuary. More architectural features adorn the Mata de Santa Cruz with a high

18th-century artificial waterfall. Nearby is yet another park open to the public, the Penedo da Saudade, with a famous view.

The city, which would be stifling if it weren't for its gardens and the open spaces provided by the river, extends also to the other bank of the Mondego. The Gothic Church of Santa Clara—where Queen Isabella stayed, and near where the beautiful Inés de Castro took shelter during the period of her doomed love affair—is now more than half submerged in the waters which have already carried away the old palace and convent. The remains of the queen were moved to the convent of Santa Clara-a-Nova higher up the hill, where they still repose in a tomb of solid silver. Her original Gothic tomb, surrounded by polychrome stone figures of her nuns and of the Apostles, is in the choir at the end of the church.

Before leaving Coimbra you must take the children to visit Portugal dos Pequeninos. It's an immense garden containing replicas of all kinds of dwellings and monuments typical of Portugal and her former colonies, all built to the scale of the world of a five-year-old child.

East and South of Coimbra

Located on the high cliffs bordering the river—23 km. (14 miles) northeast of Coimbra on N110—whose every bend reveals a new landscape, the town of Penacova is a window opening onto the valley. Here you'll find carved toothpicks, fashioned out of the soft wood of the willow tree.

Almost immediately west of Penacova, in a hidden valley, is the psychiatric hospital of Lorvão in the old monastery whose reputation used to be so impressive that even the Moors respected its privileges. The two daughters of King Sancho retired to this monastery, and are now interred here in their precious tombs. Once a retreat for pious and wealthy ladies who decorated the stalls and panels of its choir with their coats-of-arms, Lorvão also has some admirable bronzes and iron grillework, as well as a small museum off the chancel.

On a side road from Ceira, a few miles southeast of Coimbra, stands the lovely church and former Benedictine convent of Semide. The fine carpet tiles, pair of tall painted angels, countrified canvases, a beautiful organ, and good polychrome statues in the church are all well worth seeing. The convent buildings have been used for the last 50 years for what is obviously a well-run boarding school for homeless boys, who are thrilled to show visitors around.

But even more striking than the treasures of Semide are the pilgrimage chapels among the oaks and arbutus of the Serra da Lousã to the south. White sanctuaries rise among the trees around an old castle, crouched at the bottom of a heavily wooded valley. This is the full Romantic landscape, an ideal locale for solitary hermits, with peaks below racing clouds, and mountain torrents roaring in the deep gorges. The little town of Lousã is noted for its *solars,* or large town houses, particularly the Casa da Viscondessa de Lousã with a high central Baroque pediment.

To the south—about 21 km. (13 miles) by N1—near Condeixa, which features 17th-century mansions and houses in lovely gardens, are the ruins of Conimbriga, a city of the Luso-Roman epoch. Menaced by the barbarian tide of the Visigoths, the city attempted to fortify itself by building a wall haphazardly constructed of rocks, bricks and pieces of old statues. The attempt was futile—the city was razed in 458, and its ruins gradually became submerged by a layer of soil from which olive trees sprouted. Fifteen centuries slipped by before excavations uncovered columns, thermal baths, fountains, and, above all, a collection of mosaics. Wandering in the diggings will give a very good idea of the layout of a Roman provincial settlement, and how it went about its daily life. A museum supplements these impressions and documents the discoveries made in the area, and delightful copies of little Roman lamps are on sale. Nearby you can see the ruins of an aqueduct.

A little further south—about 26 km. (16 miles) on N1/E50—the town of Pombal evokes the name of the Marquis of Pombal, the famous minister of Joseph I. Pombal subjected his tyrannous energy to the service of this easy-going king; he rekindled the Portuguese economy and the spirit of nationalism in its people, and rebuilt the city of Lisbon after the earthquake of 1755. He died, disgraced, in the town which bears his name. On the hilltop is a 12th-century castle of the Knights Templar, recently restored, from which you can enjoy a marvelous panoramic view. From here you can go south to Leiria.

Coastal Beira

We return to the north of the Beira region, and the city of Aveiro. Crisscrossed by canals, it was an important fishing port of the 16th century, brought into prominence by the discovery of Newfoundland. The finest buildings of the city date from this era, especially the churches and the opulent Convent of Jesus. The Infanta Santa Joanna, daughter of King Afonso V, lived here in the 15th century. The most powerful princes of the epoch sought her hand in vain for she was determined to become a nun. Her tomb of inlaid marble is amazing in its richness and delicacy. The convent with its golden chapels houses a large collection of 15th- and 16th-century religious art.

It is possible to take pleasant boat rides on the lagoon, which, however, can be a bit misty. Indeed, Aveiro's chief diversion is fishing in the lagoons (or *rias*), followed by feasting on the local kind of fish chowder called *caldeirada à pescador*. The narrow wooden bridges over the *rias* are a curious feature of this area. The Fabrica Aleluia pottery factory will copy any picture, photograph, etc., on to tiles or plaques for you.

In 1575 a violent tempest resulted in the obstruction of the entrance of the port of Aveiro, and the city began to die, in a commercial sense, from slow strangulation—a long strip of land, isolated, low and swampy, formed where the waters of the River Vouga stagnated, creating a vast lagoon which now changes shape as capriciously as a jellyfish, subject only to the whims of the rains and the tides. A strange universe—composed of mist and seaweed, of reeds and sea birds bobbing on the water as nonchalantly as if they were perched on their nests, of ponds hollowed out like wash basins among the meadows—evokes the atmosphere of the *polders* of Holland. However, Aveiro and its surroundings have become very prosperous again.

Here you'll find dikes which serve as highways for hundreds of bicycles, irrigation canals, and boats which seem for all the world to be sailing in the middle of the pastures. The sky is gray and murky, the wind damp. Fresh-water fish jostle their salt-water brothers in the thousands of inlets of the salt-marshes. The natives comb the lagoon with enormous wooden rakes drawn by oxen, harvesting a seaweed rich in iodine, which they use to fertilize their fields. The *moliceiros*—boats whose prows are curved into the shape of a swan's neck—furrow the placid waters, poled along by half-naked boatmen, from dawn to dusk, bringing home boatloads of black crabs, eels and seaweed.

In 1808 another tempest broke open the sandbanks which had been blocking the channel of Aveiro, and the lifegiving tides swept once again across the bar. But in the meantime the nearby port cities of Ovar and Murtosa to the north, and Ílhavo to the south had grown used to their land-locked way of life; they had become livestock breeding and dairy centers—occupations which they elected to continue. Nevertheless, Ílhavo still maintains its Museum of the Sea, where you'll find a striking survey of all the life and history of this amphibious area—an area where, at Aveiro, they dance on the linked pontoons of the boats during the March Festival, and where, at Praia de Mira and Torreira, they live in odd dwellings called *palheiros,* fashioned from the old hulls of boats. In Ovar, as well as the fishermen's houses, there is the pilgrimage chapel of Calvario.

On the Costa Nova do Prado, you bathe in the open sea or, if you don't mind the seaweed, choose the calmer waters of the polluted lagoon. The whole of this strange part of Portugal is marked by pyramids of glistening salt from the salt pans, drying in the sun and wind. At certain times of the year these pyramids are thatched with straw against the winter rains, breaking up the flatness of the landscape in an extraordinary way.

The Pousada da Ria, 40 km. (25 miles) northwest of Aveiro, is situated on a calm lagoon, near a Nature Reserve, for this part of the coast is a haunt of innumerable sea birds.

The castle of Vila da Feira, a few miles northwest of Ovar, is one of the best-preserved and most romantic fortresses in all of Portugal, set against a background of great trees.

South of Ílhavo are the historic porcelain works of Vista Alegre, with a fascinating museum (open only in the afternoon) showing examples of everything the factory has produced and a shop where you can buy the porcelain. This remarkable firm was founded in 1824 by José Ferreira Pinto Basto and has remained in the same family ever since. Several of the craftsmen, too, are descended from the original workers. Visitors who admire Baroque should be sure to ask for the chapel to be unlocked as it is filled with fine features. Built at the end of the 17th century, the chapel was part of the original Quinta on which were later erected the porcelain works, schools, and a model village for the employees, in which many still live.

Further south by N109, the Mondego valley slips toward the sea. Here, due west of Coimbra, is the river's broad estuary at Figueira da Foz, where the coast is low and sandy. The alluvial deposits which have come down to the shore from the mountains and silt deposited by the tide have combined to form the fine sandy beaches of Figueira da Foz, and Praia da Mira 35 km. (22 miles) to the north.

One of the most important cod-fishing ports of Portugal, Figueira is a lively seaside resort with swimming pools, a casino and all the essential holiday amusements plus an archeological museum. If you have any leisure time left, see the Casa do Paço: it's decorated with 6,888 tiles of Delftware which were washed up on the beach after a shipwreck. Figueira is also a good spot from which to take side trips into the Serra da Boa Viagem and to Cape Mondego.

Seventeen km. (10½ miles) inland on N11, towards Coimbra, is the great ruined castle of Montemor-o-Velho, rising above rice fields. The little village has a lot of atmosphere, and was the birthplace of some famous men in the past.

PRACTICAL INFORMATION FOR
THE THREE BEIRAS

WHEN TO COME. Summer is delightfully pleasant in the mountains of the Serra da Estrela. While a scorching sun beats down on the plains and beaches, you relax in the cool heights among groups of stunted trees.

TOURIST OFFICES. There are local tourist offices in the following towns: **Águeda,** Rua Central de Sargentos (tel. 034 62413); **Arganil,** Praça Simões Dias (tel. 039 22850); **Aveiro,** Praça da Republica (tel. 034 23680); **Buarcos,** Largo Tomás de Aquino (tel. 039 25019); **Caldas da Felgueira,** Praça Prof. Dr. José Veiga Simão (tel. 032 94348); **Caramulo,** Estrada Principal (tel. 032 86437); **Castelo Branco,** Alameda da Liberdade (tel. 072 21002); **Coimbra,** Largo da Portagem (tel. 039 23799); **Covilhã,** Praça do Municipio (tel. 075 22170); **Curia,** Largo da Rotunda (tel. 034 52248).

Figueira da Foz, Edifício Atlantico (tel. 039 22935/22126) and subsidiary at Rua 25 de Abril (tel. 039 22610); **Figueiró dos Vinhos,** Ave. Padre Diogo Vasconcelos (tel. 039 52178); **Fundão,** Ave. da Liberdade (tel. 075 52770); **Gouveia,** Ave. 1° de Maio (tel. 075 42135); **Guarda,** Praça Luis de Camões (tel. 071 22251); **Ílhavo,** Rua Arcebispo Pereira Bilhano (tel. 034 22395); **Lousã,** Edifício da Câmara, Rua João de Cáceres (tel. 039 99502).

Luso, Rua Dr. António Granjo (tel. 034 93133); **Manteigas,** Praça Dr. José Maria Bote 1 (tel. 071 47129); **Monfortinho,** Termas de Monfortinho (tel. 072 44223); **Oliveira de Azeméis,** Praça José da Costa (tel. 034 64463); **Oliveira do Hospital,** Edificio da Camara (tel. 038 52522); **Ovar,** Praça da Republica (tel. 034 52215); **Pombal,** Praça do Cardal (tel. 036 22001); **São Pedro de Muel,** Ave. Sá e Melo (tel. 044 59152); **Seia,** Largo do Mercado (tel. 071 22272); **Vila da Feira,** Praça da Republica (tel. 034 32611); **Viseu,** Ave. Gulbenkian (tel. 032 22294).

HOTELS AND RESTAURANTS

Águeda (Aveiro). Halfway between Coimbra and Oporto, on N1, north of Águeda, *Pousada de Santo António* (E), Serem (tel. 034 521230). 13 rooms with bath. A handy stopover en route north or south; isolated.

Almeida (Guarda). *Pousada Senhora das Neves* (E). tel. 071 54283. 21 rooms with bath. In a frontier town completely enclosed with fortifications. AE, DC, MC, V.

Aveiro (provincial capital). Accommodations include numerous pensions. *Afonso V* (E), Rua Dr. Manuel das Neves 65 (tel. 034 25191/3). 80 rooms with bath. AE, DC, MC, V. *Imperial* (M), Rua Dr. Nascimento Leitão (tel. 034 22141). 50 rooms, with bath. AE, DC, MC, V. *Residêncial Pomba Branca* (M), Rua Luis Gomes de Carvalho (tel. 034 26039). 19 rooms with bath. Breakfast only. *Arcada* (I), Rua Viana do Castelo 4 (tel. 034 23001). 54 rooms with bath. Breakfast only. AE, DC, MC, V.

Restaurants. *Cozinha do Rei* (E), in Hotel Afonso V (tel. 034 26802). AE, DC, MC. *Bota Rota* (M), Rua do Carmo 64 (tel. 034 28688). *Centenário* (M), Largo do Mercado 9–10 (tel. 034 22798).

Buçaco (Aveiro). *Palace* (L), tel. 031 93101/2. 79 rooms, 64 with bath. Excellent restaurant; exclusive wines from the cellar. Tours of superb wine cellars by request. One of Europe's great hotels, with extraordinary architecture in forest setting. Good center for exploring the region. AE, DC, MC, V.

Caldas da Felgueira (Viseu). Spa. *Grande Hotel das Caldas* (M), tel. 032 94299. 106 rooms, most with bath. Sauna, pool. Wonderful green and peaceful setting by the River Mondego. Closed mid-Oct. to end May.

Canas de Senhorim (Viseu). *Urgeiriça* (M), tel. 032 67267. 53 rooms with bath. Very comfortable; with pool, tennis, and excellent food. In woodland; tastefully decorated in the old style; huge public rooms with log fires in winter. AE, DC, MC, V.

Caramulo (Viseu). Off the Coimbra-Viseu road, N2, on N230. *Pousada de São Jerónimo* (M), tel. 032 86291. 6 rooms with bath. Pool, badminton. Delightful garden. AE, DC, MC, V.

Castelo Branco (provincial capital). *Pensão Arriana* (I), Ave. 1 de Maio 18 (tel. 072 21634). 18 rooms with bath. Breakfast only. *Pensão Caravela* (I), Rua do Saibreiro 24 (tel. 072 23939). 27 rooms, 14 with bath. Breakfast only. AE, DC, MC, V.

Restaurants. *Arcadia* (I), Ave. de Liberdade. Good regional cooking. Closed Wed. *Casa de Chá* (I), Ave. 1° de Maio 55. *Lua e Sol* (I), Rua S. António 22. Owner-run; good wine.

Cernache do Bonjardim (Castelo Branco). *Estalagem Vale da Ursa* (M), tel. 074 67511. 12 rooms with bath. Charming, newly built inn overlooking lake. Pool, water sports. Excellent food.

Coimbra (provincial capital). Coimbra is not well endowed with hotels; many travelers prefer to overnight in nearby Figueira da Foz, Buçaco or Curia. Accommodations include several pensions not listed here. *Astoria* (M), Ave. Emidio Navarro 21 (tel. 039 22055/7). 70 rooms, 51 with bath. Good, old-style restaurant with Buçaco wines. AE, DC, MC, V. *Bragança* (M), Largo das Ameias 10 (tel. 039 22171/3). 83 rooms with bath. MC. *Oslo* (M), Ave. Fernão de Magalhães 23/5 (tel. 039 29071/3). 34 rooms with bath. AE, DC, MC. *Avenida* (I), Ave. Emidio Navarro 37 (tel. 039 22156/7). 25 rooms with bath. AE. *Pensão Mondego* (I), Largo das Ameias 4 (tel. 039 29087). 43 rooms, most with bath. *Residência Almedina* (I), Ave.

Fernão de Magalhães 203 (tel. 039 29161). 28 rooms with bath. Breakfast only. *Residência Domus* (I), Rua Adelino Veiga 62 (tel. 039 28584). 20 rooms with bath. Breakfast only. AE.

Restaurants. The rather limited choice of restaurants is supplemented by some modern snack bars. Do not forget to sample the delicious local wines. *Dom Pedro* (M), Ave. Emidio Navarro 58. DC, V. *Lung Wah* (M), Monte Formoso. V. *Nicola* (M), Rua Ferreira Borges 35. *Pinto d'Ouro* (M), Ave. João das Regras 68. Specializes in chicken. Just across the bridge. *Piscinas* (M), Piscinas Municipais. The best, particularly at lunchtime. AE, DC, MC, V. *Santa Cruz* (M), Praça 8 de Maio.

Covilhã (Castelo Branco). *Pensão Solneve* (M), Rua Visconde Coriscada 126 (tel. 075 23001). 38 rooms, most with bath. MC. *Pensão Residência Montalto* (M), Praça do Municipio (tel. 075 25091). 15 rooms with bath. Breakfast only. MC. *Pensão Restaurant A Regional* (I), Rua das Flores 4 (tel. 075 22596). 18 rooms, some with bath.

Curia (Aveiro). Famous spa. Numerous small hotels and pensions are open during the season. *Hotel das Termas* (M), tel. 031 52185/7. 40 rooms with bath. Pool, park setting with boating lake and lovely walks. Open all year. AE, DC, MC, V. *Palace* (M), tel. 031 52131/2. 122 rooms with bath. Magnificent pool, tennis, other sports activities; excellent restaurant. A grand hotel in the old style. Closed Oct. through May. DC, MC.

Figueira da Foz (Coimbra). Casino. Popular summer resort with marvelous beach, yacht harbor. As well as the main hotels listed below, there are many small hotels and pensions, most open summer only. *Albergaria Nicola* (E), Rua Bernardo Lopes 59 (tel. 033 22359). 24 rooms with bath. AE, DC, MC. *Estalagem da Piscina* (E), Rua Sta. Catarina 7 (tel. 033 22420). 20 rooms with bath. Pool. Closed Nov. through Apr. AE, DC, MC, V. *Grande* (E), Ave. 25 de Abril (tel. 033 22146). 91 rooms with bath. AE, DC, MC, V.

Aparthotel Atlantico (M). 70 good service apartments with spectacular sea view. Recommended. Bookings at Grande Hotel above. AE, DC, MC, V. *Aparthotel Sottomayor* (M). Also has 60 good service apartments with fine sea view. Bookings at Grande Hotel. DC, MC. *Costa da Prata* (M), Esplanada Silva de Guimarães (tel. 033 26610). 66 rooms with bath. Breakfast only. AE, DC, MC, V. *Hotel da Praia* (M), Rua Miguel Bombarda 59 (tel. 033 22082). 65 rooms with bath. Breakfast only. AE, DC, MC, V. *Internacional* (M), Rua da Liberdade 20 (tel. 033 22056). 55 rooms with bath. Breakfast only. AE, DC, MC, V. *Wellington* (M), Rua Dr. Calado 23–7 (tel. 033 26767). 34 rooms with bath. Breakfast only. AE, DC, MC, V.

Restaurants. There are numerous good restaurants on the promenade and in the town. Fish is especially recommended. *Tamargueira* (M). On the beach. For inexpensive, straightforward Portuguese food served indoors in cork-lined dining room or outdoors on terrace; with its own live shellfish pool. AE, DC, MC. *Teimoso* (I). Also serves reasonably priced, simple Portuguese dishes. About 5 km. (3 miles) out on the Cabo Mondego road. Also has rooms.

Forte da Barra (Aveiro). *Pensão Jardim* (I), tel. 034 36745. 10 rooms. Excellent food and friendly owners.

Fundão (Castelo Branco). *Estalagem da Neve* (E), Rua de São Sebasti-
ão (tel. 075 52215). 6 rooms, 4 with bath. Pool. AE, DC, MC. *Fundáo* (M),
Rua Vasco da Gama (tel. 075 52051). 50 rooms with bath. Breakfast only.
AE, DC, MC, V. *Pensão Tarouca* (M), Rua 25 de Abril 41 (tel. 075 52168). 19
rooms, 4 with bath.
Restaurant. *Herminia* (M), Ave. de Liberdade 125. New; good food.
AE, DC, MC.

Guarda (provincial capital). Near Spanish border. *Residência Filipe*
(E), Rua Vasco da Gama 8 (tel. 071 22658/9). 25 rooms, 7 with bath. AE,
DC, MC, V. *Hotel do Turismo* (M), Ave. Coronel de Carvalho (tel. 071 22205).
105 rooms with bath. Pool, disco. AE, DC, MC, V. *Pensão Aliançia* (M), Rua
Vasco da Gama 9 (tel. 071 22135). 30 rooms, 16 with bath. Breakfast only.
Restaurants. *Aliança* (M), Rua Mouzinho de Albuquerque 6. *Belo Hori-
zonte* (M), Largo de São Vicente. Closed Sat.

Ílhavo (Aveiro). *Albergaria Arimar* (E), Ave. Mario Sacramento (tel.
034 25131). 11 rooms with bath. MC.

Luso (Aveiro). Famous spa. In addition, there are several small hotels
and pensions. *Grande Hotel das Termas do Luso* (M), Rua dos Banhos
(tel. 031 93450/2). 157 rooms with bath. Excellent pool, tennis, disco.
Closed mid-Oct. through Apr. DC, MC, V. *Eden* (M), Rua Emidio Navarro
(tel. 031 93171). 56 rooms with bath.
Restaurants. *O Cesteiro* (M), Rua José Duarte Figueiredo. Closed Wed.
V. *Regional* (M), Rua Dr. Lucio Abranches.

Mangualde (Viseu). *Estalagem Cruz da Mata* (E), Estrada Nacional
(tel. 032 62556). 12 rooms with bath. On edge of town. *Senhora do Castelo*
(M), tel. 032 63315. 85 rooms with bath. Magnificent location and views.
Winter sports nearby. AE, DC, MC, V.

Manteigas. (Guarda). Spa. *Casa de São Roque* (M), tel. 075 47125. 6
rooms with bath. Country house. Dinner available. *Hotel de Manteigas*
(M), just outside town (tel. 075 47114). 26 rooms with bath. Set in moun-
tain scenery. AE, DC, MC, V. *Pensão Serradalto* (M), tel. 075 47151. 15 rooms,
in the village.
Pousada de São Lourenço (E), tel. 075 47150. 11 rooms. In Serra da
Estrela mountains 13 km. (8 miles) north of village. Stunning views. AE,
DC, MC, V.

Mealhada (Aveiro). *Motel Quinta dos 3 Pinheiros* (M), tel. 031 22391.
35 rooms with bath. Pool; good restaurant. Excellent overnight stop on
the road between Lisbon and Oporto. AE, DC, MC.
Restaurants. There are several reasonable restaurants beside the main
Lisbon–Oporto highway. Try the local specialty, *leitão* (roast suckling
pig).

Murtosa (Aveiro). *Pousada da Ria* (E), Bico do Muranzel, Torreira
(tel. 034 48332). 10 rooms with bath. Pool. On remote but polluted lagoon,
nature reserve, 40 km. (25 miles) from Aveiro. Lovely views. AE, DC, MC,
V.

Nelas (Viseu). *Albergaria de São Pedro* (M), Bairro das Toicas 4 (tel. 033 94585). 69 rooms with bath. Breakfast only, recommended. AE, DC, MC, V.

Oliveira de Azeméis (Aveiro). *Estalagem de São Miguel* (E), Parque la Salette (tel. 031 64144). 14 rooms with bath. In a park, with fine views. Excellent service. AE, DC, MC, V.
Restaurant. *O Campones* (M), Rua 25 de Abril. Wonderful regional food and wines. Closed Sun. MC.

Ovar (Aveiro). *Estalagem Xoupana* (E), Bertuge-Várzia (tel. 056 53468). Comfortable rooms and excellent restaurant. AE, DC, MC.
At **Torrão de Lameiro,** 5 km. (3 miles) southwest on N327. **Restaurant.** *Vela Areinho* (I), tel. 056 52848. Good, simple food, including shellfish. Highly recommended.

Pinhel (Guarda). *Pensão Falcão* (I), tel. 071 42104. 24 rooms with bath.

Póvoa das Quartas (Coimbra). Near Oliveira do Hospital, on N17 halfway between Coimbra and Guarda in scenic mountain spot. *Pousada Santa Bárbara* (E), tel. 038 52252. 16 rooms with bath. Rooms are sunny and attractive; garage. AE, DC, MC, V.

Sabugal (Guarda). *Albergaria Santa Isabel* (E), Largo do Cinema (tel. 071 92412). 45 rooms with bath. Comfortable. Breakfast only.

São Pedro do Sul (Viseu). Health resort and spa. *Lisboa* (M), tel. 032 71250. 40 rooms with bath. Breakfast only. *Hotel Vouga* (I), Estrada Nacional 63 (tel. 032 71263). 38 rooms with bath.

Seia (Guarda). *Estalagem de Seia* (E), Ave. Dr. Afonso Costa (tel. 038 22666/22682). 35 rooms with bath. Good central base for exploring the area. *Pensão Camelo* (M), Largo Marquês da Silva 86 (tel. 038 22530). 25 rooms, with annex, most with bath. Breakfast only. *Serra da Estrela* (M), Largo Marquês da Silva (tel. 038 22573). 21 rooms with bath. Breakfast only.

Termas de Monfortinho (Castelo Branco). Well-known spa. *Astoria* (M), tel. 077 44205/6/7. 94 rooms, 29 with bath. Open only May to mid-Nov. Tennis, disco. *Fonte Santa* (M), tel. 077 44104. 49 rooms, 41 with bath. Set in grounds. Open May to mid-Nov. Also several small pensions available.

Termas de Monte Real (Leiria). Spa. *Hotel Monte Real* (I), Parque das Termas (tel. 044 62151). 114 rooms, 59 with bath. Tennis. Closed end Nov. to end May. Several pensions also in the area.

Vila da Feira (Aveiro). *Pensão Ferreira* (I), Rua Dr. Vitorino de Sá (tel. 056 32859). 9 rooms.
Restaurants. *Caçador* (M). *Pedra Bala* (M). Both serve good local food and wines.

Viseu (provincial capital). *Grão Vasco* (E), Rua Gaspar Barreiros (tel. 032 23511). 88 rooms with bath. Pool, attractive gardens, good cuisine. AE, DC, MC, V. *Maria I* (M), Alto do Caçador (tel. 032 26143/5). 45 rooms with bath. Recommended. DC, MC. *Avenida* (I), Ave. 28 de Maio 1 (tel. 032 23432). 40 rooms, 32 with bath. *Pensão Rossio Parque* (I), Largo Major Teles 55 (tel. 032 22285). 14 rooms, most with bath. Several pensions.

Restaurants. *Alvorada* (M), Rua Gaspar Guerreiro 24. *Cortiço* (M), Rua Augusta Hilario 47 (tel. 032 23853). Local specialties. MC. *Gruta* (M), Rua D. Duarte 25. *Trave Negra* (M), Rua dos Loureiros 36. MC. *A Parreira* (I), Ave. da Belgica 2. Local setting.

CAMPING. There are campsites at the following places: Agueda de Baixo; Arganil; Aveiro; Castelo Branco; Coimbra; Coja; Cortegaça; Figueira da Foz (and at Gala); Fundão; Guarda; Ílhavo; Mira (Dunas de Mira); Murtosa (Praia da Torreira); Oliveira de Azeméis (La Salette); Oliveira do Hospital (2 sites); Ovar (Furadouro São Jacinto); Pedrogão; Penacova; São Pedro do Sul; Vages; and Viseu (Fontelo).

PLACES OF INTEREST. Museums are usually open daily, except Mondays and public holidays, 10–5, but check the times locally. Some close for up to 2 hours for lunch. Entrance fees are between 150$00 and 300$00. Apart from the items listed below, almost all of the places have interesting old churches to see as well.

Almeida. Massive **fortress,** northeast of Guarda, right on the frontier, on N332. Some old houses covered with azulejos.

Anadia. Paço da Graciosa, 18th-century, with superb azulejos, about 24 km. (15 miles) north of Coimbra.

Aveiro. Aveiro Museum, in former Convent of Jesus, Rua Santa Joana (tel. 034 23297). Main interest is with Princess Joana, who lived here in late 1400s. The church has her tomb, and a glittering interior. The museum is fine for Baroque art. An interesting combination of museum and convent.
Hunting Museum. Parque D. Pedro V.

Belmonte. Centum Vellas, Roman tower. **Castle,** 13th–14th century, with magnificent views over the Serra da Estrela.
Monastery by the hotel has pretty cloisters and unusual ceramic groups of Testament scenes.

Buçaco. Military Museum. Tracing events in the Peninsular War that happened close by. Just outside forest wall, by the Queen's Gate.

Caramulo. Fundação Abel de Lacerda Museum. Wide-ranging and worthwhile collection—medieval art, tapestries, porcelain, works by Portuguese and other artists of the 19th and 20th centuries, including Dali, Miró, Chagall, Leger, Picasso, and Dufy. Also fascinating vintage cars.

Castelo Branco. Francisco Tavares Proença Museum. Small general interest museum, established in former bishop's palace. Combination of

Roman items, tapestries, paintings, and folk artefacts. Lovely 17th-century **gardens** round the museum.

Coimbra. Machado de Castro Museum. Very fine collection of paintings, early polychrome sculpture, tiles, pottery, medieval plate, etc. Guided tours.
Monastery of Santa Cruz. 12th-century; Manueline decor, tiles, wood carving, interesting tombs; 16th-century Cloister; remarkable carved stalls in upper choir. 18th-century octagonal relic chapel reached from cloisters.
Old Cathedral (Sé Velha). 12th-century fortress-like building, with gilded retable, carvings in interior; fine 13th-century cloisters, much restored.
Old University (Universidade Velha). Chapel, Manueline with lovely 18th-century organ loft, tiles and Manueline decorations. **Library,** one of Portugal's most beautiful Baroque (1724) interiors. **University Museum of Sacred Art,** small museum of church objects, beside the chapel. The square which these buildings surround has marvelous panoramic view over the Mondego.

Condeixa-a-Nova (Conimbriga). Roman ruins of 3rd–5th centuries, still being excavated. Good **museum** with items found on the site.

Covilhã. Romanesque **chapel of São Martinho.**

Figueira da Foz. Casa do Paco. Enormous collection of Dutch pictorial tiles. **Dr. Santos Rocha Municipal Museum,** Rua Calouste Gulbenkian. A grab bag of Roman remains, paintings, pottery, furniture, in a new building with the public library. Best in archeological items.

Guarda. Cathedral, mainly 15th century, thus with plenty of Manueline elements. Fine views to be had from the roof.
Regional Museum, Rua Gen. Alves Roçadas. Arms, archeological items, paintings, and local history. May be closed for reorganization.

Idanha-a-Velha. Roman remains of Egitânia, about 6 km. (4 miles) south of Medelim, off N332. Reputed birthplace of Wamba, the Gothic king. Worth a visit for the archeology buff. Excavated pieces in the church. Ask for the key from house near the tower.

Ílhavo. Museum of the Sea.

Lorvão. Small but interesting museum off the chancel of the monastery church.

Mangualde. Palácio do Conde de Anadia, 18th-century palace with fine azulejos.

Monsanto. Castle, ruins of a medieval fortress on rocky hill. Fantastic views from top of keep over Serra da Estrela and Carmona Dam lake. Remains of **Romanesque church** (belfry), and tombs cut into the rock. Just east of Medelim on N239.

Sabugal. Castle, 13th-century and everyone's idea of how a castle should be, with a formidable five-sided keep. Ask at the town hall for admission.

Viseu. Almeida Moreira Museum, private house filled with pretty things.

Cathedral, various periods, with fine 17th-century facade. In the upper choir the Treasury exhibits medieval pieces of sacred art.

Grão Vasco Museum. A large and interesting collection, with excellent painting and sculpture, including primitives of the Viseu school (16th-century).

Old Town, Lovely old paved lanes, with Renaissance houses and Baroque churches. Worth exploring.

Vista Alegre. Porcelain museum. Open P.M. only.

SPECIAL EVENTS. For further details and exact dates, consult local tourist offices. **January.** *Fair of St. Sebastian,* with processions, Vila da Feira, mid-month. **March–April.** *Annual Fair* at Aveiro. Procession of boats at night on the lagoons at Ovar, Thursday in Holy Week. **April.** Folk pilgrimage to *Nossa Senhora do Almurtão* at Idanha-a-Nova, late April. **May.** Historic procession of the *Marafonas* at Monsanto, 3. *Queima das Fitas,* the famous burning of the ribbons at Coimbra, end of May.

June. Annual festival and *Fair of St. James,* with popular celebrations, at Covilhã, 22. *Eve of St. John* celebrations at Figueira da Foz, with athletics, folk dances, processions, high jinx of all sorts, 23–24. **July.** *Festival of the Holy Queen* at Coimbra, a nocturnal procession from Santa Clara convent, folk dances, first two weeks in July in even-numbered years. **September.** Grape harvest festivals, athletic events, other entertainment, at Curia, mid-month.

USEFUL ADDRESSES. Travel Agent. *Wagons-lits/Thomas Cook,* 89 Ave. Navarro, 3000 Coimbra (tel. 039 25333/20222). Closed Sat. **Car Hire.** *Avis,* Rail Station, Coimbra (tel. 039 34786).

OPORTO

Owing to its situation at the mouth of a great river, the pre-Roman settlement of Cale, on the left bank of the Douro, became a Roman stronghold and a thriving commercial center, with a hard-working and enterprising citizenry. Later, its standing was further strengthened by a ruling priesthood, who maintained the Christian faith throughout the barbarian and Moorish invasions, and the upheavals of the wars of liberation.

Laid open to the plundering raids of the Moors, the Normans, and the Asturian kings, the township, fastened into the steep rock overlooking the port, or Porto, as the city is called in Portuguese, learned to be self-sufficient the hard way. It closed in upon itself on the windswept height above the river, dominated by its first cathedral.

When, in the 11th century, the Princess Teresa was given in marriage to the Burgundian Count Henry, she brought in her dowry the lands between the rivers Minho and Douro, a domain to be known henceforth as the County of Porto and Cale, or Portucale. Their son, Afonso Henriques, was the first king of Portugal. The capital was Braga, where the count lies buried. His widow offered the old city to a French bishop, Hugues, who misused his churchman's authority to gain political power. Once assumed, that power was firmly held by Braga's bishops, who long played a leading part in the history of the country and, indeed, are still called Primates of Portugal.

On the vast terrace in front of Oporto cathedral, an inscription in stone recalls that on this site, in 1147, Pedro Pitões, Bishop of Braga, summoned together the French, English, and German crusaders, whose storm-driven ships had been thrown back on the coast. He made a rousing speech, urging the men-at-arms to sail southward, and help the young King Afonso Henriques to take Lisbon from the Moors.

At a time when the future capital of Lisbon was merely a Moorish fortress, Oporto was already a flourishing commercial town, trading by sea in fish and salt and wine, a model of simple living and hard work. Devout but sharply rejecting all priestly intereference; having a due regard for success, money, and social standing, but refusing to bow to empty rank; for 800 years, Oporto fought against the power of bishops and landlords, but freely undertook, in the name of God and country, the most thankless tasks and the hardest ordeals.

One of the most tireless and enterprising of all Portuguese, Henry the Navigator, was born in Oporto. Here, he planned and carried out his first undertaking, the manning and arming of the ships that were to conquer Ceuta, the foremost Christian stronghold in Africa. Of the great adventure of discovery that followed, it was Lisbon that took the greater share of the spoils, spending her booty on the building of Jerónimos and Madre de Deus, both churches of outstanding beauty. More self-effacing, it was enough for Oporto to know that hers was the honor. There is an old saying that "Coimbra sings, Braga prays, Lisbon shows off, and Oporto works." It is true to this day, and it is in this light that Oporto is to be seen and respected, though better by daylight.

Oporto, with some half million inhabitants, is the country's second city but its economic center. It likes to call itself the capital of the north. It is a debatable word, for the feeling of the town is deeply, nobly provincial, in the best sense of strong and lasting tradition. It is indeed a northern town, a watercolor in gray, with fogs, soft drizzling rains, cloud-filtered sunshine, a climate for fine gardens, renowned for camellias and roses, for family life in well-ordered homes. But it is also a sprawling, modern, wealthy city, with massive new developments on the outskirts, a bustling and fashionable commercial area in the heart of town, recently converted into a pedestrian precinct, and there are now numerous shopping centers.

Discovering Oporto

After you have negotiated the great spaghetti tangle of routes into the city, you may very well be taken aback with what greets you. The center of town, around the railway station and at the crossroads of the main streets, is depressingly undistinguished. It is best to turn away from the drab main avenue, crowded with buses, clanging with trams.

Better start exploring at the old Morro da Sé, that headland of barren rock on which Lisbon's liberation was decided. Slum-clearance seems to have been overdone, as perfectly respectable granite buildings were blown up and streets traced straight through the wreckage, but the great drafts of air, sucked in from the sea through the narrow, sand-banked mouth of the Douro, now freshen the wide open space in front of the cathedral. A Baroque stone pillory stands on the cathedral square.

Dark and brooding, fortified with battlements, the 12th-century Sé is entered through a Baroque door, while the 14th-century Gothic cloister is brightened by azulejos portraying the Song of Songs. The 17th-century altar, with retable and tabernacle, is in silver, so finely worked that it was 100 years in the making. During the invasion of Napoleon's armies, this

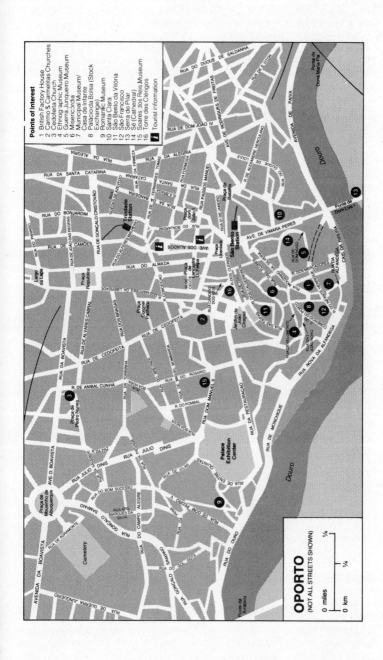

Points of Interest
1 British Factory House
2 Carmo & Carmelitas Churches
3 Cedofeita Church
4 Ethnographic Museum
5 Guerra Junqueiro Museum
6 Misericórdia
7 Municipal Museum/
  Casa do Infante
8 Palácio da Bolsa (Stock
  Exchange)
9 Romanic Museum
10 Santa Clara
11 São Bento da Vitória
12 São Francisco
13 Serra do Pilar
14 Sé (Cathedral)
15 Soares dos Reis Museum
16 Torre dos Clérigos
i Tourist information

OPORTO
(NOT ALL STREETS SHOWN)

0 miles ¼
0 km ¼

treasure escaped pillage through the foresight of the sacristan, who covered it with a thick layer of whitewash.

In a transept stands a statue of Notre Dame de Vendôme, which has spent 700 years within the church, since her arrival with a French crusader from Touraine. As in so many Portuguese churches, the sacristy is lovely, with 18th-century pictures of the life of Christ in Rococo gold frames.

The Old Quarters

Leaning over the long stone balcony that fronts the Sé, the traveler has a bird's eye view of the river and the town, with its countless church towers. Below him, at the foot of the cathedral, lies the old quarter, where he can still see long broken stretches of old walls and narrow cobbled streets, winding steeply up to the safe haven of the church, both dating from a time when the town lived in fear of attack by both land and water.

These noisy alleys swarm with shrill-voiced and good-natured working people. This area is still a hideout of small handcrafts of all kinds, of junk shops amidst the street sale of fish and vegetables.

"Local color is the poverty of other people." Barredo is dying, soon to be reborn in order and cleanliness. It may well become, mirrored in the bronze waters of the river, the most beautiful place in town. For the city planners are growing careful. In the past 40 years, the fashion for skyscrapers in steel and glass, so alien to the landscape, had replaced or overshadowed the fine old buildings in granite. Fortunately, in the space between the docks of the Ribeira and the Sé, Oporto has retained the dignity of an old-fashioned etching.

To be within safe reach of God and money, houses were built around the churches and warehouses. As more people thronged to town, the narrow houses grew upwards, piling story upon story in a crazy scaffolding of garrets, and backward in depth; the old tile roofs are studded with skylights over the dark back rooms. The houses have a plaster wash of earthy colors, dull green, yellow ocher, rust red. But the palaces and churches are in granite, with a glaze of earthenware tiles, bright blue and white patterns form a strange but attractive picture within the stern framework of gray stone.

If you look up above street level, you will see the long rows of balconies and the flowers that grow in the shadow cast by wrought iron or wooden fretwork, among the hanging laundry. You will see the sheer drop of houses falling downward to the river, and what may have seemed a commonplace town will be seen all at once in its true light, a network of perspectives, of lines linking past to present, like the new bridge that swoops upwards to support the old battlements.

When the morning mists at last drift away from the sun, the graphite sparkles, the glazed tiles shine, the window panes glitter and Oporto takes on a different aspect.

The Treasures of Oporto

Since Oporto is a merchant city, with no use for noble aristocratic layabouts, she has few of the fine patrician houses that help make the charm of Lisbon. In the 18th century, a bishop with a fondness for pomp and a weakness for show built the Baroque episcopal palace, now municipal offices, which offsets the Romanesque simplicity of the cathedral.

An Italian, Nicolas Nasoni, built in 1755 the famous Torre dos Clérigos at the expense of the Oporto clergy. The most outstanding landmark in the city, its finely chiseled height rises above the oval Baroque church and provides a superb view; he also remodeled the 17th-century Carmelitas church and built a few handsome private houses.

The Palácio das Carrancas, now the Soares dos Reis Museum, holds a collection of paintings, among which are two fine Clouets; sculptures, of which the best is by Soares dos Reis, gold and silver work, some splendid 16th-century Limoges enamels, and furniture, much of it English.

The Ethnographic Museum, in a fine mansion designed by Nasoni, records the folklore of the province, its costumes and handicrafts, its way of life, its songs and dances. The Guerra Junqueiro Museum, near the cathedral, was given to the city by the poet's wife and daughter, with the contents which had been collected by the owner over the years. There is lovely furniture, sculpture, silver, pewter, European and Oriental ceramics as well as a number of Nottingham alabasters. The Romantic Museum in the Quinta da Macieirinha, where Charles Albert of Sardinia lived after his exile in 1849, is a perfect example of the period. Lace-edged net curtains drape the windows, papier-mâché tables decorate the long drawing room, and there are charming watercolors on the walls. The shaded garden is noted for its rare camelias.

Nor has Oporto more regard for her fine old streets, Rua das Flores or Rua de Belmonte, with stone coats-of-arms over the house doors. The Rua das Flores holds all the flavor of old-time Oporto, grocers still sell beans or rice from burlap sacks, and drapers pile bolts of cloth behind huge oak counters: nothing has changed, neither the brass scales nor the dark back shop with its odor of calico and brown sugar. In the same street, you will find the best silversmiths and jewelers of a province renowned for its fine handicrafts. But between midday and two everything closes in Portugal's strictest lunch break.

In a room by the white-painted granite Baroque church of the Misericórdia is one of the mysteries of the history of art. Who painted the *Fons Vitae,* presented by King Manuel? Some say Holbein, others Jean de la Pasture, Van der Weyden, Metsys or Van Orley. It is perhaps an unknown Portuguese primitive. Whoever the artist it is a strange and disquieting work of art, showing Christ on the cross, His blood flowing down on the kneeling D. Manuel I, his queen and his two children, all clad in brilliant colors.

Among the many churches, the oldest is the 12th-century Romanesque Cedofeita, founded, according to legend, by the Suevian king, Theodomir. The finest, and by far the richest, is one dedicated to the little brother of the poor, São Francisco, in spite of the fact that his order had met with a frosty welcome in Oporto, where begging was not held in high esteem. However, the friars were upheld by the king, and it became the fashion for noblemen to be buried, at a price, within the church walls. Little by little, the bare Gothic nave and side chapels disappeared under the gilt wood carving that crept like ivy up the pillars, overrunning the vaulted arches, and strangling the altars. This frenzy of garlands and cherubs, of flying birds, was overlaid with five hundred pounds' weight of gold leaf. Other fine Baroque churches are the Carmo, Grilo, São Bento da Vitória and, above all, see the golden cave of Santa Clara which is not far from the cathedral. Romanesque outside, the interior is one of the richest in the country. The ceiling over the chancel is covered with cherubs and flying angels, and the pair of tiny organs are fascinating. Ask the sacristan to take you into the upper and lower choirs behind the grilles at the end of the church. They, too, have painted ceilings and amusing old canvases.

In the lower part of the city, near São Francisco, already mentioned, the British Factory House in the Rua do Infante Henrique, is the only one remaining in Europe of the many commercial centers which English merchants set up abroad over the centuries. It is a fine old building, still owned and run by the English Port wine firms.

Next door to São Francisco is another must—the 19th-century Palácio da Bolsa (the Stock Exchange), with a glistening, ornate Moorish Hall, based on the Alhambra.

Two other major sights are the central railroad station of São Bento, whose waiting room is lined with remarkable 1930s azulejos; and the Municipal Museum, with much material on the age of Prince Henry the Navigator.

Oporto Bridges

History has shown that a thrifty middle class will back the most costly undertakings, when it has reason to believe that it will get its money's worth. A hundred years ago, the need for a bridge began to be felt. The dense river traffic was a livelihood to over half the town. The width of the Douro and its unforeseeable changes of current, kept the city of Oporto at a difficult distance from the huddle of Port wine lodges and warehouses on the southern bank, on the former site of the old Roman port of Cale (today the new town, or Vila Nova de Gaia). The growing exchange between the two harbors demanded a safer passage than that afforded by barges.

In 1809, during the Peninsular War, a bridge of boats had given way under the crowds in flight from Soult's advancing troops, and hundreds of people had been drowned. In 1876, the French engineer Eiffel built the Ponte de D. Maria Pia, a railway bridge of some elegance, a single arch of ironwork "all in Brussels lace," one of the most outstanding engineering feats of the times. Three years later, an Eiffel-trained engineer started to build the bridge of Dom Luis, with upper and lower roads, which took six years to finish.

As Oporto spread out, becoming the greatest industrial center of the country, there was a growing need for yet another outlet for cross-river traffic. In 1953, a third bridge, the Ponte da Arrábida, was built, a far-flung span of soaring concrete almost three hundred yards in length, like the others a masterpiece of its time, and with them forming a fitting framework for the great river. And now a new railway bridge is under construction next to the Ponte de D. Maria Pia.

The Environs of Oporto

Oporto was born of the Douro, and owes her thriving commerce to the river. But this fine watercourse which derives its name, Rio do Ouro (River of Gold), to the nuggets once found on its bed, is unsafe, given to sudden risings of the waters and to dangerous storms. Twice within 50 years, the level rose to the lower platform of the bridge of Dom Luis, and the dwellers in the flooded riverside houses got out by way of the 14th-century battlements above. The levels the water reached can be seen outside the Sandeman Port wine lodge in Vila Nova da Gaia.

The Douro washes down from Spain vast amounts of silt which, flowing out to sea, are checked by the sand bar, thus choking the mouth of the river with ever-growing dunes that cut off navigation, and have resulted in many spectacular shipwrecks. After several vain attempts to clear a passage for ships, an artificial harbor was built on the coastline. It is the port of Leixões, which serves as a dock for the few passenger ships, cargo boats, fishing fleets, and sailing craft of all kinds. During the year, some five million hampers of sardines are discharged at the wharves, to be sent to the nearby canning factories in Matosinhos.

Not far from Leixões is the airport of Pedras Rubras, under an hour by plane to Lisbon, two hours from London, and now with direct flights to many European and American cities.

The British Connection

Oporto, whose name means both a port and a wine, is now but a link with either. It has become a hub for the coasting trade. The grapes are grown in vineyards 160 km. (100 miles) away, in the upper reaches of the Douro, and are carried by tanker-lorries down river to Vila Nova de Gaia, there to be made into the world-famous wine.

In 1703, a trading agreement was made between England and Portugal, by the terms of which the Portuguese market was to give priority to English wool, in exchange for a first choice of Portuguese wines. The Methuen Treaty gave rise to heated opposition, except in Oporto, which owes to it both her riches and her renown.

Following the treaty, the town welcomed the arrival of British merchants, who would oversee the blending of the wine and, often many years later, the shipping of the casks. These men, coming with wives and families, settled in the country for good, while keeping to the British way of life. Marrying among themselves, they sent their children back home to school, and founded one of those extraordinary commercial aristocracies, expatriate and bilingual, which was to become a feature of 18th- and 19th-century Britain, thereby firmly establishing her trade throughout the world.

These 18th-century settlers gave Oporto a taste for plain rosewood, mahogany and simple polished silver, replacing the heavily carved furniture and the chased silver with a dull finish then in use. To this day, Valongo makes Sheraton-style furniture, and Beiriz the thick pile carpets, which had brought into formal Portuguese houses the look of quiet English comfort. And, of course, the wine merchants had given Oporto her mellow dessert wine, matured, blended and reinforced over the years, to ship home to Britain, although France is now the main consumer.

The Aristocrat of Wines

The story of Port wine is absorbing and eventful. In the late 18th century, Pombal's attempt to control both its output and its price gave rise to bloody riots. In the 19th century, the vines were attacked by a blight that cost a year's livelihood to the whole countryside. For 200 years, a fruitful rivalry existed between the great companies, many of which bear English names: Sandeman, Cockburn, Croft, Dow, Warre, Graham, Taylor, alongside the Portuguese firms of Borges, Barros, Fonseca, Gonzalez Byass, Ferreira, and Ramos Pinto.

These names are written large on the tiled roofs of the huge Port lodges in Vila Nova de Gaia, where visitors are given a friendly welcome. Some firms have on show on the river an old *rabelo,* a highprowed sailing boat which used to be steered with poles and an outsize rudder down the eddying water of the Douro. In the half light of the old lodges, Port wine slowly ages in the oak barrels, to a fullness of body ranging from sweet to semidry, in every shade of color from amber yellow to ruby red.

We discuss the production of Port a little in our earlier chapter on wine, and will not repeat ourselves here, but any visitor interested in wine and its subtleties would do well to take advantage of being in Oporto to visit one of the lodges. There you can buy a bottle of your favorite Port, or, if you want to find out about the wine the firm will be glad to sell you a selection of bottles to cover a wide range of tastes. As in all countries with a tradition of good wine, the merchants of Oporto, however busy, are open-hearted and open-handed, always ready to welcome a stranger. Almost all the Port-wine companies show visitors the immense casks standing in rows in the airy, light cellars—which are not cellars, but great warehouses—and explain some of the mysteries of making Port.

Above the lodges by the upper level of the D. Luis Bridge, the elegant, circular church of Nossa Senhora da Serra do Pilar has a rare 17th-century circular cloister, and a superb view of Oporto from the terrace in front.

The Coast Road

Southward a string of quiet family beaches studs the coastline to Espinho, an increasingly fashionable resort with a casino, which has now become the center of a highly sophisticated complex of luxury amusements, an excellent swimming pool, and two championship golf courses of international standard plus a 9-hole course right by the sea. The long sandy beaches south of Oporto are very popular with the locals, but it is wise to remember that the Atlantic can be dangerous for bathers in rough weather, when red flags are hung out in warning. The result of this is that most hotels, and every resort of any size, have pools.

Oporto families relax at the mouth of the river, at Foz do Douro, along the flowery promenades that border the river bank from Oporto to Matosinhos. There the vacationer will find small beaches, restaurants and snack bars, and in Leça, a salt-water swimming pool built into the rocks. Also, in a pinewood near the sea at Anjeiras, an excellent campsite.

On the coast road north from Oporto, anyone with taste for architectural melodrama will enjoy the stern stateliness of Leça do Balio, a Gothic church crowned with battlements, as much a prison as a church, by the old monastery of the Order of Hospitalers. In it took place, in the 14th century, the wedding of King Fernando and the faithless Leonor Teles, a match that was to end the first Royal dynasty. Oddly enough, because of the beauty of its setting, Leça do Balio, its harshness softened with flowers, is often chosen for the big weddings of Oporto. Outside the church is a Manueline cross.

The wide granite highway that leads to Vila do Conde is shaded with trees and bright with roses. The huge convent of Santa Clara, founded in 1318, and its beautiful tombs, the aqueduct with its 999 arches, the wharves of the Ave river, all give the town a distinguished look. It is a center for lace-making and visitors are welcomed to the school for this craft at Rua Joãquim Maria de Melo, 70. Nearby, the beach offers a long sweep of fine sand and fresh sea air.

Póvoa de Varzim owes its beauty to the sea. Formerly a fishing village, it now boasts a casino, a luxury hotel, two heated swimming pools, and other amenities similar to Espinho, with speed boats for hire. But only in summer—the rest of the year it is left to the fishermen who, wearing rough sweaters of raw wool embroidered in red with Solomon's seal, crosses, anchors, and lobsters, continue in all weathers their age-old life of work and danger. Birthplace of the great Portuguese novelist Eça de Queirós (1845–1900), Póvoa de Varzim also has an excellent Museum of Ethnography and History.

Two Romanesque churches in the nearby countryside are worth a visit: São Pedro de Rates and Rio Mau, especially the former, which has a remarkable 12th-century facade and a fine interior.

The coastal route north of Póvoa de Varzim is described in our chapter on Minho.

Inland from Oporto

The Douro and its contributaries water a pleasing variety of landscapes, picturesque settings for country fairs; vine growing dominates along the upper Douro, while the green valleys of the Sousa and the Tamega are distinguished by meadows and woods.

Between the rivers lies the old town of Penafiel, with its gargoyles and coats-of-arms. The Quinta da Aveleda, a fine old country house set in a beautiful park, makes a light and pleasant table wine. Penafiel, a point of departure for several rewarding side trips, is interesting in itself for the Renaissance parish church, the Baroque Misericórdia and typical granite houses.

Amarante, a town on the River Tamega, flowing between tree-shaded banks and spanned by a Regency bridge, deserves to be better known. It has a fine church, São Gonçalo, renowned for its columns painted with gold and flowered garlands winding up them, and an extravagant organ supported on a merman with two black tails. In the town, the painted wooden balconies and wrought-iron gates and window bars give the town a stately and outlandish charm.

Amarante is a thriving agricultural center, and the fair of São Gonçalo is among the most colorful in Portugal. Every year, on the first Saturday and Sunday in June, spinsters and unmarried men get together, to offer each other the phallic-shaped cakes sold on that day; this half-joking meeting is sometimes rewarded by a tardy courtship. The town is, in fact, renowned for its cakes and sweets; its specialty, the *doçe de São Gonçalo,* is a small round jelly made with eggs and sugar.

For the lovers of art, the Convent of São Gonçalo houses a museum which prides itself on its fine paintings by Amadeu de Sousa Cardoso. Born in the nearby countryside, this painter, who shared a studio with Modigliani and sat for *The Portuguese* by Braque, belonged to the movement known

as the Paris School. He died in 1918, leaving behind him a body of work
that helped show the way to postwar art.

Amarante is a good center from which to visit Travanca, which lies in
a hollow and has an interesting 12th-century church, once part of a Benedictine monastery. It is also a jumping-off point for Freixo de Baixo, with
a Romanesque church, and the Serra do Marão which reaches 1,019 meters (3,343 feet) at the Alto de Espinho.

Castelo de Paiva, also known as Sobrado de Paiva, is a center for trips
to the Paiva and Cinfães valleys, and to the Serra de Montemuro. An impoverished Marquess of Paiva became the husband of a mistress of Napoleon III, for whom the Emperor constructed the palais on the Champs-
Elysées which accommodated the Travelers Club for many years. The only
great courtesan of the 19th century to acquire a genuine title of nobility,
she bettered her performance by later marrying the Prince of Henckel-
Donnersmarck, first ambassador of the German Reich to the French Republic.

South of Sobrado de Paiva lies Arouca, with a wonderful Cistercian convent, now a school. In the church is a series of great 18th-century statues
of the nuns, unforgettable in their stylized dignity. The museum includes
some delightful pictures.

Before leaving the region we should mention the great River Douro
again, this time for itself alone, for it is the central fact of life here. Not
only a source of the fertility of the region, it's also increasingly a source
of power as the eight dams up to the frontier are completed. One of the
most striking sights of the whole valley is the point at which the Tamega
joins the Douro at Entre-os-Rios.

PRACTICAL INFORMATION FOR OPORTO

TOURIST OFFICE. There is a National Tourist Office in Oporto, 43
Praça D. João 1 (tel. 02 25805/28433/319281). Among its other activities
it organizes guided visits, excursions into the Minho region, and has information about boat trips on the Douro.

HOTELS. In addition to those listed below, Oporto has numerous other
hotels, residências, albergarias, pensions and a youth hostel which fall into
the Inexpensive category. One of the major problems for car-borne visitors
to Oporto is that of parking. It is extremely difficult to find parking space
near hotels, and you should check with the hotel before arriving, if possible, as to where you can find space.

Infante de Sagres (L), Praça D. Filipa de Lencastre 62 (tel. 02 28101/8).
83 rooms with bath. Solid comfort, central. Good restaurant. AE, DC, MC,
V.

Meridien (L), Ave. da Boavista 1466 (tel. 02 668963). 227 rooms with
bath. Disco, sauna, shops. Parking. In newly developed area with good
shopping centers nearby. AE, DC, MC, V.

Porto Atlantico (L), Rua Afonso Lopes Vieira 66 (tel. 02 694941/9).
58 rooms with bath. Pool. AE, DC, MC, V.

Porto Boega (L), Rua do Amial 607 (tel. 02 400148). 116 rooms with bath. Pool, tennis. A little out of town. Parking available. AE, DC, MC, V.

Porto Sheraton (L), Ave. da Boavista 1269 (tel. 02 668822). 253 rooms with bath. Shops, sauna. Oporto's newest hotel, in same area as Meridien and Porto Atlantico. Pool. Parking. AE.

Batalha (E), Praça da Batalha 116 (tel. 02 20571/4). 142 rooms with bath. Parking available. AE, DC, MC, V.

Castor (E), Rua dos Doze Casas 17 (tel. 02 570014). 58 rooms with bath. Disco. In quiet residential area some distance from the center. AE, DC, MC, V.

Corcel (E), Rua de Camões 135–7 (tel. 02 380268). 62 rooms with bath. AE, DC, MC, V.

Dom Henrique (E), Rua Guédes de Azevedo 179 (tel. 02 25755/8). 111 rooms with bath. Disco, shops. In 18-story octagonal tower; spectacular views from 16th-floor lounge and 15th-floor restaurant, but somewhat lacking in atmosphere. AE, DC, MC, V.

Inca (E), Praça Coronel Pacheco 52 (tel. 02 384151). 62 rooms with bath. Very central, excellent restaurant. AE, DC, MC, V.

Ipanema (E), Rua do Campo Alegre 156–174 (tel. 02 668061). 150 rooms with bath. Central. AE, DC, MC, V.

Miradouro (E), Rua da Alegria 598 (tel. 02 570717). 30 rooms with bath. Parking available. AE, DC, MC, V.

São Gabriel (E), Rua da Alegria 98 (tel. 02 323982). 29 rooms with bath. DC, MC.

Vice-Rei (E), Rua Julio Dinis 779 (tel. 02 60124/6). 27 rooms with bath. DC, MC.

Grande Hotel do Porto (M), Rua da Santa Catarina 197 (tel. 02 28176/8). 100 rooms with bath. For those who like the old style. AE, DC, MC, V.

Império (M), Praça da Batalha 127 (tel. 02 26861/6). 95 rooms with bath. DC.

São João (M), Rua do Bonjardim 120 (tel. 02 21662). 14 rooms with bath. Central AE, DC, MC, V.

Tuela (M), Rua Arquitécto Marquês da Silva 180 (tel. 02 667161/4). 197 rooms, many with bath. Parking available.

YOUTH HOSTEL. *Pousada de Juventude do Porto,* Rua Rodrigues Lobo 98 (tel. 02 65535).

CAMPING. *Parque de Campismo de Prelada,* Santa Casa da Misericórdia, Rua Monte dos Burgos, Prelada, (tel. 02 812616).

RESTAURANTS. Oporto's cooking is rich and heavy. The traditional dish is tripe, cooked with beans, chicken and sausage. It is a dish which has earned the people of Oporto the nickname of "tripeiros" (tripe-eaters) and dates from the time the city was under siege during the Napoleonic Wars. There are some good-value small restaurants on the riverside, or Ribeira. In fact the town has a huge number of restaurants and snack bars. Note that most of the expensive restaurants in the center are closed on Sundays.

Churrascão Gaúcho (E), Ave. Boavista 313 (tel. 02 698206). Good grill. Closed Sun. AE, DC, MC.

Cozinha Real do Fado (E), Rua Arménia 72 (tel. 02 382666). Fados every night. AE, DC, MC.

Dona Filipa (E), Hotel Infante Sagres, Praça D. Filipa de Lencastre 62 (tel. 02 28101). Old style hotel restaurant with Portuguese cuisine. AE, DC, MC.

Escondidinho (E), Rua Passos Manuel 144 (tel. 02 21079). For a perfect meal of regional specialties and French dishes. Closed Sun. AE, DC, MC, V.

Foco (E), Rua Afonso Lopes Vieira 86 (tel. 02 667248). Varied cooking, modern setting. AE, DC, MC.

Lagosteiro (E), Rua Conde Burnay 140 (tel. 02 566678). Good fish and shellfish. Closed Sun. AE, DC, MC.

Linos (E), Ave. Dr. Antunes Guimarães 265. At the very top of the price category. AE, DC, MC.

Portucale (E), Rua da Alegria 598 (tel. 02 570717). Top of apartment block with superb view. AE, DC, MC, V.

Regaleira (E), Rua de Bonjardim 87 (tel. 02 26465). Near the Infante Sagres hotel. Closed Wed. AE, DC, MC.

Abadia (M), Rua do Ateneu Comércio do Porto 22 (tel. 02 28757). Good fish. Closed Sun.

Chines (M), Ave. Vimara Peres 38 (tel. 02 28915). Chinese food. AE.

Mal Cozinhado (M), Rua Onteirinho 11 (tel. 02 381319). Typical setting with good regional cooking; dinner only, sometimes with fado. Closed Sun. MC.

Palmeira (M), Rua do Ateneu Comércio do Porto 36 (tel. 02 315601). Good value, for Portuguese cuisine. Closed Sun.

Taverna do Bebodos (M), Cais da Ribeira (tel. 313565). Local setting, excellent value. Closed Sun., public holidays. Amusing street market on river bank outside.

Tripeiro (M), Rua de Passos Manuel 195 (tel. 02 25886). Just the place to try tripe, but check which days it's on the menu. Closed Sun.

Alzira (I), Viela do Buraco 3 (tel. 02 25004). Good cooking, large portions.

Neptuno (I), Rua Rodrigues Sampaio 133 (tel. 02 27937). Simple, good seafood. AE.

CAFÉS AND WINE BARS. Among cafés the *Imperial, Majestic* and *Brasileira* are the best known. For a restful glass of Port try the *Solar do Vinho do Porto* near the Palácio dos Desportos.

PLACES OF INTEREST. Hours are normally from 10 A.M. to 5 P.M. but with a longish closure over lunch, sometimes as much as 2 hours. Most are closed Mon. and public holidays. Entrance fees vary—mostly between 150$00 and 300$00.

Botanical Gardens, Rua do Campo Alegre 1191.

Casa do Infante, Rua da Alfandega. Open Mon. to Sat. 2–7.

Ethnographic Museum, Largo São João Novo. Local arts and handicrafts; archeological remains. Open Mon. to Sat. 10–5.

Guerra Junqueiro, Rua de Dom Hugo 32. Well-known Portuguese poet's house, with his furniture and ornaments. Open Mon. to Sat., 11–5.

Municipal Museum, Rua da Alfandega. Open Mon. to Fri. 9–12, 2–5:30.

Romantic Museum, Rua de Entre Quintas 220. Charming house filled with Regency and early Victorian pieces; lovely gardens. Closed 12:30–2.

Soares dos Reis Museum, Carrancas Palace, Rua D. Manuel 11. Large collection of paintings, sculpture, ceramics, furniture and jewelry. Open Mon. to Sat. 10–5, but some galleries are often closed.

Torre dos Clérigos, Rua dos Clérigos. A marvelous view from the top of this 18th-century tower which dominates the city.

SPECIAL EVENTS. During **June**—20–30—*Festivals of the Popular Saints,* particularly on the eve of the feast of São João (St. John) on 24, when the whole city takes part and walks the streets all night holding flowers of garlic, and hitting passers-by on the head with plastic hammers—an evening not to be missed! There are bonfires, and roast kid washed down with vinho verde.

August 25 sees the *Festa de São Bartolomeu* and the Procession in Paper Costume, which takes place in the suburb of Foz do Douro. The remains of a once-famous pilgrimage, these are very colorful, ending in a "colossal, collective bathe" when Neptune and everyone else washes away the Devil.

SHOPPING. Good new shopping centers (*centro comércial*) are appearing in Oporto, with lots of shops on several floors. For the widest range of good buys try the *Brasilia* or the *Dallas.* **Crafts.** Silversmiths abound in modern Oporto. *Reis Filhos,* Rua 31 de Janeiro 239, can show you heavy, elaborately decorated table services based on indigenous motifs and executed in their own workshops. Lalique crystal can be purchased here, too. The shop also handles gold items, various types of jewelry, and a collection of antiques. *Pedro A. Baptista,* Rua das Flores 235, deals in antique silver as well as the modern variety, and has a fine selection of antique furniture as well. Gold-plated filigree work is a regional specialty that is modest in cost yet ideally suited for memorable gifts.

Perfecta, Rua Santa Catarina 93, shows gold-filigree ships in its windows together with intricate bracelets and powder boxes.

For decorative knick-knacks you might try *Moveis, Estofos, Decorações* on the Rua 31 de Janeiro. For colorful pottery, there's *Mosaicos Cerâmicas* on the Rua dos Clérigos, opposite the Torre dos Clérigos. Next door there's a fascinating shop stacked with coarse cottons, brightly designed for interior decoration. Lacy napkins and embroideries are on display at *Candida Celeste Nogueira Alves,* Rua Boa Hora 15. *Vista Alegre* porcelain is displayed in their showroom at Rua Càndido dos Reis 18.

For sturdy leather bags, bright feminine gadgets, and trinkets of straw filled with flowers or covered with fruit, wander into *Ribeiro,* Rua 31 de Janeiro 185.

Birdcages hang from the ceiling, brushes stand against the door, guns and shells and hardware are strewn everywhere at *Casa Pereira* on Rua Sá da Bandeira 96. Baskets for all purposes and attractive espadrilles in any size can be found by browsing through at least a dozen shops along the upper half of Rua Alexandre Braga. Stop and treasure hunt for amusing gifts at *Casa Fernandes Tinoco,* Rua Santa Catarina 24–30. A modern, attractive store, it shows massive jewelry, copper plates, woodcarving, and leather cases with files and needles.

Clothes. Also on Rua Santa Catarina, near the Grande Hotel, is *Confiança*, with a wide selection of readymade blouses, men's shirts, scarves, bright trinkets, pocketbooks, and beachgear. Next door is *Beigel* which specializes in furs, though for the more modest shopper, it's a good choice for imaginative flowered jewelry and silk scarves.

For soft Shetland sweaters and sports wear in general, try *Vicente*, Rua 31 de Janeiro 174. *Corte Inglês* down the street at 140, carries woolens and conservative sports shirts for men. *Cotrim*, at 29, stocks more colorful sports articles, sweaters, socks, and bolts of finest poplin. You can have shirts made to order here in a week. Scattered up and down this thoroughfare are several women's shoe shops. Most popular is *Gonçalves* at 96 who make elegant shoes to measure.

Books. A favorite bookstore is the *Livraria Britanica*, Rua da Boa Hora 43, which stocks American and English bestsellers in hard and paperbacks. Others are the conveniently located *Livraria Figueirinhas* on the Praça Liberdade, and the *Livraria International* at Rua 31 de Janeiro 43.

Pharmacy. Across the street from the popular café *A Brasileira*, in Rua Sá da Bandeira, the *Castilho* pharmacy stands ready for every emergency whether it be dietetic or cosmetic. Their huge bath sponges are a practical buy.

USEFUL ADDRESSES IN OPORTO. Consulates. *American,* Rua Julio Dinis 826–3° (tel. 02 63094/690008); *British,* Ave. Boa Vista 3072 (tel. 02 684789).

Travel Agent. *American Express,* Star Travel Service, Ave. dos Aliados 202 (tel. 02 23637/311863).

Poste Restante (General Delivery), Praça 1 de Dezembro.

Car Hire. *Avis,* Rail Station (tel. 02 22373), will meet reservations. Five other outlets in town, including Grand Hotel, Hotel Inca, and Airport (tel. 02 223733—Avis general phone for Oporto). *Hertz,* Rua de Santa Catarina 899 (tel. 02 9481400).

PRACTICAL INFORMATION FOR
THE ENVIRONS OF OPORTO

TOURIST OFFICES. There are local tourist offices in the following towns: **Amarante,** Rua Candido dos Reis (tel. 055 422980); **Espinho,** Rua 6 (tel. 02 920911); **Matosinhos,** Rua França Junior 1 (tel. 02 934414); **Miramar,** Rua Alvares Cabral; **Penafiel,** Rua Álvares Cabral 222; **Póvoa de Varzim,** Ave. Mouzinho de Albuquerque 166 (tel. 052 624699); **Vila do Conde,** Rua 25 de Abril and Rua 5 de Outubro (tel. 052 631472); **Vila Nova de Gaia,** Jardim do Morro, Rua Rocha Leão (tel. 02 304524).

HOTELS AND RESTAURANTS. There are countless small beaches along the coast, each with several adequate hotels or pensions. Worth mentioning (in addition to those listed below) are Cortegaça, Furadouro and Granja.

Amarante (Oporto). *Navarras* (M), Rua António Carneiro (tel. 055 424036). 58 rooms with bath. Pool. Breakfast only. AE. *Amaranto* (I), Edificio Amaranto (tel. 055 422106). 35 rooms with bath. Breakfast only. *Caçador* (I), Rua 5 Outubro (tel. 055 423126). 11 rooms. Restaurant with excellent food. *Silva* (I), Rua Candido dos Reis 53 (tel. 055 423110). 22 rooms, some with bath. Breakfast only.

Restaurants. There are several café-restaurants. *Zé da Calçada* (E), Rua 31 de Janeiro (tel. 055 422023). Terrace. Also has 7 rooms.

In the **Serra do Marão**, 26 km. (16 km.) away at 1,400 meters (4,600 ft.), *Pousada de São Gonçalo* (E), tel. 055 461113/4. 18 rooms, 14 with bath. Charming, with spectacular view. AE, DC, MC, V.

A Ver-O-Mar (Oporto). 3 km. (2 miles) from Póvoa do Varzim. *Estalagem de Santo André* (M), tel. 052 681881. 50 rooms with bath. Pool, disco. Peaceful; recommended. AE, DC, MC, V.

Espinho (Aveiro). With beach and a casino. Accommodations include several pensions. *Praia Golfe* (E), Rua 6 (tel. 02 720630). 139 rooms with bath. 2 championship golf courses; excellent pool, also nearby Granja pool; monoplanes for hire. AE, DC, MC, V. *Apartamentos Solverde* (M), Rua 21, no 77 (tel. 02 722819). 83 service apartments for 4 persons. AE, DC, MC, V. *Mar Azul* (M), Ave. 8 (tel. 02 720824/5). 18 rooms with bath. Noisy.

Restaurants. There are plenty of reasonable restaurants, snack bars and cafés. *Casino* (E). Dinner only. AE, DC, MC. *America* (M). For shellfish. Dinner only. Closed Thurs. in winter. MC. *Cabana* (M). Excellent seafood. Closed Mon. in winter. AE, DC, MC. *Cartuxa* (M). DC, MC.

Foz do Douro (Oporto). Suburb of Oporto. *Boa Vista* (M), Esplanada do Castelo 58 (tel. 02 680083). 39 rooms with bath. Pool, disco, shops, sauna. AE. *Pensão Mary Castro* (M), Rua das Motas 48 (tel. 02 680141). 12 rooms with bath. Breakfast only.

Restaurants. There are many restaurants along the promenade. *Dom Manuel* (E), Ave. Montevideu 384 (tel. 02 672304). Overlooks the sea and promenade; recommended. AE, DC, MC. *Varanda do Sol* (E), Rua Coronel Peres 244 (tel. 02 686302). Pleasant view. AE.

Leça do Balio (Oporto). *Estalagem Via Norte* (E), Estrada Via Norte (tel. 02 9480294). 12 rooms with bath. Pool, disco. AE, DC, MC.

Le ça Da Palmeira (Oporto). **Restaurants.** *Chanquinhas* (E), Rua Santana 243 (tel. 02 9951884). Fish and shellfish; bar and fireplace. Closed Sun. AE, DC, MC. *Boa Nova* (M), tel. 02 9952182. Good shellfish and peaceful sea view. MC. *Garrafão* (M), Rua António Nobre 50 (tel. 02 9951660). Own shellfish; old-style and excellent. Closed Sun.

Matosinhos (Oporto). Mainly known for the many small restaurants specializing in seafood. *Porto Mar* (I), Rua Brito Capelo 167 (tel. 02 932104/6). 32 rooms with bath. Breakfast only. Pools, camping ground. AE, DC, MC.

Restaurants. *Majara* (M), Rua Tomás Ribeiro 264 (tel. 029 33732). Closed Tues. AE, DC, MC. *Proa* (I), Ave. Norton de Matos (tel. 02 930022). Closed Mon. Excellent shellfish. AE.

Miramar (Oporto). *Mirassol* (M), Ave. Vasco da Gama 3 (tel. 02 7622665). 25 rooms with bath. Disco. 18- and 9-hole golf courses. AE, DC, MC.

Póvoa de Varzim (Oporto). Casino, golf course. *Vermar Dom Pedro* (E), Ave. dos Banhos (tel. 052 61041/5). 208 rooms with 12 deluxe suites. 2 heated pools; grill room, restaurant, bar, nightclub, tennis. AE, DC, MC, v. *Costa Verde* (M), Ave. Vasco da Gama 56 (tel. 052 681531). 48 rooms with bath. Breakfast only. AE, DC, MC, v. *Grande* (M), Passeio Alegre (tel. 052 62061/3). 105 rooms with bath. On the sea. DC, MC.

Restaurants. There are several seafood restaurants, but best check price lists first. *A Casa dos Frangos* (M). Try for good-value meals, especially chicken. *O Marinheiro* (M), tel. 052 682151. On edge of town. Excellent, typical setting. AE, DC, MC. *Tourygalo* (M). Similarly good value. Closed Thurs.

Praia de Lavadores (Oporto). Small beach on the coast 7 km. (4 miles) west of Vila Nova de Gaia, just below Oporto. **Restaurant.** *Casa Branca* (M), tel. 02 7810269. Excellent food. AE, DC, MC, v.

Vila do Conde (Oporto). *Estalagem do Brasão* (E), Ave. Coronel Alberto Graça 144 (tel. 052 64016/7). 24 rooms with bath. Disco. AE, DC, MC, v. *Motel de Sant'Ana* (M), Azurare (tel. 052 61694). 34 units. Pool; restaurant. AE, DC, MC, V.

Restaurants. *O Pinhal* (M). Regional food. *São Pedro* (M). More regional dishes.

CAMPING. There are campsites at the following places: Amarante (Quinta dos Frades); Canidelo; Cortegaça; Esmoriz; Espinho (Solverde, Lugar dos Mophos); Gondomar; Madalena (2 sites); Matosinhos (Angeiras); Vila Nova de Gaia (Praia da Madelena. Lugar da Marimha); Vila do Conde (Avore).

PLACES OF INTEREST. Museums are usually open daily, except Mondays and public holidays, 10–5, but check times locally. Some close for an indeterminate lunch, anything up to two hours. Entrance fees are between 150$00 and 300$00. Apart from the items listed below, almost all places have interesting churches to visit as well.

Amarante. Church and Museum of São Gonçalo. The church, part of the former convent, dates from 1540, and is a fascinating blend of Renaissance and Baroque with older elements. The museum has the usual mixture of sacred paintings and sculpture, but with the special interest of modern works by Amadeu de Sousa Cardoso. The museum is in the buildings beside the church—once part of the convent, now the town hall.

Arouca. Convent of Santa Maria. Former Cistercian foundation. Full of fascinating details—remains of Queen Mafalda (1194–1252), early 1700s carved choir stalls and statues, Baroque architecture (rebuilt after 18th-century fire). Fine museum of religious paintings and sculpture in adjoining convent.

Leça Do Balio. Monastery Church, formerly Knights Templar stronghold. Romanesque, built 1336, with earlier sections (cloister). Interior rather bare, restored during brutal period of Portuguese restoration in the 1940s.

Póvoa De Varzim. Combination old fishing village and modern resort. **Municipal Museum of Ethnography and History,** Rua Visconde de Azevedo (tel. 052 310290). Small but interesting local collection.

Vila Do Conde. Convent of Santa Clara. 16th-century church with fine Renaissance tombs. Apply at convent for guided tours.
Lace Making Center and School, Rua Joãquim M. de Melo 70

SPECIAL EVENTS. There are countless festas, romarias, bullfights and other local diversions in the summer months in this area. For further details and exact dates consult local tourist offices. **March–April.** Processions at Póvoa de Varzim on Good Friday and Easter Sunday. **May.** Pilgrimage to *Nossa Senhora da Hora,* Matosinhos, Sunday after Ascension. Pilgrimage with celebrations to *Senhor da Matosinhos,* Matosinhos, Whitsun.

June. *Romaria of São Gonçalo,* a large annual fair and folk pilgrimage at Amarante, first weekend of June. *Feast of São João,* the patron saint, at Vila do Conde, 23–24, with costumed procession of the *rendilheiras* (lace-makers). *Festival of São Pedro* (St. Peter) at Póvoa de Varzim, 28–30. **August.** *Festival of the Assumption* at Póvoa de Varzim, with blessing of fishing boats, huge procession, fireworks, etc., 14–15. **September.** *Festival of Our Lady of Sorrows,* long Sunday procession, Póvoa de Varzim, midmonth.

MINHO

Minho, the sea on one side and Galicia on the other, is Portugal's liveliest and most colorful province. It takes its name from the river that forms its northern border with Spain. The countryside is green and smiling, the farmlands tended with loving care. No tiniest patch of land is wasted; vines twine round the poplar trees, and grape arbors high above your head form cool, shady tunnels along the road. You will also pass underneath other, equally fragile, arches of triumph, made of woven reeds and paper flower garlands, lighted at night by lamps strangely reminiscent of fireflies. These are the *arriais minhotos,* which herald coming events such as fairs, processions and dancing. There is not a summer Sunday in Minho that doesn't feature these three traditional festivities, generally organized somewhere in between a church and a flowing stream. They are, of course, preceded by the regular Sunday Mass held in all the countless churches. And even the most obscure hamlet usually has, in addition to its parish church, one or two shrines or sanctuaries somewhere out among the vineyards or in the hills.

Some of the Minho churches—notably at Fonte Arcada and Friestas—are exquisite Romanesque jewels, their imposing columns adorned with peacocks and griffins, with ox-heads chiseled in the stone. Granite abounds in Minho, and the tireless quarriers of the region—they are much in demand the world over—have been digging since time immemorial in the apparently inexhaustible Gerês quarries.

You will pass, set in carefully tended miniature fields, graystone houses whose only decoration is the vine branches that cast their shade over the entrance, with swarms of children playing in the yard. It frequently hap-

244

pens that the parcels of land are so divided up among the various heirs that each remaining section can no longer provide a sufficient living for the family. In such cases, it is not uncommon for the head of the family, or perhaps one of the sons, to emigrate temporarily to some other country. Early in this century, they usually went to Brazil. Then the trend shifted to Venezuela for a while. These days they have gone to France, Switzerland, or Germany. Some come back no better off than before; but most have managed to save enough to buy a bit of land or to build a house. In fact, the money sent back from abroad by these absent workers forms a very important part of the region's economy.

During the grape harvest the roads are vivid with black and golden fruit hanging high from the branches of the many trees—for in Minho the stakes on which the grapes grow are placed against the trees, so that oaks, poplars, and cypresses seem to have given themselves over to the bearing of grapes. The vine grows everywhere, crowning little white cottages, winding between small gardens and cornfields, and wreathing old tower walls. It engulfs all the lanes so that they become long green tunnels. Filtering through the leaves, the sun makes dancing shadows on the hot dust raised by passing carts, drawn by the amber-colored oxen. The potters of Barcelos like to model these oxen, with their lyre-shaped horns and lustrous coats, and in every shop you will find little models made of heavy, glazed pottery. More frivolous are the pink roosters and flower-dotted chickens of the local ceramists. The native art of Barcelos is an apt expression of this land, which is so like a box of toys upset on a grassy lawn.

Hearts of Gold and Filigree

Minho is the province where one finds the most colorful costumes still, the liveliest holiday celebrations, the most attractive countryside, and some of the most interesting architecture. It differs from the rest of the country in its vivacity and flair for living, which is all the more remarkable as it is also comparatively the poorest. Life would be grim in Minho if the people did not know how to enjoy themselves as well as how to work very hard.

The big holiday of the year, the *romaria* of Viana do Castelo, takes place in August and lasts for a solid week. It includes everything—bullfights, parades in which mythological characters mingle with Biblical figures, and fireworks sparkling out over the river. Like all people with frugal means, Minho folk delight in candles, carpets of live flowers underfoot, firecrackers whose sole purpose in life is to produce noise. Both in big towns and in tiny crossroads hamlets, you will discover exquisite churches along with cobble-stoned squares for holding the fairs, and performing the local dances, as well as large natural granite floors for threshing corn.

Along the streets and amid the squares, the regional costumes stand out by the very freshness and originality of their colors and design. Unfortunately its very distinctiveness has caused the Minho costume to be tastelessly imitated, and cheap, vulgar versions of it are on sale at market stalls, during festivals and such occasions. The authentic Minho dress deserves to be jealously guarded in all its beauty, including as it does hand-woven fabrics, pure flaxen linen touches, and solid gold jewelry. The art of filigree work is very ancient, and especially a craft of Minho. All kinds of devices are fashioned out of the twisted gold wire, but one of the most popular is the heart, which turns up in all sorts of guises, notably on earrings. In some ways the effect is Moorish, echoing the damascening that became one of the great industries in Toledo.

Here a bit of further advice is not amiss: if you are shopping for embroidery, ceramics, filigree jewelry, etc., pay particular attention to quality. In the market stalls as in the small shops, you will usually find the most mediocre wares displayed side by side with the finest.

Discovering Minho—The Coast

Most of the places you'll want to see here are all fairly close together—Minho is a compact province. There are, also, many interesting peripheral spots, such as the Baroque church at Santo Tirso; interesting old border citadels at Vila Nova da Cerveira, Valença do Minho—both with pousadas inside their fortifications—and at Melgaço; and the late 18th-century Brejoeira palace near Monção. As you near certain villages, you will be attracted by odd-looking rectangular granite boxes, in reality silos, perched up on four stilts to hinder rats from getting at the grain. These are called *espigueiros*. They cover an entire hill below the castle in the remote town of Lindoso, beyond Ponte da Barca.

But before venturing inland to explore the ancient cities of the Minho, it would be worth taking a look at the long coastal road that runs from Oporto to the Spanish frontier at the River Minho, route N13 all the way, via Vila do Conde and Póvoa de Varzim.

From the dunes of Ofir to the Spanish border, the Minho coast sparkles with beaches whose effect is a combination of clean winds, gentle mists, and a sun that is more bright than scorching, plus the sea-wrack borne in on the tides. The seaweed gatherers literally comb the surf looking for this iodine-rich fertilizer. The *sargaçeiros* at Fão and Apulia (south of Ofir) are a picturesque sight with their brief white tunics, plunging out into the waves to bring in the precious seaweed with their great rakes.

A great deal of this route runs not only beside the sea, but through spreading town and vacation developments. The first two on the trip are Ofir, on the south bank of the estuary of the River Cavado, and Esposende on the north bank. Ofir has a wonderful beach, plus good hotels; Esposende, like many places up the coast, started as a small fishing village, expanded considerably, but kept the old kernel alive.

Traveling on up the Costa Verde (Green Coast) you will reach the large resort of Viana do Castelo (around 30 km., 18½ miles). This lovely old town lies at the mouth of the River Lima and at the foot of a mountain accessible both by road and cable car: on the top rises the basilica of Santa Lucia with a good hotel alongside overlooking the great estuary and the Atlantic. In the 16th century, Viana do Castelo rivaled Oporto as a maritime center. In the square, King Manuel's Town Hall, from whose arcades the crowds could enjoy tournaments and *Pavanes,* was finished by João III, whose coat of arms it bears. The Renaissance loggias of the Misericórdia or Hospice of Mercy (the work of João Lopes) have tall caryatids and an aura of Venetian gracefulness. The stone fountain, also in Renaissance style, harmonizes perfectly with the noble proportion of the old emblazoned dwellings with their dusky walls and gleaming granite surfaces, scattered through this former haven of prosperous shipbuilders and sea-captains. The coast is still guarded by the prehistoric fortress from which the place takes its name—a reminder of the heroic 49-day siege in 1827 by the Oporto rebels.

Visitors coming to Viana do Castelo for the annual Pardon of Our Lady of Sorrows in August will carry away with them unforgettable memories. Best book well ahead for this, or you may have to sleep in your car.

Viana's river is the Lima, whose current is so gentle that in ancient times it was called "the river of forgetfulness." But the Atlantic Ocean brought fame and fortune to the city long ago when ships from Genoa and Venice dropped anchor in its port. The lords of the area quickly became absorbed in maritime trade, investing fortunes in fishing fleets and dealing with traders from all over the world. By the 16th century, Viana was so renowned and opulent that King Manuel occasionally lived there. The Távoras Palace dates from the 16th century, the Palaces of the Cisnes and of the Barbosa Maciéis, the latter now the Municipal Museum, were built in the 18th. This naturally has a large collection of Viana pottery, with its delicate blue and pearly-white coloring, as well as good furniture and sculpture.

The city is rich in old granite houses with iron balconies and Manueline windows. The chapels and hospices are fancifully ornate, and these architectural designs are faithfully reproduced in the beautifully elaborated local embroideries. The white-on-white is the most elegant, but the motifs of flowers and hearts are also carried out in red or blue on a white ground.

The road continues northward along the coast, passing through dunes, pine groves, and a fair amount of summer development. From Viana there is a railroad too, paralleling route N13, all the way to the mouth of the Minho. There are beaches of varying degrees of acceptability en route, with a good one at Vila Praia de Ancora and again at Moledo. If you keep your eyes open for small side roads as you go along, you will find that some of them lead down to fairly isolated beaches.

The Minho now forms the frontier with Spain, and there are a string of border towns to visit, all of them showing signs of old fortifications: Caminha, with a town hall on the main square, once part of the defenses; Vila Nova da Cerveira, whose castle houses an imaginative pousada; São Pedro da Torre, with its restored Roman bridge; and Valença do Minho, a major crossing point, with a rail and road bridge over into Spain, a fortified hill enclosing two little villages, each also walled, a pousada with magnificent views, and generally rewarding to explore.

Inland Minho

We begin our exploration inland from the Minho coast with routes running east from Viana do Castelo. Two roads go up the green valley of the River Lima. That on the north bank passes the Solar de Bertiandos, a large country house almost on the road, with a Gothic tower, a Renaissance center and early Baroque wings. This part of the Minho contains a large number of country houses, whose owners take in guests. The Portuguese name is *Turismo do Habitaçao*. The rooms, all with bath, are comfortable and breakfast is included but not always dinner. However, every town has reasonably good restaurants and this is an agreeable way of seeing how the Portuguese landowners live on their country estates.

Ponte de Lima is a lovely town, the wide river crossed by a many arched Roman bridge as well as a modern one downstream for today's traffic. Between the bridges, a splendid avenue of old plane trees shades a wide river-side walk, on which the "New Fair" has been held since the 12th century, on the 2nd and 3rd weekends of September. The town has delightful, rambling streets, 18th-century houses and a battlemented tower.

Returning over the old bridge to the north bank, the road upstream passes the ancient Benedictine convent of Refóios de Lima. The church here is filled with splendid golden woodwork and the adjoining convent, though abandoned, is used as a farm.

Further east is another well-situated riverside town. Ponte da Barca, this time reached by a Gothic bridge, is much smaller than Ponte de Lima, but it is at the crossing of four main roads. That to the east follows a mountainous route to Lindoso with the *espigueiros*. To the north through Arcos de Valdevez, near which is one of the best known country houses, the Paço da Gloria, which takes guests, to Monção, which can also be reached by a riverside road from Valença do Minho. Monção is a cheerful town which still pays fond tribute to the memory of its stalwart heroine, Dieu-la-Deu, who in 1638 stood up to the Castilian attackers. Local sights feature her statue, her house, and the place where she lies buried. Her name also graces a fruity-flavored wine that tastes marvelous along with a dish of Minho river lampreys cooked either *à l'escabèche* (in a peppery sauce) or in *matelote*-style (in a herb-flavored stew with red wine).

Eastward of Monção, in the remote angle of the frontier, almost entirely surrounded by Spain, lies Melgaço, with its castle keep and famous for its hams; southwards is Castro Laboreiro, like many villages around here, with thatched rooftops straggling out over the rocky flatlands, and the shepherds in rough homespun garments, their flocks guarded against wolves by great shaggy dogs.

Further south and to the east of Lindoso lies the Peneda-Gerês National Park, and the great system of lakes and dams, mostly along the River Cavado. We describe this area and the route into it from Chaves at the end of the Trás-os-Montes chapter but, of course, it would make an excellent trip in the reverse direction, out of Braga, taking the best part of a day to go up and see the magnificent views and perhaps explore the National Park a little. Here the mountains look totally savage and untamed. Gaudily painted houses reflecting the tenacity of man's hope cling close to the rock, and there are still wild stretches of land where nature has been allowed to go its unmolested way. In these great valleys, mountain torrents rush down in winter and spring between the jagged crests of the Serra do Gerês, and wild boar, wolves, civet cats and a singular breed of wild horses roam at will.

Braga and Bom Jesus

The road south from Ponte de Barca, N101, goes straight to Braga, the provincial capital. It is a very ancient city, for to the Celtic Bracara was added the name Augusta after the Roman conquest in 279 B.C., when it became a bustling town at the crossroads of five military routes. Capital of the Sueves, it kept its importance under the Visigoths and for long withstood the Moorish attacks. Braga's archbishops were known sometimes to wield greater authority than the kings themselves. Archbishop Diego de Sousa beautified the town with churches, palaces, calvary crosses and fountains in the 16th century, Braga's golden age, and two centuries later another archbishop made the city into one of the main centers of Portuguese Baroque art.

A busy regional focus, Braga has exploded over the last few years and is still growing fast. The ancient center of the town is now swamped in noisy surrounding streets, apartment blocks and a kind of Noah's Flood of traffic.

The originally Romanesque cathedral presents an equally impressive blend of styles, seen at their best in the chapels—the delicate wrought-iron tracery in the Capela de São Giraldo, the intricately carved stonework in the apse of the Sé, next to the statue of Our Lady of the Milk. The museum off the cloisters has a fascinating collection including a 14th-century crystal cross set in bronze, pure gold altar vessels, richly embroidered 18th-century vestments and a charming group of Our Lady in an elegant hat with the Holy Child, riding on a donkey, patiently led by St Joseph. There is also a great deal of quite worthless religious bric-à-brac. (It is part of the appeal of most treasuries attached to the larger Portuguese churches, that they contain as much devout detritus as they do genuinely interesting and attractive pieces.) From the magnificent upper choir, which you will cross as part of the visit to the separated parts of the museum, you will see the wildly Baroque organs, supported by cloven-hoofed satyrs, which reach to the roof. The choir is redolent with Brazilian wood and gilding.

Beyond the cathedral, housed in a former palace, is the Biscainhos Museum, with bright, elegant 18th-century rooms furnished in period style, and displaying silver and porcelain to the best advantage. At the back is an evocative formal garden, with some exceptionally interesting decorative tiles. This is one of the neatest, most engaging museums in Portugal.

In the Braga suburb of São Jerónimo Real—3½ km. (two miles), off route 201—is the unusual Chapel of São Frutuoso, rebuilt in the 11th century in the original form of a Greek cross. The adjoining Baroque church has superb stalls in the upper choir and a lovely sacristy. Nearby in the village of Tibães are the great gardens and buildings of the first Benedictine monastery in Portugal, painful in their desolation; for only the splendid church is kept up, with fine untouched Baroque gold work and lovely statues and choir stalls.

An interesting triangular route can be followed from Braga, which will lead you to three important places of pilgrimage, all of them also fascinating for their Baroque elements, or for their fine views. The first of the three is Bom Jesus do Monte, around five km. (three miles) away, a densely wooded hill that many people visit Braga specifically to see. The church itself is a late example of the characteristic Minho Baroque, built between 1784 and 1811, and makes effective use of gray stone ornaments round doors and windows in the dazzling whitewashed walls. But the really splendid thing about Bom Jesus is the stairway up to the shrine, also a marvel of Baroque art, but of an earlier date, started in 1723. The stairway folds in and out like a gigantic fan. Fountains placed along the various resting-places represent the five senses, with water splashing out from the eyes, ears, nose, mouth, and breasts of the stone statues. Next comes the Virtues, following up the seemingly endless steps. At last you emerge onto a pleasant, restful esplanade under the welcome shade of trees, where the air is cool and refreshing and in winter camellias bloom. In small chapels on the way up is a series of tableaux with lifesize figures illustrating the Stations of the Cross.

If you don't want to climb up the great staircase—which would mean that you would miss seeing the chapels and statuary on the way up—you can take the funicular for a few escudos, or drive up the winding road (or a combination of any of these). There are restaurants, refreshments and a couple of hotels beside the sanctuary, so the visit can be made into an attractive trip from Braga.

Another four km. (2½ miles) further along the same road is the shrine at Monte Sameiro, much later in date, though also dedicated to the Virgin. This is a terraced platform with fieldglasses, through which, if you are lucky with the visibility, you can survey the city of Braga, lying below, and right over the countryside to distant Monte Santa Luzia above the Atlantic.

The wildly Baroque chapel of Santa Maria Madelena on the Serra da Falperra—5½ km. (3½ miles) out of Braga on route 309—a hill that is alive with hoopoes in the spring, completes the pilgrim triangle in the hills east of Braga.

Also east from Braga, and a little beyond the triangle described above, the round-shaped dwellings of prehistoric Celtic towns, citanias—Sabroso, Briteiros—huddle behind triple protecting walls. In the rock round about, there are still traces of the grimly determined people who lived out their laborious existences here. Their implements have now found their way into the museum of Guimarães, but their dogged, resolute spirit lives on in their descendants on this frugal soil.

Between Braga and the coast, west along N103, lies Barcelos. Here the dukes built a castle in the 15th century to guard the Roman bridge over the Cávado. The ruins stand next to the austere parish church, so very different from the elegant 18th-century octagonal Church of Senhor da Cruz, whose gilded pulpit is fixed to a wall of splendid azulejos. Don't miss the colorful throngs on a market Thursday in Barcelos, where you are quite likely to find some good local ceramics laid out in the huge square, surrounded by fine buildings. Though if you are driving be warned that not only is it almost impossible to park on fair day, you may never get across the bridge in the middle of town.

Barcelos is the home town of the pottery cockerel which has almost become a symbol for Portugal itself. The legend that goes with it tells of a pilgrim to Santiago da Compostella, who was accused of robbery. He invoked the help of St. James (Santiago) and, pointing to the judge's dinner of roast fowl pleaded "If that cock doesn't crow they'll string me up" . . . and of course it did and they didn't.

Also interesting are the Pinheiros manor, the Gothic pillory and the many old houses with their heraldic designs. A small archeological and ceramic museum has been set up in the Palace ruins which contains, among other items, a 14th-century Crucifix *O Senhor do Galo,* commemorating the famous cock.

Guimarães

Southeast of Braga, on route N101, is the fine ancient town of Guimarães. Minho was actually the cradle of present-day Portugal, the nucleus from which the kingdom grew. It was made possible through the grateful generosity of a sovereign of León. When Afonso Henriques was born in Guimarães, in 1106, the realm of his father, Henry of Burgundy, was a mere dukedom. But he extended his domain far south of Lisbon, so the high turret of Guimarães in which Afonso first saw the light of day is represented on the Portuguese king's coat-of-arms, along with six other strongholds recaptured from the Moors.

Guimarães is today a provincial town, proud of its glorious past, rich in treasures of silver and stone carvings collected in the museums. The chief industry is linen weaving.

The town is a delightful blend of medieval and Renaissance architecture, among which is the 15th-century former City Hall with its arcades and the esplanade at the foot of the castle. On days when fairs are held, horse traders and linen merchants set up their stalls, among wicker hampers, pitchers of green wine, and stoneware. The famous fair of São Gualter is held in August, that of São Torcato is in July. Monte da Penha towers some 2,000 feet above the town. There are two pousadas here, one in the center of town and the other, the Pousada de Santa Marinha, in beautifully restored monastic buildings, with a fine view over the city.

In every way the castle is the focus of the city. Surrounded by a park, the great tenth-century fortified keep rises on a spur that juts into the town. Below the castle, surrounded by cypress trees like massive candles, is a tall statue of the Founder King, a figure weighed down with armor, his face beneath a splendid helmet. Nearby is a tiny Romanesque chapel, São Miguel do Castelo, the very one in which he was baptized, and stretching out around the hill a greatly changed version of the same vista that he must often have surveyed.

At the foot of the hill the totally restored Gothic palace of the dukes of Bragança contains lovely tapestries, carpets and furniture, and two canvasses by Josefa of Obidos.

Back in town, the street of Santa Maria comes almost straight out of the Middle Ages: granite archways, wooden balconies, paving stones underfoot. Directly in front of the collegiate church of Nossa Senhora da Oliveira (Our Lady of the Olive Branch) is the spot where Wamba was tilling the soil on the day that two messengers sought him out to inform him of his election as king of the Visigoths. In disbelief, he thrust his olive-branch stick into the earth, declaring that only if this stick were to bear leaves would he accept the proferred crown—whereupon the stick promptly sprouted foliage. And so Wamba became a king. In the tenth century, on the site of this miracle, a devout believer constructed an abbey. There has been much rebuilding on the site, but the remaining structure is a fine combination of Gothic and Romanesque, set in a square that is surrounded by Gothic houses.

The Alberto Sampaio Museum is housed in parts of this complex of buildings, the cloister and chapterhouse among them. There are many beautiful and historically important pieces here, foremost among which is the tunic worn by João I at the crucial Battle of Aljubarrota, and a very fine triptych, enameled and in silver gilt, depicting the Holy Family and scenes of medieval life—look for the inset of shepherds at the Nativity—said to have been captured in the same battle from the King of Castile's abandoned tent.

There is a lot else to see in Guimarães: the Largo do Toural, an attractive square, with its cobbles set in wave patterns and surrounded by fine Classical houses; the church of São Francisco, whose chancel is decorated with 18th-century azulejos, and which has an interesting sacristy; and especially the Martins Sarmento Museum (open from 2 to 5 P.M.) in the Gothic cloister and annexes of the Convento de São Domingos, containing rich finds from the prehistoric settlements of Briteiros and Sabroso, impressive sculptures strangely reminiscent of Epstein and Moore. There are also Lusitanian and Roman stone sarcophagi, a strange miniature bronze chariot, various weapons and ornaments, and the famous Pedra Formosa. But it is the Colossus of Pedralva that arrests the attention—a huge prehistoric granite figure of brutal power.

PRACTICAL INFORMATION FOR MINHO

TOURIST OFFICES. There are tourist offices in the following towns. **Arcos de Valdevez,** Ave. Marginal (tel. 058 66100); **Barcelos,** Rua Duques de Bragança (tel. 053 82882); **Braga,** Ave. Liberdade 1 (tel. 053 22550); **Caldelas,** Ave. Afonso Manuel (tel. 053 36124); **Esposende,** Rua 1° Dezembro (tel. 053 961354); **Gerês,** Ave. Manuel F. da Costa (tel. 053 65133); **Guimarães,** Ave. da Resistência ão Fascismo 83 (tel. 053 42450).

Moledo, Ave. Couto dos Santos (tel. 058 92154); **Monçao,** Largo do Loreto (tel. 051 52757); **Ponte de Lima,** Praça da Republica (tel. 058 942335); **Santo Tirso,** Praça de Municipio (tel. 052 52914); **Valença,** Ave. da Espanha (tel. 051 23374/6); **Viana do Castelo,** Palácio das Távoras, Rua Candido dos Reis (tel. 058 22620/24971); **Vila Praia de Áncora,** Rua Miguel Bombarda (tel. 058 911384); **Vila Nova da Cerveira,** Ave. Manuel S. Lebrão (tel. 051 95376).

HOTELS AND RESTAURANTS

Afife (Viana do Castelo). Good beach, windy at times. **Restaurants.** *Praia* (I). Café-restaurant. *Praia Mar* (I). Café-restaurant serving large portions; pleasant sea view.

Arcos De Valdevez (Viana do Castelo). *Casa do Requeijo* (E), tel. 058 65272. 2 rooms with bath; 3 independent apartments with bath, living room, kitchen. Country house; dinner available. *Paço da Gloria* (E), tel. 058 941477. 10 rooms. Famous 18th-century house with monumental gardens, pool; lunch and dinner available. English owner.

Barcelos (Braga). *Albergaria Condes de Barcelos* (E), Ave. Alcaides de Faria (tel. 053 82061/2). 30 rooms with bath. AE, DC, MC, V. *Pensão Bagoeira* (I), Ave. Dr. Sidónio Pais 57 (tel. 053 82236). 20 rooms. Good regional food—try the spring lamprey for a treat. *Pensão Dom Nuno* (I), Ave. D. Nuno Álvares Pereira (tel. 053 81084). 27 rooms with bath. Breakfast only. AE.
Restaurant. *Turismo* (M), Rua Duque de Bragança.

Braga (provincial capital). *Turismo* (E), Ave. João XXI (tel. 053 27091/4). 132 rooms with bath. Modern, with rooftop pool. Disco. AE, DC, MC, V. *Caranda* (M), Ave. da Liberdade 96 (tel. 053 77027). 100 rooms with bath. Good new hotel with excellent restaurant. AE, DC, MC, V. *João*

XXI (M), Ave. João XXI (tel. 053 22146). 28 rooms with bath. AE, DC, MC, V.

Restaurants. *Conde Dom Henrique* (M), Rua do Forno 17 (tel. 053 23408). Just behind the cathedral; slightly severe dining room, but excellent food and attention. Closed Wed. V. *Inácio* (M), Campo das Hortas (tel. 053 22335). Dishes of the region, but rather mediocre service. *Ragú* (M), Ave. João XXI 789. There are also plenty of cafés and snack bars.

At **Bom Jesus do Monte,** 6 km. (4 miles) out of town. *Hotel do Elevador* (E), Parque do Bom Jesus do Monte (tel. 053 25011/4). 25 rooms with bath. Comfortable rooms and good, old fashioned restaurant. At a sanctuary high above Braga with panoramic view of the region. Well worth an expedition for lunch. *Sul Americano* (I), tel. 053 22515. 28 rooms, some with bath. AE, DC, MC.

At **Sameiro,** another high sanctuary, along the crest of the hill. **Restaurant.** *Casal de São José* (M). For a pleasant break among the pinewoods.

Caldelas (Braga). Spa. *Grande Hotel Bela Vista* (M), tel. 053 36117. 69 rooms with bath. Tennis. Closed Jan. through May. AE, DC, MC, V. *Pensão Universal* (M), tel. 053 36236. 20 rooms. With wonderful grill and meat dishes in adjoining restaurant. Open all year. Various other pensions. *Grande Hotel de Caldelas* (I), Ave. Afonso Manuel (tel. 053 36114). 61 rooms. Closed Oct. through May.

Caminha (Viana do Castelo). Picturesque old town overlooking the Minho. *Pensão Galo de Ouro* (I), Rua da Corredoura 15 (tel. 058 921160). 10 rooms, with annex of 5 rooms, restaurant.

Restaurants. *Remo* (M), Ave. Dr. Dantas Carneiro (tel. 058 92459). MC. At **Lanhelas:** *Casa da Arte* (M).

At **Seixas:** *Foz do Minho* (M), tel. 058 92301. *Napoleon* (M), Lugar de Coura (tel. 058 922115). AE, DC.

Caniçada (Braga). *Pousada de São Bento* (L), tel. 053 57190/1. 10 rooms with bath. Pool, tennis, excellent food. 24 km. (15 miles) northeast of Braga in lovely country. AE, DC, MC, V. *Casa da Cruz do Real* (E), tel. 053 57452. 4 rooms with bath. Country house with wonderful mountain views. Meals available.

Esposende (Braga). *Estalagem do Zende* (L), Estrada Nacional 13 (tel. 053 961855). 12 rooms with bath. Good restaurant. Disco. Reasonably near beach. AE, DC, MC, V. *Nelia* (M), Ave. Valentim Ribeiro (tel. 053 961244). 42 rooms with bath. Recently refurbished; near beach. AE, DC, MC, V. *Suave Mar* (M), Ave. Eng. Arantes e Oliveira (tel. 053 961445/6). 45 rooms with bath. Pool, tennis; pleasant. MC, V.

Restaurant. *Nelia* (E), Rua 1 de Dezembro.

Gerês (Braga). Spa resort at 1,830 meters (6,000 ft.), with water sports, National Park and Nature Reserve. There are several hotels, pensions and restaurants, mostly on Avenida Francisco da Costa. *Hotel do Parque* (M), Ave. Manuel Francisco da Costa (tel. 053 65112/65151). 60 rooms, most with bath or shower. Pool; tennis. Closed mid-Oct. to mid-May. *Hotel das Termas* (M), Ave. Francisco da Costa (tel. 053 65143/4). 31 rooms with bath. *Universal* (I), tel. 053 65141. 90 rooms.

Gondarém. (Viana do Castelo). *Estalagem da Boega* (E), Quinta do Outeiral (tel. 051 95231). 30 rooms with bath. Lovely old house with views of the Minho. Pool, tennis. Close to Vila Nova da Cerveira.

Guimarães (Braga). Apart from those listed, the town is not well provided with hotels or restaurants. *Pousada de Santa Maria da Oliveira* (L), tel. 053 412157. 16 rooms with bath, 6 suites. Appealing 18th-century palace in center of old town. Large dining room, fine for lunch when sightseeing. AE, DC, MC, V. *Pousada de Santa Marinha* (L), tel. 053 418453. 53 rooms with bath. Ancient monastery commissioned by Dom Afonso Henriques, beautifully restored, in delightful setting. Opened in 1986, about two miles outside town. AE, DC, MC, V. *Fundador Dom Pedro* (M), Ave. D. Afonso Henriques 740 (tel. 053 412683). 54 rooms with bath, 9 suites. Modern and a little out of town by the rail station. Breakfast only. AE, DC, MC.
Hotel do Toural (I), Largo do Toural 15 (tel. 053 411250). 30 rooms, some with bath. Breakfast only.
Restaurants. *Jordao* (M), Ave. D. Afonso Henriques 55. Good food. Closed Tues. *Nicolino* (M), Largo do Toural 106–9. Excellent service and good food. *Vira Bar* (M), Largo 28 de Maio. Good local dishes. AE.

Lanhelas (Viana do Castelo). *Casa da Anta* (E), tel. 058 921434. 4 rooms with bath. Country house on River Minho. Dinner available. *Casa do Ribeiro* (E), São Cristovão do Selho (tel. 053 410881). 5 rooms with bath. Country house in wooded property. Dinner available. *Paço de São Cipriano* (E), Tabuadelo (tel. 053 481337). 5 rooms with bath. Battlemented country house. Dinner available.

Melgaço (Viana do Castelo). Spa. *Pensão Boavista* (M), Estrada Nacional 202 (tel. 051 42464). 28 rooms, 10 with bath. Closed Oct. through May. *Hotel das Aguas* (I), tel. 051 42262. 60 rooms, most with bath. Closed Oct. through May. *Rocha* (I), tel. 051 42356. 31 rooms, 4 with bath. Closed Oct. through May.

Monção (Viana do Castelo). Famous for lamprey dishes in early spring. Ferry boat to Spain across the Minho. *Albergaria Atlantico* (M), Rua General Pimenta de Castro 13 (tel. 051 52355/6). 24 rooms with bath. AE, DC, MC. *Residência Mané* (M), Rua General Pimenta de Castro 7 (tel. 051 52355). 8 rooms with bath. Restaurant. AE, DC, MC, V. *Central* (I), Praça Deu-La-Deu (tel. 051 52314). 23 rooms. Plus 6 rooms in annex.
Restaurants. *Chave d'Ouro* (M), Largo de Estação. *Escondidinho* (M), Praça Dieu-la-Deu.

Monte da Penha (Braga). Near Guimarães. *Hotel da Penha* (M), tel. 053 414245. 18 rooms, some with bath. Recently modernized. Good restaurant.

Ofir/Fão (Braga). Seaside resort. *Estalagem do Parque do Rio* (L), Pinhal de Ofir (tel. 053 981521/4). 36 good rooms with bath. Peaceful and secluded, particularly well designed and built by its architect owner. Wonderful swimming pool; tennis. Shops. AE, DC, MC, V.
Ofir (E), Ave. Raul de Sousa Martins (tel. 053 961383/5). 200 rooms with bath. Also family apartments. Tennis, riding, pool, shops. On long,

safe, sandy beach. AE, DC, MC, V. *Pinhal* (M), Estrada do Mar (tel. 053 961473/4). 89 rooms with bath. Disco, tennis, 2 heated pools, shops. 300 meters from beach; and, with a name like that, pines—naturally. AE, DC, MC, V.

Restaurant. In **Fâo.** *Martins do Frango* (I). For excellent grilled chicken and shellfish.

Ponte da Barca (Viana do Castelo). *Pensão Freitas* (I), Rua Conselheiro Rocha Peixoto (tel. 058 42113). 14 rooms.
Restaurant. *Restaurant Bar do Rio* (M). Good cuisine and peaceful atmosphere, overlooking bridge and river.

Ponte de Lima (Viana do Castelo). There are several *Casas da Habitação*—old buildings, farmhouses and palaces with rooms with bath for hire. Minimum stay is usually three nights. The local Tourist Office will advise you of addresses and details. *Pensão São João* (I), Rua do Rosario 6 (tel. 058 941288). 11 rooms, some with bath. Breakfast only.
Restaurant. There are also several cafés. *Encanada* (M), Praça Municipal. Panoramic view. Closed Thurs. AE. *Monte da Madalena* (M). MC.

Riba de Ave (Braga). *Estalagem de São Pedro* (E), Ave. Narciso Ferreira (tel. 052 93138). 7 rooms with bath. Attractive.

Valença do Minho (Viana do Castelo). Charming town. *Pousada de São Teotónio* (L), tel. 051 22252. 16 rooms with bath. Inside old fortifications with superb view of the River Minho and Tuy in neighboring Spain. Restaurant has magnificent food. 1 km. (½ mile) from Spanish border on road to Vigo. AE, DC, MC, V.
Lara (M), Lugar de S. Sebastião (tel. 051 22348). 54 rooms with bath. Breakfast only.
Restaurants. *Mané* (M), Largo da Esplanada. Closed Fri. AE, DC, MC. *Muralhas* (M), Largo Verissimo de Morais. MC.
At **Monte do Faro**, 7 km. (4 miles) east. *Residência Monte do Faro* (M), tel. 051 22411. 6 rooms. Well-known restaurant. Worth a visit for its peaceful siting, and spectacular views over nearby Spain. AE, DC, MC, V.

Viana do Castelo (provincial capital). *Hotel de Santa Luzia* (L), tel. 058 22192. 47 rooms. Completely refurbished; pool, tennis. Wonderful woodland location overlooking sea, river and city. AE, DC, MC, V. *Afonso III* (E), Ave. Afonso III 494 (tel. 058 24123/7). 89 rooms with bath. Disco, tennis, pool at short distance; central. AE, DC, MC. *Casa do Ameal* (E), Miadela (tel. 058 22402). 3 rooms with bath; 4 apartments. Country house. Dinner available.
Albergaria Calatrava (E), Rua José Espregueira (tel. 051 22011). 15 rooms with bath. Breakfast only. AE, DC. *Parque* (E), Parque da Galiza (tel. 051 24151/5). 123 rooms with bath. Pool; central location with panoramic restaurant. AE, DC, MC, V. *Rali* (I), Ave. Afonso III 180 (tel. 058 22176). AE, MC, V. *Viana Sol* (I), Largo Vasco da Gama (tel. 058 23401). 71 rooms with bath. Pool. Several pensions.
Restaurants. *Luziamar* (E), Praia de Cabedelo. With pool. *Alambique* (M), Rua Manuel Espregueira 86 (tel. 051 23894). Good local food and decor. Also has 24 rooms. Closed Tues. AE, DC, MC. *Os Três Potes* (M), Beco

dos Fornos 7 (tel. 058 23432). Fados and folklore. Closed Mon. MC, V. *Os Três Arcos* (M), Largo João Tomás da Costa 25. Excellent seafood.

Vila Nova da Cerveira (Viano do Castelo). A good point from which to explore the area. Ferry boat to Spain across the river. *Pousada de Dom Diniz* (L), tel. 058 95601. 29 rooms with bath, 3 suites. Set within fine 14th-century castle walls of picturesque town overlooking the River Minho. Most attractive. Disco. AE, DC, MC, V.

Vila Nova de Famalicão (Braga). *Moutados* (M), tel. 052 23500. 59 rooms with bath.
Restaurant. *Iris* (M), Rua Adriano de Bastos (tel. 052 22001). 18 km. (11 miles) southwest of Braga on N14. Lovely old solar, with excellent food. Good for lunch break if driving through (the town itself is of little interest). Best to book. AE, DC, MC, V.

Vila Praia de Âncora (Viano do Castelo). Good, safe, sandy beach. *Meira* (M), Rua 5 de Outubro 56 (tel. 058 91111). 45 rooms with bath. Disco. and excellent restaurant. AE, DC, MC, V.
Restaurants. *Lirios Verdes* (M), Ave. Dr. Ramos Pereira (tel. 058 911113). Delicious seafood and sea view. MC. *Sereca da Gelfa* (M), tel. 058 911630. Excellent seafood. Also has 6 rooms with bath; tennis, pool, camping and adjacent self-service restaurant.

CAMPING. There are campsites at the following places: Braga (Parque da Ponte); Caldas das Taipas; Caminha (Mata do Camarido); Esposende (Fão); Gerês (Vidoeiro); Guimarães (Parque das Taipas and Pena); Viana do Castelo (Cabedelo and Orbitur); Vila Praia da Âncora; Vilar de Mouros.

PLACES OF INTEREST. The Minho abounds in old aristocratic palaces and buildings in every town. If you ask, you will be able to enter and visit many of them. As well as the items listed below and in the chapter, most towns also have interesting churches to see, too many to list. Museums are usually open daily, except Mondays and public holidays, 10–5, but double check times locally. Some close for up to two hours for lunch. Entrance fees are between 150$00 and 300$00.

Barcelos. **Archeological Museum** and **Regional Museum of Ceramics,** Paço dos Duques (tel. 053 82071). The archeological section, in the remains of the ducal palace, is small but has some interesting items—the ceramic museum in the basement is the better of the two.

Bom Jesus do Monte. Baroque religious fantasia, 5 km. (three miles) from Braga (refer to text for description). Close by are two more shrines worth visiting, Monte Sameiro and Serra da Falperra (also refer to text).

Braga. **Biscainhos Museum,** Rua dos Biscainhos (tel. 053 27645). Excellent small "country house" museum—porcelain, furniture etc.—beautifully kept, with fine formal garden, and helpful guided tours.
Cathedral Treasury. Guided tours of a sprawling collection, housed in many rooms. Tour takes in the Upper Choir. Plenty to see in the rest of

the cathedral, too, especially the Chapel of Glory (fine tiles) and the King's Chapel.

Dom Diego de Sousa Museum, Largo do Paço. Roman archeological items from the region, and medieval sacred art.

Guimarães. Alberto Sampaio Museum, in the Convent of Nossa Senhora da Oliviera buildings, Rua Alfredo Guimarães (tel. 053 42 465). One of Portugal's finest museums, imaginatively installed in buildings that are notable for themselves. Plenty of valuable and interesting historical items.

Castle. Formidable 10th-century keep, a symbol of Portugal's birth.

Martins Sarmento Museum, Rua de Paio Galvão (tel. 053 42969). Archeological finds, mainly Roman, from regional excavations. Also the prehistoric Colossus of Pedralva. Open only 2–5.

Palace of the Dukes of Bragança (tel. 053 42273). Totally restored palace at the foot of the castle hill, with tapestries, carpets, furniture, armor, etc.

Lousado. Railway Museum.

Ponte de Lima. São Francisco des Terçeiros, Ave. 5 de Outubro. A church museum in both senses—a museum in a desanctified church, and a museum of sacred objects. Lots of Baroquery, fine carved church furniture. Guided tours morning and afternoon except winter months, then afternoons only.

Rates. Church of São Pedro, 12th-century, magnificent Romanesque building. Tricky to find, inland from Póvoa, about 12 km. (7½ miles) by N206.

Refoios do Lima. Former **Benedictine convent church** on a side road just north of Ponte de Lima, off N236. Magnificent gilded woodwork. The ruined conventual buildings are being transformed into an Agricultural College for 300 students.

Viana do Castelo. Misericórdia. Glorious 1589 hospital, with Baroque church next door.

Municipal Museum, Largo de São Domingos. Housed in the 18th-century palace of the Barbosa Maciéis family, this is as much to be seen for the building and its magnificent azulejos (1720s) as for the contents—furniture, sacred art, ceramics, etc. Also a courtyard with stone carvings.

SPECIAL EVENTS. For further details and exact dates, consult local tourist offices. **March–April.** Braga has the most impressive *Holy Week* processions in Portugal. **May.** *Festival of the Cross* at Barcelos, with religious ceremonies and fair with exhibition of local ceramics, 2–5. One of Portugal's biggest wingdings. **June.** Costumed *Procession of King David and the Shepherds* at Braga, traditional fair with celebrations, 23–24. **July.** *Handicraft Fair* at Vila do Conde.

August. *Fair of São Gualter* (St. Walter) at Guimarães, 1st Sun. in month, for 4 days. Annual pilgrimage at São Bento da Porta Aberta, Gerês, 10–15. *Festival of Santa Rita da Cassia* at Caminha, with processions, dancing and fireworks. *Pardon of Nossa Senhora da Agonia (Our Lady of Sorrows)* at Viano do Castelo: one of Portugal's most extraordinary religious demonstrations, with people in regional costumes, processions, folk dances, fair, bullfights, fireworks and evening festivities on the River Lima, Fri., Sat. and Sun. closest to Aug. 20. *Romaria of St. Bartholomew of the Sea* at Esposende, 23–24. Strange age-old customs mark this festival as they do on the same dates in Ponte da Barca. Annual pilgrimage to *Nossa Senhora de Sameiro* at Braga, last Sun. in month.

September. Porto de Ave, Póvoa de Lanhoso, *pilgrimage* to 17th-century chapels, 1st Sun. *New Fair* (dating from 12th century) at Ponte de Lima, mid- to late month.

SHOPPING. Local fairs can give good value in textiles, light clothing, shoes, baskets and pottery. **Crafts.** Barcelos is a noted ceramic center. The potters' taste runs mainly to figurines of the little amber-colored oxen so typical of the region, with their lyre-shaped horns. These sturdy glazed terracotta beasts are on sale everywhere, along with pink or blue roosters. Hand embroidery and gold filigree jewelry comes from Viana do Castelo.

USEFUL ADDRESSES. Travel Agent. *American Express,* Star Travel Service, Ave. D. Afonso Henriques 638, Guimarães (tel. 053 415750).

Car hire. *Avis:* Rua Gabriel Periera Castro 28, Braga (tel. 053 72520); Hotel Afonso III, Viana do Castelo, Guimarães (tel. 058 23994).

TRÁS-OS-MONTES

This remote and beautiful province in the extreme northeast of Portugal has become easier to reach in recent years by the construction right on its eastern side of road and railway bridges over the River Douro at Barca de Alva on the Spanish frontier, some 65 km. (40 miles) north of Guarda, taking the road through Pinhel. Incidentally, the railway line from Oporto to Barca de Alva along the great valley of the Douro is one of the most scenically rewarding in the country. But all the local rail routes are fascinating; that to Chaves via Vila Real, and the others to Bragança and Mirando do Douro can all provide long and excellent chances to get to know the changing landscape—long the journeys certainly are, as the trains stop at every small town.

The region is still almost unknown to travelers and attracts very few package tours, as the distances involved are great, the roads few and mostly serpentine to excess. But adventurous travelers will find themselves richly rewarded by the splendid countryside and interesting towns which, in spite of much ugly new building, keep their medieval centers and still retain many country customs which have disappeared elsewhere.

First-class accommodations are limited in Trás-os-Montes, but there are pousadas at Bragança, Miranda do Douro, and Alijó, and that in the Serra do Marão, between Amarante and Vila Real, though not technically in the province, can be used for exploring the southwestern part of the region. Good hotels and golf courses can be found at the spas of Pedras Salgadas and Vidago. The Hotel Trajano at Chaves, the Albergaria Cabanelas at Vila Real, the Estalagem do Caçador at Macedo de Cavalheiros, and the Hotel Bragança right in the town of that name, are all reasonably good

259

and, as everywhere in Portugal, the estalagems and pensions are clean and neat, though certainly simple, and the most basic restaurant always has good food and local wine.

Noble Port Wine

Bound to the south by the Douro flowing between its high steamy banks, the only place in the world which can produce the grapes from which Port is made, Over (or Behind) the Hills—which is the meaning of Trás-os-Montes—is bordered to the east and north by Spain and to the west by the River Tamega and the Serras do Barroso and Gerês.

The temperamental, shifting Douro meanders along a valley where the summer temperatures can soar to over 100° F. at the bottom and be almost cold, by contrast, in the hills above. Tiered terraces appear to cling for dear life to the cliffs of schist. The blackened lava has been crushed by patient hand labor and molded into long barricades that are held up by dry stone retaining walls. Proudly tended vineyards, on which countless hard and anxious hours of pruning and spraying have been spent, are rich in fruit and foliage. These are noble vines, the luxurious aristocrats of the country's grapes, yet so very frail and susceptible to the slightest caprice of weather or insect.

But the grape harvests make up for all the painstaking toil and hardship. The great luscious bunches hang in all their velvety splendor—deep black, royal purple, with here and there a tinge of carnelian. The grapes must be gathered with infinite care—only a perfectly intact fruit yields the precious Port wine. The heaped baskets weigh anywhere from 125 to 160 pounds, and must be carried carefully on men's backs, for no wheeled vehicle could cope with the vertiginous slopes. With straps securing their precious burdens in place, the processions of *borracheiros* leaning on long sticks, and accompanied by whistles and fifes, thread their way down toward the wine presses.

In small farms here, the grapes are still trodden by human feet, to keep the seeds from getting mashed and also to draw out every last bit of rich goodness from the skins. But all the big Port wine firms are now using mechanical winepresses, which have been developed in recent years. When the must begins to form, the juice ferments and seethes, and the foamy froth finally overflows the vats. For the people of the valley this is the year's high point, when the combined effects of vast weariness, the high hopes for the new vintage that has rewarded their hard labors, and not least the sheer intoxication of the new wine, all combine to create a genuinely bacchanalian atmosphere.

Vila Real to Mirandela

Vila Real, the first sizeable town you'll come to in the province if traveling inland from Oporto, is filled with 16th- and 17th-century houses, their portals decorated with coats of arms. The cathedral of São Domingos is a Romanesque-Gothic building, but if you are interested in Baroque architecture, look for the Clerigos church, also called the Capela Nova. This is fan-shaped, filling the angle between two streets which meet at the doorway set between two heavy columns. The pediment is surmounted by a pair of archangels flanking St. Peter.

But for really fantastic Baroque, you should visit the Solar de Mateus, a little way out of town to the east. The extraordinary U-shaped facade, with high decorated finials at each corner, is now known all over the world, from being reproduced on the label of the vast numbers of bottles of Mateus wine that are exported every year. The huge portal is approached by a double staircase. Set back to one side is the chapel with an even more extravagant facade. The interior is open to the public and contains elegant furniture, rare books, and historic letters, with Wellington and Frederick the Great among the correspondents.

A few miles further along the Vila Real–Sabrosa road from Mateus, at Panóias, are the ruins of a Roman sanctuary dedicated by its governor, Caio Calpurnio, to the gods of the underworld. This rock temple was only part of a much vaster complex.

South of Vila Real—on the far side of the mountains and across the river at Régua, where the demarcated region for the port wine vineyards starts—lies Lamego, once ideally located for the Moors of Spain, who used to bring their wares there. Beside the largely 12th-century cathedral and numerous Renaissance and Baroque churches, the former Episcopal Palace (now the Regional Museum) contains a fine collection of paintings, tapestries and sculptures. Lamego is specifically famous for the great pilgrimages that take place there at the beginning of September, when large numbers of the faithful climb the splendid monumental staircase up to the Baroque Nossa Senhora dos Remedios. If you, too, make the climb, you can rest at the top under the chestnut trees and enjoy the view over the town to the distant mountains.

If you take the main road northeast out of Vila Real (N15) towards Bragança, you will find that the formerly twisting road has been straightened out for most of its length of 132 km. (87 miles) and you drive through exceptionally fine, high countryside. The rolling arable land continues to Murça, which contains the largest of the prehistoric Iron Age pigs which can be found all over Trás-os-Montes. This particular granite boar stands on a plinth in the middle of town, very odd and—even to the archeologists—quite inexplicable.

On through superb country, brilliant with young barley in the spring, pale gold after harvest, with huge sweet chestnuts and tall cherry trees growing in sheltered hollows—the few villages solid and dark, quite unlike the cheerful white-washed hamlets further south.

Mirandela, exactly halfway to Bragança, is an attractive town on the River Tua, crossed by a fine medieval bridge of 17 arches. Another strange 18th-century house, that of the Tavoras family, now used as a town hall, dominates the place. The great facade rises in the center, with elaborate pediments and Baroque ornaments.

Bragança

Beyond Mirandela the road passes among groves of poplars and willows, through Macedo de Cavaleiros, which has an attractive estalagem, until the great castle of Bragança appears in the distance, 2,000 feet above sea level. The approaches to Bragança have unhappily been spoiled by numbers of ugly new buildings, but the core of the medieval city is untouched. The modern and comfortable, if characterless, Pousada of São Bartolomeu is just off this road in from Vila Real, on the edge of town, with a perfect view across a wide ravine to the crenelated walls and keep of the castle, floodlit at night.

Bragança is a name to conjure with for the British, as Catherine of Bragança married one of her most colorful kings, Charles II. It was a marriage of convenience and Charles, whose sexual appetites were omnivorous, treated her with little more than formal courtesy. She returned to Portugal after his death and functioned as an extremely efficient regent during the illness of her brother, King Pedro II. Although this great noble family took their name from the town, their connections with it have left almost no traces. Catherine herself was born in Vila Viçosa and died in Lisbon. The Bragança Pantheon in the Lisbon church of São Vicente de Fora will probably provide the history buff with more to interest him.

The castle at Bragança contains a well-displayed military museum, but be careful on the battlements if you are walking round them on a windy day. Nearby is the pentagonal Domus Municipalis, a City Hall dating from the 12th century, an exceedingly rare survival of a Romanesque civic building. The key can be obtained from an old lady in one of the cottages close by, as can the key of the parish church alongside. This has a superb painted ceiling, as have most of the other churches in the town. Another prehistoric granite boar stands below the castle keep, this one with a high medieval stone pillory driven through its body. The huddle of small houses round the castle, themselves surrounded by a wall, is a good example of the way in which medieval communities nestled close to their castles for protection, and to supply the defenders with produce and necessary craftsmanship.

Turning right to go back down into town, you will pass the church of São Bento, with a fine Mudéjar vaulted ceiling and a retable that has recently been regilded. More of the prehistoric pigs can be seen in the Abade de Baçal Museum in the former episcopal palace, along with some charming furniture, fine silver and attractive canvases—including a Dutch painting of Orpheus enchanting the animals with his lute. The Abade de Baçal, Francisco Manuel Alves, who died in 1947, was a remarkable local priest who devoted his life to the antiquities of the region, and who wrote a number of books on his researches, which included the first serious study of the *Marranos,* the Jews who fled from the Spanish Inquisition into these remote parts and practiced a curious mixture of Jewish and Christian rites.

At least two other churches in town are of interest. The cathedral, a former Jesuit church, has a lovely Gothic roof; nearby is the Misericórdia, an ancient hospital, whose chapel has a towering retable, featuring a welcoming Virgin.

Bragança—which could well be your first town in Portugal if you drove in from Spain—via Quintanilha, on a scenic, slightly basic, back road—is not a town to take up too much of your time. The inside of a day will easily exhaust its sights, so you should think of it as just an overnight stop.

Down the Spanish Border—Miranda do Douro

South of Bragança route N218 leads through fine, high, cultivated country, passing the town of Outeiro with the ruins of a castle, and eventually reaching Malhadas, a center for the breeding of the Miranda cattle, especially adapted to the climatic extremes of this region. Visitors are welcome at the State Farm in the village.

Six km. (four miles) further on the dark bulk of the Renaissance cathedral of Miranda rises above the walled town, as the driver approaches across an unusually level tract of land. At the entrance, the excellent Pousada de Santa Caterina has been built above the great gorge of the Douro which forms the frontier with Spain. (If you wish to approach Portugal from Spain at this point, Miranda is due west of Zamora.) Below is a manmade lake and the international bridge. Overhead wheel extraordinary birds, including Egyptian vultures. As one of the city gates is almost at the door of the pousada, this is an ideal place to stay.

Houses from the 14th and 15th centuries line the narrow cobbled streets around the cathedral (mid 1500s), built at a time when the city must have been exceptionally prosperous, for the architect of this splendid church was Diogo de Torralva, who also designed the cloister of the Filipes at Tomar. The interior is rich with a fine high altar retable and unusual choir stalls with paintings in grisaille. Ten beautiful chandeliers light the nave. The little statue of the Menino Jesus de Cartolinha—Child Jesus in a Silk Hat—stands in a glass case in the transept. The image, which is about two foot high, wears a 19th-century suit with a jaunty top hat. Other outfits given by the local people, who are very fond of this statue and proud of its oddity, are attached to the sides of the case.

The city is so remote that the townsfolk speak a dialect, and still perform characteristic local dances such as the *Pauliteiros,* in which men in white kilts, black shirts, and flower-decked hats, strike the sticks they hold to mark the rhythm of the complicated steps. The *Galandum* for both men and women is danced to the sound of square tambourines. The older men and women continue to wear heavy black cloaks in the winter, which can be very cold in this high countryside. Linen is still woven in the local cottages. These costumes and local artefacts can be seen in the da Terra de Miranda museum near the cathedral.

The city was at one time Wellington's headquarters in the Peninsular War, and from the terrace outside the cathedral there is another view of the deep gorge across which, according to tradition, the Commander was slung in a basket when the war moved into Spain.

South of Miranda there are a couple of Templar castles to be seen. One is at Penas Róias, on a side road northeast of Azinhozo (N219). Here there is a high tower, with a very small village round its base. The other is at Mogadouro, formerly a silk center and border stronghold. It is now a market town with the ruins of a Templar fortress. The main church and former Franciscan monastery have some attractive contents.

Continuing down route N221, just before Barca de Alva, you will reach the oddly named Freixo de Espada-à-Cinta (Ash tree of the Girded Sword). The road goes through high wooded country, until a tall heptagonal tower rears up from a cluster of houses in the wide, fertile valley below. Again, a rash of new buildings has disfigured the outskirts, but the main square presents an attractive architectural ensemble. The parish church, Igreja Matriz, is a find for anyone interested in the fantastications of the Manueline style—inside are some exceptionally good paintings; the high tower seen on the approach to the town stands beside the church, all that remains of the town's fortifications; opposite the church is a delightful Misericórdia, with an imposing facade.

A turning off N221, just 14 km. (nine miles) before Freixo, on N220, brings you to another interesting town, Torre de Moncorvo. It lies near one of the largest deposits of iron ore in Europe, and is grouped round an enormous church with a high, solid tower. Mainly 16th century, the interior of this great building does not belie the splendid exterior. Three naves, separated by elephantine columns, lead the eye to the golden high altar, enhanced by fine choir stalls.

Due north of Moncorvo, first on N325, then N102, is the village of Vila Flor, with an intriguing country museum in the Solar dos Lemos. This time there is not only another prehistoric boar, but also an Iron Age granite cat, with a medley of oddities such as an early typewriter, radios and walking sticks, with one or two pieces of fine furniture. An International Cultural and Scientific Institute has headquarters in the Solar.

This route, if followed north, would lead you back to Macedo Cavaleiros and, eventually, Bragança. Or you could wander through the network of smaller roads westwards—routes N214 etc.—to arrive at Vila Real.

Bragança Westwards—Chaves and Montalegre

If you decide to turn westwards, back towards the Atlantic from Bragança rather than turn southwards and follow the Spanish frontier, you will be opting for a fascinating route—undeniably tiring to drive, but with some tremendous things to see along the way.

You take N103 out of Bragança—in fact, you will be on N103 all the way—heading for Chaves. You will actually be paralleling the *other* Spanish border, the northern one. This is one of the most spectacular roads in the country, winding at first through laughing uplands (how do uplands laugh?) to reach Vinhais, with two churches embedded in the great Baroque facade of the former convent of São Francisco. The route runs along a watershed, with the mountains of Spain to the north, and the distant mass of the Serra da Estrela to the south. Shortly before reaching Chaves, high on a crest you will see the ruins of the 13th-century Monforte castle, plus a natural phenomenon, the Bulideira, a huge block of stone that can be set rocking by a push of the hand but cannot be toppled.

Chaves is sited just ten km. (six miles) south of the frontier post at Vila Verde da Raia. It was captured from the Moors in 1160, centuries after the Romans, who built the still-used bridge over the River Tamega, had left the peninsula. So the city is one of the oldest in the country. The castle, with high tooth-battlemented keep, was built in the 14th century by King Diniz. It is surrounded by narrow, windy streets of elegant houses, most of which have lovely ironwork balconies on the top floors, as indeed do many of the houses in the northern part of the country. In the main square is the Misericórdia church, lined with huge panels of blue-and-white azulejos depicting scenes from the New Testament, and which reach right up to the painted ceiling.

Chaves has some hot springs, valued by the Romans, which still function and ensure the town a small reputation as a spa. If you have time to turn south from Chaves, on N2, you will find Vidago and Pedras Salgadas, two more spas. Local tradition claims that the holy but hot waters in these spas were cast up from the entrails of the underworld.

35 km. (22 miles) after Chaves the road reaches Baraca and the beginning of the great system of lakes and hydroelectric dams. A short side trip should be made here, turning right up N308 to Montalegre. The ruined castle can be seen for miles around and, conversely, the views from it are

very fine. The little town itself has nothing else to offer, but the detour will be rewarded by the castle alone.

After leaving Montalegre the return to the main route can be on the westward arm of the triangle, to take you back to N103. From here on the road follows the edge of the great lake system, winding along the edges of drowned valleys in a ceaseless series of long loops. It can be extremely exhausting for the driver, but rewarding for everyone else in the car, as the views are mostly spectacular. The area stretching away to the north is the Peneda-Gerês National Park. Allow plenty of time to stop frequently and take in the panoramas in all directions, some of them spreading for many miles over deep ravines and to distant mountains.

There are at least two points where you could make a sortie from route N103 up into the park area. One is from the Venda Nova Dam, for 15 km. (nine miles) to the Paradela Dam, with great views over the River Cavado. The other from just before Cerdeirinhas on route N308 to Gerês itself, an attractive little spa with waters that are good for liver complaints. The region around here, deep in the National Park, is heavily wooded and rocky. You can, if you want, continue on up to the Spanish frontier.

In these hills, the pilgrimage church of Nossa Senhora da Abadia, flanked by low 18th-century arched pilgrim houses, is the scene of an enormous *romaria* at the end of May. The local villagers decorate their churches and chapels, carpets lovingly made of flowers are laid where the procession is going to pass and the festivities end with fireworks and dancing to the local band.

From Cerdeirinhas the route now runs for 30 km. (18½ miles) through rocky heights and down tree-clad slopes to reach Braga, the capital of Minho, lying in its wide plain.

PRACTICAL INFORMATION FOR TRÁS-OS-MONTES

TOURIST OFFICES. There are local tourist offices in the following towns: **Bragança,** Ave. 25 de Abril (tel. 073 22272); **Chaves,** Rua de Santo António 213 (tel. 076 21029); **Freixo de Espada-A-Cinta,** Largo Dr. Guerra (tel. 07962104); **Lamego,** Ave. Visconde Guedes Teixeira (tel. 054 62005); **Régua,** Largo da Estação (tel. 22846); **Torre de Moncorvo,** Paços do Concelho (tel. 079 22288); **Valpaços,** Rua do Mercado Municipal; **Vidago,** Largo Miguel de Carvalho (tel. 076 97470); **Vila Real,** Ave. Carvalho Araujo (tel. 059 22819).

HOTELS AND RESTAURANTS

Alijó (Vila Real). *Pousada do Barão de Forrester* (E), Rua José Rufino (tel. 099 95467). 11 rooms with bath, in modern building in ancient village. Excellent local cuisine and wine. AE, DC, MC, V.

Restaurant. *Adega do Souto* (M). Just outside town. *Pelourinho* (I). Fine bargain eating.

Bragança (provincial capital). *Albergaria Santa Isabel* (E), Rua Alexandre Herculano 67 (tel. 073 22427/8). 14 rooms with bath. In the old city. DC, MC. *Pousada de São Bartolemeu* (E), Estrada de Turismo (tel. 073 22493). 15 rooms with bath. Delightful, the best place to eat. Lovely view of castle and old city. Not in center. 32 km. (20 miles) from border. AE, DC, MC, V. *Bragança* (M), Rua Arantes e Oliveira (tel. 073 22578/9). 42 rooms with bath. AE, DC, MC. Several pensions.

Restaurants. We suggest that you eat at the pousada. Alternatively, try *Florida* (E), Rua Alexandre Herculano. *Plantório* (E), Estrada das Cantarias (tel. 073 22426). AE, DC, MC. *Arca de Noé* (M), Ave. do Sabor. Closed Fri. *Boite Cruzeiro* (M), Praça da Sé 12. *Tulipa* (M), Rua Dr. F. Felgueras.

Carvalhelhos (Vila Real). Spa. *Estalagem de Carvalhelhos* (E), tel. 092 42116. 10 rooms, 5 with bath. Charming.

Chaves (Vila Real). Spa. *Estalagem do Santiago* (M), Rua do Olival (tel. 076 22545/6). 30 rooms with bath. *Trajano* (M), Rua Candido dos Reis (tel. 076 22415/6). 39 rooms with bath. DC, MC. *Hotel de Chaves* (I), Rua 25 de Abril (tel. 076 21118). 36 rooms, 11 with bath. *Pensão Jaime* (I), Rua Joãquim José Delgado (tel. 076 21273). 61 rooms, many with bath.

Restaurant. *O Pote* (M), tel. 076 21226. Modern, family-run spot with very acceptable food, and friendly service. On the road into town from the east. Closed Mon.

Lamego (Viseu). *Albergaria do Cerrado* (E), tel. 054 63164. 30 rooms with bath. Breakfast only. Out of town. AE, DC, MC, V. *Estalagem de Lamego* (E), Monte Raposeira (tel. 054 62162). 7 rooms, 5 with bath. *Motel Turissera* (M), Estrada Florestal (tel. 054 62082). 18 units with bath. *Parque* (I), Senhora dos Remedios (tel. 054 62105/6). 32 rooms with bath. Outside the town, by pilgrimage church of Nossa Senhora dos Remedios. AE, DC, MC, V. *Residêncial Solar* (I), Largo da Sé (tel. 054 62060). 25 rooms with bath. Recommended; excellence of rooms belied by simple entrance. Breakfast only.

Restaurants. *Aviz* (M), Rua do Gremio. *Turiserra* (M), Estrada Florestal. Closed Mon.

Macedo De Cavaleiros (Bragança). *Estalagem do Caçador* (E), Largo Manuel Pinto de Azevedo (tel. 078 42356). 26 rooms, 8 with bath. Attractive place.

Restaurant. *Costa do Sol* (M). Excellent food. Just outside town. Also has rooms.

Miranda Do Douro (Bragança). *Pousada de Santa Catarina* (E), tel. 073 42255. 12 rooms with bath. Overlooks the great gorge and dam on the Douro. Very well managed. Good restaurant. AE, DC, MC, V. *Pensão Planalto* (I), Rua 1 de Maio (tel. 073 42362). 42 rooms, most with bath. Restaurant attached.

Restaurants. *O Mirandês* (I). Excellent budget value. *Santa Cruz* (I), Rua Abade de Bacal 61. Good regional cooking.

Mirandela (Bragança). *Pensão Globo* (M), Ave. N.S. do Amparo (tel. 078 22711). 30 rooms with bath. Breakfast only. *Pensão Jorge V* (M), Fontes Frias (tel. 078 23126). 29 rooms, most with bath. Breakfast only. *Mira-*

Tua (I), Rua da Republica 20 (tel. 078 22403). 31 rooms with bath. Breakfast only. AE, DC, MC, V.

Restaurants. *O Grês* (M), Ave. N.S. do Amparo (tel. 078 22670). Near river and old bridge. Very good food. Closed Sun.

At **Aldeia do Romeu.** *Restaurante de Maria Rita* (M). With delicious food and charming little museum nearby.

Mogadouro (Bragança). *Pensão Estrela do Norte* (M), Ave. de Espanha 65 (tel. 079 52426). 27 rooms with bath. Breakfast only.

Restaurant. *A Lareira* (M), Ave. N.S. do Caminho (tel. 079 52363). French cooking; highly recommended. Closed Mon. Also has 10 rooms.

Pedras Salgadas (Vila Real). Well-known spa. *Pensão do Parque* (M), Parque (tel. 059 44108). 58 rooms without bath. *Pedras Salgadas* (I), Parque (tel. 059 44156). 146 rooms, 80 with bath. Closed mid-Oct. through May.

Pinhão (Vila Real). *Pensão Ponto Grande* (M), Rua Central 103 (tel. 054 72456). 14 rooms with bath. Recommended. Good restaurant adjacent.

Régua (Vila Real). *Pensão Columbano* (I), tel. 054 23704. 70 rooms, 56 with bath. Breakfast only.

Restaurants. *Arco Iris* (M), Ave. Sacadura Cabral. MC. *Castelo Negro* (M), Rua da Ferreirinha. *Romaninho* (M), Ave. de Ovar.

Torre De Moncorvo (Bragança). **Restaurant.** *Adega Regional O Lagar* (I), Rua Adriano Leandro 16. Regional food and good local wine, in spacious former wine store.

Vidago (Vila Real). Spa; with several small hotels and pensions. *Palace* (E), Parque (tel. 076 97356/8). 115 rooms, 64 with bath. Good restaurant with fixed menu. Tennis, golf, pool, badminton, disco; coiffeur. DC, MC.

Vila Flor (Bragança). *Pensão Restaurante Campos* (I), Ave. Marechal Carmona (tel. 078 52311). 10 rooms with bath.

Restaurant. *Sanctuário* (M). Good home cooking. Splendid view.

Vila Real (provincial capital). *Albergaria Cabanelas* (E), Rua D. Pedro de Castro (tel. 059 23153). 24 rooms with bath. Restaurant; good snack bar below. AE, DC, MC, V. *Mira-Corgo* (M), Ave. 1 de Maio (tel. 059 25001). 46 rooms with bath; 30 apartments. Breakfast only. Pool. AE, DC, MC, V. *Tocaio* (I), Ave. Carvalho Araujo 45 (tel. 059 23106/7). 52 rooms with bath. AE, DC, MC.

Restaurants. *Espadeiro* (M), Ave. Almeida Lucena (tel. 059 22302). AE. *O Montanhês* (M), Lugar das Avores.

Vinhais (Bragança). *Pensão Ribeirinha* (I), Rua Nova (tel. 073 72490). 18 rooms. Breakfast only.

Restaurants. *Nova Lisboa* (M), Rua Morais José Sacramento. *Sintra Transmontana* (M), Rua dos Frades.

CAMPING. There are campsites at the following places: Chaves (São Roque, Rua São João de Deus); Lamego (Dr. João de Almeida); Mirandela (Tres Rios/Maravilha); Mondim de Basto; Vila Flor; Vila Real.

PLACES OF INTEREST. Notable buildings and museums are perhaps a bit scarcer in Trás-os-Montes than elsewhere in Portugal, but there is still quite a lot to see. As the region is comparatively so poor, buildings tend to be in worse shape than elsewhere, but that can add a touch of extra faded attraction. Museums are usually open daily, except Mondays and public holidays, 10–5, but check locally for times, especially important around here. Most close for up to two hours over an indeterminate lunch. Entrance fees are between 150$00 and 300$00. As well as the places listed below and in our text, there are also numerous churches to see. Many will be closed and you'll need to find the keyholder's whereabouts in a nearby cottage or garden.

Aldeia do Romeu, Mirandela. Charming little **museum.**

Bragança. Abade de Baçal Museum, Rua Abilio Beça. Very agreeable small museum, with antiquities of the region, Roman funerary steles, paintings, costumes, Iron Age pigs, and general ethnographic material.
Castle, with a military museum in the small rooms all the way up the inside of the keep; surprisingly well displayed.
Domus Municipalis. Unusually shaped 12th-century city hall, rare Romanesque survival. Key from one of small houses in front of the building.

Chaves. Regional Museum and Military Museum. Housed in the castle keep. More archeology, coins, African art, militaria.

Lamego. Lamego Museum, Largo de Camões. Paintings (16th to 18th centuries); glorious tapestries (mainly Flemish); sacred art, vestments, etc., from the former Convent of Chagas.

Vila Flor. Solar dos Lemos. Country museum with Iron Age granite animals. Closed 12.30–2.30 and Tues.

Vila Real. Ethnographic Museum. Regional display; worth visiting if you're in town.
Solar de Mateus, the famous house, known from the labels on millions of bottles of wine, 3½ km. (2 miles) east of town on N322. Quite long guided tour of fine interior—library, rich furniture, carved ceilings, Baroque chapel.

SPECIAL EVENTS. For further details and exact dates, consult local tourist offices. **July.** *São Tiago's Fair* at Mirandela, with traditional dancing, games and fireworks, late July, early Aug. **August.** *Festival of St. Barbara* at Miranda do Douro, mid-month. **September.** *Pardon of Nossa Senhora dos Remedios* at Lamego, with both religious and secular festivities, as well as processions in local costumes, early in month. *Pilgrimage to Nossa Senhora do Nazo,* 11 km. (7 miles), and folk dances by the *pauliteiros,* Miranda do Douro, early in month. Grape harvest festivals in the Upper Douro valley, near Miranda do Douro, late Sept./early Oct. **No-**

vember. The people from roundabout stream to the *Todos os Santos Fair* at Chaves, first week.

MADEIRA

When the Portuguese seafarers sent out by Henry the Navigator in 1419 sailed in sight of a wooded island some 900 km. (560 miles) southwest of Lisbon, they named it *ilha da madeira* (island of wood). The following year they returned to Madeira to begin its colonization in the name of Portugal. A more romantic if unreliable legend is that the first people to land there were two English lovers, Robert McKean and Anne d'Orset, fleeing from Anne's angry aristocratic parents.

So began the history of Madeira—no traces of any previous civilization are evident on the island—and the volcanic terrain was brought under cultivation after extensive burning of the natural forestation to grow first cereals, then sugar cane, and, from the beginning of the 17th century, vines for wine production.

In the early 19th century, during the Napoleonic Wars in Europe, the island was twice occupied by British troops, but has otherwise remained unmolested. Shortly after Portugal became a republic in 1910, Madeira and the other smaller islands of the archipelago achieved self-government under a special statute and became an "autonomous" region in 1976. The islanders are fiercely proud of their independence to this day.

It is still possible to approach Madeira by sea, although there are few cruise liners these days, and indeed this will give you the best perspective of the island. However, you are more likely to come in over the sea by air, land at the now enlarged runway of Santa Catarina Airport, and take a taxi along the steep-sided coastal road to the capital, Funchal, 20 km. (12 miles) away.

Madeira delights the traveler at first sight. The words "Enchanted Island," often used to describe it, take on real meaning as a panorama of

colors and shapes unfold—flowers everywhere, steep but richly green terraced slopes, all combined with the warm, semi-tropical air and a comfortable sense that as a visitor you are welcome.

Everyone who is involved in tourism on Madeira is well disposed towards visitors, and they almost all speak good English. The island's government is keen to make the tourist industry pay, and who can blame
them. They have ideal conditions: breathtaking scenery, unpolluted sea,
fresh fish, a wonderful selection of home-produced fruit, and a climate
with only gentle variations, winter and summer, day and night.

It is hard to make up your mind what to do first on this tiny island,
only 57 km. (35 miles) long and 22 km. (13 miles) wide. There's so much
to see and do: browse around the old parts of Funchal, shop for Madeira
wine, local embroidered goods, or wickerwork, or take walks along the
irrigation canals (*levadas*) which criss-cross the terrain, giving access to
otherwise inaccessible areas.

Life on the Terraces

Madeira is a steep mountaintop, the tip of a long-extinct, submerged
volcano thrusting up from the sea. On its southern slope Funchal rises
in semi-circular tiers, spreading out and up into the surrounding vegetation. It is a wonderful sight by day, and even more so at night when the
city lights up.

Funchal has something over one-third of the island's population, about
100,000 inhabitants. There are a few smaller towns such as Machico,
where the explorers first landed, Ribeira Brava and Câmara de Lobos on
the south coast, São Vicente and Porto Moniz on the north coast—all
these are becoming more developed.

The rest of the population is scattered, living a lonely, hardworking life
on patches of land carved into seemingly impossible terraces. Peasants
from the Portuguese province of the Minho, and some from Flanders, were
the first settlers, followed by many others of different origins. Today, many
Madeirans are fair with light eyes. They are thickset and hardy, and in
the countryside wear knitted oiled wool caps covering their ears to keep
out the mist and rain.

While human settlers were able to work on the rocky slopes, animals
were not, and neither horses, nor mules, nor donkeys were domesticated
as beasts of burden. All was, and still is, done on foot—wicker baskets
were made for carrying most goods, and skins for the grape juice for wine-
making. The tourist is well advised to follow this example—the best way
to explore can be on foot—and high heels are neither advisable nor necessary, except to go to the casino!

Apart from the production of Madeira wine, the two main industries
are wickerwork and embroidery, and these have been developed into a sophisticated handicraft business which keeps many Madeirans in work.
You will want to squeeze at least a bread basket into your luggage, so attractive are the wicker goods which range from simple table mats to enormous pieces of furniture. The main center for this work is Camacha, to
the northeast of Funchal.

If you visit this part of the island in spring, you will see fields full of
curious-looking tree stumps, like overgrown denuded vines. These are the
willow trees which have been stripped of their branches, which can be seen

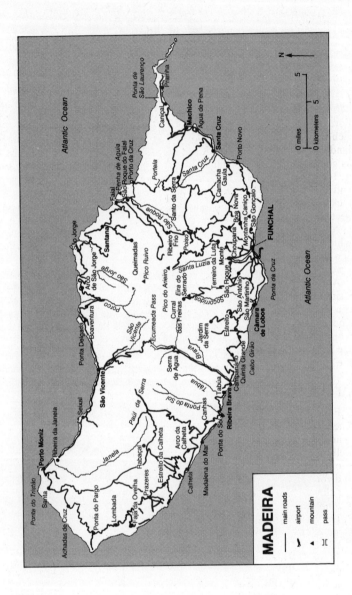

MADEIRA

—— main roads

✈ airport

▲ mountain

)(pass

stacked up to dry against a convenient wall or fence, their bark having been peeled off by water or steam. These supple branches are woven into the shapes and forms you can buy in the Camacha warehouse or all over Funchal.

Embroidery work is said to have been started on Madeira over 100 years ago by an Englishwoman, Mrs. Phelps. She opened a school to teach needlework to help the women of Funchal whose families were suffering hardship because of a blight that killed a year's harvest of grapes. It is possible, however, that the art of embroidery was brought to the island by the Flemish settlers centuries before.

However little they know about Madeira, most people have heard of Madeira wine. Its history is long, as the island's vine stock was first imported from Crete at the beginning of the 15th century and planted in the rich volcanic soil along the sunny south coast. Gradually more and more land was given over to vineyards as the resulting wine became recognized as good quality, and a commercial treaty between England and Portugal in 1660 encouraged export until the trade reached its height in the 18th and 19th centuries. The problems of blight and phylloxera were valiantly tackled in the 1870s by the ancestors of families whose names are still connected with the wine business, such as Blandy and Leacock.

A whole tradition surrounds the vintage, the picking of the grapes, which begins in late August and goes on until early November. Madeira is a fortified wine—that is, grape alcohol is added after fermentation, a practice that was started in the last century to aid preservation of the wine.

An official Wine Festival takes place in September, when tourists can visit villages and participate in the picking and mashing of the grapes. You can taste the wine at any time, however, in the Madeira Company's Wine Lodge near the Tourist Office on Avenida Arriaga, Funchal's main street, where there is also a small museum. You can also visit the Museum of the Madeira Wine Institute, which controls production and quality for the island's main industry, in Rua 5 de Outubro.

Funchal

Funchal is an ideal holiday resort: everything is within easy distance. There are no beaches on Madeira, except one very small one at Prainha near the eastern tip of the island, far from Funchal, but all hotels have well-maintained sea-water swimming pools, and there is a large public pool complex, the Lido, just west of town. Wherever you stay, you will find yourself in a garden or a banana grove, and there is something flowering all year round, whether it be bougainvillea, jasmine, orchids, jacaranda, hibiscus or a dozen other semi-tropical species.

The port of Funchal, once home to cruise liners, is now busier with cargo containers and pleasure craft lying at anchor in the new marina, from where boat trips up and down the coast can be arranged. The town's main avenue is bustling, even noisy with traffic at certain times of day, but much restructuring of the town center is being done to make life more pleasant for the visitor.

Back from the commercial center are straggling streets climbing up away from the sea, quiet squares paved with black and white mosaic, and a number of architectural gems to remind you of Funchal's 500-year history. On the main square, the blue-mauve blossoms of the jacaranda trees

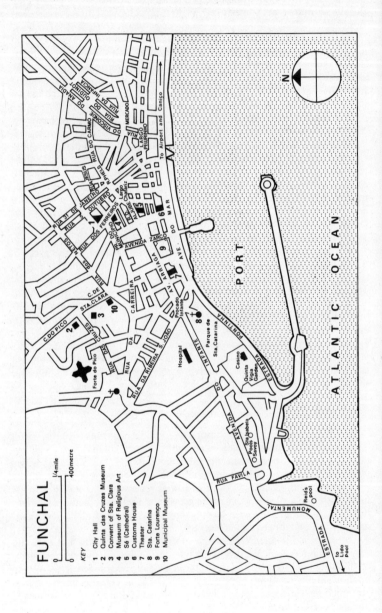

FUNCHAL

0 ¼mile
0 400metre

KEY
1 City Hall
2 Quinta das Cruzes Museum
3 Convent of Sta. Clara
4 Museum of Religious Art
5 Sé (Cathedral)
6 Customs House
7 Theater
8 Sta. Catarina
9 Forte Lourenço
10 Municipal Museum

in full spring flower are so bright that they draw the eye away from the buildings—the Jesuit church, the town hall in black basalt with white-washed walls, overlooking the picturesque old town, and the Museum of Sacred Art, once the bishop's palace, which is well worth a visit. In it are gathered together, from all the churches in the island, 15th- and 16th-century retables and paintings of the Portuguese and Flemish schools. The chapel was the first place of worship put up by the settlers, many of whom came from Bruges; it was therefore to the artists of their home town that they entrusted the painting of the holy pictures. These were paid for not in money but in sugar, long the main wealth of the island, as may be seen by the coat-of-arms of Funchal, with its five sugar loaves.

The Sé (late 15th-century cathedral) is at the end of Avenida Arriaga. It has a beautifully simple exterior, in contrast with a fairly elaborate interior. Make sure to see the choir stalls, retable, and the carved ceiling made from local juniper tree wood; the church treasury includes a vermeil crucifix, gift of King Manuel I of Portugal.

Sugar has also left its trace in the beautiful Quinta das Cruzes, now a museum and the former dwelling place of Zarco, discoverer, with Tristão Vaz Teixeira, of the island. The furniture is made of wood from Brazil (mahogany or rosewood) in a shape called *caixa de açucar,* for the cupboards and chests and boxes were made from the crates used to ship the raw sugar.

There, as in the case of many other country houses or *quintas* in Madeira, full of fine old English furniture and silver and East India Company china, the gardens are still the greatest beauty. Orchids of several varieties are a delight, and even the most lukewarm nature lover will be dazzled by the lush display of flowers from all parts of the world. Plants and flowers can be bought from these gardens.

The church of the Convent of Santa Clara contains the tomb of Zarco. The convent itself was founded by Zarco's two daughters, who are buried in the cloisters. It was the nuns from this foundation who used to take refuge in Curral das Freiras from the attentions of marauding pirates.

Away from the town center, in the modern hotel zone west of Funchal, is another attractive small church, the chapel of Nossa Senhora da Penha de França. It lies on the street of the same name, almost hidden in a lush garden. Built in 1662, it has an interesting history, being a center of pilgrimage until the end of the 18th century. Although it is usually closed during the week, an English Mass is said on some Sundays.

The English Church, on Rua de Quebra Costas, is very active, and the resident Chaplain is always glad to have visitors. It is set in quiet gardens away from the bustle of the town. The church also boasts a well-stocked library with more than 2,500 books.

Many other buildings can be glimpsed just by strolling around the old part of town or near the waterfront. The Customs House, facing the harbor on a picturesque street, is a national monument, but was actually used for its original purpose until fairly recently.

Funchal also has many parks and gardens which are well maintained and a joy to walk through. In addition to savoring the sight and the scent of the flowers, you will probably see dozens of curious, almost tame lizards sunning themselves on the paths. The Parque de Santa Catarina, on the way from the main hotel area to the center of Funchal, is especially delightful. One glorious garden which should not be missed is the Jardim

Botânico, in the hills northeast of the town, on the road to Camacha. You can also get there by bus from Avenida do Mar. Here the plants are well laid out and marked (in Portuguese and Latin) and there is a wonderful view over Funchal Bay.

Don't forget to visit the open-air market (*Mercado dos Lavradores*) on the eastern side of town, especially in the mornings when it is at its busiest. All the locally grown fruit and vegetables are sold there, from the humble but ever-present banana to more exotic varieties such as avocados (*abacates*), custard apples (*anonas*) and passion fruit (*maracujá*). This fruit is also used to make soft drinks and to flavor ice cream. The fresh fish you will be offered in the restaurants is also on sale, notably the black *espada* or scabbard fish, fearsome-looking but delicious to eat, which is fished from the deepest ocean waters and is very plentiful.

Exploring the Island

The visitor who stays the whole time in Funchal may miss what most of the island is about. One way of getting an interesting perspective of Madeira is to take one of the many boat trips which are offered from the marina. What an inaccessible place it must have seemed to those early explorers! The mountainous terrain ends abruptly at the sea with many rocky inlets and some incredibly high cliffs such as Cabo Girão, rising 580 meters (1,900 ft.) above sea level.

To tour the island by land, you can take one of the organized bus trips—though not recommended if you suffer from motion sickness!—or hire a car from one of the several agencies. Distances are not great, but they are deceptive, as the roads are mostly narrow, steep and tortuous and in some places not well surfaced. You need three days to see all the island, if you are based in Funchal.

It is well worth the effort, however. The scenery of the interior is stunning, with peaks rising to over 1,800 meters (6,000 ft.) and a jagged landscape; the north coast is wild and less inhabited, the western end is wooded and cool, and the eastern tip is a land of barren reddish rock stretching away into the deep blue ocean.

Monte and Terreiro da Luta

Monte is now a suburb of Funchal, six km. (four miles) inland on the road to Choupana. The church of Nossa Senhora do Monte, set in beautiful gardens, is the burial place of the Austro-Hungarian Emperor, Charles I, who died here in 1922. Two km. (a mile) up the road is Terreiro da Luta, with a breathtaking view from the Monument of Our Lady of Peace over the Bay of Funchal. From either place you can take the famous "toboggan" rides back to town. These *carrinhos de cesto* are actually padded wicker sofas mounted on wooden runners, controlled by two white-suited men gripping ropes with which they guide the conveyance, either pulling or steering from behind. It is an exhilarating ride over narrow cobbled back streets, often quite steep, which gets you back to Funchal in about half the time it took to drive up the road. This mode of travel was once the only form of transport on Madeira, first for goods and later for people. Man-powered carriages were once common, until they were taken over by ox-drawn vehicles. Sadly, even these are now rarely seen.

Choupana and Camacha

About 29 km. (18 miles) to the north of Funchal via Terreiro da Luta, the highway climbs to around 1,500 meters (5,000 ft.). Just below the top, turn right for Choupana, set amid pines and eucalyptus; then go on to Camacha, a charming mountain village and the center of the wicker industry. The basket-makers' cooperative oversees the handicraft from the cutting of the willows to the finishing touch of varnish. The warehouse-shop is well stocked with beautifully made goods, and there is a restaurant and bar.

Continuing through the pinewoods, you will reach Caniço, where there is the Jardim do Sol bar-restaurant. Turn right for Funchal.

Eira do Serrado and Grande Curral

About 19 km. (12 miles) to the northeast take the road to the Pico dos Barcelos (five km., three miles, from Funchal, panorama), continue to Eira do Serrado, 1,026 meters (3,366 ft.) overlooking the Grande Curral, crater of an extinct volcano.

It is in Curral das Freiras that the traveler will come upon the true grandeur of Madeira. Leaning out over a seemingly bottomless pit, he will discover, hundreds of feet below, a village hidden from pirate marauders by the surrounding mountains. The name derives from the early days of island settlement, when nuns from the Convent of Santa Clara in Funchal used to take refuge up here when the town came under attack.

The imposing mass of Pico Ruivo overlooks the basalt mountain range, its jagged ridges towering against the sky like strange dream cities. Colorful roads wind around the mountainside, affording an overall view of the wonderful landscape; a ray of sun pierces the mist, revealing small houses nestling higher than the eagles and fields no bigger than straw mats clinging to the steep ridges. Streams run down every slope into this central reservoir; the water channeled in *levadas* bordered by a narrow footway, feeds a network of irrigation canals reaching to every cultivated corner of the island. This wild, lost valley is particularly impressive when the mist wreathes the surrounding peaks.

Câmara de Lobos and Cabo Girao

Eight km. (five miles) west of Funchal is Câmara de Lobos—the name means "chamber of sea-lions" as these animals used to thrive in the area. Here fishermen drag their boats up on the stony beach and hang out their nets from mast to mast. Well placed between Funchal and the vineyards rising in tiers on the sunniest slope of the island, the town is rapidly losing its colorful simplicity and is turning into a tourist mecca. Sir Winston Churchill liked the place and painted it (you can buy postcards of him caught in the act), but one wonders if he would do so today.

Go five km. (three miles) along the main road which winds towards Estreito through the vineyards, and turn left at the sign to Cabo Girão. The road ends on a terrace providing a sweeping view of the entire headland, one of the highest cliffs in the world. Below you can see the slender ledges which have somehow been terraced for cultivation.

Continuing along the coastal highway you will come to Campanário and Ribeira Brava, a good sized seaside town with a pleasant pebble beach. Turn inland up the canyon and climb to Encumeada Pass, 1,000 meters (3,300 ft.) high and 42 km. (26 miles) from Funchal. Just south of there, near Serra de Agua, is Madeira's only pousada, which has dramatic views. It is small, with a restaurant. This is an ideal spot for those keen on walking, painting or photography.

The highway continues on to São Vicente on the north coast.

Santa Cruz and Machico

The coastal highway leads east from Funchal via the Montanha lookout point and Caniço (see above) to Santa Cruz (19 km, 12 miles), which has an interesting 16th-century town hall.

Some ten km. (six miles) further on, the road leads to Machico, its fine stony beach and 15th-century church. Legend says that the previously mentioned English lovers, in flight from her disapproving family, were shipwrecked on the shore and after her death he, soon afterwards, died of grief. The ship's crew survived, and built a raft, but were captured by Barbary pirates, who sold them into slavery; it is said that one of the men sent word to Portugal, so that Zarco could chart his course to the island. In fact, Zarco and his sailors landed there long afterward, in 1419, at the very mouth of the river that flows out through the strand of Machico, and found the great cedar tree under which the lovers were buried. This beautiful outlying valley, the attractive fishing port, and the nearness of the long headland of São Lourenço—with its theatrical sunsets—are all making Machico another tourist center.

At Prainha, near the eastern tip of the island, lies Madeira's only sandy beach, small and rather cove-like, below the hilltop chapel of Our Lady of Charity.

The highway now extends beyond Caniçal into the tip of Madeira Island, Ponta de São Lourenço, where the landscape is quite different from that of the green interior—barren rock contrasting rather beautifully with the deep blue of the ocean.

The Interior and Porta da Cruz

The center of the island is mountainous, separating the north and south coasts. There is a good highway to the top of Pico de Arieiro (1,830 meters, 6,000 ft.). From Curral das Freiras a road leads through the Lombo Grande to the island's loftiest peak, the Pico Ruivo (1,890 meters, 6,200 ft.), a good five hours' hike. An alternative recommended itinerary: by car to Queimadas de Santana, a quaint village with thatched roofs, then two hours on foot. It's advisable to hire a guide, owing to sudden thick mists. At the top there is a Tourist Office refuge, or *casa de abrigo*.

Porta da Cruz lies 38 km. (24 miles) from Funchal on the north coast via Poiso (1,490 meters, 4,900 ft.). An alternative route is through Caniço and Santo da Serra, emerging at the Poiso turn-off junction. From Portela you look out over Porto da Cruz and Faial, separated by the Penha d'Aguia cliff. There is a fine view on the way down of the sea, and mountains. Return trip via Santana, the road winds towards Ribeiro and Poiso. The whole area is rich in plant life.

The North Coast

This region has magnificent scenery, more untamed than the south coast. The most direct route is the road described above going through Monte, Terreiro da Luta, and Poiso, and then down again through Santana. Follow right along the north coast via Ponta Delgada (the road takes a brief swerve inland), São Vicente to Porto Moniz at the island's north-westernmost point. This is a charming little village with two or three restaurants and a couple of pensions which appear to be the locals' only livelihood. On a somewhat exposed stretch of coastline, the once famous natural swimming pools are not much used. Return by descending in a southerly direction, then going eastwards via Ribeira Brava. Calheta has a parish church with a mudejar ceiling, and there is a side trip to the 25 cascades of Rabaçal, the highest of which plunges down from over 90 meters (300 ft.).

A new road has been opened from near Rabaçal northwest to the coast at Porto Moniz. It crosses high, barren country which may be shrouded in mist but is still a short cut avoiding the long drive around the south coast. If you choose to approach Porto Moniz from the São Vicente road, or return that way, you have a treat in store. The road clings to a cliff face, passing under many dark, dripping tunnels, with spectacular views. One waterfall literally cascades over the road.

Porto Santo

An hour and a half away by fast hydrofoil, or just 15 minutes by plane, lies the only other inhabited island of the Madeira archipelago—Porto Santo. Quite different in character from the main island, it has a chalky soil, no high mountains, and is fringed by a golden beach. This is where the Madeirans go for their beach outings or holidays, and it is well worth the trip over for a day.

Porto Santo has a drier climate than Madeira, and in fact suffers frequent droughts, making the locals depend to a large extent on produce brought over from the main island. It is an ideal place to take long walks, lie on the beach where in summer months the facilities are quite good—there is even a windsurfing center—or eat fresh fish in one of the several restaurants around the island. There is no public transport, but taxis are cheap, and you can also hire bicycles in the small main town, Vila Baleira.

The town has some historical interest too. Christopher Columbus went to Porto Santo, where he met and married Isabel Moniz, the daughter of the island's administrator. The house where he is supposed to have lived stands behind the parish church, which has a 17th-century painting of Mary Magdalene at the feet of Christ.

PRACTICAL INFORMATION FOR MADEIRA

WHEN TO COME. There is no one outstandingly "best" season for Madeira: all are pleasant. The year-round climate is temperate, although the humidity level is usually quite high. The thermometer never really soars, thanks to the cool mountain air that immediately makes its presence felt when a passing cloud covers the sun, or just as you begin on the third winding curve up among the exotic trees. Flowers bloom virtually the whole year round.

August is not the most favored month, since sometimes the island is enveloped in a shroud of mist called the *capacete*. But the springtime is wonderful, and so is the fall. Most of the rainfall comes then, in heavy showers, but rarely in prolonged periods.

Whatever time of year you go, remember that it is always much cooler up on the mountains, and that the north coast may be more windy than the south.

TOURIST OFFICES. The Regional Tourist Office in Funchal is at Ave. Arriaga 18 (tel. 091 29057 or 091 25658); open Mon. to Sat. 9–7, Sun. 9–1. This office has currency exchange facilities. There are also small offices at the airport, in Machico, and on Porto Santo.

MAGAZINE. The *Madeira Island Bulletin* is a useful publication in English, giving details of events and names of shops and restaurants.

TELEPHONE CODE. The telephone code for Madeira (and Porto Santo) is 091. This code must be used when calling from outside the island, but not when you are already on the island.

HOW TO GET TO MADEIRA. By Plane. From the U.S. the route is via Lisbon. *TAP Air Portugal* runs several flights a day by Boeing 737 from Lisbon to Funchal, taking 1 hour 40 mins. *TAP* also operate flights from London to Funchal twice a week.

By Ship. There are no regular passenger services between Lisbon, Madeira and the Azores, but Funchal is a port of call on many cruises from other places. One company, *Empresa Nacional Madeirense,* runs a cargo ship once a week from Lisbon to Funchal and will carry a few passengers.

HOW TO GET TO PORTO SANTO. By Plane. *TAP's* regional airline has a frequent service—practically a shuttle—from Funchal's Santa Catarina airport, taking 15 mins. The timetable varies according to season: best check at the Tourist Office in Funchal.

By Hydrofoil. The *Independência* hydrofoil service runs from Funchal to Porto Santo, taking 90 mins. It runs once daily in winter and twice daily in summer, when it is possible to make the round trip within a day. Tickets should be bought in advance from the office in the marina.

One word of warning: the crossing can be quite rough, even though the *Independência* travels at speeds of up to 30 knots (60 km. per hour). No refreshments are served on board.

FUNCHAL HOTELS AND RESTAURANTS   •

Hotels. As well as conventional hotels, Funchal has a good choice of albergarias, apartment hotels and pensions. Albergarias are older style establishments with character, usually serving breakfast only. Apartment hotels consist of apartments all equipped with baths and kitchenettes, with mini-markets nearby. Funchal has a large number of pensions with accommodations at reasonable prices; all rooms have baths and most serve only breakfast.

Hotels in the Deluxe price category are all of international class and in superb locations, mostly on the outskirts of Funchal.

Deluxe

Casino Park, Ave. do Infante (tel. 091 33111). 400 rooms with bath, 22 suites, 32 studios. Conference facilities for 650 people; pool, disco, tennis. Gaming rooms in casino open 4 P.M.–3 A.M. Bring your passport. Designed by Oscar Niemeyer, principal architect of Brasilia. AE, DC, MC, V.

Madeira Palácio, Estrada Monumental (tel. 091 30001). 260 rooms with bath, 18 suites. Conference facilities for 250. Heated pool, disco, tennis. AE, DC, MC, V.

Madeira Sheraton, Largo António Nobre (tel. 091 31031). 500 rooms with bath, 19 suites. Conference facilities. 3 pools, tennis, disco. AE, DC, MC, V.

Reid's, Estrada Monumental (tel. 091 23000). 168 rooms, 12 suites. 150 rooms with bath, 15 suites. Conference facilities for 300 people. 2 heated seawater pools, bathing jetty, nightclub, 10 acres of superb sub-tropical gardens. Famous for over half a century, full of atmosphere but well modernized, including airconditioning. Tennis, all facilities. AE, DC, MC, V.

Savoy, Ave. do Infante (tel. 091 22031). 347 rooms with bath, 12 suites. Conference facilities and banqueting. Seafront bathing area including two heated pools and children's pool. Tennis, disco. AE, DC, MC, V.

Expensive

Alto Lido, Estrada Monumental (tel. 091 29197). 115 rooms. Apartment hotel with pool and nightclub. AE, DC, MC.

Catedral, Rua do Aljube 13 (tel. 291 30091). 25 rooms with bath. Albergaria in city center, with roof terrace. AE, DC, MC.

Do Mar, Estrada Monumental (tel. 291 31001). 135 rooms. Apartment hotel. Pool, nightclub. AE, DC, MC.

Girassol, Estrada Monumental (tel. 291 31051). 132 rooms with bath. Heated pool, sports facilities, nightclub. AE, DC, MC, V.

Monte Rosa, Rua de João Tavira (tel. 291 29091). 38 rooms with bath. Albergaria. AE, DC, MC.

Navio Azul, Estrada Monumental (tel. 291 25580). 42 rooms, 4 suites. Apartment hotel with pool. AE.

Penha da França, Rua Penha da França (tel. 291 29087). 35 rooms with bath or shower. Albergaria in charming old estate with fine garden and pool. Bar with snacks; light suppers served. Recommended.

Quinta do Sol, Rua Dr. Pita 6 (tel. 291 31151). 105 rooms with bath, 11 suites. Next door to Country Club's pool, tennis courts and 18-hole putting course, all available to residents. Also own fresh-water pool. AE, DC, MC, V.

Santa Isabel, Ave. do Infante (tel. 291 23111). 68 rooms with bath, 10 suites. Rooftop pool with sun terrace. AE, DC, MC, V.

Raga, Estrada Monumental (tel. 291 33001). 159 rooms with bath. Pool, nightclub. AE, DC, MC, V.

São João, Rua da Maravilhas 74 (tel. 091 46111). 192 rooms with bath, 16 suites. 2 pools, nightclub. Airconditioned. AE, DC, MC, V.

Vila Ramos, Azinhaga da Casa Branca 7 (tel. 291 31181). 104 rooms with bath, 6 suites. Pool, disco. AE, DC, MC, V.

Moderate

Buganvilia, Caminho Velho da Ajuda (tel. 291 31015). 106 rooms. Apartment hotel with pool, restaurant, nightclub. DC.

Carmo, Travessa do Rego 10 (tel. 291 29001). 80 rooms with bath. Sauna, rooftop pool with sun terrace. In city center.

Casa Branca, Caminho Velho da Ajuda (tel. 291 30043). 41 rooms. Apartment hotel with pool. DC, MC.

Duas Torres, Estrada Monumental (tel. 291 30061). 118 rooms. Apartment hotel with pool, tennis, restaurant and nightclub. AE, DC, MC.

Estrelícia, Caminho Velho da Ajuda (tel. 291 30131). 148 rooms with bath. Pool, nightclub. AE, DC.

Florassol, Estrada Monumental 306 (tel. 291 33121). 94 rooms. Apartment hotel with pool and restaurant. AE, DC, MC.

Golden Gate, Ave. Arriaga 21 (tel. 291 20081). 35 rooms with bath. Popular but noisy. AE.

Gorgulho, Rua do Gorgulho (tel. 291 30111). 115 rooms. Apartment hotel with pool, tennis, nightclub. AE, DC, MC.

Greco, Rua do Carmo 16 (tel. 291 30081). 28 rooms. Pension. MC.

Lido-Sol, Estrada Monumental (tel. 291 29006). 39 rooms. Apartment hotel with pool and restaurant.

Madeira, Rua Ivens 21 (tel. 091 30071). 26 rooms with bath. 5 suites. Pool. Breakfast only. AE, DC, MC.

Mimosa, Caminho Velho da Ajuda (tel. 091 31021). 100 rooms. Apartment hotel with pool and restaurant. DC.

Monte Carlo, Calçada da Saúde 10 (tel. 091 26131). 45 rooms with bath, 3 suites. Pool. AE.

Orquídea, Rua dos Netos 71 (tel. 091 26091). 70 rooms with bath. In city center. AE, DC, MC.

Santa Maria, Rua João de Deus 26 (tel. 091 25271). 83 rooms with bath, 8 suites. Back rooms are quieter. Pool, good restaurant; central.

Inexpensive

Astoria, Rua João Gago 10 (tel. 091 23820). 16 rooms. Pension.

Colombo, Rua da Carreira 182 (tel. 091 25231). 25 rooms. Pension.

Flamenga, Rua dos Aranhas 45 (tel. 091 29041). 35 rooms.

Monumental, Estrada Monumental 306 (tel. 091 26117). 24 rooms. Pension just outside town, near the big hotels.

Parque, Campo da Barca 15 (tel. 091 25208). 22 rooms.

Phelps, Largo do Phelps 4 (tel. 091 25214). 18 rooms. Pension.

Santa Clara, Calçado do Pico 16B (tel. 091 24194). 14 rooms. Pension in fine old house with garden, outside the center.

These pensions only serve breakfast.

Restaurants. Here is a small selection of the hundreds of restaurants in and around Funchal. As the local cooking is invariably good, it is worth while being adventurous and trying others on impulse, bearing in mind that menus can be limited in the cheaper ones. Many restaurants advertise in the *Madeira Island Bulletin,* a useful publication in English available at the Tourist Office.

Expensive

Caravela, Ave. do Mar 15. With splendid sea view. AE, DC, MC, V.

Charola, Rua Dr. Pita 6A.

Golfinho, Largo de Corpo Santo 21. Specializes in seafood. In old part of city. AE, DC, MC, V.

Kon-Tiki, Rua do Favilla 9 (tel. 091 28737). Interesting food; reservations recommended.

Miami, Caminho do Amparo.

Reid's Hotel Grill, (tel. 091 23001). For a special meal in luxurious surroundings. Excellent international cuisine; dress formal; dinner only; reservations required. AE, DC, MC, V.

Romana, Largo do Corpo Santo 15. Top quality restaurant in old part of city. Closed Sun. AE, DC, MC, V.

Taverna Real, off Rua Fernão de Ornelas. Madeiran and Austrian food in splendidly restored 15th-century wine cellar. Fados; dinner only. Closed Sun.

Moderate

A Seta, Estrada do Livramento 80. Fun place with good food, on outskirts of city.

Café Berlin, Estrada Monumental 219. German owned, with garden. Recommended.

Cervejaria Coral, Rua António José Almeida. Outdoor terrace in city center. Local "Coral" beer is excellent.

Espadarte, Estrada da Boa Nova 5. Towards Botanical Gardens. Friendly.

Minas Gerais, Ave. do Infante 2. Old-established central café-restaurant.

Patio, Ave. Zarco 21. Tables set in elegant covered patio. Highly recommended. Next door to arts complex and English bookshop.

Tahiti, Rua das Pretas 19. Small and friendly, with good local cooking and natural foods.

Inexpensive

Apolo, in the Cathedral Square. Good, generous meals; papers and films on sale.

O Bau, Estrada Monumental. Beyond Hotel Girassol. Small, friendly; delicious local food.

Estrela do Mar, Largo do Corpo Santo 1–7. Very good seafood and own lobster tanks. AE, DC, MC, V.

Gavina's, Rua do Gorgulho. Near Lido complex. Fine simple fish menu in unpretentious surroundings overlooking the sea. AE, DC.

A Gruta, Estrada da Pontinha. A cave in the old defensive walls, with outdoor patio overlooking the harbor.

Joe's Snack, Rua Penha da Franca. In garden of Quinta da Penha da França. Salads and light meals, lunch only. **Joe's Bar** beneath, open in the evening; friendly atmosphere.

Hotels and Restaurants Around the Island

(All hotel rooms have private bath)

Calheta. Restaurant. *Estrela* (I). Simple local food.

Camacha. Restaurants. *Café Relógio* (M). Regional dishes. Wicker-work for sale. *José Nobrega* (M), Sítio da Igreja. Wickerwork shop has a restaurant and bar.

Câmara de Lobos. Restaurants. *Capoeira* (M), Estrada de Câmara de Lobos. *Coral Bar* (M), Largo da Republica 2. Good fresh fish and salads. *Ribamar* (M). Regional food.

Caniço. *Apartment Hotel Inter-Atlas* (M), Garajau (between Funchal and Caniço), (tel. 091 932421). 133 rooms. 2 pools, restaurant, nightclub. AE. *Pensão Residência Galomar* (M), Caniço de Baixo (tel. 091 932443). 36 rooms. Pool, tennis, restaurant. *Tourist Complex* (M), Caniço de Baixo (tel. 091 932232). 47 units.
Restaurant. *O Boeiro* (E). Figueirinhas. Local specialties and steaks. AE, DC, MC, V. *Jardim do Sol* (M).

Faial. *Casa de Chá do Faia* (M), Lombo de Baixo. Superb setting in the hills near Santana. Well-cooked regional food. Comfortable.

Machico. *Atlantis* (L), Água de Pena (tel. 091 962811). 266 rooms with bath, 24 suites. 2 pools, tennis, nightclub, all facilities. Marvelous views. AE, DC, MC. *Dom Pedro* (E), Estrada de São Roque (tel. 091 962751). 218 rooms with bath, 14 suites. Heated pool, tennis, nightclub, private beach, windsurfing. AE, DC, MC. *Matur Tourist Complex* (E), Água de Pena (tel. 091 962511). 368 serviced apartments and villas. 2 pools, tennis, restaurant, nightclub. Bridge club, all facilities. AE, DC, MC. *Residêncial Salomar* (E), (tel. 091 932443). 44 rooms with bath. Pool; breakfast only.
Restaurants. This town is growing, and you will find other reasonable restaurants as well as the following. *Facho* (M), Praça Salazar. Excellent local dishes. Also has a few rooms with bath. AE, DC, MC. *Luigi* (M). Real Italian food. AE, DC, MC. *Mercado Velho* (I). Good local food, also snacks. AE, DC, MC.

Porta da Cruz. Restaurant. *Penha d'Ave* (I).

Porto Moniz. *Lar da Baia* (I), (tel. 091 85106). 11 rooms. *Pensão Fernandes* (I), (tel. 091 85147). 10 rooms. Bar, restaurant. Homely, but good value.
Restaurant. *Cachalote* (I). Rustic building on rocks by the sea; fine for fish.

Ribeira Brava. *Bravamar,* (tel. 091 952224). Brand new; 36 rooms with more planned.
Restaurant. *A Parada* (I).

Santa Cruz. Restaurant. *Varanda* (M). At the airport, with good view.

Santo da Serra. 9-hole golf course. **Restaurant.** Comfortable club house with snack bar. Check if open at your hotel or Tourist Office.

Serra de Agua. *Pousada dos Vinháticos* (E), tel. 62344. 10 rooms with bath. In scenic location high in central mountains. Reservations recommended for this state-run inn. Restaurant also open to non-residents.

São Vicente. Restaurant. *Galeão* (I). A good place for lunch on a drive.

Porto Santo

The island has two good-quality hotels, a couple of pensions and some holiday apartments for hire. Most of the villages have small restaurants with good cooking. The only town is Vila Baleira. The many beaches are sandy and clean and wide.

Porto Santo (E), tel. 091 982381. 91 rooms with bath, 2 suites. Pool, tennis, restaurant. AE, DC, MC. *Praia Dourada* (M), tel. 091 982315. 35 rooms with bath. AE, DC, MC. *Pensão Central* (M), tel. 091 982226. 12 rooms with bath. *Pensão Palmeira* (I), tel. 091 982112. 23 rooms with bath.

Restaurants. *Baiana* (M). Snack bar and café; regional food. *Toca do Pescador* (M), Ponta da Calheta. Good fresh fish.

PLACES OF INTEREST. The following museums and other places of interest to visitors are all in or near Funchal. There are very few buildings of note around the island, the main sights are those of landscape and the evidences of the Madeirans' hard work to tame it to man's will.

Cathedral (Sé), Ave. Arriaga. Memorable choir stalls and roof. Treasury of Sacred Art.
Convent of Santa Clara. Fine cloisters.
Customs House. Closed weekends.
English Church, Rua de Quebra Costas. A 10-minute walk from the center of Funchal. Library open every morning except Mon.
Fire Brigade Museum, Estrada Luso Brasileiro 10.
Jardim Botânico (Botanical Gardens). A short drive up the Camacha road from Funchal. Well worth a visit for the plants and the views over the bay.
Madeira Company's Wine Lodge and Museum, Ave. Arriaga 28. Also tasting rooms and sales.
Madeira Wine Institute Museum, Rua 5 de Outubro.
Municipal Museum, Rua da Mouraria. Natural history; aquarium. Open Mon. to Sat. 9:30–5, Sun. 12–5.
Museum of Sacred Art, Rua do Bispo 21. Open Tues. to Sun. 10–12, 2–5.
Photographic Museum. Rua Carreira 43. Afternoons only.
Quinta das Cruzes, Calçada do Pico 1. Up Calçada de Santa Clara from the Municipal Museum. Villa built by Zarco, with furniture, chinaware and garden. Open Mon. to Sat. 2–5, Sun. 12–5 (check times with Tourist Office).

EXCURSIONS. By Bus. Bus trips can be an excellent way to see the island for those who do not suffer from motion sickness. They are organized by *Agência Abreu,* Rua Gorgulho 1, Funchal (tel. 31077), and by *Panorama Viagens e Turismo,* Rua Dr. Brito Camara 3A (tel. 29194). Or ask at your hotel or at the Tourist Office.

By Boat. If you are to experience Madeira to the full a boat trip is essential. Details and times of such trips are available at the Tourist Office in Funchal or at offices at the Marina, where tickets for the *Independência* to Porto Santo can also be purchased. *Amigos do Mar,* Calçada Cabo Queira (tel. 23941) organize fishing trips.

SPECIAL EVENTS. Many Madeiran villages celebrate religious holidays with processions and pageantry; included below are some important pilgrimages and romarias. For further details and exact dates, consult local tourist offices. **February** or **March.** Carnival festivities. **April.** Flower Festival. **June.** Bach Festival, for music lovers. *São Pedro* at Ribeira Brava, June 28–29.
August. Madeira Wine Rally. Pilgrimage to *Nossa Senhora do Monte,* 6 km. (4 miles) from Funchal, Aug. 14–15. **September.** Grape Harvest festivities. *Nossa Senhora do Loreto,* in Calheta. **October.** Festival of *Senhora dos Milagres* at Machico. **December.** Christmas and New Year's Eve celebrations. Book accommodations far in advance for the New Year (*São Silvestre*) celebrations: the huge fireworks display over Funchal is world famous.

SHOPPING. Embroidery. The best Madeira embroidery is handworked on Irish linen, cambric, organdy, cottons and even French silks. It can be bought at the *Instituto do Bordado, Tapeçaria e Artesanato,* Rua Visconde de Anadia and at several shops around Funchal, for instance, *Casa Oliveira,* Rua da Alfandega 11, who have their embroidery workrooms on the premises. As well as the work produced by official companies, you can find local women selling their cruder but no less attractive handiwork at streetmarkets all over the island.
Ferreira, Ornelas & Co., 59 Rua Dr. Fernão de Ornelas, have hand-embroidered gifts, table and house linen, dresses and even wine. *Brasão e Freitas,* Rua do Conselheiro 39, specializes in tapestries and *Madeira Gobelins,* Rua da Carreira 194, is noted for art needlework and *Patricio & Gouveia,* Rua Visconde de Anadia 24, a big variety of goods on several floors. The *Casa do Turista,* Rua do Conselheiro Silvestre Ribeiro 2, in spite of its name, has one of the best selections of regional goods in Funchal.
Flowers. For flowers, which can be packed for export, go to *A Estufa* in the shopping center near the cathedral, or *A Rosa,* Rua Impératriz dona Amélia 126, in Funchal.
Food. Fruit, vegetables and even fish are sold at the *Mercado dos Lavradores,* the market on the eastern side of Funchal, just north of Rua de Santa Maria. Mornings are best.
Wickerwork. Attractive wickerwork goods can be bought at Camacha, the main center of the craft, northeast of Funchal, and at numerous shops in Funchal itself.

Wine. A wide variety of wines is produced on Madeira, a pleasant surprise for those who know Madeira wine only as an ingredient in cooking. A very dry *Sercial,* chilled, makes a delicious apertif, while the rich *Malmsey* is a good after-dinner drink. Wine can be bought at the Madeira Company's Wine Lodge, Ave. Arriaga 28, and at many shops in Funchal.

OPENING TIMES. Normal shopping hours are 9–1, 3–7. However, most of the shops and cafés in the big new shopping mall, *Centro Comércial do Infante,* Ave. Arriago 75, in Funchal are open 10 A.M.–10 P.M. Banks are open 8:30–11:45, 1–2:45. *Câmbios* (currency exchanges) have longer hours.

SPORTS. For further details of sports facilities ask at local Tourist Offices. **Tennis.** Several hotels have courts, including Reid's, Savoy, Vila Ramos, Duas Torres, Gorgulho, Galomar, Atlantis, Dom Pedro, and Matur. There are also courts at the Reis Magos Tourist Complex, Caniço de Baixo. **Golf.** The *Santo da Serra Golf Club,* about 20 km. (12 miles) northeast of Funchal, has a nine-hole course (5,244 yards), with an 18-hole course due to open. **Walking.** The interior is excellent walking country, but it is advisable to have a guide for the high mountains. The paths along the irrigation channels (*levadas*) have been mapped out and can make delightful walks. Ask at the Tourist Office for details. **Swimming.** All hotels have pools, mostly sea-water. There are public pools at the Lido complex, a short bus ride to the west of Funchal. Sea bathing is possible from some hotels. **Windsurfing.** Available from the private beach at the Dom Pedro hotel at Machico, and on Porto Santo beach. **Deep Sea Fishing.** *Amigos do Mar,* Calçado Cabo Queira (tel. 23941), organize excursions. Or ask at Tourist Office.

USEFUL ADDRESSES. Consulates. *American,* Ave. Luis de Camões, Edificio Infante, Bloco B4, Apt. B (tel. 091 47429). *British,* Ave. de Zarco 2, Box 417 (tel. 091 21221).

Travel Agents. *American Express,* Star Travel Service, Ave. Arriaga 23, P.O. Box 543, Funchal (tel. 091 32009); Ave. Dr. Gregório Pestana Junior 10, Vila Baleira, Porto Santo (tel. 091 982459).

Airports. Santa Catarina, Funchal (tel. 091 52933); Porto Santo (tel. 091 982355); *TAP Air Portugal* (tel. 091 30151 or 091 22415, or, at the airport, tel. 091 52021).

Car Hire. As driving can be fairly hazardous, inexperienced drivers are advised to hire a driver as well: they are excellent and safe. *Avis:* Largo António Nobre 164, Funchal (tel. 091 25495); at the hotels Reid's, Casino Park, Atlantis; on Porto Santo, (tel. 091 82381). *Atlas:* Ave. Infante (Shell Garage), Funchal (tel. 091 23100). *Hertz:* M.I. Nunes Lda, Rua Ivens 12, Funchal (tel. 091 26026); also at airport. *InterRent:* Estrada Monumental (Hotel Duas Torres), Funchal (tel. 091 25619).

Taxis. Cabs can be hired in Funchal at Ave. Arriaga, Praça do Município, and outside the Reid's, Palácio and Sheraton Hotels. Other towns all have convenient pick-up places.

THE AZORES

Strung out across some 500 km. (300 miles) of the Atlantic, the nearest island 1,500 km. (900 miles) west of Lisbon, the furthest 2,000 km. (1,200 miles), the Azores (Açores in Portuguese) consist of nine volcanic islands adrift in the Atlantic. Though European by virtue of their Portuguese administration, the islands are fundamentally different from their mother country, and indeed from the rest of Europe, in terrain, climate and way of life, chiefly as a result of their isolation and volcanic origin. Even in the hurly-burly of the 20th century they remain largely unspoilt, a land apart. After the 1974 revolution, the constitution of 1976 gave the Azores a large measure of autonomy, with their own legislative assembly and government. This situation was reinforced under a revised constitution agreed in 1982.

The Carthaginians were the first peoples to settle the islands, probably reaching them in the fourth century B.C. But their subsequent history remained obscure until well into the Middle Ages. In 1351 the islands appeared for the first time on a map (Italian), but it was almost another 100 years before they were colonized in any serious way. Having visited the islands initially in 1431/2 under the impetus of Prince Henry the Navigator, the Portuguese established a settlement on Santa Maria, the most easterly of the group, in 1450. Further colonization followed, this time by the Flemish, when the Portuguese presented Faial, one of the more westerly islands, to Isabella of Burgundy in 1466. And in fact a number of the first "captains" or governors of the islands were Flemish, including one Josse van Hurtere who gave his name to Horta, the capital of Faial.

Though the archipelago was to offer vital staging posts for the Portuguese in their early epic voyages of discovery across the globe, and despite further successful colonization, the islands remained largely untouched by events in Europe for almost the next 500 years, some notable exceptions aside. In 1591, for example, Sir Richard Grenville fought a famous and bloody naval battle with the Spanish, and in the 18th century Captain Cook used the islands as a revictualling point during his voyaging around the world.

In fact it was as a maritime base that the islands enjoyed their greatest period of sustained significance when, in the 19th century, the Azores became both a whaling center of importance and an anchorage and safe harbor for the many thousands of sailing ships plying the great north Atlantic trade routes. As a result of this permanent coming and going, many islanders were tempted away and left to settle and work in California, Bermuda, Venezuela and New England, where there is still a sizeable population.

To some extent the Azores' role as a mid-Atlantic haven has continued today. Many yachtsmen use the islands as a convenient stopping point while a number of cruise ships also call in here, though their visits tend to be brief. In World War II, when the U.S. Air Force built a large airport on Santa Maria to help ferry men and supplies to the Allies, the islands regained their strategic importance. And for about 20 years after the war trans-Atlantic airlines used the islands as a refuelling point. A small number of airlines flying to and from South America continue to do so today. But for the most part, the Azores are no longer either a stop-over point of importance or a significant trading area. Thus, while tourism is inevitably on the increase, the tranquil tempo of life on the islands remains largely undisturbed.

Mist-Shrouded Peaks

Legend has it that the Azores are the sunken peaks of the lost Continent of Atlantis, whose ancient civilization was destroyed in a calamitous and terrible upheaval. But the islands are probably among the world's newer land masses, thrown up out of the Atlantic by intense and violent volcanic activity. And indeed their volcanic nature is everywhere evident; from the blackness of the beaches, innumerable lava flows, geysers and mineral springs to the *caldeiras* (formed by explosions of extraordinary violence) and crater lakes, these last forming one of the islands' most lovely and dramatic features.

Though most of the Azorean volcanoes are now extinct, unhappily for the islanders volcanic activity and earthquakes are by no means a thing of the past. At the beginning of 1980, a severe earthquake hit the islands of Terceira and São Jorge, both in the central group, though fortunately causing few casualties. And São Miguel (which is to the north of Santa Maria) and Faial both suffered badly as a result of volcanic activity earlier this century.

The volcanic nature of the group is also eloquently attested to by the towering mist-shrouded peaks all the islands possess, though none more dramatically than Pico in the central group whose highest peak climbs 2,320 meters (7,611 ft.) into the ever-present clouds.

Volcanoes, earthquakes, towering mountains and steep rugged coasts might seem at first sight to indicate that life on the Azores must be hardy in the extreme. In fact, quite the opposite is true. The islands enjoy an extremely temperate climate that is never less than mild all year round, if perhaps also a little rainy. But this combination of balmy warmth and regular rainfall conspires to make the Azores very fertile. Consequently a wide range of crops is possible as well as extensive dairy farming. And, as one might expect, the surrounding seas teem with fish of many kinds. Vegetation on the islands is fundamentally European in character, though some African species are found, but its density and luxuriance are almost tropical. Wild flowers abound and there is a wide variety of sea and land birds, including numerous buzzards. Vinegrowing, helped by the volcanic soil, is an important activity, especially on Pico, Graciosa and Terceira. The local *Vinho de Cheiro* has a peculiarly delicious tang.

Life on the islands is simple. Most Azoreans are fishermen or farmers, performing tasks that have remained largely unchanged in their essentials for hundreds of years, as is shown by the numbers of windmills. Though there are a few industries such as straw and woodworking and the manufacture of earthenware pottery, they are small scale and unimportant when measured against the contributions of both fishing and farming to the islands' economy.

The Eastern Islands—Santa Maria and São Miguel

The first of the islands to be discovered by the Portuguese in 1431, Santa Maria, is the southernmost in the archipelago, roughly rectangular in shape and covers some 155 square km. (60 square miles). Columbus called in here in 1493 on his return from the West Indies and the tiny chapel at Anjos in Vila do Porto, where his crew prayed and gave thanks for their safe delivery stands to this day. The chapel also contains a triptych that belonged to Gonçalo Velho, captain of one of the other ships in Columbus's little fleet.

The landscape is varied with wooded hills, green fields and many orchards. There are numerous small and secluded beaches. Although of volcanic origin, the island is mainly formed of limestone and her quarries provide much of the building material used in the islands. The marine fossils are unusually varied. Red clay, found in abundance, has provided the basis for a thriving ceramics business in Vila do Porto, the capital.

Santa Maria's other claim to fame is the large airport built by the United States at the western extremity of the island during World War II. Though little used now, it is interesting that the impetus behind its construction was the invocation by Great Britain in 1944 of the Treaty of Alliance between Britain and neutral Portugal. On the face of it a perfectly acceptable diplomatic justification for building an airport on neutral soil, the remarkable thing is that the treaty was signed in 1386.

Vila do Porto, principal port as well as capital, is filled with shining whitewashed houses. There is a convent (São Francisco) with a beautiful golden retable and some 17th-century glazed tiles in the church. Near Vila do Porto and Pedras de São Pedro, as well as Covas near Almagreira, there are some unusual grottoes in which, in the old days, people hid their goods and grain to prevent them being stolen by marauding pirates.

Other places to visit include the bay of São Lourenço in the northeast, where there is a pretty sandy beach with a little island opposite it (Ilhéu do Romeiro) and Santo Espirito to the south of the bay. The parish church here is both characteristic and attractive. The ethnological museum at Santo Espirito contains an amusing collection of local objects.

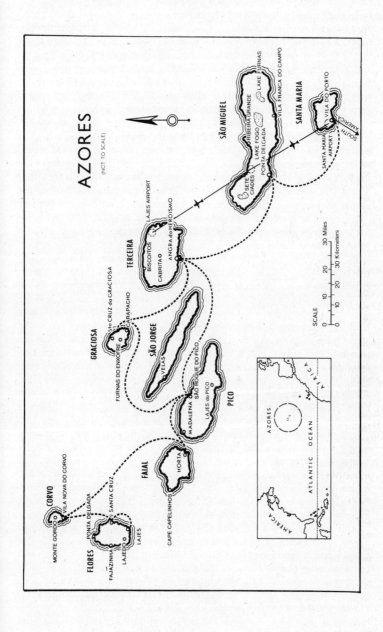

AZORES
(NOT TO SCALE)

São Miguel is the largest and most important of the islands, comprising an area of some 1,300 square km. (500 square miles). Sixty-four km. (40 miles) long, it is no more than 16 km. (ten miles) across at its widest point. It was discovered at the same time as Santa Maria and settlement began in 1439 by order of King Alfonso V. Ponta Delgada on the south coast has been the capital since 1546.

São Miguel is distinguished principally by its remarkable abundance of vegetation and deeply blue crater lakes. It has tea plantations and large areas of pineapple grown under glass; in addition, the development of farming and stock breeding has helped to make it one of the most prosperous islands in the archipelago.

Two excursions, both from Ponta Delgada, enable visitors to enjoy the beautiful features of São Miguel. The first trip, about 40 km. (25 miles) in all, is to the two lakes of the Sete Cidades (Seven Cities). The lakes are in the hollow of a crater with a circumference of about 12 km. (eight miles) and adjoin one another. But while one reflects the gorgeous blue of the sky, the other is as vibrantly green as the luxuriant plant life that borders its shores. There are many other lakes in the area as well, and some splendid views from the nearby heights. Capelas, along the coast, is the center of the tobacco fields.

The second trip is to Furnas and totals about 80 km. (50 miles). The road from Ponta Delgada starts off amid greenhouses full of ripening pineapples and goes on through Ribeira Grande, with tea plantations, on the north coast where there are sulphur mud baths and numerous geysers. It is one of the oldest settlements in the Azores. Try to visit the Town Hall and the Church of Nossa Senhora da Estrela. The church has in the upper choir a glass case containing hundreds of small figures molded in rice-flour and gum arabic, representing scenes from the Old and New Testaments. From the Santa Luzia observation point there is a fabulous view over the north coast and the Sete Cidades mountain mass.

Continue along the coast to the Santa Iria observation point and veer obliquely south. From the Pico do Ferro observation point there is an unparalleled view of the Furnas Valley.

The next stop is Furnas itself, whose many mineral springs and geysers have made the town a leading resort spa. It has the world's only naturally warm pool of ferruginous waters. But the region also has magnificent gardens, pineapple and tea plantations, and the famous Terra Nostra Park, which contains a notable collection of ancient trees and superb ferns. From Furnas there are side trips into the mountains, to Povoação (with more luxuriant plant life and rich farm lands) and to Lake Furnas.

Returning to Ponta Delgada along the south coast, you pass through a number of picturesque villages of which the most characteristic is Vila Franca do Campo. There is a Gothic church here with a basalt facade and the pilgrimage chapel of Nossa Senhora da Paz up a series of formal stairs, shining white against the green of the fields. The procession of São Miguel, in this village, is a curious survival of medieval social organization, when representatives of the various types of workers and artisans carry their patron saint through the streets. Off the shore, the strange rock towers of the little island of Vila Franca form a natural swimming pool.

In the center of the island is the Lagoa do Fogo, also worth a visit, and now within a nature reserve which includes the Lombades Gorge, which is covered with luxuriant vegetation, and a smaller lake, the Lagoa do Porto.

Ponta Delgada itself is of interest principally because of its site, running parallel to the lovely bay. But it also possesses features of architectual interest. The parish church of São Sebastião, behind a triple Baroque portal, contains pre-Reformation English embroidered vestments in the sacristy. Other points of interest are the Carlos Machado museum, the Esperança convent with a festival on the 5th Sunday after Easter, the former Jesuit church of the Colégio and the church of São José.

The Central Group

The first island of the central group is Terceira. It lies 87 km. (54 miles) to the northwest of São Miguel and is the most easterly of the group, the other islands being Graciosa, São Jorge, Pico and Faial. Terceira is the most densely populated of all the Azores. It is roughly oval-shaped and is some 16 km. (ten miles) long and 19 km. (12 miles) wide.

Terceira's name is derived from the fact that it was the third island to be discovered by the Portuguese. But it was actually settled in 1450 by Jácome de Bruges who, as his name implies, came from the Low Countries. Vasco da Gama stopped here after his epoch-making voyage to India in 1493. Terceira is also the site of the principal airport of the Azores, at Lajes, with international traffic.

The countryside, which is frequently obscured by mists, is very fertile and is divided into a patchwork of fields called *cerrados,* separated either by loose stone walls or by hedges of hydrangeas. The interior has a number of small lakes and geysers and, at Algar do Carvão, curious underground caves which are very deep and contain wonderful stalactites and stalagmites. The wild cattle from Bagacina and Pico do Cabrito are of interest to stock breeders. The single-storied houses all have sash windows, unlike those elsewhere in Portugal.

The capital of Terceira is Angra do Heroísmo, the name commemorating the bravery shown by the inhabitants against the Spanish who occupied the town in 1582. The city, now largely rebuilt after the 1980 earthquake, is grouped around the splendid 16th-century castle of St. John the Baptist. But other places of interest in this large and prosperous town are the Colégio church—which has the finest collection of Dutch 17th-century tiles outside Holland—the museum in the Convento de São Francisco, the Misericórdia church and the 17th-century Palácio Bettencourt where the Public Library is installed.

Among the many places to visit are Cabrito in the center, where there are a number of underground warm-water lakes, the crater of Guilherme Moniz (14 km., nine miles, in circumference) and the Biscoitos vineyards on the north coast, planted in fertile laval soil. There are also a number of mountain ranges of considerable drama including the Serra do Cume in the east and the Serra de Santa Barbara in the west.

Praia da Vitória, a well laid out town, has an 18th-century Christmas crib in the parish church, in a Baroque gold side chapel. The Church of São Sebastião in the Vila de São Sebastião, on the road between Angra and Praia da Vitória, is the most interesting on the island. Built in the 15th century, with fine Gothic features, it is one of the very few churches with frescoes.

Terceira is also home to one of the more intriguing religious events in the Azores. From Pentecost to the end of the summer, every village and hamlet collect offerings for the poor and place them in ornate and brightly-decorated little buildings which somewhat resemble summer houses; they are called *impérios*. The festival is climaxed by bull runs through the narrow streets of the towns.

Of the other islands in the central group, the smallest and most isolated, away to the northwest of Terceira, is Graciosa. It is only 18 km. (11 miles) long and seven km. (four and a half miles) wide and is the flattest of all the Azores.

The capital, Santa Cruz da Graciosa, is on the northeast coast. It has an exceedingly handsome parish church and a good ethnographical museum with special emphasis on wine growing.

However, the most interesting and unusual feature on Graciosa is the Furna do Enxofre, or Caldeira, a bizarre and rather sinister volcanic phenomenon. It consists of a tunnel in the rocks of the Caldeira hills in the south of the island leading down to a sulphurous lagoon some 90 meters (100 yards) below the surface. It is best seen around midday, when a little sunlight penetrates. The Termas do Carapacho, a few miles to the southwest on the sea, is a spa famous for its wealth of medicinal waters.

São Jorge lies some way to the south of Graciosa and is the most distinctively shaped of all the islands being 53 km. (33 miles) long but no more than eight km. (five miles) wide. A range of hills forms the spine of the island, reaching over 900 meters (3,000 ft.) at its highest point at Pico da Esperança. The island is covered by a thick mantle of farmlands and deep blue hydrangeas. In fact, though it is rather wild and rocky looking, São Jorge produces excellent dairy products. The cheese is particularly good.

The buildings in many of the villages and in Calheta and Velas, the two main towns, are washed a blinding white. But be warned that there are no hotels on the island, though there is a good *estalagem* in Velas, several *residências* and simple but clean rooms to be had in many houses. One spot worth a visit is the wonderful garden of the Quinta do Areeiro belonging to the Cunha da Silveira family. The parish church in Velas was built in 1460 under the terms of the will of Prince Henry the Navigator, and is still of great architectural interest. Also worth seeing is the 17th-century Town Hall. The church in Manadas, halfway between Velas and Calheta, is a perfect example of 18th-century Portuguese Baroque, with tiled panels of the Life of St. Barbara and beautiful vestment chests in the sacristy.

Lying a few miles to the southwest of São Jorge is Pico, 50 km. (30 miles) long by 14 km. (nine miles) wide. It is a harsh and rocky island. The coast is heavily indented and has a large number of islets, caves, and grottoes, including the Furna da Malha near the capital, Lajes dó Pico, a natural tunnel some two km. (one and a quarter miles) in length.

Pico is the most obviously volcanic of all the islands. Whole villages have been built from laval matter, there are many reefs made from lava, and porous calcinated lava is everywhere visible. This positive surfeit of laval soil and volcanic ash has also ensured that the island is the most important and productive wine growing center in the Azores. A nature reserve has been created on this strange island.

Lajes do Pico has a number of fine 17th- and 18th-century buildings and the church of São Pedro is the oldest on the island. There is also a whaling museum here in the Casa dos Botes.

Pico's sailors are in fact the finest in Portugal. Like their counterparts on Faial, they harpoon whales by hand. Lookouts on the cliffs herald the arrival of the whales. The men then push off from the shores in their light, swift boats, stealthily advancing on their victims. However, like their prey, the whalers of Pico are a dying breed. On the last Sunday in August the Festa dos Baleiros, or Whalers' Festival, takes place, attracting people from all over the island.

The island's main feature is the great peak that towers over the center, its top constantly swathed in a white blanket of cloud. At 2,319 meters (7,611 ft.), it is the highest mountain in Portugal. There is a track that passes between hedges of rose bushes that goes almost to the top, but the last part of the ascent has to be made on foot. You'll need to take a guide and try to start at daybreak (spend the preceding night at Madalena). On a clear day the view takes in Faial, São Jorge, Graciosa and Terceira.

Faial, separated from Pico by a wide channel, is the most westerly of the central group. It is also one of the most important of all the islands, chiefly on account of its port, the largest in the Azores. This is at Horta, the capital. Ferry boats make the crossing to and from Madalena on Pico, several times a day.

The island is roughly circular in shape and measures some 21 by 16 km. (13 by 10 miles). Like the other islands, it is extremely fertile. And indeed the many magnificent hydrangea hedges that adorn Faial have caused it to be commonly called the Blue Island. However, the thousands of camellias that grow in the Flemish Valley, a renowned beauty spot, are almost equally spectacular. But the landscape is also extremely dramatic in places, nowhere more so than at Capelhinos on the northwestern corner. It was here in 1957 that the last major volcanic erruption in the Azores occurred. It lasted for one terrifying year, and there are still a number of houses, as well as the lighthouse, lying half-buried under the lava and ash. Further dramatic evidence of the erruption is provided by the *misterios,* veins of hardened lava, and by the exhibits in the Volcanic Museum.

Less awesome volcanic phenomena are to be found around the great crater lake of Cabeço Gordo, the highest point of the island. The calm surface of the lake reflects the vast clumps of hydrangeas surrounding it. Today the area is a nature reserve.

At Horta the dock walls carry hundreds of paintings, signatures and phrases inscribed there by sailors who have passed through over the years, and it is still a busy and lively port. Near the port and next to the old fort there is a splendid view of neighboring Pico from the esplanade. There is another notable view from the terrace in front of the Carmo church, which is lined with large tiled panels amidst golden altars. The town also has some good museums, including the Museum of Sacred Art in the Rua Serpa Pinto. You might also wish to see the Public Library in a 17th-century building.

Nature lovers should visit the Quinta de São Lourenço, three km. (two miles) from Horta, where there is an extraordinary range of plant life.

The Western Group—Flores and Corvo

Flores and Corvo are the most westerly and remote of the Azores. They were discovered by the Portuguese in 1452 and settled in the 16th century. Both islands were later to play an important role in Portugal's struggle against Spain. In 1582 Sir Walter Raleigh, co-opted by the Portuguese in the fight against the common enemy, used Flores as a base for his fleet.

Flores' name comes from the profusion of flowers found on the island, and while it is highly fertile—the local plums are delicious—and much farming is done, the terrain is in fact extremely rugged. There are a considerable number of lakes in the extinct volcano craters in the center of the island, all of which provide excellent fishing. A further characteristic local feature are the waterfalls which splash straight down into the sea. Many people consider this the most spectacularly beautiful of all the islands. The many lakes in the center of the island are eye-catching, particularly the Lagoa Funda, with sandy shores bordered by hydrangeas below the foothills of the mountains.

The capital, Santa Cruz das Flores, is a typical fisherman's settlement. There are boats drawn up on the beach and nets and lobster pots galore. The town has many churches, of which the most interesting is São Pedro. There is also an ethnological museum.

On the opposite side of the island is Fajãzinha. It is here that you will find the waterfalls that cascade directly into the sea. But there is also a charming 18th-century church, Nossa Senhora dos Remedios.

Corvo is the smallest of all the islands and is a mere 26 km. (ten miles) square. The population of about 400 lives a semi-communal existence. There is one town, Vila Nova do Corvo. Its cottages are all built in the same simple style along narrow lanes called *canadas*. Farming and fishing are the only occupations. Two adjacent lakes to the north are formed from extinct volcanic craters; little islands dot their blue waters.

PRACTICAL INFORMATION FOR THE AZORES

TOURIST OFFICES. There are local tourist offices on the following islands. **Faial,** Rua Vasco da Gama, Horta (tel. 092 22237); Rua Marcelino Lima, Horta (tel. 092 23801); Graciosa, Praça Fontes Pereira Melo, Santa Cruz da Graciosa (tel. 095 72125); Pico, Rua Conselheiro Terra Pinheiro, Madalena (tel. 095 92500); Rua Capitão Mor Garcia Madruga, Lajes (tel. 095 97405). **Santa Maria,** at airport, (tel. 096 82155); **São Miguel,** Ave. Infante D. Henrique, Ponta Delgada (tel. 096 25743); **Terceira,** Rua Rio de Janeiro 47-A, Angra do Heroísmo (tel. 095 23393).

GETTING TO THE AZORES. By Plane. Though no longer *every* day, there are frequent flights from New York, Montreal and Lisbon, to Lajes airport on Terceira. There is a regular daily service between Ponta Delgada on São Miguel and Lisbon. The airport on Santa Maria is used for flights to and from South America. Faial Airport at Castelo Branco also has some international flights.

There are regular airlinks between all the islands—even tiny Corvo, which now has a helicopter service. Local weather conditions govern schedules so it's best not to have too rigid a timetable.

By Boat. There are no regular sailings between the Azores and the European mainland. Though there *is* a Portuguese cargo boat, the *Pauline*

Marie I, which plies between Lisbon and New Bedford, Mass., taking some passengers, and calling in at the Azores and Madeira. Apply *Mutualista Açoreana,* Rua do Ouro 181–6, Lisbon 1100. And a number of cruise lines call at Ponta Delgada in São Miguel and Horta in Faial. The majority are operated by *P&O* out of Southampton in Britain, but *Cunard's* QE 2 occasionally calls in here as do a number of cruises from Miami. None, however, stays for long.

HOTELS AND RESTAURANTS

Faial. At **Horta.** *Estalagem de Santa Cruz* (E), Rua Vasco da Gama (tel. 092 23021). 25 rooms with bath. AE, DC, MC, V. *Fayal* (E), Rua Cônsul Dabney (tel. 092 22181). 83 rooms with bath. Pool, disco, snack bar. AE, DC, MC. *Residêncial São Francisco* (M), Rua Conselheiro Medeiros 13 (tel. 092 22957). 29 rooms with bath. Breakfast only. *Pensão do Infante* (I), Praça do Infante, Angústias (tel. 092 22837). 19 rooms with bath. Breakfast only.

Restaurants. *Central* (M), Rua Serpa Pinto 15. *A Lagoa* (M), Rua da Conceicão 18. *O Lima* (M), Rua Serpa Pinto 9. *Peter's Bar* (M). Friendly place. *Royal 1908* (M), Rua Tenente Valadim. *O Tripeiro* (M), Rua do Mar. *Café Sport* (I), Rua Tenente Valadim. Well-known yachting haunt along the quay.

At **Praia do Almoxarife. Restaurant.** *Praia Mar* (I), Largo Silva Leal.

Flores. At **Lajes.** *Estalagem das Flores* (I), tel. 092 52496. 6 rooms with bath. Simple.

At **Santa Cruz.** *Francesca* (M). Excellent cooking at this hotel; recommended. *Residêncial Toste* (M), Rua Senador André Freitas (tel. 092 22119). All rooms with bath. *Residêncial Vila Flores* (M), Rua Senador Andrê Freitas (tel. 092 52190). 9 rooms with bath. Restaurant.

Graciosa. At **Santa Cruz da Graciosa.** *Residêncial Santa Cruz* (M), Largo Barão Guadalupe (tel. 095 72345). 20 rooms with bath. Simple and friendly.

Pico. At **Lajes do Pico.** *Acor* (M), tel. 092 97243. All rooms with bath. Breakfast only. *Castelate* (I), tel. 092 67304. All rooms with bath.

Restaurants. *Lagoa* (M). *Lajense* (M). *Ramiro* (M).

At **Madalena.** *Aparthotel Caravelas* (M), tel. 092 92500. Good rooms and apartments near sea. *Residêncial Pico* (M), Biscoitos (tel. 092 92392). 32 rooms with bath. Good restaurant. *Mini Bela* (I), tel. 092 92263. Some rooms with bath. Breakfast only.

Restaurants. *Café Acor* (I). *Golfinho* (I).

At **São Roque do Pico.** *Pensão Acor* (I), tel. 092 67438. 13 rooms with bath. Breakfast only.

Restaurant. *O Cadete* (I).

São Jorge. In **Velas,** the capital. Rooms in private houses are available—ask in the *Roma* restaurant. *Estalagem das Velas* (E), tel. 095 42632. 24 rooms with bath. Good restaurant. *Australia* (M), tel. 095 42210. All rooms with bath. *Beira Mar* (M), Rua Dr João Pereira. *Residêncial Neto* (M), Rua Dr. José Pereira (tel. 095 42403). 9 rooms with bath. Pool.

Restaurants. *Roma* (M). Lunch only. *Arcadia* (I), Rua São João. *Solmar* (I), Rua Cândido Reis. *Velense* (I), Rua Dr. José Pereira.

At **Calheta.** *Solmar* (M), Rua Domingos Oliveira (tel. 095 46120). All rooms with bath.

Restaurants. *Continental* (M), Rua Padre Joãquim Moreira. *Os Amigos* (I), Relvinha.

Santa Maria. At **Vila do Porto.** *Aeroporto* (I), tel. 096 82211. 47 rooms with bath. Restaurant. At airport nearby.

Restaurants. *Atlântida* (I), Rua Teófilo Braga 71. *Central* (I), Rua Luis Bettencourt.

At **Praia Formosa.** *Praia* (M). *Soturmar* (M).

São Miguel. At **Ponta Delgada.** *Avenida* (E), Rua Dr José Bruno Tavares Carreiro (tel. 096 25725). 80 rooms with bath. Restaurant. AE, DC, MC. *Infante* (E), Ave. Infante Dom Henrique (tel. 096 23331). 39 rooms with bath. DC, MC. *São Pedro* (E), Largo Almirante Dunn (tel. 096 22223). 30 rooms with bath. Recommended. AE, DC, MC. *Canadiano* (M), Rua do Contador 24A (tel. 096 27421). 50 rooms with bath. Breakfast only. AE, DC, MC. *Gaivota* (M), Ave. Marginal (tel. 096 23286). Service apartments. DC. *Loreto-Sol* (M), Largo do Loreto 40 (tel. 096 27281). Another apartment hotel, with fully equipped apartments for 3 to 4 people. *Residêncial America* (M), Rua Manuel Inácio Correia 58 (tel. 096 24351). 23 rooms with bath. Breakfast only. MC. *Residêncial Central* (M), Rua Machado Santos 82 (tel. 096 24491). 40 rooms with bath. Breakfast only. *Sete Cidades* (M), Rua Contador 20 (tel. 096 27344). 32 rooms with bath. Breakfast only. DC, MC.

Restaurants. Ponta Delgada also has many good inexpensive seafood restaurants. *O Corisco* (E), Rua Manuel da Ponte. Excellent seafood spot. MC. *London* (E), Rua Ernesto do Canto 21. AE, DC, MC. *Solar Açoreano* (E), Rua Eng. José Cordeiro 55. One of the few fado places in the islands. *Cavalo Branco* (M), Rua do Meio Moio. Superb regional cooking; try the *alcatra,* a meat or fish dish, cooked overnight in a cool oven. Closed Mon. *Coliseu* (M), Ave. Roberto Ivens. Closed Tues. MC.

At **Fajã de Cima.** *O Casarão* (M), tel. 096 26813. 15 rooms with bath. MC.

At **Furnas** (Spa). *Pensão Açoriano* (M). 15 rooms with bath. *Terra Nostra* (E), tel. 096 54133. 38 rooms with bath. Natural warm-water pool, golf, tennis. AE, DC, MC.

Restaurants. *Terra Nostra* (E), tel. 096 54143. At Lagoa das Furnas; here you can eat food cooked in the natural hot waters of the geysers. Recommended; booking essential. AE. *O Retiro* (M). Opposite the Terra Nostra hotel in Furnas itself. Recommended.

At **Lagoa do Fogo.** *Caloura Motel* (I), Agua de Pau (tel. 096 93240). 20 units with bath, pool; on sea within a Nature Reserve. MC.

At **Mosteiros.** *Pousada Bom Repouso* (M), Largo da Igreja (tel. 096 95103).

At **Sete Cidades. Restaurant.** *Cavalo Branco* (M). Closed Mon.

Terceira. At **Angra do Heroísmo.** *Albergaria Cruzeiro* (E), Praça Dr Sousa Junior (tel. 095 24071). 42 rooms with bath, 5 suites. Restaurant. AE, DC, MC. *Angra* (E), Praça Velha (tel. 095 24041). 86 rooms with bath. MC.

Beira Mar (M), Rua São João 1 (tel. 095 25188). 15 rooms with bath. Restaurant, disco. *Monte Brasil* (M), Alto dos Coves 8 (tel. 095 22440). *Sé* (M), Rua de Janeiro 25 (tel. 095 22180). *Zenite* (I), Rua da Rosa 12 (tel. 095 22260). Last three serve breakfast only.

Restaurants. *Marcelino's* (E), Rua São João 47. *A Ilha* (M), São Sebastião. Fados. *Confianca* (M), Rua Santo Espirito 102. One of the many small places serving regional dishes. *Lusitana* (M), Rua S, Pedro 63. Regional food. MC. *Pico* (M), Rua Santo Espirito 106. More regional specialties. *Ladeira* (I), Rua João de Deus.

At **Praia da Vitória,** Cabo da Praia. *Nove Ilhas* (M), tel. 095 53135. 9 units with bath. Comfortable; on beach. AE, DC, MC.

At **São Mateus da Calheta. Restaurant.** *Beira Mar* (E). Seafood specialties.

At **Praia da Vitória.** *Apartments Praia da Vitória* (M), Rua de Jesus 70 (tel. 095 53015). Good service apartments.

Restaurants. *O Brasão* (M), Santa Rita. Excellent cooking. Closed Mon. *Garça* (M), Rua Serpa Pinto 67. Lovely view. Steak house. *Sousa* (M), Travessa Formosa 5. Closed Mon.

CAMPING. São Jorge. Urzelina; Faja Grande; Velas.

PLACES OF INTEREST. Museums are usually open daily, except Mondays and public holidays, 10–5, but double check the times on the spot. Some close for lunch. Entrance fees are between 150$00 and 200$00.

Faial. Museu, Palácio do Colégio, Horta. Local handicrafts including lace, tulle embroidered with straw and articles in whalebone.

Museum of Sacred Art, Church of S. Francisco. Horta. **Fort of Santa Cruz,** Horta. **Volcanic Museum.** Flemish valley filled in late winter with flowering camelias.

Flores. Museu de Etnologia (Ethnological Museum), Santa Cruz das Flores. Local handicrafts of all kinds.

Graciosa. Santa Cruz. Ethnological Museum with special emphasis on viniculture.

Furno do Enxofre. Underground lake.

Pico. Casa das Botes, Lages do Pico. Whaling museum, with objects in whalebone, log books of old whaling expeditions and one of the original whaling boats propelled by oars or sails.

Santa Maria. Museu de Etnologia (Ethnological Museum), Santo Espirito. **Forestry Park,** Vila do Porto. Rare specimens.

São Jorge. Town Hall, Velas. 17th-century building with 16th- and 17th-century documents.

São Miguel. Carlos Machado Museum, Rua João Moreira, Ponta Delgada. Open Tues. to Sun.; closed Sat. and Sun. mornings, holidays and lunchtimes.

Municipal Museum, Rua Conde de Botelho 13, Vila Franco do Campo. Closed for lunch, Aug. and Sept. Other months only open Sun. 2–5:30 P.M.

São Sebastião. Pre-Reformation English embroidered vestments in sacristy.
Pineapple Plantation, Rua Dr. Augusto Arruda, Abelheira, Fajã de Baixo. The various stages of pineapple cultivation under glass can be seen.
Ribeira Grande. N.S. da Estrela. Hundreds of small biblical figures in glass case in upper choir.
Vale das Furnas. Terra Nostra Park. Silvicultural collection. Natural hot springs.
Ribeira Seca. Museu do Chá.

Terceira. Museu, Angra do Heroísmo. Weapons, pottery and porcelain, furniture and paintings, musical instruments and large ethnological collection. Open Mon. to Fri.; closed for lunch.
Algar do Carvão. Deep underground caves.
Castle of St. John the Baptist.
Palácio Bettencourt. 17th century; now the public library.
Vila de São Sebastião. Gothic parish church with rare frescoes.

SHOPPING. Crafts. For local arts and crafts, try *Jovial,* Rua Walter Bensaude 2, Horta, on **Faial.** Ponta Delgada, capital of **São Miguel,** has the greatest choice of shops: *Capote & Capelo,* Rua Dr. Gil Mont'Alverne Sequeira 20 (tel. 096 25525); *Gil M. Teixeira & Irmão, Lda.,* Rua dos Mercadores 42 (tel. 096 24236); *Arte & Manhas,* Rua António Manuel Inacio Correia 54; *C. Lampião,* Rua dos Mercadores 101; *A Utilitaria,* Rua Machado Santos 105 (tel. 096 22096). In Praia da Vitória on **Terceira** two shops specializing in local crafts are: *Casa Vitória,* Rua de Jesus 115; *Centro Regional,* Ave. Alvaro Martins Homem 7 (tel. 095 52422).
Food/Wine. Try the passion fruit liqueur, *Liqueur do Ezequiel,* Ribeira Grande on **São Miguel.**

SPECIAL EVENTS. There are a good many religious festivities throughout the year. The islanders dress in traditional costumes and there is much singing and dancing. For further details and exact dates, consult local tourist offices.
January. Festival of Santo Amaro, Praia Almagreira, Santa Maria, Jan. 15.
May. The 5th Sunday after Easter sees the celebration of *Cristo dos Milagres* in Ponta Delgada, São Miguel. All the islands celebrate Pentecost.
June. The *S. Joaninas* are run by the municipalities of most islands, June 23–29, and give a fascinating picture of the folklore and religious traditions of the islands. Late June/early July sees the celebration of *Cavalhadas* in Ribeira Seca, São Miguel.
August. *Nossa Senhora da Guia,* the patron saint of fishermen, is fêted on Faial. Festival of Santa Maria, Vila do Porto, Aug. 15. Lajes, on Pico, hosts the *Festa dos Baleiros* (Whalers' Festival) on the last Sunday of the month. The end of the summer also sees the bull runs that climax the summer-long dedications to the Holy Spirit on Terceira.

SPORTS. For further details of sports facilities ask at local Tourist Offices. A Sea Week, starting on the first Sunday in August, is held on Faial, with all water-based sports and activities connected with the sea. **Sailing** and **Windsurfing.** Facilities for these exist on Faial, São Miguel and Terceira. Note that these sports can be made dangerous by turbulent seas and often rough weather, but certain sheltered places such as the harbor of Ponta Delgada, São Miguel, are superb. **Rowing.** On Faial. **Water Skiing.** Apply to *Amilcar Quaresma,* Largo Cardeal Costa Nunes, Madalena, Pico (tel. 092 92227), or *Pescatur,* Rua João Francisco Cabral 49, 1° E, Ponta Delgada, São Miguel (tel. 096 22691). **Scuba Diving.** On Faial. **Fishing.** Pico has excellent fishing and plenty of boats for hire. Terceira also has sea fishing. Big-game fishing is available from Faial, Pico and São Miguel; on Pico, contact *Amilcar Quaresma* (address above), and on São Miguel, contact *Pescatur* (address above). Fully equipped modern boats are available for hire from April to November. **Swimming.** Terceira has a natural pool. **Underwater Exploration.** Boat trips round the island of Santa Maria, from Vila do Porto, Ave. Kopke (tel. 096 82137).

Tennis. Clube de Ténis, Horta, Faial (tel. 092 22181); Clube de Ténis, Madalena, Pico (tel. 092 92145); Clube de Ténis, Faja de Cima, São Miguel (tel. 096 27751). Both tennis and **football** can be played on Terceira.

Golf. São Miguel has a nine-hole golf course at Furnas, and there is an 18-hole course on Terceira, at Algar do Carvão.

Shooting. There is good shooting on Pico, Faial, and particularly on Graciosa with plenty of wood pidgeon, rabbits and quail.

Riding. Centro Hipico, Rua Margarida de Chaves 34, Ponta Delgada, São Miguel (tel. 096 25993).

USEFUL ADDRESSES. Consulates. *American,* Ave. Infante D. Henrique, Ponta Delgada, São Miguel (tel. 096 22216). *British.* Rua Dr Bruno Carreiro 26-A, Ponta Delgada, São Miguel (tel. 096 661191).

Airline. *TAP Air Portugal,* Largo Prior do Crato, Angra do Heroísmo, Terceira (tel. 095 24489); Airport (tel. 095 52111). **Inter-Island Airline.** *Sata-Serviço Açoreano de Transportes Aereos, E.P.,* Largo Cons. Jacinto Candida, Santa Cruz da Graciosa (tel. 095 72456); airport, (tel. 095 72458); offices on all the principal islands.

Shipping Company. *Companhia de Transportes Maritimos,* Ave. Infante D. Henrique, Ponta Delgada, São Miguel (tel. 096 26301), and branches in the principal islands.

Travel Agents. *American Express,* Star Travel Service, Rua Serpa Pinto 74, Praia da Vitória, Terceira (tel. 095 52623). *Ornelas,* Ave. Infante D. Henrique, Ponta Delgada, São Miguel (tel. 096 22236), and branches on all the principal islands.

Car Hire. *Açorauto,* delivery and return at Lajes Airport (tel. 095 52373), Rua Serpa Pinto, Praia Vitória (tel. 095 52373); *Auto-Turistica,* Angra do Heroísmo (tel. 095 24222). There are several other firms on São Miguel, Santa Maria, Pico and Faial. *Micauto,* Ave. Infante D. Henrique 109, 9500 Ponta Delgada (tel. 096 24382).

ENGLISH-PORTUGUESE VOCABULARY

If you have a reading knowledge of Spanish and/or French, you will find Portuguese easy to read. However, Portuguese pronunciation can be somewhat tricky. Despite obvious similarities in Spanish and Portuguese spelling and syntax, the Portuguese sounds are a far cry—almost literally so—from their ostensible Spanish equivalents. Some of the main peculiarities of Portuguese phonetics are the following.

Nasalized vowels: if you have some idea of French pronunciation, these shouldn't give you too much trouble. The closest approach is that of the French *accent du Midi,* as spoken by people in Marseille and in the Provence area, or perhaps an American Midwest twang will help. Try pronouncing *"an," "am," "en," "em," "in," "om," "un,"* etc., with a sustained *"ng"* sound (e.g. *"bom"-"bong,"* etc.).

Another aspect of Portuguese phonetics is the vowels and diphthongs written with the tilde: *ã, ão, ães.* The Portuguese word for *"wool," "lã,"* sounds roughly like the French word *"lin,"* with the *"–in"* resembling the *"an"* in the English word *"any,"* but nasalized. The suffix *"-tion"* on such English words as "information" becomes in Portuguese spelling *"ção,"* pronounced *"-sa-on,"* with the *"-on"* nasalized: *"Informação,"* for example. These words form their plurals by changing the suffix to *çoes,* which sounds like *"-son-ech"* (the *"ch"* here resembling a cross between the English *"sh"* and the German *"ch":* hence *"informaçoes"*).

The cedilla occurring under the *"c"* serves exactly the same purpose as in French: it transforms the *"c"* into an *"ss"* sound in front of the three so-called "hard" vowels ("a," "o," and "u"): e.g. *graça, Açores, açúcar.* The letter "c" occurring without a cedilla in front of these three vowels automatically has the sound of "k": pico, mercado, curto. The letter "c" followed by "e" or "i" is always "ss," and hence needs no cedilla: nacional, Graciosa, Terceira.

The letter "j" sounds like the "s" in the English word "pleasure." So does "g" except when the latter is followed by one of the "hard" vowels: hence, generoso, gigantesco, Jerónimo, azulejos, Jorge, etc.

The spelling *"nh"* is rendered like the *"ny"* in *"canyon":* cf. *"senhora."*

The spelling *"lh"* is somewhere in between the *"l"* and the *"y"* sounds in *"million":* cf. *"Batalha."*

In the matter of syllabic stress, Portuguese obeys the two basic Spanish principles: 1) in words ending in a vowel, or in "n" or "s" the tonic accent falls on the next-to-the-last syllable: fado, mercado, azulejos; 2) in words ending in consonants other than "n" or "s," the stress falls on the last syllable: *favor, nacional.* Words in which the syllabic stress does not conform to the two above rules must be written with an acute accent to indicate the proper pronunciation: sábado, república, politécnico.

It is the "hushed," or unvoiced, vowels and consonants that make spoken Portuguese so elliptical and so complicated to follow for the untrained ear. You will find the intonations of Portuguese speech and the rise and fall of Portuguese voices quite fascinating.

VOCABULARY

BASICS

yes	sim
no	não
please	por favor
thank you	obrigado
thank you very much	muito obrigado
excuse me, sorry	com licença, desculpe
I'm sorry	desculpe-me
Good morning or good day	Bom dia
Good afternoon	Boa tarde
Good evening or good night	Boa noite
Goodbye	Adeus

NUMBERS

1	um, uma	18	dezoito
2	dois	19	dezanove
3	três	20	vinte
4	quatro	21	vinte e um
5	cinco	22	vinte e dois
6	seis	30	trinta
7	sete	40	quarenta
8	oito	50	cinquenta
9	nove	60	sessenta
10	dez	70	setenta
11	onze	80	oitenta
12	doze	90	noventa
13	treze	100	cem
14	catorze	110	cento e dez
15	quinze	200	duzentos
16	dezaseis	1,000	mil
17	dezasete	1,500	mil e quinhentos

DAYS OF THE WEEK

Monday	Segunda-feira
Tuesday	Terça-feira
Wednesday	Quarta-feira
Thursday	Quinta-feira
Friday	Sexta-feira
Saturday	Sábado
Sunday	Domingo

MONTHS

January	Janeiro	July	Julho
February	Fevereiro	August	Agosto
March	Março	September	Setembro
April	Abril	October	Outubro
May	Maio	November	Novembro
June	Junho	December	Dezembro

COLORS

Red	Vermelho
Blue	Azul
Black	Preto
White	Branco
Green	Verde
Gray	Cinzento
Yellow	Amarelo
Orange	Cor de laranja
Brown	Castanho

USEFUL PHRASES

The most important phrase to know (one that may make it unnecessary to know any others) is: "Do you speak English?"—in Portuguese, *Fala inglês?* If the answer is *Nao,* then you may have recourse to the list below.

How are you?	Como está?
How do you say in Portuguese?	Como se diz em Português?
Tourist Office	Turismo
Fine	Optimo
Very good	Muito bem (muito bom)
It's all right	Está bem
Good luck	Felicidades (boa sorte)
Hello	Olá
Come back soon	Até breve
Where is the hotel?	Onde é o hotel?
How much does this cost?	Quanto custa?
How do you feel?	Como se sente?
How goes it?	Que tal?
Pleased to meet you	Muito prazer em o (a) conhecer
The pleasure is mine	O prazer é meu

I have the pleasure of introducing Mr. . . .	Tenho o prazer de lhe apresentar o senhor. . . .
I like it very much	Gosto muito
I don't like it	Não gosto
Many thanks	Muito obrigado
Don't mention it	De nada
Pardon me	Desculpe-me (Perdão)
Are you ready?	Está pronto?
I am ready	Estou pronto
Welcome	Seja benvindo
I am very sorry	Desculpe (Lastimo muito)
What time is it?	Que horas são?
I am glad to see you	Muito prazer em o (a) ver
I don't understand	Não entendo
Please speak slowly	Fale lentamente por favor
I understand (or) It is clear	Compreendo (or) Está claro
Whenever you please	Quando quizer
Please wait	Faça favor de esperar
I will be a little late	Chegarei um pouco atrasado
I don't know	Não sei
Is this seat free?	Está vago este lugar?
Would you please direct me to . . . ?	Por favor indique-me . . . ?
Where is the station, museum . . . ?	Onde é a estação, museu . . . ?
I am American, British	Eu sou Americano, Inglês
It's very kind of you	É muito amavel
Please sit down	Por favor sente-se

EVERYDAY NEEDS

cigar, cigarette	charuto, cigarro
matches	fosforos
dictionary	dicionário
key	chave
razor blades	laminas de barbear
shaving cream	creme de barbear
soap	sabonete
city plan	mapa da cidade
road map	mapa das estradas
country map	mapa do país
newspaper	jornal
magazine	revista
telephone	telefone
telegram	telegrama
envelopes	envelopes
writing paper	papel de carta
airmail writing paper	papel de carta de avião
post card	postal
stamps	selos

SERVICES AND STORES

bakery	padaria
bookshop	livraria
butcher's	talho
delicatessen	charcutaria
dry cleaner's	limpeza a seco
grocery	mercearia
hairdresser, barber	cabeleireiro, barbeiro
laundry	lavandaria
shoemaker	sapateiro
stationery store	papelaria
supermarket	supermercado
toilet	casa de banho

EMERGENCIES

ill, sick	doente
I am ill	estou doente
My wife/husband/child is ill	Minha mulher/marido/criança está doente
doctor	doutor/medico
nurse	enfermeira/o
prescription	receita
pharmacist/chemist	farmacia
Please fetch/call a doctor	Por favor, chame o doutor/medico
accident	acidente
road accident	acidente na estrada
Where is the nearest hospital?	Onde é o hospital mais proximo?
Where is the American/British Hospital?	Onde é o Hospital Americano/Britanico?
dentist	dentista
X-ray	Raios-X

PHARMACIST'S

pain-killer	analgésico
gauze pads	compressas de gaze
bandage	ligadura
bandaid	pensos rápidos
scissors	tesoura
hot-water bottle	saco de água quente
sanitary pads	pensos higiénicos
ointment for bites/stings	pomada para picadas
coughdrops	pastilhas para a tosse
cough mixture	xarope para a tosse
laxative	laxativo
thermometer	termómetro

TRAVELING

plane	avião

hovercraft	hovercrafte
train	comboio
boat	barco
taxi	taxi
car	carro/automovel
bus	autocarro
seat	assento/lugar
reservation	reserva
smoking/non-smoking compartment	compartimento para fumadores/não fumadores
rail station	estação caminho de ferro
subway station	estação do Metropolitano
airport	aéroporto
harbor	estação marítima
town terminal	estação/terminal
shuttle bus/train	autocarro/comboio com ligação constante
sleeper	cama
couchette	beliche
porter	bagageiro
baggage/luggage	bagagem
baggage trolley	carrinho de bagagem
single ticket	bilhete de ida
return ticket	bilhete de ida e volta
first class	primeira classe
second class	segunda classe
When does the train leave?	A que horas sai o comboio?
What time does the train arrive at . . . ?	A que horas chega o comboio a . . . ?
When does the first/last train leave?	Quando parte o primeiro/ ultimo comboio?

HOTELS

room	quarto
bed	cama
bathroom	casa de banho
bathtub	banheira
shower	duche
toilet/Men/Women	toilete/Homens/Senhores
toilet paper	papel higiénico
pillow	almofada
blanket	cobertor
chambermaid	criada/empregada de quarto
breakfast	pequeno almoço
lunch	almoço
dinner	jantar
Do you have a single/double/ twin-bedded room?	Tem um quarto individual/ duplo/com duas camas?
I'd like a quiet room	Eu gostava de um quarto sossegado
I'd like some pillows/blankets	Gostava de mais almofadas/ cobertores

What time is breakfast?	A que horas é o pequeno almoço?
Is it served in the room?	É servido no quarto?
Come in!	Entre!
Are there any messages for me?	Há algum recado para mim?
Would you please call me a taxi?	Por favor chama-me um taxi?
Please take our bags to our room	Por favor leve as nossas malas para o nosso quarto

RESTAURANTS

menu	carta
fixed-price menu	preço fixo
wine list	carta de vinhos
house wine	vinho da casa
waiter	criado/empregado
Waiter!	Faz favor!
bill/check	conta

ON THE MENU

Starters

mixed hors d'oeuvre	acepipes variados
melon	melão
pâté	pasta de figado
soup	sopa
a rougher version of pâté	terrine
smoked ham	presunto
smoked fish	peixe fumado

Meats

lamb	borrego	mutton	carneiro
steak	bife	pork	porco
beef	carne de vaca	roast beef	carne assada
kebab	espetada	sausage	salsichas
pork cold cuts	carnes frias de porco	salami	salame
		veal	vitela
fillet steak	bife de lombo	brains	miolos
chop	costeleta	liver	figado
rib steak	entrecosto	tongue	lingua
leg of lamb	perna de borrego	kidney	rim
ham	fiambre	sweetbreads	moleijas
bacon	bacon/toucinho fumado	tripe	dobrada

Poultry and Game

duck	pato	boiling fowl	galinha para
duckling	pato novo	cozer	
pheasant	faisão	chicken	galinha
wild boar	javali	spring chicken	frango

goose	ganço	turkey	perú
partridge	perdiz		
guinea hen/fowl	galinha da guiné		

Fish

eel	enguia	whiting	pescada
cod	bacalhau	perch	perca
sea bream	pargo	salmon	salmão
monkfish	peixe espada	trout	truta
sea bass	robalo	salmon trout	truta salmonada
mackerel	cavala		

Shellfish

prawn	gamba	lobster	lavagante
scallop	vieira/salmeira	crayfish	lagostim
shrimp	camarão	mussel	mexilhão
crawfish	lagosta	sea urchin	ouriço do mar
mixed shellfish	mista de mariscos	clam	ameijoas

Vegetables

globe artichoke	alcachofra/	zucchini	courgette
asparagus	espargos	(courgette)	
eggplant	beringela	watercress	agrião
carrot	cenoura	chicory	chicoria
mushroom	cogumelo	spinach	espinafres
cabbage	couve	broad bean	favas
sauerkraut	choucroute	kidney bean	feijão verde
cauliflower	couve flor	(green)	
white haricot		leek	alho Frances
bean	feijão manteiga	green/red	pimento verde/
French bean	feijão verde redondo	pepper	vermelho
lentil	lentilha	rice	arroz
turnip	nabo	lettuce	alface
onion	cebola	tomato	tomate
potato	batata	Jerusalem	alcachofra/
pea	ervilha	artichoke	topinambo

Fruit

pineapple	ananaz	melon	melão
blackcurrant	groselha preta	peach	pessego
cherry	cereja	nectarine	pessegos carecas/
lemon	limão		nectarinas
strawberry	morango	pear	pera
raspberry	framboesa	apple	maçã
blackberry	amora	apricot	aplerce
orange	laranja	plum	ameixa

| grapefruit | toranja | greengage | rainha claudia |
| water melon | melancia | prune | ameixa seca |

Desserts

fritter	filhó/sonho	fruit salad	salada de fruta
caramel custard	pudim de	water ice	sorvete
	caramelo	pie/tart/flan	tarte/flam
cake	bolo	with whipped	com natas
ice cream	gelado	cream	
chocolate	mousse de	assorted	pastelaria
mousse	chocolate	pastry	

Sauces etc.

mayonnaise	maionaise	fried, sautéed	salteado 'com
with oil and	com azeite e		manteiga
vinegar dress-			
ing	vinagre	lightly roasted	levemente assado
braised, fried	frito	roast	assado
smoked	fumado	rare	mal passado
browned under	gratinado com	medium (steak)	normal
grill with	queijo	well-done	bem passado
grated cheese		braised on	grelhado na
curried	com caril	charcoal	braza

Index

In this Index, AZ = Azores; H = Hotels & other accommodations; MA = Madeira; R = Restaurants.

General Information

Geographical and Practical Information

Fodor's Travel Guides

U.S. Guides

Alaska
American Cities
The American South
Arizona
Atlantic City & the
  New Jersey Shore
Boston
California
Cape Cod
Carolinas & the
  Georgia Coast
Chesapeake
Chicago
Colorado
Dallas & Fort Worth
Disney World & the
  Orlando Area

The Far West
Florida
Greater Miami,
  Fort Lauderdale,
  Palm Beach
Hawaii
Hawaii (Great Travel
  Values)
Houston & Galveston
I-10: California to
  Florida
I-55: Chicago to New
  Orleans
I-75: Michigan to
  Florida
I-80: San Francisco to
  New York

I-95: Maine to Miami
Las Vegas
Los Angeles, Orange
  County, Palm Springs
Maui
New England
New Mexico
New Orleans
New Orleans (Pocket
  Guide)
New York City
New York City (Pocket
  Guide)
New York State
Pacific North Coast
Philadelphia
Puerto Rico (Fun in)

Rockies
San Diego
San Francisco
San Francisco (Pocket
  Guide)
Texas
United States of
  America
Virgin Islands
  (U.S. & British)
Virginia
Waikiki
Washington, DC
Williamsburg,
  Jamestown &
  Yorktown

Foreign Guides

Acapulco
Amsterdam
Australia, New Zealand
  & the South Pacific
Austria
The Bahamas
The Bahamas (Pocket
  Guide)
Barbados (Fun in)
Beijing, Guangzhou &
  Shanghai
Belgium & Luxembourg
Bermuda
Brazil
Britain (Great Travel
  Values)
Canada
Canada (Great Travel
  Values)
Canada's Maritime
  Provinces
Cancún, Cozumel,
  Mérida, The
  Yucatán
Caribbean
Caribbean (Great
  Travel Values)

Central America
Copenhagen,
  Stockholm, Oslo,
  Helsinki, Reykjavik
Eastern Europe
Egypt
Europe
Europe (Budget)
Florence & Venice
France
France (Great Travel
  Values)
Germany
Germany (Great Travel
  Values)
Great Britain
Greece
Holland
Hong Kong & Macau
Hungary
India
Ireland
Israel
Italy
Italy (Great Travel
  Values)
Jamaica (Fun in)

Japan
Japan (Great Travel
  Values)
Jordan & the Holy Land
Kenya
Korea
Lisbon
Loire Valley
London
London (Pocket Guide)
London (Great Travel
  Values)
Madrid
Mexico
Mexico (Great Travel
  Values)
Mexico City & Acapulco
Mexico's Baja & Puerto
  Vallarta, Mazatlán,
  Manzanillo, Copper
  Canyon
Montreal
Munich
New Zealand
North Africa
Paris
Paris (Pocket Guide)

People's Republic of
  China
Portugal
Province of Quebec
Rio de Janeiro
The Riviera (Fun on)
Rome
St. Martin/St. Maarten
Scandinavia
Scotland
Singapore
South America
South Pacific
Southeast Asia
Soviet Union
Spain
Spain (Great Travel
  Values)
Sweden
Switzerland
Sydney
Tokyo
Toronto
Turkey
Vienna
Yugoslavia

Special-Interest Guides

Bed & Breakfast
  Guide: North America
1936...On the
  Continent

Royalty Watching
Selected Hotels of
  Europe

Selected Resorts
  and Hotels of the U.S.
Ski Resorts of North
  America

Views to Dine by
  around the World